# PETER
## DISCIPLE · APOSTLE · MARTYR

# THE LIBRARY OF HISTORY AND DOCTRINE

The aim of this international Library is to enable scholars to answer questions about the development of the Christian tradition which are important for an understanding of Christianity today.

# PETER
## Disciple · Apostle · Martyr

A Historical and Theological Study

OSCAR CULLMANN
Dr. Theol., D.D. (Edin.), D.D. (Manchester)
*Professor in Basel and Paris*

Translated from the German by
FLOYD V. FILSON

SECOND REVISED
AND EXPANDED EDITION

*Philadelphia*
The Westminster Press

Library of Congress Catalog Card No. 62–10169

To
the University of Manchester
and especially to its Theological Faculty
in expression of thanks for the
Conferring of the Degree of
Doctor of Divinity

'I believe in one holy catholic
and apostolic Church'

'You are "Rock", and on this Rock
I will build my Church'

'Built upon the foundation of
the Apostles and Prophets'

'I pray for those who believe
through the word of the Apostles'

# TRANSLATOR'S PREFACE

PROFESSOR CULLMANN'S book on Peter deserves attentive reading by English-speaking Christians. We possess few thorough studies of Peter's career and position in the Church. Hundreds of lives of Jesus are available, and scores of lives of Paul, but there are few thorough presentations of the life and work of Peter, and none is up to date. This book therefore meets a definite need.

The usual discussion of Peter centres almost entirely on the question of his ecclesiastical office. Professor Cullmann gives a more balanced study; he includes also the significant role that Peter played in formulating the message of the Apostolic Church and in carrying out the missionary task of the first generation of Christians.

Recent excavations under St Peter's Cathedral in Rome, and the explicit papal announcement that the burial place of Peter has been found, have caused increased attention to the subject of Peter's residence in Rome and his supposed martyrdom there. This book examines carefully the literary, liturgical, and archaeological evidence for the Roman residence and martyrdom of Peter.

No discussion of the work of Peter can ignore the claim that Peter was the first Pope, whose successors continue to hold the same ruling authority that he held. Professor Cullmann sketches the history of the interpretation of Matthew 16:17–19, which is the key passage on this subject. He then considers carefully the historical meaning of this passage, and goes on to state its theological significance for the Church today. His book is thus an important contribution to the ecumenical discussion of our time.

The author is constantly concerned to be fair to all sides. He is determined to go no further than the evidence permits. A few readers may wish that he had adopted a more polemic tone. Most of us, however, will be grateful for this calm and friendly spirit, and will find that it makes his argument the more compelling.

By reading the manuscript, offering suggestions, and answering questions, Professor Cullmann has helped greatly in the preparation of the English edition of his work. He has assured me that I have understood his thought and rendered it faithfully. My hope is that I have given it an effective English form, for the book has something vital to say to students of the Bible, church history, theology, and the ecumenical movement.

FLOYD V. FILSON

*McCormick Theological*
*Seminary, Chicago*
*January* 15, 1953

## ON THE SECOND EDITION

The first edition of Professor Cullmann's book on Peter led to wide discussion of its content and conclusions. This second edition has undergone extensive revision which shows the course of the debate, deals with criticisms, and clarifies the presentation in the light of Professor Cullmann's continued study of the issues. The book remains the most thorough and informative study of Peter by any Protestant scholar, and the fair-mindedness of the author makes his work a useful aid to scholarly ecumenical discussion.

F. V. F.

*May* 1, 1961

# CONTENTS

# FOREWORD TO THE FIRST EDITION

BEFORE I decided that in order to pay a debt of thanks, as well as to express respect and friendly fellowship in a common task, I should dedicate this book to the University of Manchester and especially to its theological faculty, I had intended to dedicate it to my Roman Catholic friends, and particularly to the theologians among them. With them I sincerely feel myself united not only on the basis of general human esteem but also in questions of our Christian faith. However, I gave up this intention, because the final section of my work quite naturally will fail to win the approval of their Church, and so I feared that this dedication might in some way be misunderstood. I can assure them, nevertheless, that during the preparation of the final chapter I recalled many a conversation that I had had with them. I also kept in mind new objections that my discussions might evoke in them. Thus while writing that closing section I often found myself carrying on a silent discussion with them as absent members in a personal conversation.

My previous publications concerning Primitive Christian theological thought have found much genuine understanding even in Roman Catholic circles. Therefore I dare to hope and wish that my discussion of the very thing that separates us—for in the present investigation this comes quite frankly to expression, along with much that may win their assent—may do no harm, but may rather render a service to the conversation that Christian confessions have with one another.

This discussion must be continued in spite of the papal encyclical *Humani Generis*, and perhaps particularly as a result of it. If I am well informed, the admonitions of that document do not have in view those discussions with non-Roman Catholic Christians in which each side clearly represents its own standpoint. Indeed, we promote mutual and improved understanding only if we do not pass over in silence that which separates us. Where men, fully aware that they invoke the same name, make a sincere effort to listen to one another, they need not fear to speak also concerning the themes on which, as far as human eye can see, agreement is not possible. I often note, in discussions between representatives of the various confessions, that both parties take anxious pains to speak only concerning those questions regarding which there exists a common basis of discussion. The other questions are studiously avoided, even though as a rule the conversation necessarily reaches a point where it should move on to precisely those other questions for which the common basis is lacking. When this point is reached, one should go back to the reason for this lack of a common basis, not—let me repeat—to fight for one's position and not, indeed, with the illusory purpose of converting one's partner, but rather to listen to him. My purpose would not be furthered if certain things which I say were to be used as a polemic against the Roman Catholic Church. For I hold that in addition to the ecumenical achievements of recent decades it is precisely the simple discussion between Roman Catholic and Protestant theologians that is one of the encouraging events in the church history of our time.

It is in this spirit, and on the basis of the exegetical and historical principles which control the entire work, that I have written the latter part of this book. I hope that it will call forth numerous utterances, from both camps, concerning the fundamental questions over which Christendom is divided. In earlier times there was much discussion of them. Since then, however, men on both sides have become so accustomed to the fact that they do not agree in their point of departure that they often consider it unnecessary to speak about the matter at all—and what is worse, they neglect even to think about it. Apart from the fact that under these circumstances such discussions of individual questions or doctrines as have taken place in recent years are more or less futile, this procedure gives rise on both sides to prejudices and misunderstandings. Their removal should be our first aim, and indeed as much for reasons of scientific study as of faith. A resumption of the discussion concerning the primacy of Rome is also advisable because the arguments are no longer the same as they were in the sixteenth and seventeenth centuries.

In the present study I have purposely avoided raising the doctrinal question until the final chapter. This book as a whole is meant to be *a contribution to the science of history*, and in particular to that part which deals with the beginnings of the Christian faith and the Christian Church. If a librarian should be in doubt as to how to catalogue it, I should like to help him out of his perplexity at once. In spite of the sub-title and in spite of my personal interest in the theological question concerning Peter— an interest which I, even as a historian, make no attempt to conceal—this book belongs neither in the field of dogmatic theology nor in the literature of ecumenical debate nor even in the field of apologetics, but in that of the history of Primitive Christianity.

It is a historical study concerning the Apostle Peter that I here present.[1] But the history of Peter runs on without a break into the *evaluation* of this history which occurs in the continuing *historical* development. This evaluation, however, is likewise theological in nature, and the history of Peter has become the object of a dogmatic pronouncement by the Roman Catholic Church. Thus in a historical study which seeks to deal with Peter, the theological problem, on the one hand, is not to be avoided; yet this theological problem, on the other hand, can only be studied in the closest connection with the history.

May the faithful application of strictly historical methods, which I have taken care to use in dealing with this question, furnish a basis for the debate on the one hand between non-Christian and Christian historians, and on the other hand between Christian theologians of separate denominations who join in confessing One Catholic and Apostolic Church, but differ in the way they believe it is realized at the present time.

For varied assistance in preparing this volume for publication I owe hearty thanks to Candidate Georg Sauer.

OSCAR CULLMANN

*Easter*, 1952

---

[1] This seemed to me the more necessary since we have but few scholarly works on Peter. Monographs on Paul are much more numerous. Recent *general* works on Peter include, on the Protestant side, F. Sieffert, *Realenzyklopädie für Theologie und Kirche*, 3rd ed., Article on 'Peter', Vol. 15, pp. 190 ff.; F. J. Foakes-Jackson, *Peter, Prince of Apostles: A Study in the History and Tradition of Christianity*, 1927; W. Brandt, *Simon Petrus*, n.d. (popular in character); E. Fascher, *Realenzyklopädie des klassischen Alterthums*, Pauly-Wissowa, Article on 'Peter', columns 1335 ff.; on the Roman Catholic side, C. Fouard, *S. Pierre et les premières années du christianisme*; L. Fillion, *Dictionnaire de la Bible*, Article on 'S. Pierre'; A. Tricot, *Dictionnaire de Théologie catholique*, Article on 'S. Pierre', 1935; M. Besson, *S. Pierre et les origines de la primauté romaine*, 1928 (beautifully illustrated); M. Meinertz, *Lexikon für Theologie und Kirche*, Article on 'Petrus', 1936; recently, John Lowe, *Saint Peter*, 1956; P. Gächter, *Petrus und seine Zeit*, 1958.

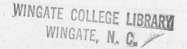

# FOREWORD TO THE SECOND EDITION

IN THE Foreword to the first edition I expressed the hope that the application of historical methods, which I was careful to use in my book, might provide the basis on which non-Christian and Christian historians, and above all Christian theologians now divided into separate confessions, could renew discussion of an old problem. This hope has been largely fulfilled. I therefore express my thanks to my Roman Catholic dialogue partners. In their articles and in special books devoted to criticism of my book they have represented their point of view with all firmness, but almost without exception they have carried on their debate with me on the high level of scientific integrity. They have not singled out this or that one point, but in an objective way have discussed all parts of my study. From secular historians also, and from Protestant theologians, I have received many stimulating and constructive reviews. From them I have tried to learn, especially in those cases where they reject my interpretations. The only unfruitful evaluations are those which come to a book from the narrow basis of *one* fixed formulation of the question and so are closed to all those problems which, though discussed in the book, lie outside that narrow horizon.

Therefore I would wish for this new edition that the question of the 'genuineness' of Matt. 16:17–19 may not push into the background all other questions. This has occurred in too many instances. Among such other questions are my treatment of the role of James, my position concerning the excavations under the Church of St Peter in Rome, and especially the interpretation of the important fifth chapter of First Clement. The latter problem, when mentioned at all, is often disposed of in a characteristically hasty way by pointing out that the author used hellenistic patterns. A series of critics were unable to derive[1] anything from my entire book except that I maintain the 'genuineness' of Matt. 16:17–19. But if in forming their judgment these scholars limit themselves to my study of this passage, should not even they seek to further profitable

---

[1] Often, unfortunately, with the somewhat primitive prejudice, whose day one would have thought was past, that to pronounce something 'spurious' is a mark of scientific method, while results of the opposite kind are suspicious signs of an 'uncritical' attitude! It is understood that I take seriously *relevant* new arguments against the genuineness.

discussion? Should they not at least join with many other reviewers in earnestly considering my proposal to transfer the verses in question, whose connection with the scene at Caesarea Philippi I also deny, into the framework of an ancient tradition concerning discourses at the Last Supper? In particular, the new argument by which I now support this thesis in the T. W. Manson memorial volume and in this present second edition should show that it involves no great difference of method whether one seeks this framework in a resurrection appearance, as do many proponents of 'spuriousness', or in the Passion Story. For this latter solution I think that I have now found still clearer traces in a considerable number of passages.

I intend to devote a separate volume, entitled *Peter and the Pope*, to the theological question of primacy in the narrower sense. Therefore I planned at first merely to revise my book slightly for this second edition, without making any basic changes. But since the historical and exegetical problems constitute its chief content, it became evident that in view of the numerous studies which, in addition to actual reviews of the first edition, have appeared on the historical problem of Peter, a complete and thorough revision of almost the entire volume was unavoidable. On the one side, Catholic theologians have studied anew the relation between James and Peter; they have rightly recognized its importance for the primacy. On the other side, K. Heussi, dealing with the question whether Peter was in Rome and continuing his polemic against H. Lietzmann, has now, in a series of writings directed against K. Aland and myself, reasserted with still greater vehemence[2] his thesis that the apostle 'never set foot in the city on the Tiber'. The debate concerning the results of the excavations under the Church of St Peter in Rome has led to important publications, and the excavations themselves still continue. Finally, new and significant studies have also appeared on Matt. 16. As a result, the footnotes especially have had to be considerably increased, in order to deal with at least the most important of these works. They show that along almost the entire line of the historical, archaeological, and exegetical discussion, the battle-fronts usually are not so drawn that in any given case Roman Catholic scholars hold one view while Protestant scholars hold the opposite one. This is a heartening sign, full of promise for ecumenical discussion as well as for the advance of freedom of study. In this regard there seems to be only one exception among the problems treated in the historical section

---

[2] Whether his review of my book, which appeared in the *Deutsches Pfarrerblatt*, 1953, can be characterized as relevant, or even as fair, the readers of that article can decide, if at the same time they are acquainted with my book.

of my book; this is the question about James, on which a definite Roman Catholic consensus can be observed.

In spite of all the mutual striving for objectivity, the essentially theological primacy question naturally continues to cause division along confessional lines, although there is no unity in the way the Roman Catholics establish the primacy or in the way the Protestants reject it. I have made the least change in the discussions which conclude the book and deal with this debate. This is not because I have not tried here also to learn from the discussion; on the contrary, it is because I intend, as already mentioned, to devote a separate volume to it in order to do justice to the large number of Roman Catholic positions. Since however I hold firmly to my basic thesis of the difference between the unrepeatable apostolate and the ongoing leadership of the Church, I have decided to let this last section stand; for the time being I have limited myself to improving statements in it which are erroneous or open to misunderstanding. In my later volume I hope to treat the problem anew in such a way as to consider more vigorously the Roman Catholic arguments against me. The question as to the manner of succession will require fresh treatment in connection with the problem of tradition; with this problem I have dealt elsewhere. My present studies of the eschatology of the New Testament should clarify still further points. But it can only aid in the essential task if, for the present, purely historical questions about Peter, which furnish the foundations for the theological questions, receive further discussion. Since the emphasis still rests on them in this second edition, I hope that my book about Peter in its new form may continue to facilitate orientation and promote pertinent discussion.

I owe hearty thanks to my sister for the preparation of the manuscript for this edition, and to my assistant, the Rev. Willy Rordorf, for the reading of the proofs and for additional help of many kinds.

OSCAR CULLMANN

*October*, 1960

# PART ONE

# The Historical Question

B

THE SOURCES for our knowledge of Peter consist mainly of the writings of the New Testament. For the final period of his life we shall have to use both archaeological and liturgical evidence and texts of the Apostolic Fathers and the Church Fathers.

We can group the information we have concerning Peter under the following headings: (1) Peter the Disciple; (2) Peter the Apostle; (3) Peter the Martyr. In the section that deals with the Apostle we shall speak also of his theological views; in that dealing with the martyrdom we shall have to raise the radically important question concerning the stay of Peter in Rome.

# I

# Peter the Disciple

## 1. Name, Origin, Call

AS SOURCES concerning Peter the Disciple only the canonical Gospels are to be considered. The apocryphal gospels add only legendary material.

The fantastic attempt to deny the historical existence of Peter and to explain 'the Christian Peter as the humanized form of the Persian Petros or Mithra' needs no refutation. It deserves mention only as a curiosity.[1]

We begin with the question as to the *name* of Peter; it is linked with the question of his role in the circle of the Twelve.

The original name of the apostle is Symeon or Simon. Symeon[2] is a Hebrew name much used among the Jews. We find this Semitic form used of Peter, however, only in Acts 15:14 and II Peter 1:1.[3] The Gospels use the Greek name Simon. This did not originate, as has been supposed, by rendering into Greek the Hebrew name. It is rather 'native Greek'[4] and is already attested by Aristophanes. It is probable that the original Hebrew name Symeon was later replaced by the Greek name of similar sound. However, it does not seem to me at all impossible that Peter, like his brother Andrew, had been given a Greek name from the outset, especially since this is true of Philip, who according to John 1:44 comes from the same place, Bethsaida, and still more since Hellenistic influence is attested precisely for this region.[5] It is not impossible, therefore, that Peter, as was customary in the Dispersion and as we probably must assume for Paul-Saul, had been given from the outset both the Hebrew name Symeon and the Greek name Simon of similar sound.

[1] See A. Drews, *Die Petruslegende*, 1924.    [2] שמעון.
[3] In Acts 15:14 this form is purposely used, since the speaker is James. In II Pet. 1:1 the reading 'Simon', Σίμων (B) is almost certainly secondary. The latest scholar to oppose identifying Symeon (Acts 15:14) and Peter is E. Fuchs (*Zeitschrift für Theologie und Kirche*, 1951, p. 350).
[4] See F. Blass—A. Debrunner, *Grammatik des neutestamentlichen Griechisch*, 7th ed., 1943, Par. 53, 2, and Fick-Bechtel, *Die griechischen Personennamen*, 1894, pp. 30, 251. See also A. Deissmann, *Bibelstudien*, 1895, p. 184, note 1 (Eng. Tr., *Bible Studies*, 1901, p. 315, note 2).
[5] See below, p. 24.

In addition to this name he has a descriptive title: *Kepha*. This is an Aramaic word and means 'stone', 'rock'. Thus *Kepha* is not, as we might be inclined to believe, a proper name.[6] It is not a given name in ordinary use among the Jews, but is rather a common noun. In the New Testament we find this title at times in its Aramaic form, that is, merely *transcribed* in Greek letters; this is usually the case in Paul's letters (Gal. 1:18; 2:9; 2:11,[7] 14; I Cor. 1:12; 3:22; 9:5; 15:5). At times, however, it is *translated* into Greek: *Petros*. Paul writes *Petros* only once, in Galatians 2:7, 8,[8] perhaps because he here cites an official document, in the Greek translation of which the form *Petros* was used. The Gospels say at times *Simon*, at times *Petros*, at times *Simon Petros*.[9] The Syriac translations write *Simon Kepha*. Where in Greek environment the word is preserved in its Aramaic spelling, it is supplied at the end with the Greek final *-s* in order to give it a Greek ending: *Kephas*. According to the Septuagint of Jeremiah 4:29 and Job 30:6, the preferable Greek translation would be *Petra*,[10] which means 'rock'. Since, however, this word is feminine in Greek and has the feminine ending *-a*, the New Testament chooses for the translation a less usual Greek word which has the Greek masculine ending *-os*: *Petros* (John 1:42). There is no essential difference in meaning between *Petros* and *Petra*, for even if originally *Petra* designated live rock while *Petros* meant rather the detached stone, this distinction was not strictly observed.[11] The preference for the form *Petros* may have been due

---

[6] This is wrongly asserted by Th. Zahn, *Kommentar zum Neuen Testament, Das Evangelium des Matthäus*, 4th ed., 1922, p. 540; but he gives no example to support his view. M. J. Lagrange, in *L'Evangile selon S. Matthieu*, 5th ed., 1941, p. 324, also considers it possible.

[7] The completely unfounded idea that Gal. 2:11 is talking about another Cephas, who is entirely different from Peter and belongs to the Seventy disciples, appears in ancient times in Clement of Alexandria, *Hypotyposeis*, V (Eusebius, *Ecclesiastical History*, I, 12, 2), then in the lists of apostles (see Th. Schermann, *Propheten- und Apostellegenden nebst Jüngerkatalogen*, 1907, pp. 302 ff.), and in recent times in J. M. Robertson, *Die Evangelienmythen*, 1910 (German tr. of Part III of *Christianity and Mythology*, 1900), p. 103, and D. W. Riddle, 'The Cephas-Peter Problem and a Possible Solution' (*Journal of Biblical Literature*, 1940, pp. 169 ff.).

[8] In opposition to all the textual evidence A. Merx, *Die vier kanonischen Evangelien nach ihrem ältesten bekannten Text*, II, 1, *Das Evangelium Matthäus*, 1902, p. 161, regards 'Peter' (Πέτρος) as secondary in these passages and assumes that in them too 'Cephas' (Κηφᾶς) was the original reading.

[9] The Fourth Gospel prefers to say: *Simon Petros*.

[10] Elsewhere in the Septuagint πέτρα translates צור and סלע. See Hatch-Redpath, *A Concordance to the Septuagint and the other Greek Versions of the Old Testament*, 1897–1900. The Aramaic word כפא (Kepha) is translated by λίθος ('stone'), as A. Dell shows, in his article on 'Matthäus 16:17–19' (*Zeitschrift für die Neutestamentliche Wissenschaft*, 1914, pp. 19 f.), by the evidence of the Jerusalem Gospel and the Sinaitic Syriac. Nevertheless, it remains true that *Kepha* in Aramaic means both 'stone' and 'rock'. Therefore the results that A. Dell draws from the translation λίθος are to be rejected. See the following note.

[11] In Homer, *Odyssey*, 243; Hesiod, *Theogony*, 675; and Wisdom 17:17 (LXX)

in part to the fact that in Aramaic there was a proper name *Petros*, which perhaps had the meaning 'first-born'.[12] This, however, is not certain.

In any event, the fact that the word *Kepha* was translated into Greek is significant. It confirms the fact that the word is not a proper name; proper names usually are not translated. The attempt has indeed been made to prove that even in pre-Christian times the name Peter existed as an abbreviation for the Latin Petronius and that it occurs in the Jewish author Josephus,[13] but the attempt at proof has failed.[14]

It is only because Peter has become for us today a familiar proper name that we are often tempted to forget that *Kepha* is a common noun. But this fact is important if we desire to judge rightly the bearing of the fact that Jesus gave Peter this title. It corresponds to Jewish custom to choose as titles words which somehow point to the promise in a particular situation and lay an obligation on their bearer. We know such examples from the Old Testament,[15] and in a similar way Jewish disciples also received from their Rabbi a title. [16] Jesus himself gave such a title not only to Peter but also to the sons of Zebedee: *Boanerges*, which is explained in Mark 3:17 to mean 'Sons of Thunder'.[17] In order to understand what an impression the giving of a name to Peter must have made on him and on the other witnesses of this event, we would do well to translate the word *Kephas* not with the word Peter, which for us today is all too familiar and has become too rigidly fixed as a proper name, but with the English word 'rock', and so call him Simon Rock.[18]

πέτρα is used with the meaning 'stone', 'piece of rock'. That the two words are interchangeable is said also by Galen, XII, 194. A. Dell, *op. cit.*, pp. 19 f., is probably wrong, therefore, in emphasizing that *Kepha* and *Petros* mean 'stone' and not 'rock'.

[12] J. Levy, *Neuhebräisch-chaldäisches Wörterbuch*, 1876 ff.; Dalman, *Aramäisch-neuhebräisches Wörterbuch*, 2nd ed., 1922; Strack-Billerbeck, *Kommentar zum Neuen Testament aus Talmud und Midrasch*, Vol. I, p. 530.

[13] Josephus, *Antiquities*, 18, 6, 3. In reality what is involved here is a textual error for πρῶτος ('first').

[14] The attempt has been made by A. Merx, *op. cit.*, pp. 160 ff. See also A. Meyer, *Jesu Muttersprache*, 1896, p. 51. It has been opposed by A. Dell, *op. cit.*, pp. 14 ff.: 'The proper name Peter does not appear at all in pagan literature; it first appears in Tertullian.' There was, on the contrary, as already mentioned (note 12), an Aramaic name פטרוס (*Petros*), which perhaps is to be connected with פטר (*peter*) 'firstborn'. The theory that the Greek *Petros* was first derived from it and gave occasion for a false retranslation *Kepha* into Aramaic is quite impossible, in view of the fact that in Paul's letters Cephas is already the usual designation and Peter clearly was only a later derivation from it.

[15] Gen. 17:5 ff., 15; 32:28; Isa. 62:2; 65:15. See also on this point Justin, *Dialogue With Trypho*, 106, 3.

[16] See P. Fiebig, *Gleichnisreden Jesu*, 1912, pp. 53 ff.

[17] See on this point E. Preuschen, 'Die Donnersöhne' (*ZNW*, 1917, pp. 141 ff.) and F. Schulthess, 'Zur Sprache der Evangelien' (*ZNW*, 1922, pp. 243 ff.).

[18] H. Pernot, in his French translation of the Gospels (1943), rightly chooses the word *roc*, and it seems to me unjustified that this suggestion has been received with some scoffing.

According to the unanimous witness of the Gospels, the giving of this name goes back to Jesus. It will not do to ascribe it to the fellow-disciples, who supposedly gave him this name of honour only later, on the basis of the fact that he was the first who saw the risen Lord.[19] For we hardly can assume that in this event the name would have become firmly established in the way that we find it really did.[20] In saying this we have not yet said whether it was actually given to him in the situation described in Matthew ch. 16. The agreement of the Evangelists concerning the basic fact is the more noteworthy in view of their absolute divergence about the circumstances in which the name was given. According to the basic passage, Matthew 16:18, with which we shall have to deal in detail, Jesus first gave Simon this title on the occasion when he likewise explained it more fully. This was at the moment when, according to Mark 8:27 ff., Peter uttered his so-called confession of Jesus at Caesarea Philippi. There Jesus asks his disciples, 'Who do men say that I am?'[21] The disciples report to him the various views current among the people. Thereupon Jesus asks, 'And in your view, who am I?' Peter speaks up and says, 'You are the Christ (Matthew adds: the Son of the Living God).' According to Matthew 16:17, Jesus answers, 'Blessed are you, Simon son of Jonah! It was not a man but the Father in Heaven who gave you this revelation.' Then he continues: 'And I say to you, You are the Rock, and upon this Rock I will build my Church.'

Thus in the same way that Peter gives to Jesus the name which later is regularly added to the name of Jesus, and finally becomes fixed as his proper name, 'Christ' (in Hebrew 'Messiah', that is, 'Anointed One'), so, according to Matthew, Jesus gives to Peter a descriptive title: 'Rock'.

Did Jesus really give this title to Peter on the specific occasion indi-

[19] So K. G. Goetz, *Petrus als Gründer und Oberhaupt der Kirche und Schauer von Gesichten nach den altchristlichen Berichten und Legenden*, 1927, pp. 67 f. Further, E. Dinkler, 'Die ersten Petrusdarstellungen. Ein archäologischer Beitrag zur Geschichte des Petrusprimats' (*Marburger Jahrbuch für Kunstwissenschaft*, 1939), pp. 2 ff., and 'Die Petrus-Rom-Frage' (*Theologische Rundschau*, 1959, pp. 196 f.); also, E. Hirsch, *Frühgeschichte des Evangeliums*, II, 1941, pp. 306 ff.

[20] E. Dinkler, *op. cit.*, is of course correct when he points out that Jesus during his earthly life addresses Peter as 'Simon'. But this hardly proves that he could not have given him the distinguishing title of honour 'Rock'. He also did not address the sons of Zebedee as 'Boanerges'. So too from the fact, likewise cited by E. Dinkler, that in addition to the confession 'he appeared to Cephas' (ὤφθη Κηφᾷ) we find 'he appeared to Simon' (ὤφθη Σίμωνι), we should not conclude that Peter's title was given only after Easter. It is correct, however, that only from that moment on—but in remembrance of a saying of Jesus—the title prevailed.

[21] Instead of the pronoun 'I' (με), Matt. 16:13 writes 'the Son of Man' (τὸν υἱὸν τοῦ ἀνθρώπου), according to the best textual witnesses, but since this reading awkwardly anticipates the answer, it is certainly secondary in comparison with Mark 8:27. See below, p. 180.

cated by this Gospel? We are justified in raising this question, for according to Mark 3:16 this event—without the addition of the explanation—took place upon another occasion, and John 1:42, moreover, places the giving of the name in still another setting. According to Mark 3:16 Jesus already called Peter 'Rock' at the time of the call of the Twelve;[22] according to John 1:42 he did so even earlier, on the occasion of their first meeting in Judea, although Jesus here speaks in the future tense: 'You *will be* called Cephas.' From these variations, which one can harmonize if one is determined to do so,[23] we conclude that in the process of transmission the memory of the moment in which Jesus gave Peter the title had become lost; the same is true of the setting of many other stories in the Gospels.

We must keep this in mind when we come to the detailed exegesis of Matthew 16:16 ff. In itself the time when the name was given has no fundamental significance. What is important, however, is first of all *the fact* that according to the unanimous witness of the Gospels Mark, Matthew, and John, Jesus did give this name to Peter and, second, that according to a tradition handed down only by Matthew, Jesus *explained* this name on a special occasion by his purpose of founding his Church upon the Apostle whom he designated as the Rock.

*　　*　　*

We can derive from the Gospels the following additional *biographical notes*. According to Matthew 16:17, Peter is the son of Jonah—Aramaic *bar-yônâ*, which John 1:42 and 21:15 f. indicate is an abbreviation for John. Whether another explanation, which appeals to a Jewish lexicon, is correct must remain doubtful. According to it, the Aramaic *bar-yônâ* had no connection with the name John, but meant the same as 'terrorist'.[24] In that case Peter belonged to the party of the determined enemies of

---

[22] M. J. Lagrange, in agreement with A. Loisy, J. Knabenbauer, etc., maintains in *L'évangile selon St Marc*, 6th ed., 1942, p. 65, that this is the original occasion: 'The time chosen by Mark is probably that which best accords with the facts, since from then on Simon becomes the corner stone of the building begun by Jesus.' From this moment Mark consistently avoids the name Simon, which up to this time he has regularly used. Only in ch. 14:37, in the Gethsemane scene, does Jesus say to him: 'Simon, are you sleeping?' Perhaps Mark purposely avoids having Jesus address Simon in this situation as 'Rock'.

[23] See below, p. 182.

[24] So Robert Eisler, *Jesous basileus ou basileusas*, 1929 f., p. 67, who follows Eliezer ben Jehuda, *Thesaurus totius hebraitatis*, Vol. II, p. 623. See G. Dalman, *Aramäisch-neuhebräisches Wörterbuch*, 2nd ed., 1922, 65a; probably an Akkadian loan-word. In favour of this view might be the fact that Jonah is not attested elsewhere as a shortened form of Johanan. On *bar-yônâ* see also H. Hirschberg, 'Simon Bariona and the Ebionites' (*JBL*, 1942, pp. 171 ff.).

Rome, the so-called 'Zealots', just as did Simon the 'Zealot' (Luke 6:15; Acts 1:13[25]) and perhaps Judas Iscariot.[26]

According to John 1:44 Peter comes from Bethsaida ('fisherman's city'), which according to the view that is by far the most probable is to be sought on the eastern bank of the Jordan near the point where it empties into the Sea of Gennesaret.[27] Even if the place itself was Jewish, we must note, nevertheless, that it was located in Gentile surroundings. This is indicated, indeed, as John 1:44 and 12:21 suggest, by the Greek name of his brother Andrew and of Philip, who likewise came from Bethsaida, as well as by the name of Simon himself.[28] 'Anyone brought up in Bethsaida would not only have understood Greek, but would also have been polished by intercourse with foreigners and have had some Greek culture.'[29] Thus is explained the fact that according to John 12:21 the Greeks turn to Philip, the native of Bethsaida. If the information of the Gospel of John that Peter came from that place is true, this could be related to the fact that in the account of Acts, chs. 10 and 11, Peter champions a universalistic point of view and, as we shall see, is not too far removed from Paul in his theology. This does not prevent Acts 4:13 from characterizing him and his companion John as 'uneducated'.[30] He had not 'studied' either by Jewish or by Greek standards.

Later we find that Peter has moved to Capernaum and settled (Mark 1:29 and parallels). It appears that Jesus often entered his home there, and perhaps actually lived with him for a short time (Matt. 8:14).

He was a fisherman by calling (Mark 1:16 and parallels: Luke 5:2 f.; John 21:3). He seems to carry on this work together with the two sons of Zebedee, who are described as 'partners' (Luke 5:10).[31]

According to the testimony of the Synoptic Gospels (Mark 1:29 ff. and parallels) as well as of Paul (I Cor. 9:5), Peter was married. Later stories concerning his children[32] and the martyrdom of his wife, at which he supposedly was present,[33] are legendary.

---

[25] The reading is Κανaναῖος in Mark 3:18; Matt. 10:4. This is not to be translated 'Canaanite', but 'Zealot', and the word merely transliterates the Aramaic word *qan'ānā*.

[26] Iscariot would be derived from *sicarius*='bandit'. J. Wellhausen, *Das Evangelium Marci übersetzt und erklärt*, 1909, p. 23, mentions this interpretation, but does not consider it probable. See Fr. Schulthess, *Das Problem der Sprache Jesu*, 1919, pp. 54 f.

[27] See G. Dalman, *Orte und Wege Jesu*, 3rd ed., 1924, p. 172. English translation, *Sacred Sites and Ways*, 1935, pp. 161 ff.          [28] See above, p. 20.

[29] G. Dalman, *op. cit.*, p. 177 (Eng. Tr., p. 165).

[30] ἀγράμματοί εἰσιν καὶ ἰδιῶται. F. J. Foakes-Jackson, *Peter, Prince of Apostles: A Study in the History and Tradition of Christianity*, 1927, p. 55, thinks that this judgment is to be ascribed to contempt for the Galilean accent.          [31] κοινωνοί.

[32] Clement of Alexandria, *Stromateis*, III, 6, 52; concerning a daughter, see *Actus Vercellenses*.

[33] Eusebius, *Eccles. Hist.*, III, 30, 2, who quotes Clement of Alexandria, *Stromateis*,

The Johannine account (John 1:35 ff.) permits us to sup
he joined Jesus he, as well as his brother Andrew and th
ciple, had belonged to the inner or wider circle of the d
the Baptist.[34]

## 2. *His Position in the Circle of Disciples*

We learn from the Synoptic Gospels that Peter actually occupies a
*unique* position within the group of disciples. Together with the sons of
Zebedee and his brother Andrew he belongs to the intimate circle of
those who gathered about Jesus. According to Mark 1:16 and Matthew
4:18, he with Andrew is the first disciple whom Jesus calls. Mark 5:37
notes explicitly that Jesus permitted no one else to follow him into the
house of the ruler of the synagogue except Peter and the sons of Zebedee.
On other occasions also we find him together with this pair of brothers
(see Mark 9:2 and parallels; Mark 14:33 and parallels).

But even within this innermost circle it is almost always Peter who
stands in the foreground. In the story of the miraculous catch of fish
(Luke 5:1 ff.) he clearly plays the chief role, although at the very end the
sons of Zebedee are included with him. According to Matthew 14:28,
only Peter attempts to imitate his Master in walking on the sea. Almost
always he appears as the spokesman for the Twelve. We have already seen
that it is Peter who answers when Jesus directs a question to *all* the disciples (Mark 8: 29 ff. and parallels). Correspondingly, the close of this
Markan narrative (ch. 8:33) says that Jesus *looks upon all the disciples* as
he speaks to Peter the stern word, 'Depart from me, Satan. Your thinking
is not under divine but under human control.' The reproach is obviously
directed equally to all the disciples, because Jesus knows that even the
words which Peter has addressed to him to hold him back from his path
of suffering reproduce the Satanic desire of all the Twelve. Thus here,
too, Peter appears as the spokesman of all the disciples.

The same conclusion results from the transfiguration story, Mark
9:2 ff. Here, too, it is Peter who proposes to Jesus that they erect tents
(Mark 9:5). The sons of Zebedee play on this occasion little more than the
role of extras.

It is Peter who in various situations turns to Jesus with questions

VII, 11, 63; concerning Peter's wife, see further the Pseudo-Clementine *Homily* XIII,
1, 11; *Recognitions*, VII, 25, 36; IX, 38.
[34] The hypothesis according to which 'bar-Jonah' designates Peter as a 'disciple of
John the Baptist' cannot be proved.

.ch all the disciples want answered: 'Lord, how many times shall I .orgive my brother who sins against me? As many as seven times?' (Matt. 18:21). 'Lord, do you speak this parable to us or also to all?' (Luke 12:41). 'Behold, we have left everything and followed you' (Mark 10:28 and parallels).

It also occurs that in one Gospel all the disciples ask the question, while in the parallel passage of the other Gospel it is only Peter who asks (Mark 7:17 compared with Matt. 15:15; Matt. 21:20 compared with Mark 11:21).

In Luke 22:8 Peter and John are directed by Jesus to prepare the Passover.—In Mark 14:29 Peter promises to be loyal to his Master.— Again, in Gethsemane, according to Mark 14:37 (Matt. 26:40), Jesus turns to Peter with the reproachful question whether he cannot watch one hour; but again the sons of Zebedee, who are likewise present, are included in the address.—According to Matthew 17:24 Peter is regarded by outsiders also as the special representative of the group of disciples. The people who collect the tax address their question to him.

The lists of the disciples (Mark 3:16; Matt. 10:2; Luke 6:14; Acts 1:13) do indeed vary in detail, but it is common to all of them that they give Peter the first place. The list in Matthew actually emphasizes the fact that he is the 'first' ($\pi\rho\tilde{\omega}\tau\sigma s$). Characteristic also is the expression 'Peter and those with him',[35] used to designate the group of disciples (Mark 1:36; Luke 9:32; 8:45 according to the best attested reading). Particularly striking is the word of the angel in Mark 16:7: 'Go and tell his disciples *and Peter* that [Jesus] goes before you to Galilee.'

With respect to this unique position, therefore, there is no such difference as has often been asserted between Mark and the other two Synoptic Gospels. Precisely in the Gospel of Mark, of which it has been said that although written in Rome it knows no claim for the authority of Peter,[36] he appears as the spokesman among the disciples. An examination of the passages already listed is sufficient to convince one that in reality each of the three Synoptic Gospels emphasizes in its own independent way the pre-eminent position of Peter. Even though Mark lacks the saying of Matthew 16:17 ff. concerning the Church, yet his entire presentation leaves not the slightest doubt as to the special role that this Evangelist ascribes to Peter. To try to derive a tendency hostile to Peter from the fact that he does not keep silence about Peter's weaknesses is to mis-

---

[35] Πέτρος καὶ οἱ σὺν αὐτῷ; Πέτρος καὶ οἱ μετ' αὐτοῦ.

[36] H. Strathmann, 'Die Stellung des Petrus in der Urkirche. Zur Frühgeschichte des Wortes an Petrus, Matt. 16, 17–19' (*Zeitschrift für Systematische Theologie*, 1943, pp. 223 ff.).

understand the significance of these items.[37] We have seen above [38] that at times all the disciples speak in one of the Synoptic Gospels, while only Peter speaks in the parallel passage of the other one. But we must notice that when this occurs it is not always the same Gospel that puts Peter in the foreground. Rather, we find that this emphasis upon this one disciple is found now in one and now in another of the Gospels. Thus in the Gospel of Mark (Mark 11:21) Peter takes the place of all the disciples, whereas in the parallel passage in Matthew (ch. 21:20) they ask the question concerning the withered fig tree.

Moreover, it will not do to make a basic distinction between Luke and Matthew in regard to their attitude to Peter, as though only Matthew had a special ecclesiastical interest in a permanent primacy for Peter.[39] Even if it is true that Matthew alone has the saying of Matthew 16:17 ff., and also the story of Peter's walking on the sea (Matt. 14:28 ff.) as well as the designation 'first' in Matthew 10:2, we must place on the other side the verses in which only Luke shows a positive interest in Peter; this is especially true in the story of the miraculous catch of fish (Luke 5:1 ff.). Furthermore, we must note particularly that in Luke's special material there is a parallel to the saying about the Rock in Matthew 16:18. It clearly gives to Peter for the future a unique function among his brothers: 'Simon, Simon, behold, Satan has asked for you in order to sift you like wheat. But I have prayed for you that your faith may not fail, and when you have turned again (according to another reading: turn again and[40]) strengthen your brothers' (Luke 22:31). This saying's genuineness cannot be contested with the same arguments that are used against Matthew 16:17 ff., since it does not contain the word 'church' (ἐκκλησία),[41] which many find objectionable on critical grounds. Hence it should be cited in this debate much oftener than it is. In this verse, too, Jesus says to Peter that he stands in a perilously close relation to Satan, but in this he is expressly linked with the other disciples: 'Satan has asked [God] for you (plural) in order to sift you (plural).' We have seen [42] that this is also the

[37] Above all, we cannot speak of a hostility of Mark towards Peter, such as R. Bultmann assumes in 'Die Frage nach dem messianischen Bewusstsein und das Petrusbekenntnis' (ZNW, 1919–20, p. 170). See M. Goguel, L'Eglise primitive, 1947, p. 191: 'There is no trace of an anti-Petrine attitude in Mark.'  [38] See p. 26.

[39] Thus H. Strathmann, op. cit., judges each of the Gospels on the basis of its attitude to the claim of authority for Peter, according to the somewhat artificial scheme by which he assumes that it belongs to this or that Church: Mark—Rome—no interest in the Petrine claim; Luke and The Acts—Pauline missionary area—a primacy of Peter for only a limited time; Matthew—Antioch (see B. H. Streeter)—permanent primacy; John—Asia Minor—anti-Petrine and pro-Johannine tendency.

[40] E. Stauffer, 'Zur Vor- und Frühgeschichte des Primatus Petri', Zeitschrift für Kirchengeschichte, 1943-4, p. 18, note 58, gives various reasons for preferring this reading.

[41] See below, pp. 170 f., 193 ff.         [42] See above, p. 25.

silent assumption in Mark, ch. 8, and yet in both places Jesus directs th
saying only to Peter, and particularly in giving the charge he speaks onl
to Peter: 'Strengthen your brothers.' Accordingly, it is impossible to dis
cern with certainty a bias for or against Peter in any of the Synopti
Gospels.

Thus according to all three Synoptic Gospels Peter indubitably playe
the role of spokesman among the twelve disciples. Furthermore, accord
ing to the Gospels of Matthew and Luke Jesus appointed him speciall
to carry out later the mission of strengthening his brothers. So the know
ledge of a special distinction given to Peter within the circle of disciple
is common to the entire ancient tradition behind the Synoptic Gospels
This is clear even *without taking into account the controversial passag*
Matthew 16:17 ff., which we shall discuss in detail in Part Two of thi
work. This unique position, which is attested not only in Matthew bu
also in Luke and Mark, cannot and must not be denied or even diminishe
in support of any confessional or critical tendency. We must add, howevei
that while in all these passages Peter is given prominence in the tota
group of disciples, he always appears as their spokesman in the 'dialogu
with Christ'; apart from this relation to Christ he never plays, as he doe
in the later literature, a leading role.[43]

A somewhat different picture emerges when we turn to *the Gospel o
John.* Here the outstanding role of Peter, which is unchallenged in th
Synoptic Gospels, becomes a problem, since for this Evangelist th
mysterious unnamed 'Beloved Disciple' of Jesus enters into a certai
competition with Peter. Thus here, in a way different from the Synoptics
a contemporary interest of the author concerning the position of Pete
may have influenced the presentation. However, it is noteworthy that thi
Gospel, which manifestly wishes to emphasize the particularly clos
relationship between Jesus and the 'Beloved Disciple', nevertheless no
where attempts to deny directly the special role of Peter within the grou
of disciples.[44] It only has the tendency to lessen this role, in so far as i
seeks to show that beside the unique position of Peter there is the some
what different special role of the 'Beloved Disciple'.[45] This is certainly con
nected with the receding of the entire group of the Twelve as such,
tendency which is characteristic of this Gospel's view of the disciples an
to which as a rule not enough attention is given. That in spite of thi

[43] This is rightly emphasized by J. L. Klink, *Het Petrustype in het Nieuwe Testamei
en de Oud-Christelijke Letterkunde,* Dissertation, Leyden, 1947.
[44] Peter also appears as spokesman for the other disciples in John 6:66 ff. and 13:3
[45] The Gospel of the Hebrews goes much further in opposing the special position
Peter.

manifest tendency the Fourth Gospel nevertheless accepts
pre-eminence of Peter appears to me to be a particularly
that this fact was so well known in the Primitive Church
neither be directly denied nor passed over in silence, but
mized.[46] It is only the exclusive nature of Peter's unique pos
opposed; in other respects the different character of the role ѵi the two
men is emphasized.

This appears in a particularly clear way in the Passion story, for example
in ch. 13:24 on the occasion of the Last Supper, where Peter must turn
to the Beloved Disciple, who is lying on the breast of the Lord, in order
to learn a secret of Jesus. It appears again in ch. 18:15, where the Beloved
Disciple enters with Jesus into the court of the high priest, while Peter
remains outside before the gate. But particularly in the most decisive
moment, at the foot of the cross, it is not Peter but the Beloved Disciple
who is present, and he is distinguished in a quite special way by the word
here directed to him by the Crucified One.[47] Furthermore, the author tells
how the Beloved Disciple comes first ($\pi\rho\hat{\omega}\tau\sigma$, ch. 20:4) to the grave but
does not enter, while Peter only comes after him but does go in. The
Beloved Disciple enters the grave after Peter does, but on the other hand
it is said only of this Beloved Disciple that he 'believes' at once when he
has 'seen' (ch. 20:8).[48]

These facts throw light also upon ch. 1:41, where we find as the first
disciples of Jesus two former disciples of the Baptist, an unnamed one
and Andrew the brother of Peter. Thus here Peter is not the 'first' dis-
ciple; he is not the $\pi\rho\hat{\omega}\tau\sigma$. Nevertheless, *after* these two, whose meeting
with Jesus serves rather as a kind of prelude, Peter is the first one who
comes to Jesus. In fact, the writer speaks also in verse 41 of the 'first' one,
and this could refer to Peter. Nevertheless, the manuscripts here differ
with regard to the ending of the word. Some read 'the first one' in the
nominative case ($\pi\rho\hat{\omega}\tau\sigma$); Andrew is thereby designated as the first one,
who as such finds his brother Peter. In this case it is emphasized that the
honour of being 'the first one' belongs to both former disciples of the
Baptist, the unnamed one and Andrew. The other manuscripts read 'the

---

[46] This is also recognized explicitly by D. F. Strauss, *Das Leben Jesu. Für das deutsche Volk*, 1864, p. 423.

[47] Ed. Meyer, 'Sinn und Tendenz der Schlussszene am Kreuz im Johannesevangelium' (*Sitzungsbericht der preussischen Akademie der Wissenschaften*, 1924, p. 159),
actually assumes that by the words directed to him and to the mother of Jesus the
Beloved Disciple is so to speak accepted into the family of the Lord and adopted as his
brother in the fullest sense.

[48] See O. Cullmann, '$\epsilon\hat{\iota}\delta\epsilon\nu$ $\kappa\alpha\hat{\iota}$ $\hat{\epsilon}\pi\hat{\iota}\sigma\tau\epsilon\nu\sigma\epsilon\nu$', in the volume in honour of M. Goguel,
*Aux Sources de la tradition chrétienne*, 1950, pp. 56 ff.

st one' in the accusative case ($\pi\rho\hat{\omega}\tau o\nu$). In this reading Peter receives the honourable rank of 'the first one', yet only in so far as he is the first to be found and led to Jesus by his brother, the former disciple of the Baptist. This divergence of the manuscripts shows how it was recognized even in ancient times that the Fourth Evangelist was specially interested in this question; whether he himself wrote the nominative or the accusative case—and this is hard to decide—it remains a fact that thereby, exactly as in ch. 20, he intends to point to the remarkable relationship between Peter and that unnamed disciple, who is probably identical with the Beloved Disciple and who was a disciple of the Baptist when he first met Jesus. Here also, it seems, the evangelist did not intend to deny the pre-eminent position of Peter, but he did wish to show how the unnamed disciple is 'first' in another respect, in the way he became Jesus' disciple.

This tendency is even clearer in view of the fact that here at the very beginning Andrew utters the confession of Jesus as the Messiah, while Peter only later calls him 'the Holy One of God' (ch. 6:66 ff.). Yet, as we must say on the other side, the Gospel of John expressly recognizes that Jesus gave to Peter the title of honour, 'Rock', and as we have seen,[49] the Gospel puts this event at the very beginning (ch. 1:42). We must also say that it reports the decisive confession of Peter with an emphasis all its own (ch. 6:66 ff.).

Exactly the same double attitude towards the unique position of Peter is found again in the supplementary chapter 21, which thus in this respect agrees with chapters 1 to 20. On the one side, that position is explicitly recognized, while on the other side, it is reduced by being confronted with the unique position of the Beloved Disciple. Thus, at the beginning of the narrative here reported concerning the appearance of Jesus at the Sea of Galilee, Peter is named first in the series of disciples listed.[50] On the other hand, the Beloved Disciple is the first to recognize the Lord, but Peter again is the first to go to him. Thus this paralleling of the two unique positions marks this chapter also. It finds its climax in the conversation which, following the miracle, occurs between the Risen One and Peter. This account is characteristic of the way in which the author of this chapter, who, no matter who he is, belongs to the Johannine circle, has grasped the meaning of the entire Gospel of John; he shows this grasp by putting at the end precisely this conversation as a sort of crown or climax. In doing so, he probably has emphasized much too strongly this purpose which the

[49] See above, p. 23.
[50] According to E. Stauffer, *op. cit.*, pp. 13 f., there lies at the basis of this narrative an early report, mentioned in I Cor. 15:5, concerning the appearance of Jesus to Peter alone. On this matter see below, p. 61.

Fourth Evangelist certainly had. But on the other hand, he
understood the Evangelist's conception; in a quite analogou
sets the two disciples face to face and shows how the Risen (
unique position to each one of them for the future, but gives e
a different role.[51] Peter is installed in the office of shepher
Beloved Disciple, who here only 'follows' Peter, which in Johannine
idiom[53] may also imply a spiritual attachment, it is promised that he will
outlive Peter. In this context this promise quite probably signifies that he
will have to fulfil a task which, though similar, is nevertheless, as in the
entire Gospel, of a somewhat different kind.[54]

Thus the Gospel of John, precisely because, in distinction from the
Synoptic Gospels, it has the tendency to emphasize the Beloved Disciple,
indirectly confirms the result to which we were led by the investigation
of the Synoptic passages concerning the disciple Peter: *Among the disciples of Jesus Peter, according to the united witness of the gospel tradition,
occupies a peculiarly representative position.*

This does not mean, however, that during the lifetime of Jesus he
possessed the role of *leader* in relation to his fellow-disciples. He is rather
at all times their *spokesman*, their *representative* in good as in bad action.

---

[51] M. Goguel, *L'Eglise primitive*, 1947, p. 200, takes another view. He assumes that
this dialogue serves to glorify Peter at the expense of the Beloved Disciple, and so
stands in opposition to chs. 1–20.

[52] To dispute this, as K. G. Goetz, *op. cit.*, p. 15, attempts to do, seems to me impossible. Goetz is no doubt correct when he writes that Peter is reinstated in the position
of disciple that he had lost by the three-fold denial. At the same time, however, more is
involved here than merely the confirmation of the call of a disciple. The fact that Jesus
no longer lives on earth necessarily has as its result a new task for the disciple.

[53] See O. Cullmann, 'Der johanneische Gebrauch doppeldeutiger Ausdrücke als
Schlüssel zum Verständnis des vierten Evangeliums' (*Theologische Zeitschrift*, 1948,
pp. 360 ff.).

[54] Thus R. Bultmann, *Das Johannesevangelium*, p. 547, writes that the authority of
Peter here passes over to the Beloved Disciple. E. Stauffer, *op. cit.*, p. 15, agrees with this,
but adds that this involves the authority not only of the Evangelist, as Bultmann thinks,
but also of the church leader John. This, however, confuses the difference between the
two unique positions, a difference emphasized in the entire Fourth Gospel and also in
this twenty-first chapter. The Roman Catholic scholar R. Graber, in *Petrus der Fels.
Fragen um den Primat*, 1949, pp. 37 ff., considers the meaning of John, ch. 21, to be as
follows: The question of Peter: 'Lord, but what will happen to this man (the Beloved
Disciple)' reckons with the possibility that the Beloved Disciple might be his 'successor';
but the answer of Jesus, 'If I will that he remain', is meant to reject explicitly this opinion
of Peter, because others are destined to be his successors. This artificial explanation is
much less justified than the hypothesis, well worth considering, of the first part of
Graber's work (see below, pp. 38 f., 42); it merely aims to find a Scriptural witness to
warrant the transfer of the apostolic succession of Peter to the Roman bishops. Moreover,
the assertion of Graber (p. 39) that the Beloved Disciple was undoubtedly still living at
the time of writing of John, ch. 21, is by no means proved by the argument that *after*
his death it would have been nonsense to refute the idea that he would not die. Cannot
one say, on the contrary, that precisely then it was necessary to show that the saying of
Jesus concerning 'remaining' was not proved false by the death of that disciple?

ut he gives them no commissions in the name of Jesus, and the Master nowhere entrusts to him such a function for the period of his own earthly life. The three passages, Matthew 16:16 ff., Luke 22:31 f. and John 21:15 ff., in which he is charged with a special obligation towards his brothers, all refer to the future, to the time after the death of Jesus. Thus the gospel tradition knew how to distinguish between the position of Peter before and after the death of Jesus.

In view of this fact, we must consider improbable the assertion some have made, that the pre-eminence of Peter in the circle of Jesus' disciples is merely a pre-dating of the position which he actually held only in the Primitive Church, after the death of Jesus. He is ascribed no leading position at all in relation to the group of the Twelve; on the contrary, he appears only as the most representative of the disciples. What all of them represent, do, and think, comes to particularly strong expression in his person.

One might indeed be tempted to go further and ask how this pre-eminence is to be *explained*. Is it due to the fact that by giving the name mentioned Jesus strengthened greatly Peter's consciousness of being a disciple? Or on the contrary, is it, together with the giving of the name, to be explained on psychological grounds by the character of Peter? The latter possibility has often been considered.[55] It takes its clue from the fact that during the lifetime of Jesus Peter did not show himself a 'rock' at all; on the contrary, his human weakness was very striking. The scene at the Sea of Gennesaret gives a concrete illustration of Peter's character. He is impulsive and enthusiastic; in the first burst of enthusiasm, he does not hesitate to throw himself into the sea when Jesus calls him, but his courage soon fades and fear grips him. So, too, he is the first to confess loudly his loyalty to his Master, but he is the first one who will deny him in the hour of danger. And yet, so one assumes, precisely this character, with its notable contradictions, makes Peter appear as the disciple with special psychological fitness to be the 'rock' among the other disciples. The exuberant enthusiasm, the fiery zeal of this disciple, are said to be in fact the human qualities that were necessary to deserve such a title of honour. His instability and weakness are said to be only the dark side of these qualities.

Nevertheless, it is hardly possible to give a psychological basis for the unique position of Peter and for the giving to him of this name. Indeed, we should not ask at all why Jesus singled him out as 'rock' instead of

[55] So especially by F. Sieffert in *Realenzyklopädie für Theologie und Kirche*, 3rd ed. Article on 'Petrus', Vol. 15, p. 190.

choosing another disciple.[56] According to our sources, we can only confirm the fact of this distinction.

Probably, however, it is also a mistake to say that the representative
position of the disciple Peter and the qualities mentioned were derived
*only* from the giving of the name. We can hardly say that only by this act
did he become conscious that in his person he represented, so to speak,
the totality of the disciples, even during the earthly life of Jesus. Again
we can only state *the fact*: Peter lets us see clearly everything that the call
to discipleship involves in human weakness and privilege.

To the question whether his pre-eminence is to be explained by the
giving of the name, or the giving of the name, on the contrary, by his
actual pre-eminence, there probably is no simple answer. In reality what
is involved is rather a reciprocal action. Jesus knows better than anyone
else the qualities of Peter, both the good and the bad ones, and he takes
account of them in his view of the work he intends his disciples to do. On
the other hand, however, the special distinction given this disciple as a
rock-man rests on the Master's act of sovereign decision, an act which
may have strengthened Peter in the representative role that his nature had
already given him.

For the period following the death of Jesus the question concerning
the unique position of Peter presents itself in another way. The disciple
becomes the apostle of the crucified and risen Lord. In this capacity his
unique position necessarily takes on another character. Of this we must
speak in the next chapter.

[56] K. L. Schmidt, *Festschrift für A. Deissmann*, 1927, p. 301, rightly rejects this
question as to the Why of the choice of Peter as the 'rock'. He observes that it can no
more be answered than can the question why God chose the people of Israel.

C

# 2

# Peter the Apostle

ACCORDING TO the sources at our disposal, the death and resurrection of Jesus create for Peter a completely changed situation. This is true in two respects. In the first place, from this time on his unique role appears no longer merely as that of a representative; in view of the physical absence of the Lord, it naturally appears also in the leadership of the small community of disciples. The character and the time limit of this leadership, however, must still be more exactly determined. In the second place, this unique position now rests upon a specific commission, which must be defined on various sides.

We begin with the first point.

## 1. The Leadership of the Primitive Church

In *The Book of Acts* we clearly note that Peter takes a unique position in the Primitive Church in Jerusalem. Apart from the letters of Paul, of which we speak later, The Acts is our only source. We investigate first the data of the first twelve chapters.

It is Peter who in ch. 1:15 ff. prompts the choice of the twelfth disciple.[1] It at once becomes evident here that the fact of his being spokesman for the others signifies likewise that whatever may be his authorization, he in every case presides over the little group of believers.

He it is who explains to the assembled multitude the miracle of Pentecost (ch. 2:14). 'He stands up with the Eleven', we are told, but he alone speaks. In verse 37, after his speech, the witnesses who had been present at the miracle address themselves, as the author puts it, 'to Peter and the rest of the apostles'.

In ch. 3 he performs the healing miracle on the lame man. In this narrative John is named with Peter in a most remarkable manner. All the

---

[1] P. Gaechter, 'Die Wahl des Matthias (Apostelgeschichte 1, 15-16)' (*Zeitschrift für katholische Theologie*, 1949, pp. 318 ff.), traces the choice back to a special commission given by Jesus.

manuscripts mention him. But the way in which he is introduced and plays little more than the role of an extra could lead us to suppose that his name was added subsequently to that of Peter. Particularly noteworthy in this connection is verse 4: 'Peter looked on the lame man, with John.'[2] If the unnamed Beloved Disciple of the Fourth Gospel had at this time already been identified with John, one could ask whether the mention of John with Peter does not correspond to a tendency similar to that which we confirmed in the Gospel of John.[3] Concerning this point, however, we can say nothing certain. That John actually did occupy a certain authoritative position after Peter in the Primitive Church is made certain by Paul, who in Galatians 2:9 reckons him together with James and Cephas among the 'pillars' of the Church.[4]

In the further development of the story it is Peter who defends the cause of the Gospel when the authorities take action against the apostles (chs. 4:8; 5:29). After the healing of the lame man it is Peter alone who speaks, although we are told in ch. 4:1: 'While *they* were speaking . . .' and although John is again named with Peter in verse 13. In the latter case, however, the mention of his name again limps noticeably and looks like an addition. Thus it cannot be denied that according to this entire narrative Peter as a member of the Jerusalem church occupies the place of leader.

Particularly in the case of Ananias and Sapphira, however, he exercises church discipline in the congregation (ch. 5:1 ff.).[5] Here his authority is especially noticeable. However we may judge concerning the genuineness or spuriousness of Matt. 16:16 ff., and whatever may be the meaning of the words 'bind' and 'loose',[6] in this narrative it is Peter who, as the earthly authority, holds court in the name of God, and according to verse 2 he does this publicly in the presence of the other apostles. The narrative concerning Simon the magician (ch. 8:18 ff.) also presupposes that Peter makes the decisions.

---

[2] ἀτενίσας δὲ Πέτρος εἰς αὐτὸν σὺν τῷ Ἰωάννῃ.

[3] See above, pp. 28 ff.                    [4] See below, pp. 43 ff.

[5] Ph.-H. Menoud, 'La mort d'Ananias et de Saphira (Actes 5, 1–11)', in *Aux sources de la tradition chrétienne. Mélanges offerts à M. Goguel*, 1950, pp. 146 ff., assumes that the intent of the entire section is to explain by their sin the fact of the death of the first members of the Church to die, Ananias and Sapphira. In opposition to this E. Trocmé, *Le livre des Actes et l'Histoire*, 1957, p. 197, emphasizes that the particular character of the sin stands in the foreground of the narrative, and with J. Schmitt, *Les manuscrits de la mer morte. Colloque de Strasbourg*, 1957, pp. 93 ff., he assumes that the married couple wanted to belong to the group of the 'perfect ones' which existed there as it did in Qumran. In opposition to this E. Haenchen, *Die Apostelgeschichte*, 2nd ed., 1959, p. 197, asserts that Peter does not act here like a *Mebaqqer* (inspector) from Qumran. He assumes an ancient Jerusalem tradition for the story of Ananias (not for that of Sapphira).                    [6] See below, pp. 210 ff.

Furthermore, The Book of Acts emphasizes the faith of the people
in the miraculous power of Peter in particular. They actually consider his
'shadow' capable of effecting a healing (ch. 5:15). Although it is said also
of the other apostles that miracles are done by their hands (ch. 5:12) and
that they teach (chs. 2:42; 4:33), yet after the first chapters these same
activities are carried on by Peter in a way which makes him appear, as he
did in the days of Jesus, to be particularly representative. But this, in the
changed situation after Jesus' death, can only mean that he thereby
occupies a *leading* role in relation to the Church; he stands at its head.

This authority extends also to the missionary field in Samaria, which in
the earliest days was dependent on Jerusalem. This land may be called
the original field of the Christian mission. Its actual missionaries are the
Christians who were driven from Jerusalem, most likely at the time of the
martyrdom of Stephen; they probably represented a point of view similar
to that of Stephen. In Acts 8:1 it is explicitly said that on that occasion the
Twelve were *not* expelled.[7] Therefore we probably must seek the fugitives
mainly among the Hellenists of the Church, and the Twelve appear to have
taken an attitude different from that of those men; otherwise they could
not have remained in Jerusalem. These church members driven from
Jerusalem, accordingly, are mentioned as the first missionaries in Samaria
(ch. 8:4), and among them only Philip is definitely named, although he
probably shared this work with other Hellenistic fugitives whose names
are not given. The missionary preaching of these men resulted in complete success: 'Samaria has received the word of God' (ch. 8:14). It is so
much the more astounding that the apostles who had remained in Jerusalem did not rest satisfied with this result, but later sent Peter and John
to Samaria. The Book of Acts explains the necessity for this by saying
that the Holy Spirit had not yet come upon the Samaritans (ch. 8:16),
although, as previously said in verse 12, they had already believed and
been baptized. So it was necessary that Peter and John subsequently lay
hands upon those baptized, and only then did the converted Samaritans
receive the Holy Spirit (ch. 8:17).[8] This clearly means that laying on of
hands and giving of the Spirit were regarded as connected with the
office of the Twelve; it shows that all missionary activity was at first
considered completely dependent upon the Jerusalem church.[9] This fact

---

[7] πλὴν τῶν ἀποστόλων.

[8] See O. Cullmann, *Die Tauflehre des Neuen Testaments: Erwachsenen- und Kinder-
taufe* (*Abhandlungen zur Theologie des Alten und Neuen Testaments*), 1948, pp. 7 f. (Eng.
Tr., *Baptism in the New Testament*, 1950, pp. 11 f.).

[9] P. Gaechter, 'Jerusalem und Antiochia, ein Beitrag zur urkirchlichen Rechtsent-
wicklung' (*Zeitschrift für katholische Theologie*, 1948, pp. 1 ff.), rightly stresses the dependence of the missionary area on the Jerusalem church. The conclusions, however,

is also of importance for the questions which arise when Paul's mission begins.

This dependence is here plainly presupposed. The presentation of The Book of Acts is merely allusive; nevertheless, it permits us to glimpse the state of affairs clearly enough. It gives the impression that those men driven from Jerusalem and now active as missionaries are to be put firmly in their subordinate position. I do not consider it improbable that the Fourth Evangelist opposes this view; when in connection with the mission in Samaria, he gives a saying of Jesus concerning 'the others who have worked', while the apostles 'have entered into their work' (John 4:38), he probably intends to put in the right light the work of those mostly unnamed missionaries to Samaria.[10]

For our problem it is important that on this occasion also Peter was delegated by the Twelve in Jerusalem to go to Samaria. It is true that here again John accompanies him, but his individuality does not emerge at all in the story.

The special mention of the Hellenists in The Book of Acts—their special views as well as the particular lot which befell them—proves that even in the Primitive Church itself there were different tendencies. Peter and the Twelve as a whole appear to have taken a mediating position between the Judaizers and the Hellenists. Peter, therefore, was able to hold together the different elements.[11] As soon as James appears at the head of the Church, this situation will change.

Following the events in Samaria, Peter likewise appears in missionary activity in Lydda, Joppa, and Caesarea, where he performs several miracles and baptizes the Gentile Cornelius (Acts, chs. 9 and 10). This shows that there was a Jewish Christian mission not only among the Jews, but also among the Gentiles; and according to this narrative, Peter takes the first position also as a missionary to Gentiles and explicitly justifies this mission. The role that The Acts assigns to Peter in the Primitive Church in Jerusalem has not been seriously questioned by scholars. As we shall see, the letters of Paul indirectly confirm it. But a definite objection to this picture has been raised as far as Peter's missionary activity is concerned.

which he draws for the cessation of the pre-eminence of this church from the fact that Peter, from a certain time on, left Jerusalem, cannot be defended. See below, p. 44, note 34; p. 45, note 35; p. 51, note 53. Ed. Schweizer, in *Geist und Gemeinde im N. T. und Heute* (*Theologische Existenz*, 1952), understands the connection with Jerusalem only in the sense of a connection in redemptive history.

[10] See O. Cullmann, 'La Samarie et les origines de la mission chrétienne' (*Annuaire 1953/54 de l'Ecole pratique des Hautes Etudes*); further, 'L'opposition contre le Temple de Jérusalem' (*New Testament Studies*, 1959, pp. 157 ff.).

[11] See W. Grundmann, 'Das Problem des hellenistischen Christentums innerhalb der Jerusalemer Urgemeinde' (*ZNW*, 1939, pp. 45 ff.).

It has been held both in earlier as well as in quite recent times that this story, which traces the Gentile mission back to Peter, is entirely or partly the creation of the author of The Acts, who follows the tendency to make Peter parallel with Paul in every respect. In the more recent studies, however, even when it is claimed that the author's editorial activity, determined by theological interests, plays a more or less sizeable role,[12] the fact that the Gentile Cornelius was converted by Peter is recognized, though it is transferred to another time.[13]

After his imprisonment by Herod and his liberation, and in connection with these events, Peter leaves the Holy City, but The Book of Acts gives no information concerning the place to which he goes. The author here expresses himself in a somewhat mysterious manner: he went 'to another place' (Acts 12:17).[14] The Roman Catholic exegetes—though not all of them—are accustomed to identify this 'other place' with Rome.[15] Indeed, an argument recently urged anew[16] could speak in favour of this identification; I refer to the parallel structure of the two parts of The Book of Acts. The first part (chs. 1 to 12) closes with the imprisonment of Peter; the second (chs. 13 to 28) with that of Paul. The second culminates in the arrival of Paul at Rome (ch. 28:14);[17] so one could ask whether it is not the

[12] M. Dibelius, 'Das Apostelkonzil' (*Theologische Literaturzeitung*, 1947, pp. 193 ff.); further, 'Die Bekehrung des Cornelius' (*Coniectanea Neotestamentica in honorem Antonii Fridrichsen*, 1948, pp. 50 ff.); and now, *Aufsätze zur Apostelgeschichte*, edited by H. Greeven, 2nd ed., 1953, pp. 96 ff. (Eng. Tr., *Studies in the Acts of the Apostles*, 1956, pp. 93 ff., 109 ff.), accepts as historical only the fact of the conversion of Cornelius as such, and also a vision belonging in another context; the entire treatment, however, of the basic questions as to the admission of Gentiles into the Church and as to table fellowship with Gentile Christians is to be credited to the author of Acts and his special bias. See also O. Bauernfeind, *Die Apostelgeschichte*, 1939, p. 143; J. R. Porter, 'The "Apostolic Decree" and Paul's Second Visit to Jerusalem' (*Journal of Theological Studies*, 1946, pp. 169 ff.); and E. Trocmé, *Le livre des Actes et l'Histoire*, 1957, pp. 170 ff. There is a good survey in E. Haenchen, *Die Apostelgeschichte*, 1959, pp. 301 ff. He himself does not see any historical event in the narrative, but only the Lucan faith-given conviction that God alone brought about the Gentile mission.

[13] See the historical kernel which W. Grundmann extracts in 'Die Apostel zwischen Jerusalem und Antiochia' (*ZNW*, 1940, pp. 132 ff.). He rejects the chronology of The Book of Acts and transfers the story into the period of the events that occur after Acts, ch. 12, when Peter has already left Jerusalem.          [14] εἰς ἕτερον τόπον.

[15] J. Dupont, *Les problèmes du livre des Actes d'après les travaux récents*, 1950, p. 88: 'If the apostle went to Rome at this time, one could explain the fact that Luke did not want to mention so early the city which was to represent the terminus of his story of the expansion of Christianity.' J. Belser, *Die Apostelgeschichte*, 1905, p. 156, cites another argument: he refers to Ezek. 12:3: 'remove from your place to another', where Babylon is meant. U. Holzmeister, on the contrary, in *Commentarius in epistolas Sanctorum Petri et Judae* (*Cursus Scripturae Sacrae*), 1937, p. 62: 'No argument proves that Peter left Palestine in the year 42; how much more impossible it is to prove that he reached Rome as early as that same year.' C. Cecchelli, *Gli Apostoli a Roma*, 1938, p. 100: 'Certainly it seems impossible to admit the presence of Peter in Rome before 63.'

[16] R. Graber, *Petrus der Fels. Fragen um den Primat*, p. 21.

[17] See also J. Dupont, *op. cit.* above in note 15. R. Graber, *op. cit.*, p. 21, appeals to A. Harnack, *Mission und Ausbreitung des Christentums*, 3rd ed., 1915, Vol. I, pp. 95 f.

journey of Peter to Rome that marks the climax of the first part: 'he departed to another place' (ch. 12:17). Nevertheless, the wording does not permit the identification of the 'other place' with Rome. That the name of Rome was omitted for fear of the pagan authorities, in order to keep secret the place where the head of the Church was staying,[18] might indeed be a possible explanation. Nevertheless, it is purely hypothetical, and would presuppose that The Book of Acts was written during the lifetime of Peter. Again, it is possible that Peter at this time went directly to Antioch, but the story does not say so. It is true that Galatians 2:11 speaks of his presence in Antioch, but concerning the time of his arrival in that city we learn nothing.[19] In reality, that 'other place' can be identified with any city of the Roman Empire.[20] We must reckon with the possibility that even the author himself of The Book of Acts had no definite place in mind.[21] In that case, the statement would only mean that from this point on Peter gives up his fixed residence in Jerusalem, and so also his position in the church there; one aim, among others, was probably to escape Jewish persecution. After this point Peter appears again in The Acts only in ch. 15, at the so-called Apostolic Council, concerning which we must speak later; then, strange to say, he vanishes completely from the narrative. The above-mentioned statement of Acts 12:17, 'he went to another place', thus plainly marks a transition in the activity of Peter and also in his position in the Primitive Church.

But first we must ask how far *the letters of Paul* confirm the data derived from the first twelve chapters of Acts concerning Peter's function as head of the Primitive Church in Jerusalem. In so doing we must note that the greater documentary value naturally belongs to the letters of Paul; they are a direct and earlier source. Since they nevertheless all belong to a later time than the events of Acts, chs. 1 to 12, we cannot expect to find in them many references to these earliest events in the Primitive Church. For the most part, Paul mentions Peter in connection with events that

[18] This is the thesis of R. Graber, *Petrus der Fels*, pp. 16 ff.

[19] See below, pp. 54 f.

[20] Sometimes with Alexandria: S. G. F. Brandon, *The Fall of Jerusalem and the Christian Church*, 1951, pp. 221 f., 225, 232, 242, assumes that Peter went to Alexandria. Matthew, who was connected with Alexandria, magnified Peter for this reason, while for the same reason Luke, who plays Paul off against Alexandria, pushes Peter into the background.

[21] Thus A. Fridrichsen, 'Sprachliches und Stilistiches zum Neuen Testament' (*Kungl. Human. Vetenskaps-Samfundet i Uppsala*, Aorsbok, 1943, pp. 28 ff.), assumes that it was a stereotyped manner of expression. D. F. Robinson, 'Where and When did Peter Die?' (*Journal of Biblical Literature*, 1945, pp. 255 ff.), proposes a theory that is doubtful but worthy of mention: εἰς ἕτερον τόπον would be identical with the 'place of glory', that is, Peter died in Jerusalem at that time, in the year 44; this, Robinson says, is the historical kernel which lies behind the narrative of Acts 12: 1-19.

occurred only in the later period of Peter's life, events about which, except for the Apostolic Council, The Book of Acts tells us so strikingly little. As a direct parallel between Paul's presentation and that of The Book of Acts, we thus have to consider only the Apostolic Council, and we shall see what great problems result when we compare the two passages here involved.

Yet the letter to the Galatians, in which Paul gives autobiographical statements in support of the theological thesis he there defends, does contain a short item which refers to that early period. It confirms, indirectly at least, what we have learned from the first chapters of The Acts concerning Peter's leading role in the Jerusalem church. We hear in Galatians 1:18 ff. that during Paul's first visit to Jerusalem, three years after his conversion, he desired to get acquainted with Cephas. It is true that according to this passage James the brother of the Lord, who as we shall see will later succeed Peter in the leadership of that church, is already in Jerusalem. However, when Paul first comes to Jerusalem, James plainly does not yet occupy an outstanding position. It seems likely that in his capacity as a physical brother of Jesus he already is playing a certain role *beside* Peter. For while Paul did not come to Jerusalem with the purpose of meeting James, yet he is the only one whom Paul sees apart from Peter. Obviously, even at this time, that is, three years after Paul's conversion, it was already impossible for a Christian believer to make a stay in Jerusalem without coming into contact with James.

For the position of Peter, however, it is significant that Paul, who does not yet know him personally, undertakes the journey only on his account. Quite possibly a contributing factor may have been Paul's wish to receive from Peter personal memories of his life with Jesus. Other apostles in Jerusalem, however, could have given him such reminiscences. If he nevertheless wanted to become acquainted with Peter in particular, the reason probably was that Paul, like all converts, knew that this man then stood at the head of the Mother Church in Jerusalem. To be sure, the leadership of Peter did not have as yet the character of the later 'monarchical' episcopate. The authority of his colleagues in the group of the Twelve, and probably that of James also, was too great to permit this. The role of the apostles in Jerusalem must not be confused with that of the group of Elders who later stand at the side of the bishop.[22] Of that role we

---

[22] Whether the Twelve *as a group* held the leadership is strongly doubted by H. von Campenhausen, *Kirchliches Amt und geistliche Vollmacht*, 1953, pp. 15 f., and Ed. Schweizer, *Gemeinde und Gemeindeordnung im Neuen Testament*, 1959, pp. 41 f. (Eng. Tr., *Church Order in the New Testament*, 1961, pp. 47 f.). In opposition to this, reference has recently been made to the analogy of the 'Council' of the Twelve in the Qumran sect

should probably be reminded by the added mention of John in the passages cited in The Acts. Only with this restriction can we speak of the episcopal office of Peter in Jerusalem.

The recognition of Peter's authority by Paul has the greater weight because it occurs in Galatians, in a letter, that is to say, written by Paul under special circumstances which prompted him to demonstrate in other respects his independence of the Jerusalem apostles. This independence, indeed, is clearly shown in the narrative of the conflict that broke out between Peter and Paul in Antioch (Gal. 2:11 ff.).

By the time Paul wrote his letter to the Galatians, the situation in Jerusalem had changed. Peter had long since left Jerusalem, and was now charged with the leadership of the Jewish Christian *mission*, while in Jerusalem itself James had become his successor.[23] It is therefore the more significant that Paul, in his account of that first journey to Jerusalem, nevertheless lets us see that at that time Peter still stood at the head of the Jerusalem church.

## 2. *The Mission in the Service of the Jewish Christian Primitive Church*

We have seen that according to Acts 8:14 Peter occasionally went, even in the first years of the Primitive Church, to the missionary district of Samaria. Thus gradually—above all by reason of the experiences which Acts, chs. 9 and 10, report that he had in Lydda, Joppa, and Caesarea— he may have recognized that his real apostolic task, and probably also his spiritual gift, lay less in the leadership of the established Church than in missionary activity.[24] At any rate, it is quite remarkable that the apostle who later is regarded as the personification of organized church government in reality exercised such a function for only a short time at the beginning, and then exchanged it for missionary work. Peter is not the archetype of the church official but of the missionary.[25] The two functions—church

(rejected by E. Haenchen, *Die Apostelgeschichte*, 1959, p. 129). On this question see B. Reicke, 'Die Verfassung der Urgemeinde im Lichte jüdischer Dokumente' (*Theologische Zeitschrift*, 1954, pp. 95 ff.), and *Glauben und Leben der Urgemeinde*, pp. 21 ff.; he emphasizes that the leading role of Peter and the authority of the Twelve were exercised at the same time.

[23] F. M. Braun, *Neues Licht auf die Kirche*, 1946, p. 170, already speaks in this connection of 'succession to apostles'. But on this point see below, pp. 44 ff., 229 ff., 234 f.

[24] According to W. Grundmann, 'Die Apostel zwischen Jerusalem und Antiochia' (*ZNW*, 1940, pp. 129 ff.), Peter first went, after the events reported in Acts, ch. 12, to Joppa, Lydda, and Caesarea. Thus on this view The Book of Acts places this journey in the wrong chronological position.

[25] This fact, which in what follows is attested by the New Testament, is also retained

administration and missionary work—were separated. These functions
James and Peter divided among themselves. The division probably was
not connected with any definite decision or act, as one might believe from
later tradition, which says that the apostles, in obedience to a command
of the Lord, left Jerusalem twelve years after the resurrection.[26] Although
this is not completely excluded, the division was probably made rather by
gradual and natural development. To this conclusion points the fact that
while Peter is still the head of the Church, James already plays, as we
have seen in Galatians 1:18 ff., a somewhat leading role *beside* him. According to Acts 12:17, when circumstances forced Peter to be absent, James
must already have taken his place, for in verse 17 Peter says: 'Tell this
to James and to the brothers', just as it previously was said in Acts 2:37,
in a way that corresponded to the existing situation: 'Peter and the rest
of the apostles.' Certainly the final transfer of the leadership to James is
connected with the imprisonment and liberation of Peter, as a result of
which the latter had to leave Jerusalem.[27] It must be seriously considered
whether the freer attitude Peter took towards the Law may not have played
a part in the change of leadership.[28] This possibility forces itself upon us
when we recall that at an earlier time, after the martyrdom of Stephen,
who was hostile towards the temple, his followers, the Hellenists, had had
to leave Jerusalem, while the Twelve, who did not share the radicalism of
Stephen, were able at that time to remain there, as Acts 8:1 expressly
notes. Must not something analogous have occurred this time, except that
now Peter had to leave Jerusalem, while James, who represented the
stricter Jewish standpoint, was able to remain?

Accordingly, the vague statement of the similar passage Acts 12:17,
'he went to another place', is intended simply to point out that after the
liberation of Peter his final transfer to exclusively missionary activity took
place. Preparation for the transfer had already been gradually made in the
previous period.

in the *Pseudo-Clementina*, which to be sure are cited here only as a secondary witness;
no teacher is authorized without warrant from James (*Recognitions*, IV, 35); Peter is sent
to Caesarea at the command of James to oppose Simon. There is thus no mention here of a
transfer of the central leadership from Jerusalem to Rome. P. Gaechter, 'Jerusalem und
Antiochia' (*Zeitschrift für katholische Theologie*, 1948, pp. 1 ff.), does not take account of
the actual role that James plays in Jerusalem.

[26] *Kerygma Petri*, according to Clement of Alexandria, *Stromateis*, VI, 5, 43. A. Harnack, *Geschichte der altchristlichen Literatur*, II, 1, 1897, p. 243, regards this tradition as
very ancient.

[27] So rightly R. Graber, *Petrus der Fels*, p. 23; also W. Grundmann, 'Die Apostel
zwischen Jerusalem und Antiochia' (*ZNW*, 1940, p. 129).

[28] Ed. Schweizer, *Gemeinde und Gemeindeordnung im Neuen Testament*, 1959, p. 37
(Eng. Tr., *Church Order in the New Testament*, 1961, p. 43), concurs with my assumption.

In the later apocryphal Acts of Peter, probably the only point which we should preserve as the historical basis is the fact that in the second half of the exercise of his apostolic calling, Peter actually undertook extensive missionary journeys.

We also find this new function of Peter confirmed in the letters of Paul. In I Corinthians 9:5 he speaks of the fact that 'the rest of the apostles, the brothers of the Lord, and Cephas take' their wives 'with them'. The comparison with Barnabas and Paul shows what is to be supplied: 'on their missionary journeys'.[29] Thus at a considerably earlier time Peter must already have begun to concentrate upon missionary work. Accordingly he, just like Paul and Barnabas, interrupted his missionary travels to go to Jerusalem for the so-called Apostolic Council.

At the time of this so-called Apostolic Council, as Paul presents it—that is, at the time when the two missionary districts, the Jewish Christian and the Gentile Christian, were separated on the basis of the friendly agreement of Galatians 2:1 ff.—the assumption of the leadership of the Church by James the brother of the Lord must already have been an accomplished fact. Already in this connection Paul indirectly ascribes to him the presiding role among the 'pillars'. According to the majority of the ancient manuscripts Paul here enumerates the 'pillars' in the following order: James, Cephas, John. This could be mere accident. But in a text such as this one, in which the authority of the negotiating partners is not unimportant, the order does mean something.[30] Indeed, the ancient copyists correctly sensed this. Hence arose the textual variants concerning this very point of order. The text designated by D places Peter before James in this list.[31] According to the principle that the 'more difficult reading' is the more ancient, we must regard as secondary this variant

---

[29] Thus we cannot speak of a transfer of the see from Jerusalem to Rome, as E. Stauffer, *op. cit.*, p. 32, suggests (see also P. Gaechter, in note 9 on pp. 36 f.). Paul is speaking of missionary journeys, which may have taken Peter in every direction, and so, of course, to Rome also. See below, pp. 71 ff.

[30] Gaechter rightly concentrates his discussion of my book about Peter on the subordination of Peter to James, a point which I strongly emphasize. But the argument which he uses in an attempt to weaken the pre-eminence of James (in his essay, 'Jakobus von Jerusalem', *Petrus und seine Zeit*, 1958, p. 278) is not convincing: he claims that in Gal. 2:9 Paul named James first only because he here was making a concession to the Judaizing obstructionists who appealed to James. An additional objection comes from P. Gaechter, *op. cit.*, pp. 278 and 430, and from other Roman Catholic scholars; they think that from the fact that Paul gives to Simon the name 'Rock' (*Kepha, Petros*) they may conclude that he regarded Peter and not James as the leader. But this designation, which during Jesus' lifetime was only Peter's *added* name, had become his regular name since Christ had appeared to him, and furthermore, it means more than 'leader' of the Church.

[31] It might seem suspicious that D here, in agreement with verses 7 and 8, reads Πέτρος and not Κηφᾶς, as is customary in Paul. But P[46] also, which moreover correctly reads James in the first passage, reads Πέτρος.

attested by D. For we perceive that in later times one could take offence at this putting of James before Peter.[32]

At all events we conclude, from the order in which Galatians 2:9 lists the 'pillars', that at the time of the incident reported it was no longer Peter but James who was the authoritative leader in Jerusalem.[33]

As far as the Jewish Christian missionary work dependent on Jerusalem is concerned, Peter stood at its head. For this reason Paul, in the same passage, Galatians 2:7 f., mentions only Peter as the organizer of the Jewish Christian mission, just as he regards himself as the organizer of the Gentile Christian mission: '[The leaders] saw that I had been entrusted with the gospel to the uncircumcised just as Peter had with that to the circumcised; for he who was at work in Peter to make him an apostle among the circumcised was also at work in me for the Gentiles.'

Nevertheless, in this position as leader of the Jewish Christian mission Peter was dependent upon *Jerusalem*. This explains the fact that according to Galatians 2:12 he has to fear the 'party of James' and must 'dissemble' on their account.[34] In this fact, among others, lies the difference between his mission and that of Paul; he is a missionary in the closest dependence on Jerusalem, while Paul—by an understanding, it is true,

[32] On the other hand, Codex Alexandrinus does not mention Peter at all. Perhaps an anti-Petrine tendency could be at work here.

[33] Against E. Fascher, in Pauly-Wissowa, column 1342. That James really was the authoritative leader of the entire Church is confirmed by the *Pseudo-Clementina*. See on this point H. J. Schoeps, *Theologie und Geschichte des Judenchristentums*, 1949, p. 125; *Aus frühchristlicher Zeit*, 1950, pp. 120 ff.; that as time passes James takes over the leadership in Jerusalem is emphasized also by H. v. Campenhausen, *Zeitschrift für Kirchengeschichte*, 1950/1, p. 137, and *Kirchliches Amt und geistliche Vollmacht in den ersten drei Jahrhunderten*, 1953, p. 21; further, E. Lohse, 'Ursprung und Prägung des christlichen Apostolates' (*Theologische Zeitschrift*, 1953, p. 265, note 25). On the question of the Pseudo-Clementines see also below, pp. 229 f., and the references given there in note 21. Let me say expressly, however, that in this connection I cite the Pseudo-Clementine writings only as a secondary source. I emphasize this because of the criticism wrongly brought against me from the Roman Catholic side; I am ready, it is charged, to found my assertion that James took over the leadership while Peter was still living, on such obscure sources as the Pseudo-Clementine writings. (See for example P. Gaechter, *Petrus und seine Zeit*, 1958, p. 271.)

[34] P. Gaechter, 'Jerusalem und Antiochien' (*Zeitschrift für katholische Theologie*, 1948, pp. 42 ff.), and recently *Petrus und seine Zeit*, 1958, p. 290, who is concerned that the role of Jerusalem should cease with the absence of Peter and pass over to Antioch, attempts to separate the party of James from James and minimize their role in Antioch. Peter, he says, yielded to them only 'for the sake of desirable peace'. This, however, conflicts with the fact that, as Paul explicitly writes, Peter *was afraid* (φοβούμενος) of the circumcision party. He has to fear these people! It will not do to treat this fear as a trifle, as is often done in Roman Catholic reviews of my book, as though what was involved was only a fear that there might be 'difficulties' with the party of James (who really were subordinate to Peter). For the verb in Paul's use almost always indicates fear before authorities. Moreover, this meaning also fits what we know of Peter from the Gospels (the denial). On the conflict at Antioch, see further below on p. 48.

with the Jerusalem 'pillars'—has more independence as he carries out his preaching among the Gentiles.[35]

The account in the letters of Paul informs us that there exists, in accord with the Jerusalem agreement of Galatians 2:9, a rather loose tie even between the Pauline mission to Gentiles and the Primitive Church of Jerusalem. This was the collection which Paul loyally made for Jerusalem in all the missionary churches that he founded. This collection for the Primitive Church was not only a humanitarian enterprise; it was conceived first of all as a manifestation of the unity of the Church, just as in Judaism the tax for the Jerusalem Temple represented the outward bond of unity for the entire company of Jewish believers dispersed throughout the Roman Empire. The Pauline mission, which seems to have had its centre in Antioch, nevertheless remains subordinated, at least to the extent of this tie, to the leadership in Jerusalem.[36]

[35] P. Gaechter, *Petrus und seine Zeit*, 1958, pp. 258 ff., in the already mentioned chapter, 'Jakobus von Jerusalem' (first published in *Zeitschrift für katholische Theologie*, 1954, pp. 130 ff.), tries to refute me mainly by minimizing the value of the witness Paul gives in Gal. 2:7 concerning the Apostolic Council. He reproaches me (p. 284) that I 'sketched Paul according to Paul, and so sketched him wrongly'. Paul, he says, gave a 'very one-sided account'. See also Gaechter's sharp judgment concerning Paul's attitude in the conflict at Antioch (*op. cit.*, p. 432; on this, see below, p. 49, note 45). This hyper-critical attitude towards the Pauline texts is the more astonishing since Gaechter places such great confidence in the narratives of Acts, though they are later. Where the presentation of Acts differs from that of Paul, as in the account concerning the Apostolic Council, he unhesitatingly gives the preference to Acts. Thus from the fact that in Gal. 2:7–9, in connection with the Gentile mission, Paul mentions only himself and not his fellow-worker Barnabas, Gaechter concludes (pp. 266 f.) that Paul also was wrong in naming Peter alone in connection with the Jewish mission. In this way Gaechter thinks to refute my statement that from that moment on Peter (in dependence on Jerusalem) stood at the head of the Jewish mission. On the other hand he deduces from Acts 15, on the basis of a quite complicated argument, that Peter spoke at the Council not as the leader of that mission but 'as the head of the Church' (that is, because he said on behalf of the Gentiles basically what Paul and Barnabas should have said, and did so while he himself had as yet converted no Gentiles except Cornelius).—E. Lohse, *op. cit.*, p. 265, attaches great significance, as I do, to the fact that Peter became a missionary after leaving Jerusalem.

[36] Very questionable and probably unacceptable even for many Catholic exegetes is P. Gaechter's appraisal of the collection (see especially *Petrus und seine Zeit*, 1958, pp. 283 ff.). He completely rejects the explanation which I give in agreement with Holl and Lietzmann and the great majority of scholars; he says that it had nothing to do with the temple tax and promoted a benevolent aim in a merely temporary situation. In no event is the argument valid which he introduces on p. 285, that if the collection had been set up in conscious dependence on the temple tax, one would have to be able to explain 'how Rome, which already towards the turn of the century was plainly the centre of the Church and at least in temporal succession the successor to Jerusalem, failed to continue an institution that was of such great benefit'. What is here presupposed about the succession of Rome requires proof. Moreover, the word λειτουργέω in Rom. 15:27, and the manner in which the Apostle speaks of the collection in this entire section Rom. 15:25–33, shows that Paul conceived it as a manifestation of unity. When he asks the Roman Christians in particular to pray that the collection may be *accepted* by those in Jerusalem (vs. 31), he reckons, at least in principle, with the possibility of a rejection, which would indicate that those in Jerusalem would not recognize him as belonging to

The bond created by the collection was the more necessary because now, as a result of the agreement reached at Jerusalem, there were two missionary organizations.[37] According to Galatians 2:9 this was the decision the apostles reached in Jerusalem: *the missionaries from Jerusalem were to go to the circumcised, while Paul and his fellow-workers went to the Gentiles* (with the right not to demand circumcision in their mission activities).[38] Thus there occurred even in Primitive Christianity a decisive separation, even though it took place in a peaceful way. In opposition to the later divisions, especially the great ones that go back to the sixteenth-century Reformers, this first one, in spite of the complete and mutually recognized independence, nevertheless expressed the common bond in that joint task of the collection.[39] If conflicts nevertheless occurred at a later

the Church. Paul's great concern is that this may not happen. The same section shows that the Jerusalem church is important to Paul as the centre of redemptive history (see vs. 27). Only by making the collection unimportant can Gaechter assert (*Petrus und seine Zeit*, 1958, p. 21) that Jerusalem plays no role or at least only a very secondary role in Paul's thinking! He seeks to prove that in Primitive Christianity the Jerusalem church *as such* was not charged with any mission. Indeed, he actually expresses himself in the following pointed manner: 'All the authority that it (the Jerusalem church) possessed radiated from its director' (*op. cit.*, p. 269). That is in fact the *crux of the problem*, and it is to his credit that Gaechter has expressed so clearly what is a silent presupposition of so many Roman Catholic exegetes. But even Gaechter adduces no texts that really establish this conception. It is not proved that after Peter left Jerusalem the church there ceased to be the centre and that this centre automatically was transferred by Peter to the place where he was.

[37] See on this point J.-L. Leuba, *L'institution et l'événement*, 1950, pp. 62 ff.

[38] E. Haenchen, *Die Apostelgeschichte*, 1959, pp. 408 f., without seeing in the passage the official text, correctly explains it as a concession that those in Antioch could forgo circumcision in their Gentile mission. Nevertheless, the (peaceable) separation was thereby realized and the theological question was not solved; this is somewhat obscured by Haenchen.

[39] If we look at the history of Christianity as a whole, it may be permissible, in view of the historical framework which is normative for the present work, to ask whether today also the Roman Catholic Church and the great World Council of Churches independent of Rome, frankly renouncing hope of agreement in matters of church polity and doctrine, should not at least seek to establish a similar tie in a collection for one another which both sides would undertake with conscious surrender of any higher aim, simply as a sign of the fact that the two great separate Churches nevertheless invoke the name of the same Lord. For the unavoidable abstention of the Roman Catholic Church from all non-Roman ecumenical conferences proves that as far as man can foresee, even though the effort to reach common convictions in central questions must never cease, there can no longer be a real union, at least in the points that cause that abstention. By the proposal to take a collection for one another which would explicitly demonstrate that we belong together we of course do not mean that the situation today is the same as the one at the time of the Apostolic Council. The chasm between the churches separated today is unfortunately very much deeper. For here the separation has not taken place, as it did in Jerusalem, in peace and 'with a handshake', nor with recognition that both sides are free to apply their theological principles. Nevertheless, there also, in that Primitive Christian discussion concerning circumcision, the issue in question was a doctrinal, *unbridged* difference which dealt with a *central point*, that is, the conception of grace, for the question whether it was possible to eat with uncircumcised Gentile Christians could be denied by the party of James. In this important respect, as is shown by the actual separation and the continued doctrinal discussions of this theme in the

time, this was because the separation could not be carried out in practice; the reason was that all of the local churches probably were already of *mixed* membership at the time of their origin. There naturally were no churches that were solely Gentile Christian, for in all the larger centres there were Jews; indeed, we know that Paul regularly addressed himself to them first of all. On the other hand, there were no churches that were solely Jewish Christian, for everywhere former pagans joined the existing Jewish Christian churches. This had not been taken into account in the separation decided upon in Jerusalem, and therefore conflict inevitably arose at once in Antioch.

Thus Jewish Christian missionaries could always build upon the fact that there were Jewish Christian members in the churches founded by Paul. They could use this fact to justify their interference in Pauline churches. Paul could have done the same thing in the churches that the Jewish Christian missionary organization had founded. In Romans 15:20, however, he explains explicitly that to him it was a matter of honour not to do so. This no doubt corresponded to the spirit of the Jerusalem agreement, even if the letter of it permitted an intervention in mixed congregations. Paul therefore always considered it an unjustified 'intrusion' by the Jerusalem mission when their representatives intervened in the churches he had founded, probably with the argument that they were responsible for the Jewish Christian elements that such churches contained. Paul made but *one* exception; this was with regard to the church at Rome. Therefore he feels compelled to justify urgently this step; he appeals to his need of having in the capital city a working base for his further activity in the far West—Spain. More than elsewhere he fears that this step may cause conflicts to arise in Rome, and we shall see how justified these apprehensions were.[40]

The fact that the Jerusalem agreement did not take into account the unavoidably mixed composition of the churches has been insufficiently considered, it seems to me, in recent studies. Only this fact, however, makes intelligible the entire tragic debate whose echoes we hear in all the letters of Paul. We should emphasize here without delay that in this entire

---

letters of Paul, the discussion even on that occasion did not issue in a shared conviction. If nevertheless the decision to undertake separate labours was made '*with a handshake*', this fact should provoke thought even today. The above proposal, which I made in the first edition, I have in the meantime formulated more clearly in my booklet, *Katholiken und Protestanten. Ein Vorschlag christlicher Solidarität*, 1958 (Eng. Tr., *A Message to Catholics and Protestants*, 1959), and it has already been carried out on all sides in a gratifying way.

[40] The circumstances in which the martyrdom of Peter took place ('jealousy', I Clem., ch. 5) find explanation on this basis. See below, pp. 91 ff., 105 ff.

debate *Peter himself no doubt stood nearer to Paul* than did the other members of the Jerusalem mission.[41] This emerges clearly from the way in which Paul speaks of him, and especially where he must blame him. Peter, of course, was bound by his position as the commissioned leader of the mission sent out from Jerusalem.

As far as the question about Peter is concerned, we must in any case be clear that from the time of the Apostolic Council there were two missionary organizations. On the one side was the one at whose head Peter stood. It depended directly on the Primitive Church at Jerusalem, which was now under the leadership of James. On the other side was the organization of Paul and Barnabas. It was independent of Jerusalem, and henceforth had with the Mother Church only the loose external connection provided by their joint work on the collection. We have seen that the Primitive Church in Jerusalem, even while Peter himself was still there, had claimed the right to exercise supervision over the mission in Samaria. Looked at in this light, the agreement of Galatians 2:9 meant that the Jerusalem group renounced in principle this claim of oversight with reference to the Pauline mission. *They henceforth acted as head only of the Jewish Christian mission carried out by Peter.*

This, however, means that in principle Paul was independent not only of the Mother Church in Jerusalem—towards which, however, he had the obligation of the collection—but especially of Peter. So we understand that when the conflict concerning table fellowship with converted Gentiles occurred at Antioch (Gal. 2:11 ff.), Peter does not appear in any sense as Paul's superior, but on the contrary *must accept a rebuke from him*. It may be that the Reformers, in their polemic against Rome, emphasized much too strongly the significance of this reprimand of Peter.[42] On the other hand, even the Church Fathers recognized its importance.[43] It may also be correct that Paul, in spite of this conflict, did not cease to

[41] J. L. Klink, *Het Petrustype in het Nieuwe Testament en de oudchristelijke Letterkunde*, 1947, actually assumes that Peter had to leave Jerusalem on account of his free attitude to the Gentile mission.

[42] See K. Holl, 'Der Streit zwischen Petrus und Paulus zu Antiochien in seiner Bedeutung für Luthers innere Entwicklung' (*Gesammelte Aufsätze*, III, 1928, pp. 134 ff.).

[43] Chrysostom (Homily on Gal. 2:1; Migne, *P. G.*, LI, Col. 371 ff.) and Jerome (Epistles 86–97 and Commentary on Galatians) were so offended by this event that they used the highly artificial explanation that Peter and Paul staged the whole conflict as a trick to instruct the believers! Even Augustine (Epistles 8–19) protested against this interpretation. See J. A. Möhler, 'Hieronymus und Augustinus im Streit über Gal. 2, 14' (*Gesammelte Aufsätze*, edited by J. Döllinger, 1839, pp. 1 ff.); Fr. Overbeck, *Die Auffassung des Streites des Paulus mit dem Petrus bei den Kirchenvätern*, 1877; A. M. Völlmecke, 'Ein neuer Beitrag zur alten Kephasfrage' (*Jahrbuch von St. Gabriel*, 1925, pp. 69–104).

designate Simon by his title Cephas, Rock.[44] Nevertheless, this passage proves that from the time when each begins to exercise his parallel mission, no one can speak of a 'primacy' of Peter in relation to Paul,[45] and in Corinth Paul will no more permit a Cephas party than he will any other party whatever.[46] Was it perhaps with particular reference to the Cephas—'Rock'—party that Paul wrote in I Corinthians 3:11 that no one can lay any other 'foundation' except that one which is laid, Jesus Christ?

In estimating the important event of the Apostolic Conference and the separation of missionary areas made there, we have based the preceding discussions exclusively upon the information Paul gives in his letter to the Galatians. As already mentioned, however, Peter appears but once in The Book of Acts in the period following the events of ch. 12. It is the last time before he completely vanishes from the narrative. This appearance is in ch. 15, on the occasion of the Apostolic Council there described. We must inquire whether the role that Peter here plays agrees with what we have learned from the letters of Paul.

Before doing so, however, we must ask whether the meeting of the apostles recounted in Acts, ch. 15, is the same as the one in Galatians 2:1 ff. At the outset we note one fact: the answer to this much debated question does not have for our study of Peter the same fundamental importance which it naturally possesses in the endless discussions that occur in special studies, as well as in general presentations of the history of Primitive Christianity.[47]

The question must nevertheless be raised. The detailed circumstances in the two accounts are so similar that the assumption almost forces itself upon us that both accounts must deal with the same event. If we make this assumption, undeniable differences appear between the presentation of Paul in Galatians 2:1 ff. and that of The Acts in ch. 15. These differences are hard to reconcile. It will suffice to mention here two points. According to Galatians 2:1, Paul went to Jerusalem by reason of a 'revelation'; according to Acts 15:1 ff., on the contrary, he went by commission of

[44] This is stressed by F. M. Braun, *op. cit.*, p. 84, and also by P. Gaechter, *Petrus und seine Zeit*, 1958, pp. 278, 430. See above, p. 43, note 30.

[45] The manner, however, in which Gaechter, *op. cit.*, p. 432, seeks to evade this conclusion seems to be a solution prompted by embarrassment: 'As far as the legal question is concerned, we should in any event consider whether it is completely excluded that Paul in his excessive zeal took upon himself a role which did not really belong to him.' According to Gaechter, the expression which Paul himself used in Gal. 2:11, 'to resist one to his face', means 'to make a scene', and this suggests that he acted towards Peter with 'excessive zeal'!

[46] Wilhelm Vischer, *Die evangelische Gemeindeordnung*, 1946, p. 18, writes on this very point: 'By this teaching (that Peter should have a successor in his unique office) the papal Church enlarged the schism of the Corinthian Peter party into a yawning cleft in the foundation.'     [47] For orientation see E. Haenchen, *Die Apostelgeschichte*, 1959, pp. 396 ff.

D

the Church. Furthermore—and this is the most important difference—according to Galatians 2:6, no ritual requirements of any kind are im posed on Paul for his Gentile mission.[48] The fundamental question con cerning the necessity of circumcision receives no theological settlement the only decision is the already mentioned separation of missionary fields which permits Paul to convert Gentiles without requiring circumcision of them. The conference of Acts, ch. 15, on the contrary, ends with th passing of the so-called Apostolic Decree (ch. 15:19 f.); it requires o converted Gentiles the observation of a minimum number of regulations chiefly of ritual character and having to do with meals.[49]

The difficulty that results from this last-named difference is furthe increased by the fact that in The Book of Acts itself this same 'decree is reported to Paul at a much later time, when he comes to Jerusalem fo the last time (ch. 21:25). It is reported in a manner that does not at al presuppose he had previously known of it or actually taken part ir deciding upon it. Moreover, it has been pointed out, especially in recen studies, that we really have to do with two quite different problems, which stand side by side in The Book of Acts without being clearly related to each other. On the one side is the question of the conversion of the Gen tiles and so of the acceptance of uncircumcised men into the Church on the other side is the question of table fellowship with them.

All these and other observations have long since stimulated the most varied attempts at a solution. We need not report here concerning them. I mention only the main types of explanation into which the most recen hypotheses can be divided.[50] According to one theory there is in The Book of Acts absolutely no parallel to Galatians 2:1 ff. According to a second view, while the meeting of Galatians 2:1 ff. is reported in Acts, it is reported not in ch. 15, but in ch. 11:27; this passage tells of an earlier visit of Paul and Barnabas to Jerusalem, on the occasion of which they brought help to the Christian brothers who were suffering from famine. According to the third explanation, the event of Galatians 2:1 ff. is indeed identical with that of Acts, ch. 15, but on this view the differences must be explained either through a chronological inaccuracy of The Book of Acts, or by a conscious tendency of its author, or by the way he

---

[48] ἐμοὶ γὰρ . . . οὐδὲν προσανέθεντο ('for to me . . . they imparted nothing additional').

[49] H. Schlier, Der Brief an die Galater (Meyer's Kommentar, 10th ed.), 1949, ad. loc., seeks to solve the contradiction by emphasizing 'to me' (ἐμοί): only on Paul personally was no further obligation placed.

[50] A good survey, in addition to that of Haenchen, is given by Dom J. Dupont, Les Problèmes du livre des Actes d'après les travaux récents, 1950, pp. 51 ff., and also by W. G. Kümmel, 'Das Urchristentum' (Theologische Rundschau, 1942, pp. 81 ff.; 1948, pp. 3 ff., 103 ff.; 1950, pp. 1 ff.).

combined various sources. We have mentioned here only the most
important solutions; in reality there exist an innumerable mass of
variations.[51] Indeed, it will hardly be possible to attain here to certainty,
and we can proceed only by the use of hypothesis. The most probable
one to me is still that one which sees in Galatians 2:1 ff. the same
event reported in Acts, ch. 15; it furthermore considers correct its
chronological location in Acts, ch. 15; but it transfers to a later time
the passing of the Apostolic Decree, and assumes that the author of The
Book of Acts erred in connecting the decree with his account of the
Apostolic Council.[52]

This question is of interest to us only in its relation to our study of
Peter. We must consider whether, on the assumption that in Acts, ch. 15,
we have to do with the same event as in Galatians 2:1 ff., the role of Peter
corresponds to that which he plays in the meeting Paul describes in
Galatians 2:1 ff.

First of all, we note that Peter appears here in his capacity as missionary,
and no longer as leader of the Church. This fits perfectly the picture we
formed from the letter to the Galatians. In the narrative of The Book of
Acts (ch. 15:7), Peter, it is true, stands up first to tell of his missionary
experiences, before Paul and Barnabas begin to speak. But it is James,
nevertheless, who plainly presides over the entire assembly, for he draws
the conclusion from what has been heard and also formulates the 'decree'.[53]
Even if the author of Acts was wrong in connecting this decree with this
Council, he nevertheless clearly held that James then stood at the head of
the Mother Church in Jerusalem, and this is the more important since in
the earlier chapters of The Book of Acts this role always belongs to Peter.

We further note that in Acts, ch. 15, Peter speaks simply as the representative of the mission dependent on Jerusalem. This agrees entirely
with the assumption which earlier considerations have already forced
upon us, that Peter as well as Paul and Barnabas *interrupted his missionary activity* to go to the Council at Jerusalem.

---

[51] Above all, in the third interpretation the event of Acts 11:27 ff. also is identified
with that of Acts 15:1 ff., in which case, of course, the question arises whether the date
of Acts 11:27 ff. or that of Acts 15:1 ff. is to be preferred.

[52] So on the whole, although again with various differences in chronology, H. Schlier,
*Der Brief an die Galater*, 1949, pp. 66 ff.; M. Dibelius, 'Das Apostelkonzil' (*Theologische
Literaturzeitung*, 1947, pp. 193 ff.); M. Goguel, *La Naissance du Christianisme*, 1946, pp.
323 ff.; W. G. Kümmel (see especially *Theologische Rundschau*, 1950, pp. 27 f.). See also
M. Dibelius—W. G. Kümmel, *Paulus* (Göschen), 1951, p. 118. This explanation is rejected by E. Haenchen, *Die Apostelgeschichte*, 1959, pp. 410 ff. He ascribes the four
requirements not to any ancient document but to a tradition current in the time of Luke
and falsely traced back to the Apostles.

[53] James is thus not merely one of the 'chief figures' of the Council, as P. Gaechter
writes in 'Jerusalem und Antiochia' (*Zeitschrift für katholische Theologie*, 1948, p. 41).

Among the missionaries present, it is true, he plays the leading role, since his task here is to represent the mission that reaches out from Jerusalem. In this respect the opening words of Peter in Acts 15:7 are characteristic: 'Brothers, you know that in the early days God made choice among you[54] that by my mouth the Gentiles should hear the preaching of the Gospel and believe.' Even if the words were not thus spoken by Peter, they fit the situation perfectly. Peter, as we also learn from Galatians 2:14, in his innermost heart stood much nearer to Paul than to James in the whole question of table fellowship with Gentile Christians, and probably also in his general attitude towards the Law. In this conference, where the question at issue is the position on the problem of circumcision, he refers not to his experiences as apostle to the Jews but to the less frequent cases where he has converted Gentiles. He can also claim, in spite of the presence of Paul and Barnabas, that he has been elected to preach the gospel to the Gentiles. The right to do this *within the Jewish Christian mission* we must almost certainly concede to him, unless we banish entirely into the realm of legend the history of the conversion of Cornelius or, in excessive adherence to the principle of the 'Tübingen School', ascribe it to the undeniable tendency of the author to obliterate the opposition between Jewish and Gentile Christians. We must recognize in it at least a historical kernel. Thus even before the decisive separation agreed on in Jerusalem, Peter belonged to another missionary organization than did the more independent apostle Paul.

Nevertheless, he represents a standpoint not far removed from that of Paul. To fail to take this sufficiently into account introduces great confusion into our conception of Primitive Christianity and leads to the formulation of unnecessary hypotheses. While Peter in administrative relations was dependent on the Jerusalem authorities, and for this reason has to 'fear' the 'party of James', nevertheless, in his relation to Gentile Christianity and the Law, he stands fundamentally much closer to Paul than to James.[55] It certainly contributed much to the peaceful settlement

[54] According to Foakes-Jackson and Kirsopp Lake, *The Beginnings of Christianity*, *ad loc.*, we should translate: 'that God has chosen us'. (According to Torrey the Aramaic ⊐ is the object.) See also II Esdras 19:7=Neh. 9:7: ἐξελέξω ἐν Ἀβραάμ: 'Thou didst choose Abraham.'

[55] The all too simple statement that Peter was nothing but a representative of the Jerusalem viewpoint is made under the influence of the 'Tübingen School', whose influence still continues, for example, in H. Lietzmann, 'Zwei Notizen zu Paulus' (*Sitzungsbericht der Berliner Akademie der Wissenschaften*, 1930, No. 8), and also in his *Geschichte der alten Kirche* (Eng. Tr., *History of the Early Church*, 4 vols., 1937–51). See for the opposite view E. Hirsch, 'Petrus und Paulus' (*ZNW*, 1930, p. 23). In ancient times this false picture was spread especially by the *Pseudo-Clementina*, and above all by the ancient source of the Preaching of Peter that they incorporated. See on this point H. J. Schoeps, *Theologie und Geschichte des Judenchristentums*, 1949, pp. 118 ff. I believe

of the conflict that Peter particularly, the missionary leader commissioned by Jerusalem, supported his colleagues Paul and Barnabas so powerfully at the Council.[56]

That later at Antioch, contrary to his inner conviction, he 'dissembled' due to fear (Gal. 2:11 ff.), may fit the psychological picture we get from the Synoptic Gospels—the picture of the impulsive disciple Peter, over-zealous in swearing loyalty to his Lord and yet denying him in the hour of danger. But on the other hand, it must be said in extenuation that as the missionary leader dependent on the Jerusalem church, he occupied in relation to the party of James *an infinitely more difficult position* than did the independent Paul. This conflict must have put Peter, the former and first head of the Church, in *a particularly painful dilemma*. Its difficulty we can only surmise, since we have no such extensive collection of letters from Peter as we have from Paul, and in addition, precisely by reason of his dependence on Jerusalem, he could scarcely speak so openly on this subject as Paul could.[57] We must keep this in mind in our interpretation of later events.

In any case, we dare not forget this aspect if we wish to form a correct picture of Peter the apostle. We must think of it particularly when we attempt to gain a conception of Peter's apostolic travels, concerning which we know so little. Mediators always have a particularly difficult position, and Peter, as we have seen,[58] probably had to mediate between the Hellenists and the Judaizers from the very beginning of the Primitive Church.

With regard to the Apostolic Council, which falls in the first half of this activity, our conclusion is that the data of The Book of Acts concerning *the position of Peter* agree on the whole with the earlier observations which we made independently of Acts, ch. 15. This is true, no matter how we think in detail concerning other aspects of the relation between Galatians 2:1 ff. and The Book of Acts. In any case this very point confirms the assumption that the author of The Book of Acts placed the Apostolic

that especially in the conception of the atoning death of Jesus it was Peter in particular who stood very close to Paul. This is indicated by the fact that The Acts in the first chapters seems to have preserved the memory that Peter described Jesus as παῖς ('servant'), that is, as the Isaian Suffering Servant of God. See on this point below, pp. 67 ff.

[56] It is probably Peter who chiefly deserves the praise which E. Haenchen, *Die Apostelgeschichte*, 1959, p. 409, gives to the Jerusalem church on the occasion of the Apostolic Council: 'This recognition of the Antiochene Gentile mission was in fact an astonishing thing for which the Jerusalem group deserves all honour.'

[57] A recollection of this, however, could be preserved in I Clem., ch. 5, where it says that Peter 'on account of unjustified jealousy had to suffer not one or two but manifold troubles'. Is this not a reference to the way that Peter was *constantly* torn between the two positions? See below, p. 106.

[58] See above, p. 37.

Council (except for the decree) in its correct chronological location.

Concerning the entire second half of Peter's missionary activity we know, as has been said, practically nothing but the fact that it occurred. The introduction of I Peter (ch. 1:1), whether authentic or not, seems to presuppose that he did mission work in *Asia Minor*. Nothing definite concerning it is known. His name is chiefly connected, however, with three mission centres in particular: Antioch, Corinth, and Rome.

We have heard that at the time of the incident reported in Galatians 2:11 ff. Peter was at *Antioch*, where he had to submit to the rebuke by Paul. He may already have been there at an earlier time, but we have no certain information on this point. The Book of Acts only tells that those scattered as a result of the Stephen persecution came to Antioch (Acts 11:19). Since it is reported in ch. 8:1 that the apostles were not then dispersed with the others, the assumption that Peter founded the church at Antioch, while not explicitly excluded, is nevertheless hardly probable.[59] One could ask at the most whether Peter *subsequently* did not have to confirm the conversion of the Antioch Christians, and so indirectly confirm the foundation of that church, somewhat as he did in Samaria in the position he then held as head of the Primitive Church in Jerusalem. We possess no information, however, of any such role. In any case, the assertion that Peter founded the church at Antioch appears relatively early, in Origen, and then later in Eusebius, Chrysostom, and Jerome.[60] The church of Antioch can thus make a legitimate appeal to this rather ancient tradition. It must be emphasized that in this respect Antioch can raise in principle the same claim as Rome, since this Petrine tradition for Antioch is attested at least as well, if not better. We shall have to recall this in Part Two of this book, for this question is not without importance in reference to the exclusive claim that the Roman bishop lays to Matthew 16:16 ff. Only from this point of view are we interested in the assertion that Peter founded the church at Antioch. As a historic fact, however, the claim cannot be supported.

We have already seen that it is arbitrary to identify the 'other place' of Acts 12:17 with Antioch.[61] The only certain thing, accordingly, is that Peter made a stay in Antioch. He probably also maintained rather close relations with this church, as the incident of Galatians 2:11 ff. presupposes.

---

[59] It is denied also by H. Katzenmayer, 'Die Beziehungen des Petrus zur Urkirche von Jerusalem und Antiochien' (*Internationale kirchliche Zeitschrift*, 1945, pp. 116 ff.).

[60] Origen, *Homily on Luke*, VI, c (Migne, *P. G.*, XIII, Col. 1814 ff.); Eusebius, *Ecclesiastical History*, III, 36, 2 and 22; Chrysostom, *Homily on Ignatius* (Migne, *P. G.*, L, Col. 591); Jerome, on Gal. 2:1 (Migne, *P. L.*, XXVI, Col. 340); *De viribus illustribus*, 1 (Migne, *P. L.*, XXIII, Col. 637).

[61] See above, pp. 39 f.

Indeed, his position as leader of the Jewish Christian mission necessarily brought him into particularly close connection with this church, which by reason of its racial composition was the centre not only of the Gentile Christian but also of the Jewish Christian mission.

Did Peter visit *Corinth* during his missionary travels? Neither The Book of Acts nor Paul's Letters to Corinth say so, and in any case, The Book of Acts appears to know nothing of any participation by Peter in the *founding* of this church. Its narrative in ch. 18 speaks only of the conversion of the Corinthians through the preaching of Paul; it scarcely leaves room for a parallel activity of Peter. The statements of I Corinthians also exclude Peter's participation in the founding of the church. In I Corinthians 3:6 Paul writes: 'I planted, Apollos watered, God gave the increase'; and in I Corinthians 4:15: 'Even if you have countless masters in Christ, yet not many fathers. For in Christ Jesus *I*[62] became your father through the Gospel.' Here Paul clearly considers himself the sole founder of this church.

In I Corinthians, however, there is support for the assertion often made that *later* Peter came also to Corinth and worked there as a missionary. In the first chapters of I Corinthians we are told of parties which were formed in Corinth, and ch. 1:12 mentions a 'Cephas party' in addition to a Paul party and an Apollos party and the uncertain 'Christ party'. Does not the existence of this Cephas party presuppose the presence and preaching of Peter at Corinth? The fact that this letter directed to the Corinthians makes special mention of the example of Cephas, who takes his wife with him in his missionary travel (I Cor. 9:5), could argue for this view; one could, if pressed for evidence, also cite the noteworthy fact that Paul, as he himself says (I Cor. 1:14 ff.), baptized only Gaius, Crispus, and Stephanas and his household. Could it be that he was of the opinion that to baptize with the Spirit was the business of the Twelve, as in Samaria (Acts 8:14 ff.)?[63]

On these brief indications, however, we can build at best only a hypothesis. The assertion that Peter was in Corinth has been made, as we have said, by the above-named scholars. It has also found vigorous opponents.[64]

[62] ἐγώ.     [63] See above, pp. 36 f.

[64] Among the defenders of the thesis that Peter made a stay in Corinth I name particularly Eduard Meyer, *Ursprung und Anfänge des Christentums*, Vol. III, pp. 441 (note 1), 498 ff.; A. Harnack, *Mission und Ausbreitung des Christentums in den ersten Jahrhunderten*, 3rd ed., 1915, p. 63, note 2; H. Lietzmann, 'Die Reisen des Petrus' (*Sitzungsbericht der Berliner Akademie der Wissenschaften*, 1930, pp. 153 ff.); J. Zeiller, *L'Eglise primitive* (*Histoire de l'Eglise*, Vol. 1, p. 227; Eng. Tr., *History of the Primitive Church*, Vol. 1, 1942, p. 233); recently, H. Katzenmayer, 'Das Todesjahr des Petrus' (*Internationale kirchliche Zeitschrift*, 1939, p. 85), and especially his article, 'War Petrus in Korinth?' (*Internationale kirchliche Zeitschrift*, 1943, pp. 20 ff.). Among those who oppose this view

In ancient times it first appears about the year 170, in the letter of Diony-sius of Corinth to the Romans. Eusebius cites it: 'By this exhortation you have united closely the tree of the Corinthians and that of the Romans—trees that were planted by Peter and Paul. For both [apostles] taught in the same way, in that they planted in our Corinth, and after they taught together in Italy they suffered martyrdom together.' [65] The value of this testimony is lessened at once by the manifestly false assertion, refuted not only by The Book of Acts but also by Paul, that the church in Corinth was *founded* by Peter together with Paul.

Altogether apart from this assertion of Dionysius, however, we must take a stand concerning the deduction which draws from the existence of the Cephas party in Corinth the conclusion that Peter later made a stay in this city. This conclusion is in any event not convincing. For all Jewish Christian missionaries regarded Peter as the head of their mission; no doubt they took particular pleasure in setting him up against Paul as the 'true apostle', and they probably appealed to his special relations with Jesus, as we can perceive indirectly in the letters of Paul. On this account Paul has to protest that he, too, has 'seen Christ' (ch. 9:1). But Peter himself certainly did not belong to those against whom Paul turns with particular severity in his letters to the Corinthians. He is not one of those whom Paul elsewhere characterizes as 'false brothers', who have followed him everywhere to discredit his person and above all his apostolic author-ity.[66]

In Galatians likewise the polemic of Paul does not have Peter in view. Here, too, there is no need to assume, as various historians have asserted, that Peter had been in Galatia. Nothing indicates that the incident at Antioch led to a breaking of the Jerusalem agreement and so to a break between Paul and Peter.[67] Peter himself, according to all that we have con-cluded concerning his attitude, is probably not directly responsible for the counter-mission of the 'false brothers' who sought everywhere to sabotage the work of Paul. Presumably they took particular pleasure in appealing to the name of Peter, and probably represented in some way that he had sent them. But doubtless this was not so. It is sufficient, there-

---

should be named above all W. Bauer, *Rechtgläubigkeit und Ketzerei im ältesten Christen-tum*, 1934, p. 117; M. Goguel, 'L'apôtre Pierre a-t-il joué un rôle personnel dans les crises de Grèce et de Galatie?' (*Revue d'Histoire et de Philosophie religieuses*, 1934, pp. 461 ff.); *La naissance du Christianisme*, 1946, pp. 335 ff. (Eng. Tr., *The Birth of Christian-ity*, 1954, pp. 305 ff.).

[65] *Ecclesiastical History*, II, 25, 8.

[66] So rightly E. Hirsch, 'Petrus und Paulus' (*ZNW*, 1930, pp. 63 ff.), in opposition to H. Lietzmann, *op. cit.*, in note 64 above. See also on this subject above, pp. 52 f.

[67] This is rightly emphasized by M. Goguel, against H. Lietzmann, *op. cit.*

fore, to assume that these people came into the Corinthian church that Paul had founded.

This, however, does not exclude the possibility that in the course of his journeys Peter once visited Corinth (and also Galatia). Since he stood at the head of the Jewish Christian mission, we certainly must reckon with this possibility. But it cannot be proved either from the existence of the Cephas party nor by any other indications.[68] The stay in Corinth, accordingly, can neither be definitely asserted nor denied, but it may be considered as possible.

We thus see that since our ancient sources give only extremely meagre reports, we can say nothing certain concerning this entire missionary activity of Peter.[69] It is particularly significant that these sources, the Letters of Paul and The Book of Acts, are also completely silent concerning the stay of Peter in *Rome*, which later was universally accepted. This question, however, we shall consider in connection with the special chapter which we shall devote to Peter the Martyr.

Thus far, then, we have established that *the Apostle Peter, in the first period after the death of Jesus, leads the Primitive Church in Jerusalem; he then leaves Jerusalem, where the leadership passes over to James; and from then on, by commission of the Primitive Church and in dependence on it, he stands at the head of the Jewish Christian mission.*

### 3. *The Question of the Apostolic Commission*

It still remains to answer the question which we put at the opening of this chapter: does this apostolic activity of Peter—in its two successive expressions, the leadership of the Church and the missionary preaching —go back to a special commission which Peter received from Jesus?

We have seen that as far as the unique position of Peter *during the lifetime of Jesus* is concerned, we can no longer determine how far it has its basis in his peculiar character traits, and how far in the distinction Jesus gave him by bestowing on him the name 'Rock'. We have shown that both answers must be taken into account, and furthermore that at that time

[68] H. Katzenmayer, 'War Petrus in Korinth?' (see above, note 64), uses among other things to support his argument I Clem., ch. 47, where it says that Apollos was approved by the apostles. It is claimed that he could have met Peter only in Corinth. Nevertheless, it is by no means established: 1, that Peter is here meant; 2, that he could have met Apollos only in Corinth.

[69] E. Haenchen takes a much more sceptical attitude towards the view I here maintain concerning the position of Peter as a missionary. See 'Petrus-Probleme' (*New Testament Studies*, 1961), a review article which deals with the second German edition of my book on Peter.

Peter's unique position did not yet take the form of setting him over the other disciples. For the period after the death of Jesus, however, where Peter for a time actually *led* the Jerusalem church, the question concerning his commission presents itself in another way.

The Primitive Church has the consciousness that everything which happens in it and to it belongs to the central redemptive action which is being fulfilled in Christ; all these events are an integral part of the redemptive plan of God. Thus is explained the lofty apostolic consciousness of Paul, who does everything in the conviction that he is an instrument of the God-guided Christ Event. We are not so well informed concerning the consciousness of any other apostle, but in view of the fact that the first Christians always regarded themselves as the true people of God, we may assume without question that Peter also was conscious in his action of being specially commissioned by Christ.

Does this consciousness of Peter's also rest upon the experience of a special call, as we know it does in the life of Paul? Does not such an experience, in the Primitive Christian view, belong as a matter of course to the apostolic office?[70] If so, then with reference to Peter the further question arises: Did his actual call to be an apostle come through the *incarnate* Jesus, if it refers also to the time after his death? Or did it first come from the *risen* Christ? Or must we reckon with *both*?

The saying to Peter concerning the Church (Matt. 16:16 ff.) will be discussed in detail in Part Two of this book. It must be mentioned here merely in a preliminary way, in so far as it presents a basis for a commission from the historic Jesus which Peter must carry out after Jesus' death. The action of Peter in condemning Ananias and Sapphira (Acts 5:1 ff.) could be explained very well as the fulfilment of the promise there given.

Since, however, that passage is so vigorously disputed, we shall adduce it here, as we did in Chapter One, in a merely provisional manner. Here, as there, we must say that even if we make no use of this saying, the result remains on the whole the same; the less disputed commission of Jesus to Peter to 'strengthen the brothers' (Luke 22:31 f.),[71] and furthermore, the undeniable fact that Jesus gave him the name 'Rock' (even without the reason added in Matt. 16:17 ff.), are sufficient to trace the unique position of Peter as leader of the Jerusalem church back to a commission that the earthly Jesus gave.

---

[70] See below, pp. 220 f., and the literature cited there; also, A. Fridrichsen, 'The Apostle and his Message' (*Uppsala Universitets Arsskrift*, 1947).
[71] See above, pp. 27 f.

Thus, even apart from Matthew 16:16 ff., we find it clearly possible that Peter's leading position in the Primitive Church rests upon the distinction or commission which Jesus gave to his disciple Peter even during his earthly life and which Peter has occasion to fufil only after the Lord's death.

It has of course been asserted that the saying in Luke 22:31 f., as well as all the passages in the Synoptic Gospels which give Peter a place of distinction, were later creations of the Church; in this way, it is claimed, the Church later provided a legal authorization by the historical Jesus for the leading role that Peter had actually played in Jerusalem. But we have already seen that the distinction given Peter by the name Cephas can in no case be so explained. Altogether apart from the *confirmation* that Matthew 16:17 ff. gives, we have to do here with a fact which can scarcely be disputed.

More recent studies, on the other hand, do indeed assume a special commission, but transfer it into the period after the death of Jesus, when the *risen* Christ appears and gives a commission to Peter. This commission, it is claimed, the gospel tradition later transferred back into the life of Jesus. We shall have to return to this explanation with reference to its special bearing on Matthew 16:17 ff. For the time being, however, we must say of it that at least the giving of the name Cephas cannot thus be ascribed to the Primitive Church.[72]

We possess, it is true, trustworthy traditions which attest that the *risen* Christ gave to Peter a special distinction and a special commission. Here at any rate we stand upon solid ground, and although, as I am convinced, we must acknowledge that the historical Jesus had already given Peter a special distinction, so that the question does not confront us in the form of an unconditional alternative, nevertheless for the foundation of the apostolate of Peter a *greater and more direct significance* attaches to the commission from the *Risen* One. We recall that it was an important but not the exclusive[73] prerequisite of the call to apostleship that one had seen the *risen* Lord (I Cor. 9:1; Acts 1:22).[74] So a call to a special apostolic

[72] K. Goetz and E. Dinkler take even this final step; they assume that the giving of the name is to be ascribed to the Primitive Church. See above, p. 22.

[73] H. v. Campenhausen, 'Der urchristliche Apostelbegriff' (*Studia theologica*, Lund, 1948, pp. 112 f.), rightly emphasizes how unsatisfactory is the recent custom which simply identifies apostle and witness to the resurrection. Sufficient to prove it unsatisfactory is the fact, clear from I Cor. 15:3 ff., that not all whom Paul enumerates as witnesses of the resurrection became apostles. (Note the more than five hundred brethren in I Cor. 15:6.)

[74] See K. H. Rengstorf, Article on ἀπόστολος ('apostle') in G. Kittel's *Theologisches Wörterbuch zum N. T.* (Eng. Tr., *Bible Key Words*, Vol. II, 1958). See further on this question below, pp. 221 f.

office by the *Risen* One appears almost a necessity, even if, as was doubtless true of Peter, a distinction had already been conferred by the earthly
Jesus.

In view of the great significance which the appearance as such has for
the call to apostleship, one can ask whether every appearance of the
Risen One was not regarded in itself as a 'call'. In the case of Paul, at least,
it is certain that the appearance of the Risen One, whom he sees on the
way to Damascus, coincides with his call. As far as Peter is concerned,
however, the two facts are reported separately; they are not combined
in the sources we possess concerning the appearances of the Lord that he
saw. We hear on the one hand, in I Corinthians 15:5 and in Luke 24:34,
that Christ appeared to Peter; on the other hand, in John, ch. 21, we hear
that on the occasion of an appearance at which, in addition to Peter, other
disciples also are present, the special commission is given to him to 'feed
the sheep of Christ'. It has indeed been asserted that these passages all
deal with one and the same event. Before we decide concerning this hypothesis, we desire first to evaluate separately the fact reported in I Corinthians 15:5 and Luke 24:34, to see what it teaches as to the role of Peter in
the Primitive Church.

First of all, it cannot be emphasized too strongly that according to
I Corinthians 15:5 Peter is the *first* one to whom the Lord appeared.[75]
The risen Christ thereby put the seal, so to speak, upon the distinction
which during his lifetime he had given Peter by naming him Cephas. The
passage I Corinthians 15:5, which names Peter as the first witness of the
resurrection, is perhaps the earliest Christian text that we possess; it is
older than the letters of Paul and he explicitly quotes it as a citation from
the earlier tradition transmitted to him.[76]

It is noteworthy that the Gospels do not tell of this appearance to Peter.
Even Luke gives no account of it, although he briefly mentions the fact.

[75] F. Kattenbusch, 'Die Vorzugstellung des Petrus und der Charakter der Urgemeinde zu Jerusalem' (*Festgabe für K. Müller*, 1922, pp. 328 ff.), and 'Der Spruch
über Petrus und die Kirche bei Matthäus' (*Studien und Kritiken*, 1922, p. 130), wrongly
denies this; he attempts to take the εἶτα ('then') in a non-chronological sense. For the
enumeration in I Cor. 15:5, however, the order is obviously significant. Hence A. Harnack, 'Die Verklärungsgeschichte Jesu' (*Sitzungsbericht der Preussischen Akademie der
Wissenschaften*, 1922, p. 68); K. Goetz, *op. cit.*, pp. 4 ff.; and E. Stauffer, *op. cit.*, pp.
6 ff., have given proper attention to the fact that Peter is the first one who saw the Risen
One. K. Goetz rightly points out, in opposition to F. Kattenbusch, that the words 'last
of all' in I Cor. 15:8 make it impossible to dispute the chronological element in the
enumeration.

[76] According to our previous discussion it is in any case impossible to assert with
E. Stauffer, *op. cit.*, p. 6, note 14, that 'here speaks no partisan but rather an opponent of
Peter'. Neither the authors of the formula cited nor Paul, who cites it, can be called an
opponent of Peter.

In his Gospel the Eleven report to the returning Emmaus disciples: 'the Lord has really arisen, and he has appeared to Simon' (Luke 24:34).

Was this appearance perhaps reported in the lost ending of Mark? The question forces itself upon us when we note that in two passages, and indeed in the last verses preserved for us, this Gospel makes special mention of Peter in connection with the journey to Galilee which Jesus announces is to occur after his resurrection.[77] In the former passage, Jesus says: 'When I have risen I will go before you to Galilee' (Mark 14:28). It is Peter himself who in the following verse continues the conversation with a reference to this promise. In the other passage the young man at the grave who is clothed in white announces: 'Say to his disciples *and to Peter* that he goes before you to Galilee' (Mark 16:7). In view of this one can indeed ask whether we must not postulate that a narrative concerning an appearance of Christ to Peter stood at the end of the Gospel of Mark.[78]

To assume this implies that the conclusion of Mark is lost and that it contained the narrative of the appearance to Peter that I Corinthians 15:5 and Luke 24:34 mention. This naturally remains a hypothesis, but much speaks for its correctness. It is certainly noteworthy that we possess no story concerning an event of such importance as the first appearance of the Lord, especially since it concerned the very disciple who shortly before had denied him. It may also justifiably be asked whether that event has left in the texts *preserved* any other traces, in addition to the two brief notices in I Corinthians and the Gospel of Luke.

First of all, it is believed that we possess more than a trace, that we actually possess an expansion of the actual narrative of that appearance, in the supplementary Chapter 21 of the Gospel of John.[79] It is indeed striking how, in the second part of this story, Peter is pushed into the foreground, but then, in the same way as in the corresponding passages

[77] The view championed by E. Lohmeyer, *Galiläa und Jerusalem*, 1936, that the appearance to Peter occurred in Jerusalem, would in that case become more difficult to hold.

[78] So E. Stauffer, *op. cit.*, pp. 11 f. K. Goetz, *op. cit.*, p. 73, also considers this possibility. So does N. Huffman, 'Emmaus Among the Resurrection Narratives' (*Journal of Biblical Literature*, 1945, pp. 205 ff.); to be sure, he rather arbitrarily seeks also to identify the unnamed disciple of the Emmaus story with Peter and makes Luke responsible for the transfer of the scene to Jerusalem. On the other hand, K. L. Schmidt, *Kanonische und apokryphe Evangelien und Apostelgeschichten*, 1944, p. 27; N. B. Stonehouse, *The Witness of Matthew and Mark to Christ*, 1944, pp. 86 ff.; W. C. Allen, in *Journal of Theological Studies*, 1946, pp. 46 ff.; 1947, pp. 201 ff., deny that the original conclusion of Mark has been lost. They hold rather that the words 'for they were afraid' (ἐφοβοῦντο γάρ) are the intended conclusion of the Gospel.

[79] This was already the view of Arnold Meyer, *Die Auferstehung Jesu Christi*, 1905, p. 168.

of the preceding chapters, is put parallel to the Beloved Disciple. The threefold assertion of love for his Lord and the threefold commission undoubtedly stand in intentional contrast to the threefold denial.[80] It may be that the miraculous catch of fish which is reported in the first part of the story connects also with the story of Peter's call in Mark 1:16 ff., and is intended to indicate the fulfilment of the promise there given concerning the 'fishers of men'. In its present form the chapter certainly bears the 'Johannine' stamp in both its parts, and especially in the second one; it may be, however, that a Marcan narrative concerning the appearance of Jesus to Peter lies at the basis of the story.[81] Nevertheless, it must be conceded that this assumption also is only a hypothesis, inasmuch as this entire story, as it is preserved for us in the Gospel of John, deals neither with the first appearance nor with one supposed to have been granted to Peter alone. If, however, it should prove correct that the connection of the commission given to Peter with the words referring to the Beloved Disciple is due merely to the author of the supplementary chapter, then this hypothesis would have a greater degree of probability. This would be the more likely since later eastern sources also tell of an appearance of Christ to Peter connected with a special commission.[82]

We cannot here attain complete certainty. Nor can we do so with regard to the further assumption that the gospel tradition transferred the important event of Christ's appearance to Peter back into the earthly life of Jesus, so that this event now finds expression in the narrative of Luke 5:1 ff. concerning the miraculous catch of fish at the Sea of Gennesaret,[83] further in the narrative of Matthew 14:28 concerning the walking on the sea,[84] especially in the transfiguration story,[85] and finally—concerning

[80] This interpretation, which had already been given by Ambrose and Augustine, is rejected by M. Goguel, *L'Eglise primitive*, 1947, p. 192; *Jésus*, 1950, p. 390. See on the other side J. Bernard, *A Critical and Exegetical Commentary on the Gospel According to St. John*, 1928, Vol. II, p. 690.

[81] E. Stauffer, *op. cit.*, p. 16, actually writes that 'The author of John, ch. 21, knew and used the lost ending of Mark.' See also A. Harnack, *Lukas der Arzt*, 1906 (Eng. Tr., *Luke the Physician*, 1907).

[82] See below, p. 64, note 93.

[83] So J. Bernard, *op. cit.*, p. 690, and E. Stauffer, *op. cit.*, p. 17.

[84] H. Sasse, 'Die erste Erscheinung des Auferstandenen' (*Theologische Blätter*, 1922, p. 59).

[85] Thus Wellhausen, *Das Evangelium Marci*, 1909, p. 71, already assumed, as did R. Bultmann, *Geschichte der synoptischen Tradition*, 2nd ed., 1931, p. 278, and K. Goetz, *op. cit.*, pp. 76 ff., that the transfiguration story arose from the memory of a resurrection appearance. On the contrary, A. Harnack, 'Die Verklärungsgeschichte Jesu, der Bericht des Paulus und die beiden Christusvisionen des Petrus' (*Sitzungsbericht der Preussischen Akademie der Wissenschaften*, 1922, pp. 76 ff.), and Ed. Meyer, *Ursprung und Anfänge des Christentums*, Vol. I, 1921, pp. 152 ff., hold that the transfiguration story is good tradition; they actually assume the opposite position, that this event from the earthly life of Jesus is the basis of the vision that Peter had after the Lord's death. E. Lohmeyer,

this we shall have to speak further at a later point—in the saying to Peter concerning the Church in Matthew 16:17 f. and in the commission of Luke 22:32.[86]

Not without reason, moreover, have I Peter 1:3 and II Peter 1:16 ff. been connected with the vision seen by Peter.[87]

Even if all these hypotheses are correct, it still remains puzzling that the memory of the appearance to Peter has been preserved only in scattered traces. Hence an explanation has quite properly been sought for this remarkable gap in our tradition. What interest may have been present to push into the background this unusually important event? Some have thought of a conflict between adherents of James and of Peter.[88] But this could hardly have occasioned the silence that exists in the writings in which one expects a narrative concerning these events. A more likely contributing factor could have been the inner compulsion not to be content with *one* witness for so important a fact as an appearance of the Risen One, but to introduce two or more (Deut. 19:15), so that the preference would be given to appearances before more than one witness.[89] In this connection, furthermore, one has recalled also the discussions between Jewish and Gentile Christians, such as are attested for us from the beginning of the second century and probably reach back into even earlier times. We learn from the *Pseudo-Clementina* that in Jewish Christian circles the apostolic rank of Paul was contested by pointing out that it rested only upon a vision.[90] Thus in this Jewish Christian writing the value of visions in general is denied by Peter himself.[91] If such considerations were already raised in the controversies between Paul and the Judaizers, then we definitely must reckon with the possibility that the Jewish Christian gospel tradition tended to prefer not to base the authority of

---

'Die Verklärung Jesu nach dem Markusevangelium' (*ZNW*, 1922, pp. 185 ff.), also disputes the derivation of the transfiguration story from a resurrection appearance; nevertheless, he does not consider the transfiguration historical, but holds that this narrative arose from Jewish conceptions. See now H. Baltensweiler, *Die Verklärung Jesu. Historisches Ereignis und synoptische Berichte*, 1959.

[86] See E. Stauffer, *op. cit.*, pp. 20 ff., 18 ff.; R. Bultmann, *Theologie des Neuen Testaments*, 1948, p. 46 (Eng. Tr., *Theology of the New Testament*, Vol. I, 1951, p. 45).

[87] Usually an allusion to the transfiguration story is seen here. K. Goetz, *op. cit.*, p. 89, is probably correct in opposing this view.

[88] A. Harnack, *op. cit.*, p. 70.

[89] See Lyder Brun, *Die Auferstehung Christi*, 1925, p. 22; K. Goetz, *op. cit.*, p. 74.

[90] *Homilies* 17, 19. See O. Cullmann, *Le problème littéraire et historique du roman pseudo-clémentin*, 1930, pp. 248 f. C. Holsten, *Die Messiasvision des Petrus und die Genesis des petrinischen Evangeliums*, 1867, p. 120, already explained on this basis the suppression of the report of Christ's appearance to Peter.

[91] *Recognitions*, II, 62. Peter here tells that at the Sea of Gennesaret he believed in his spirit that he saw Jerusalem and Caesarea, and when he later came to Caesarea, the reality did not correspond at all to what he had seen in vision.

Peter upon a commission given only by the Risen One. Connected with this could be the fact that the significance which in the later life of Peter attached to the appearances in general, and above all to that first appearance of Jesus, was curtailed. Recent scholars, indeed, believe that they find in Peter a special capacity for visions.[92]

However that may be, and in spite of its meagre emphasis in the Primitive Christian writings,[93] the unshakable fact remains that Peter was the first to see the Risen One. In the earliest period this certainly must have contributed greatly to his *authoritative position* in the Primitive Church.[94] For at that time there certainly existed no reason to belittle visions as a basis of apostolic authority. The enumeration of the appearances, which constitutes the content of the oldest Christian document preserved to us (I Cor. 15:3 ff.), proves on the contrary what a great value was ascribed to these events as an attestation of the resurrection. Thereby the witnesses themselves also received special distinction. It is clear that he to whom had been given the dignity of being the *first* witness of that mighty fact was regarded, just because of this chronological preferment, as the one especially commissioned by Christ to hand on this witness. Accordingly, even this first appearance of Jesus, which has sufficient documentary proof, would suffice to give the foundation for the authoritative position of Peter as the leader of the Church.[95] There is the additional point, however, as we have seen, that in John, ch. 21, we actually possess a tradition according to which Peter was explicitly commissioned by the Risen One to 'feed his sheep'. Whether this deals with the same event or

[92] K. Goetz, *op. cit.*, pp. 98 ff., recalls in this connection Acts, chs. 10 and 11; 12:9 in addition, he recalls the passage mentioned in the Pseudo-Clementine *Recognitions*, II 62, and especially the Apocalypse of Peter, which likewise presupposes that Peter was regarded as a 'seer' in a special sense; he also recalls the famous *Quo-vadis* story from the *Actus Vercellenses*, ch. 35. See also W. Grundmann, 'Die Apostel zwischen Jerusalem und Antiochia' (*ZNW*, 1940, p. 135).

[93] As attestations from *later* times should be named here: The Gospel of Peter, the Ethiopic Apocalypse of Peter, Pistis Sophia, the Syriac Treasure Cave (translation by C. Bezold, 1883, p. 71), and especially the mediaeval writing of the Arab Asch Shahrastani on 'Religious Sects and Philosophical Schools' (*Die Religionsparteien und Philosophenschulen*, German translation by Th. Haarbrücker, I, 1850, pp. 360 f.). See on this subject F. Haase, *Apostel und Evangelisten in den orientalischen Ueberlieferungen*, 1922, pp. 208 ff.; further, K. Goetz, *op. cit.*, pp. 89 f.—According to A. Harnack, 'Petrus im Urteil der Kirchenfeinde des Altertums' (*Festgabe für Karl Müller*, 1922, pp. 2 ff.), even Celsus knew of the appearance of Christ to Peter. He holds that Origen, *Contra Celsum* II, 55, refers to Peter.

[94] The importance of the first appearance of Christ for the Petrine question is also correctly understood by E. Seeberg, 'Wer war Petrus?' (*Zeitschrift für Kirchengeschichte* 1934, pp. 571 ff.). J. Klausner, *From Jesus to Paul*, translated from the Hebrew (1943), also emphasizes it strongly. In general, he ascribes to Peter the exclusive leading role in the origin of the Primitive Church.

[95] Therefore a special call separate from the appearance, such as is postulated by A. Fridrichsen, *op. cit.* (see above, p. 58, note 70), would not be absolutely necessary.

not, the deeper meaning of the special commission to Peter in John, ch. 21, is in any case already implied in the fact of the appearance to Peter that I Corinthians 15:5 reports.

We still must consider the wording of the commission as it is formulated in John 21:16 ff.: 'Feed my sheep.' It has rightly been pointed out[96] that the Damascus Document discovered in 1896,[97] which in connection with the recent manuscript discoveries in Palestine takes on particular importance,[98] speaks of the leader of the fellowship as the 'shepherd of the flock'. His duty is to proclaim the word, explain the Scripture, and exercise community discipline (ch. 13:9).

The command to feed the sheep includes the two activities which we have shown to be the successive expressions of Peter's apostolate: leadership of the Primitive Church in Jerusalem and missionary preaching. We perceive from the conceptions which lie behind John, ch. 10, that not only the leadership of the Church but also the missionary work belongs to the office of shepherd. The linguistic usage, which there designates the Jews first of all as the 'sheep', proves that both functions have primarily in view *the Jews*. In this sense Jesus speaks in the Synoptic Gospels of the 'lost sheep of the house of Israel' (Matt. 10:6), to which he knows himself to be sent; this does not exclude but is in fact the foundation for his responsibility for the 'other sheep' who do not belong to this flock (John 10:16).

We thus see that the commission given by the Risen One may be applied to the functions which the apostle Peter actually exercised successively in his relations with the Jewish Christian Primitive Church.

So we reach the conclusion that *his position probably rests in the first instance upon a commission from the risen Lord*; at the same time, however, the fact that the earthly Jesus gave him the special distinction of the name Cephas, and further the representative role of the former disciple of Jesus, helped to confer authority on him as leader of the Church and as missionary.

Even here, however, we must emphasize that in John, ch. 21, the commission to feed the sheep also has connected with it the prediction of the martyrdom of Peter. This, however, means that the commission to the

---

[96] E. Stauffer, *op. cit.*, pp. 4 ff.

[97] Published by Schechter in 1910. W. Staerk, *Die jüdische Gemeinde des neuen Bundes in Damaskus*, 1922; L. Rost, *Die Damaskusschrift*, 1933.

[98] From the almost endless literature I cite, in addition to the articles by R. de Vaux in *Revue Biblique* (since 1949) and by W. Baumgartner, 'Der palästinische Handschriftenfund', in *Theologische Rundschau* (since 1948 9), which give quite complete orientation, the comprehensive volumes by H. Bardtke, *Die Handschriftenfunde am Toten Meer*, 1952; Vol. II, 1958, and A. Dupont-Sommer, *Les écrits esséniens découverts près de la Mer morte*, 1959.

apostle Peter *has a time limitation*. That is, it is limited to *the period of the foundation of the Church*. We shall have to take this aspect into account in Part Two of the present book.[99]

## 4. *The Theological Views of the Apostle*

In view of the nature of the sources it would be a rash undertaking to try to present a 'theology' of the apostle Peter. Even if one holds that the First Epistle of Peter was written by the apostle himself, the basis for this undertaking is too small. However, some very important points can be established with a relatively high degree of certainty.

More than once I have pointed to the fact that Peter was not far removed from Paul in theology.[1] Indeed, I should go even further and definitely assert that within the circle of the Twelve he is the one who in this respect *stands closest to Paul*.

We have already emphasized his *universalism*. Contrary to a widespread but erroneous view, this is definitely attested, not only by The Book of Acts, which since the days of the Tübingen School scholars have with some justification regarded as tendential in this respect and therefore have wanted to discard as a proof, but also by Paul. Precisely in connection with the conflict at Antioch, Paul expressly recognizes that Peter in theory represents the same universal viewpoint that he himself holds. Indeed, he reproaches Peter at Antioch only because he has been untrue to his conviction out of fear of the people from James. It may even be true that his origin in the city of Bethsaida,[2] with its Hellenistic influences, had much to do with shaping this broad-minded attitude of Peter. But this attitude doubtless requires a deeper foundation.

Peter obviously learned from his Lord that the divine election of the Jewish people for a definite function does not mean that God's gracious working is limited exclusively to this one people. It was not in vain that Peter was an eyewitness. He understood Jesus' words concerning those who come from the East and the West to recline at table with Abraham, Isaac, and Jacob in the Kingdom of God (Matt. 8:11). He also understood the meaning of that scene with the centurion of Capernaum. Therefore later, in the Primitive Church at Jerusalem, he took a mediating attitude between the group of the Judaizers and that of the Hellenists, and

---

[99] See below, pp. 214 ff.
[1] See above, pp. 52, 47 f. On this subject, see E. Hirsch, 'Petrus und Paulus' (*ZNW*, 1930, pp. 63 ff.).
[2] See above, p. 24.

he was able to hold the two sections together as long as he stood at the head.[3]

But his universalism seems to me to have a still deeper *theological* anchor. This was in the understanding he achieved that Christ's death was the atoning death. Perhaps he was the first one to grasp this after Jesus' resurrection.[4] It is true that it has become common custom to regard the apostle Paul as the creator of the theology of the cross. Indeed, he did in a powerful way put his mighty spiritual gift of systematic thought at the service of the preaching of the cross, and Peter certainly never received the rabbinical training of a Paul. But I do not believe that Paul was the first one to understand the death of Jesus as an atoning death for the forgiveness of sins. On the contrary, I am inclined to ascribe to Peter this particular and fundamental insight. Although he was anything but a theologian, I think that here too he should be given a place of honour at the beginning of all Christian theology.

At this point we must keep in view the significance of the earliest Christology we possess, the explanation, namely, of the person and work of Jesus by the figure of the 'Suffering Servant of God' prophesied by Second Isaiah. This explanation, in addition to the Son of Man Christology, certainly goes back to Jesus himself.

I believe, indeed, that traces exist to show that the apostle Peter is the author of this earliest Christological explanation.

The Book of Acts proves that in the earliest times of Primitive Christianity there existed an explanation of the person and work of Jesus which we may designate somewhat incorrectly as Christology of the 'Servant of God', *ebed Yahweh*, in Greek *pais theou*; more correctly, we could call it 'Paidology'. We could even go further and assert that this is probably the earliest solution of the Christological question. To be sure, only the narrative concerning the conversion of the Ethiopian eunuch (ch. 8:26 ff.) shows explicitly that Jesus was later identified with this *ebed Yahweh*, and the memory was only faintly preserved that Jesus himself so understood his divine mission.

Apart from this narrative, however, there are other passages in The Book of Acts which, while they do not all contain an actual quotation from The Book of Isaiah, are nevertheless of the greatest importance for

[3] See on this point W. Grundmann, 'Das Problem des hellenistischen Christentums innerhalb der Jerusalemer Urgemeinde' (*ZNW*, 1939, pp. 45 ff.), and 'Die Apostel zwischen Jerusalem und Antiochia' (*ZNW*, 1940, pp. 110 ff.). W. Grundmann distinguishes, in partial dependence on E. Lohmeyer, *Galiläa und Jerusalem*, 1936, three groups in the Primitive Church: the Galilean, the Judaistic, and the Hellenistic.

[4] On what follows see O. Cullmann, *Die Christologie des Neuen Testaments*, 2nd ed., 1958, pp. 68 ff. (Eng. Tr., *The Christology of the New Testament*, 1959, pp. 69 ff.).

our question. In them Jesus openly receives the very title *ebed Yahweh*, 'Servant of God', in the Greek rendering, *pais tou theou*. In the Septuagint the latter phrase translates the expression which Deutero-Isaiah uses for the Suffering Servant of God who takes upon himself in a substitutionary way the sins of the people. There are four passages of this kind; it is significant that all four occur in the same section, in chs. 3 and 4, and that Jesus is called *pais tou theou* in no other book of the New Testament. He first appears in this capacity in Acts 3:13, where reference is made to Isaiah 52:13, then in chapter 3:26, where we really have to do with a Christological title. The expression here is Jesus—Pais, exactly as one will be accustomed later to say Jesus—Christ. Similarly one gets the clear impression in the next chapter, 4:25 ff. and 4:30, that *pais* is used almost as a fixed term; it is tending to become a proper name, just as occurred in the case of the word Christ. This confirms the existence of a very early Christology on the basis of which Jesus was called *ebed Yahweh*. It will disappear in the following period, but its use must reach back into the very earliest times.

It is probably no accident that of those four passages, the only ones in the New Testament to designate Jesus as *pais*, *two stand in a speech which is ascribed to the apostle Peter* and two in a prayer spoken in unison by the Jerusalem group of disciples when Peter is present. The Book of Acts, which has twenty-eight chapters, uses this expression in no other passage. It is probably not too bold to conclude from this fact that the author thus preserves the clear memory that it was the apostle Peter who by preference designated Jesus as the 'Suffering Servant of God'.[5] This agrees with what we know of Peter. According to Mark 8:32, he is the very one who at Caesarea Philippi showed so little understanding of the necessity for Jesus to suffer. He took Jesus aside to say to him: 'This will not happen to you', so that Jesus, who saw in him the same tempter who already had tried once to turn him from his path, had to repulse him with the words: 'Away, Satan!' We understand that the same apostle who later, according to I Corinthians 15:5, was the first to see the Risen One, thereafter in the light of the resurrection was also the *first* to preach the

---

[5] The beginnings of this explanation appear also in W. Grundmann, *ZNW*, 1939, p. 53. According to R. Bultmann, *Theologie des Neuen Testaments*, 1953, p. 51 (Eng. Tr., *Theology of the New Testament*, p. 50), this passage suggests not the Suffering Servant but the Son of David (Acts 4:25). In objection to the above assumption the influence of the theology of Luke on the speeches of Acts will be urged. But in the first place, the Servant Christology is not that of Luke, and in the second place, we must take seriously what B. Reicke writes in *Glaube und Leben der Urgemeinde*, 1957, p. 40: 'If one does not demand the impossible of this history writer and of those who handed the tradition on to him, then it must be conceded that the speeches really show a considerable striving for individual characterization.'

actual necessity of the suffering and the death of the Lord, concerning which during the lifetime of Jesus he wanted to know nothing. We understand the fact that he made the suffering and death of Jesus the very *centre* of his explanation of the earthly work of Jesus. The backward look to the denial likewise makes this easily intelligible, especially since as early as Luke 5:8 the story appears to presuppose a particular intensity in Peter's consciousness of sin.

In this connection it is interesting to recall the further fact that The First Epistle of Peter cites with emphasis the passages from The Book of Isaiah which refer to the *ebed Yahweh* (I Pet. 2:21 ff.). This observation remains of value for our study quite independently of the question whether this Epistle is genuine or not. For even if Peter did not write it, nevertheless the anonymous author who ascribed it to him was acquainted with the fact that Peter by preference applied to Jesus the conception of the Suffering Servant of God.

The Christology of the apostle Peter, if we may dare to use this expression, was quite probably dominated by the concept of the *ebed Yahweh*. If so, he who tried to turn Jesus from the way of suffering, and denied him at the decisive moment of the Passion story, was the first one who, after Easter, grasped the necessity of this offence. He could not express this conviction better than by using the designation *ebed Yahweh*; this was the more true since he must have known how great an importance Jesus himself had attached to the ideas connected with the phrase.

Thus of Peter's theological attitude we may say, though with some caution, that the rock apostle, who in Jerusalem was the leader of the first church and doubtless was the first to preach Christ there, was not merely the organizer with only practical interests, as we usually conceive him. Here too the picture of the Prince of the Church is incorrect. He certainly possesses a much greater significance in the foundation of Christian theology than we are accustomed to assume. If we had from him a large collection of letters, such as we have from Paul, it is certain that a different picture would result. It is true that he did not have the technical theological training of Paul, who studied with the Rabbis. But the great idea which Paul later worked out in systematic form very probably occurred first to the fisherman Peter.

This remains true although the same insight was revealed to Paul *independently* of Peter. For we must believe Paul when he writes in Galatians that he received his gospel neither from men nor through human mediation (Gal. 1:12). By the term gospel, Paul, in keeping with his whole theology, can only have meant its central point, the word of the cross.

Later times have often been unjust to Paul by putting him in the shadow of Peter. Theologically, however, scholars seem to me to be unjust to Peter when they put him entirely in the shadow of Paul, or regard him as Paul's antagonist, devoid of understanding for the great Pauline insights.

# 3

# Peter the Martyr

## 1. *The Problem*

EVEN IN our presentation of the missionary activity of Peter the fragmentary character of our sources drove us to inferences and hypotheses. Such measures are still more necessary in dealing with the specific circumstances of his death. It is noteworthy that the single ancient source from which we might expect information on this point, The Book of Acts, is as silent concerning the death of Peter as it is concerning that of Paul, and we have at our disposal no other ancient texts which report this event of such importance for the Primitive Church. We nevertheless must discuss the indirect witnesses from which conclusions concerning the martyrdom of Peter are drawn. The following sections must inquire whether or not these deductions are correct.

The question is the more important since it is closely connected with the problem of Peter's stay in Rome. The solution of this problem, in turn, is linked with the interpretation, so weighted with historical consequences, which the Roman Catholic Church still gives to the saying of Jesus in Matthew 16:17 ff. concerning the rock upon which the Church of Christ is to be built.

This explains also the violent emotion with which the whole discussion has been carried on ever since the stay of Peter in Rome was questioned, first by the Waldensians in the Middle Ages and in more recent times by Protestant scholars. All too often there slip into this debate conscious or unconscious considerations of a confessional kind, which belong in the realm of Protestant-Catholic controversy. In opposition to such an attitude it must be emphasized at the outset that we are dealing here with a purely historical question, which can be handled only with the objective methods of scientific historical study. To proceed thus is the more important since the question whether the papal claim of power over the Christian Church is justified is much too complex for us to answer simply by solving the problem whether Peter ever made a stay in Rome. In reality the decision can only be reached by explaining Matthew 16:18 ff.

If indeed it could really be proved that Peter never set foot in Rome at all, as many have asserted and still assert, then of course the papal claim could not be *historically* defended at all; it would have to rest content with a purely dogmatic justification,[1] which has often been declared sufficient from the Roman Catholic standpoint.[2] Only in this respect is the theological and ecclesiastical question linked with the result of historical study. The opponents of the papal claim may always be greatly tempted to make the matter easy for themselves by thinking that perhaps in this radical way the entire problem can find a relatively quick solution. On the other hand, however, we must say that if scientific reasons indicate the correctness of the later tradition, which asserts that the apostle Peter made a stay in Rome, this alone, as we have noted, is still insufficient to furnish a foundation for the papal claim.

It is fortunate, therefore, that with the passage of time those confessional and polemic considerations have largely disappeared from scholarly discussion. In recent years it has actually been Protestant or confessionally independent scholars who have carried on the debate among themselves; in this debate some answer affirmatively the question whether Peter made a stay in Rome, while others deny it.[3] In the following pages we shall first sketch briefly the history of the problem, and then investigate whether it is possible to derive from the archaeological and literary witnesses to which appeal is made at least indirect indications of a Roman stay of our apostle.

## 2. *History of the Debate Whether Peter Resided in Rome*

The question was first raised in the Middle Ages by Christians for whom the Bible was the sole norm, the Waldensians. We can understand why it was they who did so. As we have seen, the New Testament nowhere tells us that Peter came to the chief city of the Empire and stayed there. For the Waldensians, the silence of the Bible was quite decisive.[4] Later, in the year 1326, Marsilius of Padua, in his *Defensor Pacis*, expresses cautious doubts as to whether Peter was ever in Rome. He, too, appeals

[1] We may add that more or less cautious doubts have been expressed from time to time even by Roman Catholic scholars. Ellendorf goes the furthest in this sense, in *Ist Petrus in Rom und Bischof der römischen Kirche gewesen?*, 1841 (cited by F. Chr. Baur, *Paulus*, 2nd ed., 1867, Vol. II, p. 322; Eng. Tr., *Paul*, Vol. II, 1875, p. 296).

[2] See below, p. 236.

[3] For the earlier history of the problem I refer to K. Heussi, *War Petrus in Rom?*, 1936, pp. 8 ff., and F. Chr. Baur, *Paulus*, 1845, pp. 671 ff.; 2nd ed., 1867, Vol. II, pp. 316 ff. (Eng. Tr., *Paul*, Vol. II, 1875, pp. 291 ff.).

[4] Concerning the opposition by the Waldensians see P. Moneta of Cremona O. P., *Adversus Catharos et Waldenses*, V, 2, Rome, 1743, p. 411.

to the fact that from the sacred Scriptures nothing can be proved concerning this. Perhaps—but only perhaps—he did come to Rome and was bishop there; that he held such a position can be asserted with certainty only for Antioch.

For the next two hundred years we hear nothing of a real attack upon the tradition. Not until 1519–20 does an anonymous author write an essay contending 'that the apostle Peter was never in Rome'.[5] For him, too, as for the Waldensians, the chief argument is the silence of the sacred Scripture. He is not content to express doubts; like them, he goes on to direct denial. Sebastian Franck echoes his thesis and his line of argument.[6] It might seem striking, on the contrary, that the Reformers took no special interest in this problem. In their fight against the Pope they did not build upon this comfortable argument. This is the more noteworthy since they plainly had at least a trace of doubt concerning the stay of Peter at Rome.[7] Thus Luther writes: 'There are some scholars who say that Peter never came to Rome. And it is said to be difficult for the Pope to defend himself against such scholars. I will not here be judge of the question whether Peter was there or not. St. Paul alone was certainly there, as Luke writes in The Book of Acts and Paul himself in his letters; he can very well have instituted the Church and the bishops at Rome.'[8] He further reports that in Rome he saw and heard that one did not know the graves of Peter and Paul.[9] But he adds: 'And the apostles St. Peter and St. Paul may then lie in Rome or not; that makes no difference.'[10] The Protestant church historian from the second half of the sixteenth century, Flacius Illyricus, writes somewhat cautiously in 1554 that it is 'not absolutely certain' that Peter was in Rome,[11] while later in his great work, the Magdeburg *Centuries*, he speaks of the martyrdom of Peter and of Paul

[5] His pseudonym is Ulricus Venelus Minhoniensis. See Melchior Goldast, *Monarchia S. Romani Imperii*, Vol. III, 1613, where the tract is printed on pp. 1–16.

[6] See H. Oncken, 'Sebastian Franck als Historiker' (*Historische Zeitschrift*, 1899, p. 412).

[7] In any case it is incorrect when J. Zeiller, *L'Eglise primitive* (*Histoire de l'Eglise*, Vol. I, 1946 ed., p. 227; Eng. Tr., *History of the Primitive Church*, Vol. I, 1942, p. 233), writes that the denial of the Roman residence of Peter arose in the time of the Reformation, as a part of the Protestant polemic against the papal primacy.

[8] M. Luther, *Wider das Papsttum vom Teufel gestiftet*, 1545 (Weimar edition, 54), cited from E. Mülhaupt, *Luthers Evangelien-Auslegung*, 1947, Vol. II, p. 551.

[9] See below, p. 131 f.

[10] He further writes in the same passage (Mülhaupt, p. 552): 'They lie and invent hundreds and thousands of things about St. Peter himself, so that the idea has occurred to me that neither St. Peter nor St. Paul laid the first stone of the Church of Rome. Perhaps a disciple of the apostles came from Jerusalem or Antioch to Rome...'

[11] *Historia certaminum inter Romanos Episcopos etc., de primatu seu potestate papae bona fide ex authenticis monumentis collata*, p. 267. But in his writing, *Ob Petrus in Rom gewesen sei*, he completely rejects the idea that Peter had been there.

in Rome.[12] A scientifically grounded challenge to the Roman tradition about Peter is offered only at the end of the seventeenth century, by the Reformed scholar Friedrich Spanheim.[13] His arguments are in part worthy of note even today. In spite of his critical spirit, however, the eighteenth century took no great interest in this problem. Gibbon, in his great *History of the Decline and Fall of the Roman Empire*,[14] does indeed question whether any of the disciples of Jesus became a martyr outside of Palestine. In the year 1804 the Göttingen scholar in ancient philology, J. G. Eichhorn, champions the view that the stay and martyrdom of Peter at Rome were not historical events, but were erroneously deduced from 1 Peter 5:13.[15] F. Schleiermacher, in his lectures concerning church history, numbers himself among those who 'doubt the entire account of Peter's stay in Rome'.[16] Likewise, W. M. L. de Wette, in his *Introduction to the New Testament*,[17] declares that the alleged fact, already improbable in itself, is a 'saga'. The majority of the Protestant theologians at the beginning of the nineteenth century, however, affirm the tradition of the Roman stay of Peter. Chief among them are the two great church historians A. Neander and J. Gieseler. The former describes the denial of the tradition as 'hyper-criticism',[18] the latter as an expression of 'partisan polemic'.[19] So much the more impressive was the attack which the Tübingen theologian F. Chr. Baur undertook against the tradition in 1831, in connection with his Hegel-inspired view of Primitive Christianity.[20] The ensuing discussion, however, was burdened by debate over this exaggeration of the opposition between Jewish Christianity and Gentile Christianity. The thesis of Baur, therefore, was almost universally rejected.

In the following period the denial of the Roman tradition about Peter was almost universally abandoned. A man like Ernest Renan assumed as a fact Peter's stay in Rome, and in the year 1897 it was the critical Protestant theologian and historian A. Harnack who wrote the notable sentence

[12] *Centuries*, I, Book II, pp. 28 and 527.

[13] *Dissertatio de ficta profectione Petri apostoli in urbem Romam deque non una traditionis origine*. See *Works*, II, 1703, Col. 331 ff.

[14] *History of the Decline and Fall of the Roman Empire*, 1776 ff.

[15] *Einleitung in das neue Testament*, Vol. I, 1804, pp. 554 f. See also Vol. III, 1812, pp. 603 f.

[16] *Complete Works*, Section One, Vol. XI, edited by E. Bonnell, 1840, p. 69.

[17] *Einleitung in das N. T.*, p. 314.

[18] *Geschichte der christlichen Religion und Kirche*, Vol. I, 1826, p. 317.

[19] *Lehrbuch der Kirchengeschichte*, Vol. I, 2nd ed., 1827, p. 189.

[20] 'Die Christuspartei in der Korinthischen Gemeinde, der Gegensatz des petrinischen und paulinischen Christentums in der ältesten Kirche, der Apostel Petrus in Rom' (*Tübinger Zeitschrift für Theologie*, 1831, pp. 137 ff.). See also *Paulus, der Apostel Jesu Christi*, 1845, pp. 212 ff. (see the Eng. Tr., *Paul*, 1876, Vol. I, pp. 261 ff.).

that the denial of the Roman stay of Peter is 'an error which today is clear to every scholar who is not blind'. So one had the impression that the tradition was finally confirmed. Harnack was of the opinion that 'the martyr death of Peter at Rome was once contested by reason of tendentious Protestant prejudices, and then by reason of tendentious critical prejudices'.[21] Although for most persons the question appeared settled, it was raised anew by the confessionally independent historian Ch. Guignebert in 1909, in his book on 'The Primacy of Peter and the Coming of Peter to Rome'.[22] He answered the question in the negative. In Germany C. Erbes[23] and in Switzerland P. W. Schmiedel[24] likewise opposed Harnack's conclusion.

However, it seemed again that the last word had been spoken on the side of Harnack and the Roman Catholic tradition when Harnack's successor, the Protestant theologian H. Lietzmann, published in 1915 his important book, *Petrus und Paulus in Rom* (second ed., 1927). Lietzmann uses his archaeological and especially his wide liturgical knowledge to illuminate the question. He comes to the conclusion that the testimony from the year 170 concerning the graves of the two apostles at Rome must be correct. That is, the two apostles were actually buried in the two places in Rome which today are reverenced as their graves, Peter at the Vatican, Paul on the road to Ostia.

Nevertheless, this did not put an end to the dispute. It has been continued, chiefly among Protestant theologians, in connection with Lietzmann's book. In the year 1930 appeared my own essay concerning First Clement, ch. 5.[25] In it I conclude, from what we derive by inference from this text concerning the circumstances of the two martyrdoms of Peter and Paul, that Rome was the place of their martyrdom. E. Molland agreed with me,[26] and with the addition of some supplementary points A. Fridrichsen also accepted my interpretation.[27]

[21] *Die Chronologie der altchristlichen Literatur bis Eusebius*, Vol. I, 1897, p. 244, note 2.

[22] *La Primauté de Pierre et la venue de Pierre à Rome*.

[23] C. Erbes, 'Petrus nicht in Rom, sondern in Jerusalem gestorben' (*Zeitschrift für Kirchengeschichte*, 1901, pp. 1 ff., 161 ff.). In his publications concerning the date of the death of the apostles Paul and Peter (*Texte und Untersuchungen*, 1899) and concerning the graves of the apostles in Rome (*Zeitschrift für Kirchengeschichte*, 1924, pp. 38 ff.), Erbes is much more reserved in his judgment concerning the question of the Roman stay of Peter.

[24] P. W. Schmiedel's view is found in 'War der Apostel Petrus in Rom?' (*Protestantische Monatshefte*, 1909, pp. 270 ff.); also in Th. K. Cheyne's *Encyclopaedia Biblica*, IV, pp. 459 ff.

[25] O. Cullmann, 'Les causes de la mort de Pierre et de Paul d'après le témoignage de Clément Romain' (*Revue d'Histoire et de Philosophie Religieuses*, 1930, pp. 294 ff.).

[26] *Theologische Literaturzeitung*, 1937, columns 439 ff. There is also given here a good discussion of the controversy between Lietzmann and Heussi.

[27] 'Propter invidiam. Note sur I. Clém. V' (*Eranos Rudbergianus*, 1946, pp. 161 ff.).

Lietzmann's conclusion, however, was opposed by Adolf Bauer, in the series of 'Vienna Studies',[28] by Ch. Guignebert,[29] and further by H. Dannenbauer.[30] The latter actually formulated the result of his investigation in these words: 'Every little village in Palestine can claim with greater justification than can the imperial capital to be the place of Peter's death.' To the opponents of the Lietzmann thesis belong further J. Haller[31] and E. T. Merrill,[32] while G. Krüger[33] championed the traditional thesis, chiefly on the basis of First Clement.

The chief arguments of the opponents of the tradition were gathered up in 1936 by Karl Heussi in the brochure he directed against Lietzmann, *War Petrus in Rom?* ('Was Peter Ever in Rome?'). This writing, which announced as its reliable result that 'Peter never set foot in the city on the Tiber', aroused great interest. It called Lietzmann himself to the field of battle with a reply, 'Peter: Roman Martyr' (1936).[34] In the following years K. Heussi tried anew to defend his thesis that we are dealing with a legend in the assertion that Peter suffered martyrdom in Rome.[35]

The war did not put an end to the discussion. Lietzmann, who died in 1942, was of course unable to take further part in it. In 1942 M. Dibelius published an essay concerning 'Rome and the Christians in the first century'.[36] In it he too concerns himself chiefly with the most important indirect witness for the martyrdom of Peter, First Clement, ch. 5. He sides with Lietzmann, but seeks to explain the brevity of the notice chiefly by the literary character of the author.

On the Roman Catholic side also scholars have continued especially the study of I Clement 5 in connection with our problem.[37] In addition,

---

[28] 'Die Legende von dem Martyrium des Petrus und Paulus in Rom' (*Zeitschrift für klassische Philologie*, 1916, pp. 270 ff.).

[29] 'La sépulture de Pierre' (*Revue historique*, 1931, pp. 225 ff.).

[30] 'Die römische Petruslegende' (*Historische Zeitschrift*, 1932, pp. 239 ff.); 'Nochmals die römische Petruslegende' (*Historische Zeitschrift*, 1939, pp. 81 ff.).

[31] *Das Papsttum*, Vol. I, 2nd ed., 1950, pp. 1 ff., 472 ff. (polemic in a disagreeable and irritated tone).

[32] *Essays in Early Christian History*, 1924, pp. 267 ff.

[33] 'Petrus in Rom' (*ZNW*, 1932, pp. 301 ff.).

[34] 'Petrus römischer Märtyrer' (*Sitzungsbericht der Berliner Akademie der Wissenschaften*, 1936, pp. 392 ff.).

[35] 'War Petrus wirklich römischer Märtyrer?' (*Christliche Welt*, 1937, columns 161 ff.); *Neues zur Petrusfrage*, 1939; 'Eine französische Stimme zur römischen Petrustradition' (*Christliche Welt*, 1939, columns 596 ff.). On the whole controversy between Heussi and Lietzmann, see also R. Draguet, *Revue d'Histoire ecclésiastique*, 1938, pp. 88 ff.

[36] 'Rom und die Christen im 1. Jahrhundert' (*Sitzungsbericht der Heidelberger Akademie der Wissenschaften, Philologisch-historische Klasse*, 1942).

[37] M. Schuler, 'Klemens von Rom und Petrus in Rom' (*Trierer Theologische Studien*, I, 1941, pp. 94 ff.); L. Sanders, *L'hellénisme de S. Clément de Rome et le paulinisme*, 1943 (see below, pp. 98 f.); O. Perler, 'Ignatius von Antiochien und die römische Christusgemeinde' (*Divus Thomas*, 1944, pp. 442 ff.); St. Schmutz, 'Petrus war dennoch in Rom'

we should mention particularly the various studies which the Old Catholic scholar Katzenmayer published, during and after the war, in the *Internationale Kirchliche Zeitschrift*. In them he seeks in his own peculiar way to establish that both the Roman stay, which he assumes, and the death of Peter occurred long before the Neronian persecution, in the year 55.[38]

After the end of the war the chief interest, quite understandably, was directed to the excavations under the Church of St Peter in Rome. The study of the literary sources became at first somewhat more cautious, since the official publication of the result of the excavations was awaited. Since, however, these excavations permitted different interpretations, none of which is generally accepted, the study of the literary sources has received new and still greater attention. Heussi entered the field with new publications; he defined his position with reference to the most recent excavations and above all tried to support his thesis on the basis of the imperfect tense in Galatians 2:6.[39] He defended himself against the first edition of my book, *Peter* (1952), and later against the important article concerning 'Petrus in Rom' which K. Aland published in the *Historische Zeitschrift* (1957).[40] Even earlier Aland with others had taken pains to show the impossibility of Heussi's interpretation of Galatians 2:6.[41] Heussi has continued until quite recently to present his viewpoint in a new series of polemic articles; they reflect a self-confidence and bias even greater than he showed in the first phase of the discussion, which was marked by his opposition to Lietzmann.[42] In a larger work, *The Death of*

(*Benediktinische Monatsschrift*, 1946, pp. 122 ff.); B. Altaner, 'Neues zum Verständnis von I Clem. 5, 1–6, 2' (*Historisches Jahrbuch*, 1949, pp. 25 ff.).

[38] There appeared even before the war: 'Zur Frage, ob Petrus in Rom war', 1938, pp. 129 ff.; 'Das Todesjahr des Petrus', 1939, pp. 85 ff. We have already mentioned, p. 55, note 64, the essay, 'War Petrus in Korinth?' (1943, pp. 20 ff.). See also 'Die Schicksale des Petrus von seinem Aufenthalt in Korinth bis zu seinem Märtyrertod', 1944, pp. 145 ff.; 'Die Beziehungen des Petrus zur Urkirche von Jerusalem und zu Antiochien', 1945, pp. 116 ff. In further articles in the same journal the author seeks to prove that a primacy of Rome or of its bishop is lacking until the end of the third century. Unfortunately, in the essays that are of interest to us in our study, the argument is often somewhat forced, and at times is built on arguments from silence.

[39] 'Das Grab des Petrus' (*Deutsches Pfarrerblatt*, 1949, p. 82); ' "Papst" Anenkletus I und die Memoria Petri auf dem Vatikan' (*ib.*, p. 301); 'Die Nachfolge des Petrus' (*ib.*, p. 420); 'Der Stand der Frage nach dem römischen Aufenthalt des Petrus' (*ib.*, p. 501); 'Gal. 2 und der Lebensausgang der jerusalemischen Urapostel' (*Theologische Literaturzeitung*, 1952, columns 67 ff.); 'Die Entstehung der römischen Petrustradition' (*Wissenschaftliche Zeitschrift der Universität Jena*, 1952/3, pp. 63 ff.).

[40] Pp. 497 ff.

[41] 'Wann starb Petrus? Eine Bemerkung zu Gal. II, 6' (*New Testament Studies*, 1959, pp. 267 ff.).

[42] In a completely irrelevant article and without taking up my arguments, he tried at first to discredit my book: 'Oscar Cullmanns Petrusbuch' (*Deutsches Pfarrerblatt*, 1956, pp. 79 f.). In his brochure, 'The Roman Tradition about Peter Critically Considered' *Die römische Petrustradition in kritischer Sicht*, 1955), it is actually painful to see how

*Peter in Rome: Observations on Karl Heussi's Denial of It*,[43] K. Aland has described in a systematic way the content and method of Heussi's polemic. After a new and careful testing of all arguments he comes to the conclusion: '. . . as a matter of method what remains but to accept the martyr death of Peter in Rome as a fact? . . . In my view, this is the result which one must reach when one uses the methods and viewpoints which are valid for historical-critical study of the first and second Christian centuries.'

Recent general presentations of Primitive Christianity likewise tend, when they deal with the literary witnesses, to accept the Roman sojourn of Peter.[44] Particularly deserving of mention as a special study is the inquiry of the Danish scholar J. Munck, *Peter and Paul in the Revelation of John*.[45] He makes the interesting though doubtful attempt to find in Rev. 11:3-13 the oldest attestation of the martyr death of both apostles.

Heussi, by misuse of the word 'critical', accuses of 'slavery to tradition and a failure of the historical-critical sense' all who in this *purely scientific* question do not share his view (see the Foreword). As if a truly critical sense should not be valid also against scientific dogmas and especially against one's own interpretations. My thoroughly developed interpretation of I Clement 5 (first edition of this book, 1952, pp. 96 ff.) not only is not discussed, but is not even reported to the reader, and is 'dispatched' in a footnote remark that says nothing (p. 23, note 2; see below, p. 108, note 46). Although he declares in this brochure that with it he definitely concludes the debate, he continues the discussion still further, especially in attack on K. Aland: 'Petrus und die beiden Jakobus in Galater 1-2' (*Wissenschaftliche Zeitschrift der Universität Jena*, 1956/7, pp. 147 ff.); 'Ist die sogenannte römische Petrustradition bereits im Lukas-Evangelium und schon kurz nach dem Jahre 70 bezeugt?' (*ib.*, pp. 571 ff.); 'Zur Abwehr gegen Aland' (*Deutsches Pfarrerblatt*, 1958, pp. 224 f.); 'Drei vermeintliche Beweise für das Kommen des Petrus nach Rom' (*Historische Zeitschrift*, 1958, pp. 240 ff.). See also most recently his review of Th. Klauser's book, often mentioned below: 'Die römische Petrustradition im Lichte der neuen Ausgrabungen unter der Petruskirche' (*Theologische Literaturzeitung*, 1959, pp. 359 ff.).

[43] *Der Tod des Petrus in Rom. Bemerkungen zu seiner Bestreitung durch Karl Heussi* (1959).

[44] So C. T. Craig, *The Beginning of Christianity*, 1943, p. 266. P. Carrington, *The Early Christian Church*, 1957, Vol. I, pp. 186 ff.; 196; 205 ff., and noted church historians such as H. v. Campenhausen (e.g., *Verkündigung und Forschung*, 1946/7, p. 230) and C. King, 'The Outlines of New Testament Chronology' (*Church Quarterly Review*, 1945, p. 149), speak in favour of accepting the sojourn of Peter in Rome. M. Goguel, to be sure, in his great work concerning the origin of Christianity (*L'Eglise primitive*, 1947, pp 203 ff.; he gives a good presentation of the problem), inclines to strong scepticism towards the traditional thesis, but reaches no definite decision. A similar scepticism, though in its final result rather favourable to the acceptance of a late arrival of Peter in Rome and his martyrdom there, is represented by G. Miegge in his popularly written but quite instructive little book, *Pietro a Roma* (n.d.).

[45] *Petrus und Paulus in der Offenbarung Johannis* (1950).

### 3. *The Literary Sources*

What *sources* are to be considered in our study of the question of the Roman residence and martyrdom of Peter? The earliest Christian writings, the *letters of Paul*, contain no direct or indirect data whatever concerning a stay of Peter in Rome or concerning his death. At the time when Paul writes I Corinthians, Peter is making missionary journeys in company with his wife (I Cor. 9:5). That is all we hear in the letters of Paul concerning this period of Peter's life. From the mere fact of this silence we cannot infer that a Roman stay by Peter or his martyrdom there is excluded. The failure of the letters of Paul to report his *death* is no cause for wonder; we scarcely can assume that Peter died so long before Paul[46] that the latter could have spoken of it explicitly or by implication in a letter, even had he had occasion to do so. The situation is different with regard to the *stay* of Peter in Rome. There is, to be sure, no *a priori* necessity to claim that Paul must have spoken of this fact. Nevertheless, we possess from him a letter addressed to the Roman church itself, and although we must be cautious in using so-called arguments from silence, yet it must be said that if Peter were actually sojourning at the time in the church of the capital city, it would be astonishing for Paul not to refer to him at all in this letter, which greets by name numerous Roman Christians.[47]

The assertion that he purposely refrained from speaking of Peter, because the latter by his Judaizing preaching had worked in Rome in a way contrary to the teaching that Paul set forth in his letter to the Romans, shatters on the already established fact that Peter cannot be called a mere Judaizer; in reality, he stood much closer to the theology of Paul than to that of James.[48] The opposition that Romans expresses to Judaizing

---

[46] K. Heussi, indeed, thinks that Peter died as early as the year 55. He holds that when Paul wrote Galatians, Peter was no longer alive (Gal. 2:6: 'whoever they *were*'); *Theologische Literaturzeitung*, 1952, pp. 67 ff. On this question see below, p. 81, note 56. H. Katzenmayer (see above, p. 77) also accepts the early date of 55 as the year of Peter's death.

[47] Even if ch. 16 should not belong to Romans, the silence concerning Peter in the other chapters would still be amazing. (T. W. Manson gives noteworthy new arguments —especially in the light of papyrus manuscript P[46], known since 1935—in favour of the old hypothesis that ch. 16 went to Ephesus; see his essay, 'St. Paul's Letter to the Romans —and Others', in *Bulletin of the John Rylands Library*, 1948, pp. 3 ff.). Nor can this silence be explained by the hypothesis of Graber (see above, p. 39).

[48] H. Lietzmann, 'Zwei Notizen zu Paulus' (*Sitzungsbericht der Berliner Akademie der Wissenschaften*, 1930, No. 8), has proposed the probably untenable thesis that Paul wrote Romans to oppose the Jewish Christian propaganda carried to Rome by Peter, and so to avert the danger that his gospel might find closed doors at the outset. E. Hirsch, 'Petrus und Paulus' (*ZNW*, 1930, p. 63), makes extensive concessions to this thesis, but nevertheless reacts against Lietzmann's presentation, which would make of Peter a full-fledged Judaizer. In so doing Hirsch opposes at the same time Ed. Meyer's hypothesis, which sees Peter behind the false teachers in Galatia.

teachings no more presupposes a stay of Peter in Rome than does the anti-Judaizing polemic of the letters to Corinth or Galatia become intelligible only on the supposition of a personal stay of Peter in Corinth or in Galatia—although as far as Corinth and Galatia are concerned we have not excluded the possibility that Peter at an earlier time made a stay in these regions.[49] In any case, we are forced to deny that Peter was present in the Roman church *at the time when Paul wrote Romans to them*; otherwise he could not possibly have been omitted from the list of the persons addressed in this letter.

It still does not follow, be it noted, that the tradition concerning the stay and martyrdom of Peter at Rome is therefore to be entirely rejected; the conclusion applies only to the time of writing of Paul's letter to Rome. Theoretically, Peter could have been in Rome prior to the sending of Paul's letter; he could then have left the capital city, and only later have returned there and suffered martyrdom. Nevertheless, this is not probable.[50] In any case, Paul's writing forces us in our study to the following conclusion: *at the time when Paul wrote his letter to Rome, Peter was not there*; if he came there at all, this can only have happened either before or more likely, after that time.

For any stay of Peter in Rome, however, Romans 15:20 comes indirectly into consideration. We have already seen[51] that Paul here excuses himself for coming to a church which he has not founded. Such a step he previously has avoided; he probably regarded this, in keeping with the spirit of the Jerusalem agreement, as irreconcilable with the apostolic honour. In view of this fact, and in connection with what we have concluded from Galatians 2:9, we probably are justified in concluding that the parallel Jewish Christian mission of the Jerusalem group regarded the Roman church as their field, since this church, which probably arose apart from the missionary programme, had an original membership of Jewish Christians.[52] Since the Jewish population of Rome was then large—it is estimated at 30,000 to 40,000[53]—such an original membership may certainly be assumed. This is especially convincing when we consider that when Paul writes his letter to Rome, the Jewish Christians are quite strongly represented in the Roman church along with the Gentile

[49] See above, p. 57.

[50] C. Cecchelli, *Gli apostoli a Roma*, 1938, p. 64, also declares this impossible.

[51] See above, p. 47.

[52] If the Jews from Rome who, according to Acts 2:10, were present at Pentecost in Jerusalem, brought the gospel to the capital city, this too points to Jewish Christian origin. So F. J. Foakes-Jackson, *Peter: Prince of Apostles*, 1927, p. 196.

[53] J. Juster, *Les Juifs dans l'empire romain*, 1914, pp. 209 f., actually speaks of 50,000 to 60,000.

Christians.[54] Of course, we dare not conclude with finality from this fact that Peter came to Rome or even founded that church. But we must ask whether in this case it is not probable that in his capacity as leader of the Jewish Christian Jerusalem-based mission, Peter himself did not at some time come to this church, founded as it was by Jewish Christians and still containing a strong Jewish Christian membership. Such a visit is especially likely since it was the capital city which was in question. If there was a Jewish Christian mission and if Peter was entrusted with it, then his coming to Rome, while not proved by these facts, is an assumption strongly suggested, especially if at a certain time traces of internal difficulties appear.[55]

Nothing more can be derived from the letters of Paul in either a positive or a negative sense. For when, in the report of Galatians concerning the Apostolic Council (Gal. 2:6), Paul says: 'of whatever sort the esteemed ones *were*', this by no means permits the conclusion that when Galatians was written (the year 56) Peter was already dead, since otherwise the apostle could not have used the past tense![56] Actually all that Paul wishes to say in this passage is that *for the events there reported* it makes no difference what sort of people *the Jerusalem group* 'were' who made those agreements. This remark was the more in place since, as we have seen, the relationships in the leadership of the Primitive Church did not always remain the same.

\* \* \*

If anywhere in our ancient sources, we should expect a report concerning the end of Peter's life in *The Book of Acts*. As a matter of fact, however, it does not contain even the slightest indirect allusion to a stay of this apostle in Rome. For as we have seen, it is arbitrary to understand the

---

[54] M. J. Lagrange, *Epître aux Romains*, pp. xxix f., even considers it the chief tendency of the letter to instruct the Gentile Christians concerning the role of Judaism in redemptive history and to warn them against any contempt for the Jewish Christians.

[55] See below, pp. 107.

[56] K. Heussi presents this explanation as the obvious interpretation of our passage. After he had published it in the *Theologische Literaturzeitung*, 1952, columns 67 ff., he repeated it in *Die römische Petrustradition in kritischer Sicht*, 1955, pp. 1 ff. It has been rejected also by H. v. Campenhausen, *Kirchliches Amt und geistliche Vollmacht*, 1953, p. 21, note 5, and especially by K. Aland, 'Wann starb Petrus? Eine Bemerkung zu Gal. II, 6' (*New Testament Studies*, 1956, pp. 267 ff.) and 'Petrus in Rom' (*Historische Zeitschrift*, 1957, p. 506). Aland rightly emphasizes that in the following verse (vs. 7) Paul uses a perfect tense to say something about himself which includes Peter: 'that I *had been* entrusted with the preaching of the gospel to the uncircumcised, as Peter had been to the circumcised'.—It is completely arbitrary when K. Heussi (*op. cit.*, pp. 4 f.) identifies as the son of Zebedee the James named in this passage; the reference here, as in Gal. 1:19 and 2:2, is plainly to the brother of the Lord, who was certainly still alive when Galatians was written.

F

notice in ch. 12:17 as such an allusion.[57] It must be conceded at the outset that the silence of The Book of Acts constitutes a minus for the traditional view, inasmuch as thereby one of the earliest sources that could attest the tradition fails us. Nothing more, however, may be concluded from this silence; it is not permissible to go further and see in it any support for the attempt to prove impossible the fact that tradition asserts. To be sure, those whom we mentioned, in our survey of the history of the problem, as challengers of the stay of Peter at Rome take particular pleasure in citing this silence to establish their thesis.[58]

It is indeed striking that a 'history of the apostles', in whose first part Peter plays so large a role, contains no word about the *end of his life*. Doubtless *this* notable fact calls for some explanation. As to the question, however, whether or not Peter was in Rome we can draw no conclusion of any kind from this silence. For The Acts not only says nothing concerning the *Roman* stay of Peter we now are discussing; it is silent concerning his entire missionary activity, which by the evidence of I Corinthians 9:5 is an established fact, and also concerning his death.

There is the additional fact that nothing is reported concerning the martyr death of Paul, which nevertheless is not disputed. The Book of Acts ends abruptly with the mention of Paul's arrival at Rome and the remark that he remained there two years. In view of the detail with which the journeys of Paul are described in the closing chapters, this is much stranger than the silence concerning Peter. It calls even more urgently for an explanation. However, no matter what solutions have previously been given for the riddle of the abrupt ending of The Book of Acts, the different answers leave open the question as to whether or not Peter was in Rome.

These answers assume either that the author *knew nothing* concerning the unreported end of Paul's life—and probably also of Peter's—or that *he did not want to tell of it*. In the former case one must presuppose that he completed his book immediately after the close of the two years that followed Paul's arrival in Rome. In that case there would be the possibility —but only the possibility—that Peter reached Rome later and, like Paul, suffered martyrdom there.

The assumption, however, that the author completed his work exactly two years after the arrival of Paul in Rome is not probable. A long series of reasons that need not here be cited favour the view that the book was

[57] See above, pp. 38 f.
[58] K. Heussi, to be sure, does not belong in this group. For he rightly admits (*War Petrus in Rom?*, pp. 17 ff.) that from the evidence in The Acts one cannot reach a certain conclusion.

written only later, after the Neronian persecution and after the death of Peter and Paul. In this case we probably must assume that the author was as well informed concerning the end of Peter's life as concerning that of Paul. That he possessed no information about it is scarcely possible. There remains then only the explanation that he *chose* not to tell anything about it. The reason for this could be literary in character. Often, indeed, it actually is assumed that he chose to extend this book only to this point; he stopped with the arrival of Paul at Rome, whether he planned a third book[59] or not.[60] Or the reason was of theological character; on this view, to have told of these unreported events would in some way have been out of keeping with the theological aim of the book. These cases also permit no *a priori* conclusions either for or against the stay and martyrdom of Peter in Rome. For in principle both possibilities remain open: either that Peter after those two years (or possibly even earlier)[61] died in Rome as a martyr, or that after this time (possibly even earlier) he ended his life elsewhere.

Only if the further course of this investigation should prove that the very occurrence of the event in Rome gave the author a special theological reason for not mentioning the end of Peter's life—only then could his silence possibly be considered as indirect confirmation of the assumption that Peter suffered martyrdom in Rome. As a matter of fact, I shall at least propose such a hypothesis.[62] But this will be possible only by drawing upon other texts. For the time being we must say that The Book of Acts deserves mention in our study only to establish the fact that in its case one of our oldest sources fails to help us in the question as to Peter the Martyr.

Can we learn something positive from the letters that appear in the New Testament as *letters of Peter*? Whether they bear his name rightly or wrongly is of no importance for our present purpose; even if an unknown author put them under the authority of Peter, it is important to learn whether he knew that Peter had been in Rome and whether accordingly he carried through the fiction of representing himself as present in Rome.

[59] So Th. Zahn, *Einleitung in das Neue Testament*, 4th ed., 1924, pp. 16 ff., 861 f. (see Eng. Tr., *Introduction to the New Testament*, 2nd ed., 1917, Vol. III, pp. 57 ff.), and M. Goguel, *Introduction au Nouveau Testament*, Vol. III, 1922, *Le livre des Actes*, p. 340.
[60] W. Michaelis, *Einleitung in das Neue Testament*, 1946, p. 133, considers the possibility that the author could so limit his goal because his readers had been informed concerning the further course of events.
[61] *A priori*, indeed, it is not absolutely necessary to assume with regard to Peter the same reasons for silence that one does with reference to the death of Paul.
[62] See below, pp. 91 ff., 104 f.

The Second Epistle of Peter contains no reference of any kind to Rome. It only refers to the martyrdom of Peter in ch. 1:14: 'I know that the striking of my tent will come soon, as our Lord Jesus Christ has revealed to me.' This writing, however, like the later apocryphal Petrine literature, does not call for primary consideration here. This is because, in the judgment of the great majority of scholars, it is the latest document included in the New Testament. It thus comes from a later period—at the earliest from the middle of the second century—when the tradition concerning the Roman stay of Peter begins to appear elsewhere as well. We are seeking here only the *early* witnesses.

Among them The First Epistle of Peter calls for mention. At the end of its final chapter stands a greeting. Concerning this greeting it is usually assumed that whether the writing is genuine or not, it presupposes the stay of Peter in Rome: 'The fellow-elect [church] in Babylon greets you, and so does Mark my son' (I Pet. 5:13).

Even this statement, to be sure, yields no absolute certainty. It seems to me far the most probable explanation that Babylon is a cryptic name for Rome. For if the author writes from Rome, his reason for substituting Babylon for Rome may very well have been similar to that which the author of the Apocalypse of John had. Either he wishes to avoid it out of fear of the Roman authorities, or more probably, he used the term Babylon because in his day that city, which with all that it meant for the people of Israel had been so important in Old Testament prophecy, had become a theological concept which could be applied especially well to Rome.[63]

We know indeed from ancient Christian literature how popular this typological use of geographical names was. We may think, for example, of Galatians 4:26, where the Church is called the 'Jerusalem that is above', or of Hebrews 12:22, which speaks of the 'heavenly Jerusalem'. So for the author of I Peter 'Babylon', in connection with the theological ideas that he held, may be a term meaning 'exile', just as in ch. 2:11 (see also ch. 1:1) he has called the readers 'aliens and sojourners'. At the same

---

[63] K. Heussi, *War Petrus in Rom?*, p. 38, does not see the reason for such a hide-and-seek game. But for the author of the Apocalypse of John it is clear that he was *unwilling* to name Rome. Moreover, the chapter that Heussi devotes to our passage is unsatisfactory; he discusses it only on the presupposition that I Clement, ch. 5, already proves with finality that Peter was not in Rome. It will not do, however, to interpret I Peter 5:13 on the basis of this conclusion, which we shall see is not at all assured, instead of considering the source in itself. Further literature on I Peter 5:13: H. Windisch, *Die katholischen Briefe*, 3rd ed., 1951, revised by Herbert Preisker, p. 82; further, A. Schlatter, *Geschichte der ersten Christenheit*, 1926, pp. 299 ff., and B. W. Bacon, *Is Mark a Roman Gospel?*, 1919, pp. 23 ff. See also the article by G. Kuhn on 'Babylon' in *Theologisches Wörterbuch zum Neuen Testament*, Vol. I, pp. 512 ff.

time, however, it is also an expression of the capital city's power-linked corruption; this meaning connects with the Old Testament prophetic tradition, for example, Isaiah 43:14 and Jeremiah, chs. 50 and 51.[64] Since the greeting must have a definite city in mind, there could have been in the time of the writer no other place but Rome to which this figurative meaning of the ancient Babylon was applied.

The presupposition for this conclusion, of course, is that we do have here a figurative use of the word. This conclusion is rendered likely by the fact that such a use, with reference to Rome itself, is certainly attested in other writings. It occurs above all in the Apocalypse of John, where there can be no doubt that in chs. 14:8; 16:19; 17:5 ff.; 18:2 ff. Rome is meant by 'Babylon'. Perhaps the expression 'Sodom and Egypt' in Revelation 11:8 is likewise a cryptic name for Rome.[65] We further find 'Babylon' as a figurative designation for Rome in the pseudepigraphic late Jewish literature. It appears, for example, in the Sibylline Oracles V, 159, where it is said: 'The deep sea will burn, and so will Babylon itself and the land of Italy'; in the Apocalypse of Baruch 11:1; and in Fourth Esdras 3:1 ff.; 28:31.[66] Both in the Apocalypse of John and in the late Jewish texts, of course, we are dealing with writings which can hardly be earlier than our First Epistle of Peter.[67] Nevertheless, they belong to approximately the same period.[68] In addition, the word 'mystery', which in Revelation 17:5 refers to the saying concerning Babylon-Rome, appears to indicate that this covert manner of expression was already known to Christians.[69] For all these reasons, the interpretation that the word 'Babylon' in I Peter 5:13 refers to Rome is doubtless the most natural, if we approach the passage without prejudice and without first taking into account the con-

---

[64] This has been pointed out especially by E. G. Selwyn, *The First Epistle of St. Peter*, 1949, pp. 303 ff.

[65] So J. Munck, *Petrus und Paulus in der Offenbarung Johannis*, 1950, pp. 30 ff., in opposition to the majority of interpreters, who think they find in the expression a reference to Jerusalem.

[66] See on this point H. Fuchs, *Der geistige Widerstand gegen Rom*, 1938. The rabbinic passages are given in Strack-Billerbeck, *Kommentar zum Neuen Testament*, Vol. III, p. 816.

[67] E. G. Selwyn, *op. cit.*, pp. 243 and 303, believes that our passage contains the first witness to this usage of the word Babylon=Rome; he finds that usage in this passage.

[68] In the Church Fathers this use of the word Babylon is common; it occurs in Tertullian, *Adversus Judaeos*, 9; *Adversus Marcionem*, 3, 13, and is especially favoured by Origen and Augustine. See on this point H. Fuchs, *Der geistige Widerstand gegen Rom*, 1938, pp. 74 f., and B. Altaner, Article on 'Babylon' in *Reallexikon für Antike und Christentum*, I, columns 1131 ff. It should also be mentioned that two minuscule manuscripts have replaced the word Babylon by Rome in their text. (See Th. Zahn, *Einleitung ins Neue Testament*, 3rd ed., Vol. II, pp. 17 ff.; cf. Eng. Tr., *Introduction to the New Testament*, 2nd ed., Vol. II, pp. 158 ff.).

[69] So E. G. Selwyn, *op. cit.*, p. 243.

troversy concerning Peter's stay in Rome. Papias already explained the verse in this way.[70]

It must be said, however, that it is not completely certain that the expression *must* here be understood in a figurative way. We cannot fully exclude the possibility that the long famous ancient *Mesopotamian* city of Babylon was really meant. We know from Josephus[71] and from Philo[72] that this place was still inhabited in the New Testament period, although it had lost all importance, and according to another notice of Josephus that refers to the middle of the first century, the Jews had left the place to settle in the city Seleucia,[73] which in the meantime had come to outrank the ancient Babylon. So it has actually been assumed that on one of his missionary journeys Peter came to Babylon in Mesopotamia, or if not into the city itself, at least into the region of Babylonia, and wrote our letter from there.[74] One cannot completely exclude this possibility. Nevertheless, it is not probable, and it is not supported by the later Christian tradition, which knows nothing of a missionary work of Peter in these regions. To them it brings only the apostle Thomas. To this we must add the fact that the Babylonian Talmud attests the presence of Christians in this region only from the third century on.

The assumption that the author who ascribed the letter to Peter knew nothing definite concerning the places where the apostle worked, and therefore chose the nebulous distant Babylon,[75] finds no support in fact. It is improbable also because of the explicit mention of Mark. For this reason we must reject also the assertion recently advanced that the word does not refer at all to an actual city but is to be understood figuratively, as is the word 'Dispersion' in ch. 1:1, and means 'homelessness'.[76]

---

[70] Eusebius, *Ecclesiastical History*, II, 15, 2. The explanation is frequently found in later times. See Jerome, *De viris illustribus*, 8.

[71] *Antiquities*, XV, 2, 2.          [72] *Legatio ad Caium*, 282, p. 587.

[73] Josephus, *Antiquities*, XVIII, 9, 8. See on this point Th. Zahn, *Einleitung ins N. T.*, Vol. II, 2nd ed., 1900, pp. 17 ff. (Eng. Tr. of 3rd ed., see note 68 above); and H. Windisch, *Die katholischen Briefe* (*Handbuch zum Neuen Testament*, herausgegeben von G. Bornkamm), 3rd ed., revised by H. Preisker, 1951, p. 82.

[74] A. Schlatter, *Geschichte der ersten Christenheit*, 1926, p. 299; H. Dannenbauer, 'Die römische Petruslegende' (*Historische Zeitschrift*, 1932, p. 249); and others; in earlier times, Erasmus. It is often argued that the rather friendly attitude of the letter towards the State speaks against the identification of Rome and Babylon. (See J. Haller, *Das Papsttum*, Vol. I, 1951, p. 477.)

[75] K. Heussi, *op. cit.*, p. 38, note 6.

[76] So K. Heussi in 'Die Entstehung der römischen Petrustradition' (*Wissenschaftliche Zeitschrift der Universität Jena*, 1952/3, p. 71) and *Die römische Petrustradition in kritischer Sicht*, 1955, pp. 36 ff.—For this and other texts (see p. 93, note 99) Heussi has proposed a succession of different explanations, with the sole purpose of excluding the reference to Rome. The question-begging which lies at the basis of this procedure stands in noteworthy conflict with the 'critical view' which the author claims for his treatment of the problem but would like to deny to writings by opponents of his thesis.

Theoretically still another Babylon might be considered. This is the military camp in *Egypt* near the modern Cairo. It is mentioned by Strabo[77] and Josephus.[78] One can scarcely accept, however, the misguided idea that I Peter 5:13 refers to this rather obscure Babylon. The only possible support for this view is the fact that the apocryphal Gospel of Peter and the Apocalypse of Peter are of Egyptian origin.

The other cities which have been proposed, Jerusalem[79] or even Joppa,[80] have still less claim to serious consideration. It is impossible to explain how they could have been designated by the name 'Babylon'. The passage in Revelation 11:8, concerning the city which 'spiritually is called Sodom and Egypt', has been cited as an analogy at least for Jerusalem. But as we have already mentioned, this verse cannot be taken as a certain reference to Jerusalem; it possibly refers to Rome.[81] It is pure fantasy to assume, on the basis that Clement of Alexandria declares The Second Epistle of John to have been addressed to a certain Babylonia, that the reference here is to a highly esteemed lady named Babylonia, who belonged to a church in Asia Minor.[82]

We thus reach the conclusion that First Peter, whether genuine or not, quite probably means by its place reference 'Babylon' the city of Rome. It thereby presupposes a stay of Peter in Rome, although another interpretation of this reference is not entirely excluded.

Another passage from the same First Epistle of Peter (ch. 5:1) is still to be mentioned. However, it deals only with the other question, whether Peter died as a martyr. The author here speaks of himself as 'a witness of the sufferings of Christ and a partaker of the glory soon to be revealed'. This expression also is not unequivocal. Yet it probably justifies us in assuming that the author, whether Peter or someone else, refers to a sharing in Christ's sufferings, including his death. For the witness here mentioned probably refers not only to something once seen and now proclaimed, but in keeping with the demonstrably early usage of the Greek word, refers to a witness in act.[83]

(See also above, p. 77, note 42.) Reference to this method of Heussi is made also by K. Aland, in his 'Petrus in Rom' (*Historische Zeitschrift*, 1957, especially p. 510), and above all in his essay concerning all of Heussi's polemic literature on this question: 'Der Tod des Petrus in Rom. Bemerkungen zu seiner Bestreitung durch K. Heussi' (*Collected Essays*, 1959).    [77] XVII, 30, p. 807.    [78] II, 15, 1.
[79] A. Harnack, *Chronologie der altchristlichen Literatur bis Eusebius*, 1897, p. 459.
[80] Syncellus ad a. m. 5540 (ed. Bonn 627), probably in view of Acts 9: 36 ff.
[81] See J. Munck, *op. cit.*, pp. 30 ff.
[82] This proposal comes from K. Heussi, *op. cit.*, p. 39, note 6, but he himself puts a question mark after it.
[83] So also R. Knopf, *Die Briefe Petri und Judä*, 1912, p. 188; H. Windisch—H. Preisker, *Die katholischen Briefe*, 3rd ed., 1951, p. 79; also K. Heussi himself: *War Petrus in Rom?*, p. 31, note 21; likewise H. Lietzmann, 'Petrus römischer Märtyrer'

In the same connection we still must mention, of the New Testament books that should be considered in our study, *The Gospel of John.* Of especial importance is ch. 21:18 ff.: 'As long as you were young, you girded yourself and went wherever you chose; but when you have become old, you will stretch out your hands, and another will gird you and carry you where you do not want to go.' It is almost universally recognized that these words are intended as a prediction of the martyrdom of Peter, even if there should lie behind them a proverb which simply says: The young go where they choose, the old must permit themselves to be carried.[84] When the following verse says that these words indicate by what kind of death Peter 'is to glorify God', it is beyond doubt that this 'glorifying' can only mean his martyrdom. Perhaps John 13:36 ff. also belongs here: 'Where I am going you cannot follow me now; but you shall follow afterward.'[85]

It is not entirely certain whether the 'stretching out of the hands' in John 21:18 is intended to indicate a special manner of execution, by crucifixion.[86] The Greek expression makes this quite likely.[87] Concerning the place of martyrdom the prediction contains no precise information. Even if ch. 21 was only added later to the Gospel of John, we still are dealing with a text that is relatively early.[88]

We thus have at least two rather early witnesses to the essential fact

---

(*Sitzungsbericht der Berliner Akademie der Wissenschaften,* 1936, p. 399). The expression is referred only to the apostolic office, on the contrary, by F. Hauck, *Das Neue Testament Deutsch,* Vol. III, 1930, p. 203, and C. Bigg, *The Epistles of St. Peter and St. Jude,* 2nd ed., 1910, p. 186. H. Strathmann, in G. Kittel's *Theologisches Wörterbuch zum N. T.,* Vol. IV, p. 499, admits a 'sharing in Christ's sufferings', but rejects here the technical martyrological meaning. On the entire question see O. Michel, *Prophet und Märtyrer,* 1932; H. v. Campenhausen, *Die Idee des Martyriums in der alten Kirche,* 1936; H. W. Surkau, *Martyrien in jüdischer und frühchristlicher Zeit,* 1938; E. Günther, *Martyr,* 1941.

[84] So R. Bultmann, *Das Evangelium des Johannes,* 2nd ed., 1950, p. 552.

[85] A reference of this verse to the martyrdom is rejected by R. Bultmann, *op. cit., ad loc.,* and E. Dinkler, 'Die Petrus-Rom-Frage' (*Theologische Rundschau,* 1959, p. 205). K. Aland, 'Petrus in Rom' (*Historische Zeitschrift,* 1957, pp. 502 ff.) adds Luke 22:33 as a further witness from the first century: '[Peter] said to him, "Lord, I am ready to go with you to prison and to death." ' E. Dinkler, *op. cit.,* p. 206, regards it as a decided error to see here a *vaticinium ex eventu.* While I would not exclude so completely the interpretation proposed by K. Aland, this witness does not seem to me sufficiently assured.

[86] This is rejected by R. Bultmann, *op. cit.,* p. 552. See on the contrary already in Tertullian, *Scorpiace* 15: 'Peter is girded by another when he is fastened to the cross.'

[87] ἐκτείνειν ('stretch out'). See on this point W. Bauer, *Das Johannesevangelium* (*Handbuch zum Neuen Testament*), 3rd ed., 1933, p. 238. He points out that in assuming this the order of stretching out the hands and being girded is not reversed (as R. Bultmann says, *op. cit., ad loc.*), since 'the criminal had to carry the cross to the place of execution with arms spread out and chained to it'. E. Dinkler, *op. cit.,* p. 203, also assumes knowledge of the crucifixion of Peter.

[88] K. Aland, 'Petrus in Rom' (*Historische Zeitschrift,* 1957, pp. 502 ff.), in opposition to K. Heussi, emphasizes as a proof of its very early date the textual evidence of Papyrus 52, which contained this chapter.

of the martyrdom of Peter: certainly John 21:18, and possibly I Peter 5:1, to which about the middle of the second century II Peter 1:14 is added. This evidence, it is true, does not prove the 'historicity' of this manner of Peter's death, but it renders it probable.[89] For the question whether Peter was in Rome this preliminary question, whether he died as a martyr at all, is not unimportant. For in ancient times it was hardly customary to hand down accounts of the martyrdoms with no indication of place.[90] Thus we must at least assume that those who, in the texts mentioned, show that they know the tradition of Peter's martyrdom knew also the place, even though in this passage they had no occasion to name it. This fact will call for consideration in forming a judgment concerning First Clement, ch. 5.

As the last New Testament text which we need to discuss in connection with our problem we now may add *Revelation* 11:3 ff. The hypothesis has recently been proposed that the apostles Peter and Paul are meant here by the 'two witnesses', who, after they have given their witness, are attacked, overcome, and killed by the 'beast from the abyss'. In the same passage it is said that the corpses of the two witnesses continue to lie upon the street of the 'great city', where earlier their Lord had been crucified. For 'three and a half days' men of all peoples see them lying there and refuse to permit their burial. These two witnesses have so troubled the inhabitants of the earth that the latter, out of joy over their death, now send presents to one another. The spirit of life from God re-enters the two dead men; a voice resounds from heaven: 'Come up here', and they ascend to heaven in a cloud.

These witnesses, who previously were always interpreted to be Moses and Elijah, could in fact be Peter and Paul.[91] If this hypothesis is correct,

---

[89] K. Heussi raises the question whether Peter died as a martyr at all. The manner, however, in which he seeks to minimize the testimony of John 21:18 ff. is not convincing; he claims that this tradition, which he concedes the author must have found already in existence, deals with the transfer of Paul's martyr death to his rival Peter (*War Petrus in Rom?*, p. 30, note 21; *Neues zur Petrusfrage*, 1939, p. 24; see on this point more recently, 'Der Stand der Frage nach dem römischen Aufenthalt des Petrus', in *Deutsches Pfarrerblatt*, 1949, p. 503). R. Bultmann, *op. cit.*, p. 553, writes in opposition to this view that if, on the one side, one cannot establish by this prediction the historicity of the martyrdom, yet on the other side one cannot prove that verses 18 f. have the aim of establishing the legend. Against the scepticism of K. Heussi towards the New Testament witnesses to the martyr death of Peter see also K. Aland, *op. cit.*, pp. 502 ff.

[90] This is rightly stressed by H. Lietzmann, *Petrus und Paulus in Rom*, 2nd ed., 1927, pp. 235 f.

[91] This hypothesis, first clearly expressed by the Jesuit, Juan de Mariana, *Scholia in Vetus et Novum Testamentum*, Madrid, 1619, pp. 1100 f., has now been given a scholarly foundation by Johannes Munck in his monograph, *Petrus und Paulus in der Offenbarung Johannis*, published in 1950. Independently of J. Munck this thesis was also defended by the Brussels Professor L. Herrmann, 'L'Apocalypse johannique et l'histoire romaine' (*Latomus*, 1949, pp. 23 ff.), and the Catholic exegete M.-E. Boismard, *L'Apocalypse*

we probably would have here the oldest tradition concerning the two martyrdoms. The 'great city' in this case would have to be Rome.[92] We would have to assume that the two apostles, even if they did not do missionary work at the same time, did suffer martyrdom there *simultaneously*, and that contrary to later accounts, they were not buried, but their corpses continued to lie on the public street in Rome. In addition, this tradition would tell of the ascension of these two martyrs, such as possibly is attested for Paul in The Acts of Paul.

The only possible time for these events would be the Neronian persecution. This is especially true since other features of the Apocalypse of John continue to find their best explanation as references to Nero.

Although much favours the correctness of this new hypothesis concerning this passage, we nevertheless cannot regard it as a certain basis for assuming that Peter was martyred at Rome. The cryptic manner of speech of the Apocalypse inevitably makes uncertain every interpretation in terms of contemporary history. In our passage, for one thing, the names of the 'two witnesses' are not given; moreover, the designation 'apostle' is lacking, although it is correct that elsewhere in the New Testament the apostles are called 'witnesses' in crucial passages;[93] furthermore, the name of the 'great city' where the Lord was crucified is not given, and the explanation that it means Rome does not appear immediately convincing, but actually offers difficulties. The passage permits other interpretations. Thus here also only a *possibility* remains. If, however, we could identify more clearly, on the basis of another text, an early tradition of the stay and martyrdom of Peter in Rome, then this interpretation also, which in itself is possible, would acquire greater value as a testimony.

Up to this point, however, we have nowhere found a solid foundation.

---

(*La Sainte Bible*, Jérusalem), 1950, pp. 21 f., 53 f. In doing so, however, the latter tries to find in the resurrection and ascension of the two witnesses a symbol of their 'triumph with God' or even of their 'resurrection in the person of their successors'.—G. Bavaud (Fribourg) kindly calls my attention to a fourteenth-century liturgical text for the feast of Peter and Paul (June 29); it was used in the Lausanne Missal before the Reformation and can be found in Dreves, Blume, Bannister, *Analecta hymnica medii aevi*, 1886/1922, Vol. 40, p. 321. Peter and Paul, the 'two first roots of the Church', are here designated as the 'two olive trees', with a reference to Zech. 4:3, 11 and probably also to the two witnesses in Rev. 11:3. In this case this interpretation is much older than its attestation by Mariana in the seventeenth century.

[92] See above, p. 85, on 'Sodom and Egypt'. In that case the words 'where earlier their Lord was crucified' are hard to interpret. J. Munck, *op. cit.*, pp. 34 ff., knows no other escape here except either to consider the words as an interpolation or to understand them not in a geographical but in a figurative sense, which then might possibly be applied to Rome. M.-E. Boismard, *op. cit.* above in note 91, considers the words an interpolation inspired by Matt. 23:37. The manuscript evidence, however, does not justify striking out the words concerned.

[93] See J. Munck, *op. cit.*, pp. 17 f.

The New Testament attests only the fact of the martyrdom of Peter. As far as the place is concerned, even the interpretation of I Peter 5:13 has offered us thus far only a great probability, and the silence of Romans permitted us to conclude only that at a specific time Peter certainly was not in Rome.

\* \* \*

We still have two texts which contain brief references to Peter and Paul and *in point of time* at least still belong in the New Testament sphere: the First Epistle of Clement, which probably dates from the end of the first century, and the Letter of Ignatius of Antioch to the Romans, from the beginning of the second century. Of these two *First Clement* is by far the more important for our question; it is rightly regarded as the decisive literary witness, by both the defenders and the opponents of the tradition concerning the Roman stay of Peter. We therefore shall make a more detailed study of it. For if a relatively great probability is anywhere attainable for one view or the other, it must be in the fifth chapter of this writing.

The Epistle quite probably dates as early as the end of the first century. It has even been said that it is the document of ancient Christianity which can be dated with the greatest certainty; and it is usual to give the year 96 as the date of its composition.[94]

I consider this important text the most solid basis for a new and previously unconsidered[95] solution of our question. As we approach the study of it, we must emphasize at the outset a twofold necessity. On the one hand, we must read the decisive section without any prejudice; on the other hand—and this seems to me of crucial importance—we must not tear it out of the context in which it stands, as is continually done, but must explain it strictly in that setting. Hence before we speak of the section which directly interests us, I first of all sum up the content of the immediately preceding chapters.

Ch. 5, which we must study in greater detail, stands in a larger context which embraces chs. 3 to 6. Over the entire section we could place as a heading: *Concerning the Results of Jealousy*. The theme is formulated at the

[94] A. Harnack, *Chronologie*, Vol. I, p. 255: 'between 93 and 95'. Recently Ch. Eggenberger, *Die Quellen der politischen Ethik des 1. Klemensbriefes*, 1951, has thought it necessary to bring the date down into the beginning of the reign of Hadrian. This dating is connected with the much too one-sided perspective in which he regards the entire writing as an 'apology for the court'. Everything that is said concerning conditions in Corinth, he says, is fiction! With other reasons A. Loisy, *La Naissance du Christianisme*, 1933, p. 33, also transfers the writing to the years 130–135 (Eng. Tr., *The Birth of the Christian Religion*, 1948, p. 32).
[95] See the Foreword to the second edition of this book.

end of the third chapter, where, with a citation from Wisdom 2:24, the author defines jealousy as follows: '*The unrighteous and godless jealousy through which death entered into the world.*' Ch. 9:1 speaks again of strife and of the jealousy 'which leads to death'.

The writing undertakes to prove by examples that jealousy among brothers brings harmful results. The examples cited form two groups of seven.[96] The former contains examples from earlier times, and stands in ch. 4. They are taken from the Old Testament: 1. Cain and Abel. 2. Jacob and Esau. 3. Joseph and his brothers. 4. Moses and the Jew who reproaches him for having killed the Egyptian. 5. Moses and Aaron and Miriam. 6. Moses and Dathan and Abiram. 7. David (the Philistines) and Saul.

The second group comprises the examples from the *immediate* past. It too contains seven members, and it stands in chs. 5 and 6. Here, then, we come to the much-disputed passage which, on account of its importance, I give in full in translation:

Chapter 5: 'But now, to leave the examples from ancient times, let us come to the contestants of the most recent past. Let us take the noble examples of our own generation. On account of jealousy and envy the greatest and most righteous *pillars* were persecuted and contended unto death. Let us set before our eyes our excellent apostles:[97] *Peter*, who because of unrighteous jealousy had to bear not one or two but many torments, and so, after he had given his witness, went to the place of glory which was due him. On account of jealousy and strife *Paul* displayed the prize of endurance. Seven times he was chained; he was exiled; he was stoned; he became a herald both in the east and in the west; and so he received for his faith, glorious fame. After he had taught the whole world righteousness, had reached the furthest boundary of the west, and had given witness before the authorities, he thus was freed from the world and went to the holy place, as the greatest example of endurance.'—Chapter 6: 'To these men, who have lived a holy life, was joined a great *multitude of elect ones,*

---

[96] See R. Knopf, *Die Lehre der Zwölf Apostel; die zwei Klemensbriefe* (*Handbuch zum Neuen Testament, Ergänzungsband*), 1923, pp. 48 ff.

[97] The literal translation here, depending on whether one refers 'our' to 'apostles' or to 'eyes', would be either 'let us set before *our* eyes the excellent apostles' or 'let us set before *the* eyes *our* excellent apostles'. P. Monceaux, 'L'apostolat de Saint Pierre à Rome, à propos d'un livre récent' (*Revue d'Histoire et de Littérature religieuses*, 1910, pp. 225 f.), holds that only the translation 'our excellent apostles' is possible; and he thinks that this expression should be understood in the sense of 'the apostles who have preached in Rome and Corinth'. But in ch. 44:1 the expression 'our apostles' designates the apostles in general. M. Dibelius, 'Rom und die Christen im ersten Jahrhundert' (*Sitzungsbericht der Heidelberger Akademie der Wissenschaften*, 1942, p. 20), interprets ἀγαθοί ('good', 'excellent') in the sense of *fortes*, 'valiant'. See examples for this in B. Altaner, 'Neues zum Verständnis von 1. Klem. 5, 1–6, 2' (*Historisches Jahrbuch*, 1949, p. 25).

who on account of jealousy suffered many kinds of outrage and tortures and so became most glorious examples *among us.* On account of jealousy *women* were persecuted; as Danaids and Dircae they suffered fearful and horrible ill-treatment, and so they reached the goal of their steadfast course of faith and received a glorious prize—they, the physically weak ones. Jealousy has estranged *wives* from their husbands and perverted the saying of our father Adam: "This is now bone of my bone and flesh of my flesh." Jealousy and strife have destroyed *great cities* and uprooted great peoples.'

This is thus the only early text that speaks explicitly of the death of Peter, and it should be said at the outset that we do not learn much from it. We therefore must see whether and how far it is permitted to derive more from the context.

Here again seven victims of jealousy are assembled.[98] 1. The pillars. 2. Peter. 3. Paul. 4. The great multitude of the elect. 5. The martyred women. 6. The separated spouses. 7. The destroyed cities. Of these seven examples the first, sixth, and seventh are described in quite general terms; they do not permit us to think of particular concrete events. The last two evidently are intended only to complete the number of seven. In our interpretation we must take into account the deliberately artificial arrangement of this section,[99] and we must note the difficulty which Clement inevitably encountered in finding for the relatively short period of the most recent (that is, the Christian) past the number of examples that would correspond with the group taken from the Old Testament. So perhaps in the first example also we should not think of particular names when—probably in dependence on Galatians 2:9—the passage speaks of the 'pillars'. The author seems to think here in a general way of

[98] So rightly R. Knopf, *Handbuch zum Neuen Testament, Ergänzungsband,* 1923, p. 49.

[99] Even for this reason we must reject the new thesis which K. Heussi strangely continues to advance in his second reply to H. Lietzmann, *Neues zur Petrusfrage,* 1939. His thesis is that the passage concerning Peter, in paragraphs 3 and 4, can be a later *insertion.* But in this way the entire carefully constructed pattern of Clement would be destroyed. Apart from that fact, this thesis, which he proposed to supplement his original view, witnesses that he feels some uncertainty concerning his own arguments as presented in his earlier writing, *War Petrus in Rom?,* 1936. In the main chapter of that book he actually sought to show that in this passage Clement reports the vague and empty generalities that he knows about Peter, and that μαρτυρήσας ('having borne witness') does not refer to the martyr death. In his writing of 1939 he writes astonishingly that if the paragraph concerning Peter is an insertion, then μαρτυρήσας, in correspondence with the μαρτυρήσας that refers to Paul, would still be understood in the sense of a martyr death! But he further explains: Anyone who cannot accept the thesis of interpolation should hold to those other results which his earlier study of the passage brought to light! Here one gets the painful impression that *at any price* it *must* be proved that the letter of Clement cannot be used as a proof of the martyr death of Peter in Rome.— See the analogous procedure by Heussi in the interpretation of I Peter 5:13 (above, p. 86, notes 75 and 76).

apostles and leading men of the Primitive Church who have suffered martyrdom. In any case the 'conflict unto death' means martyrdom.[1] Probably the author includes Peter and Paul among these men, but in order to obtain the number seven he probably first, before he speaks of each of them separately, names them together with the others who are collectively described as pillars. These two cases, especially that of Paul, seemed to him particularly fitted to prove the thesis he seeks to establish, that envy and jealousy lead to ruin. For we wish to establish without delay this fact: we owe the mention of Peter and Paul entirely to the circumstance that the author, in order to give greater emphasis to his warning to the Corinthian church against envy and strife, used examples from the history of the Primitive Church, and chose exactly seven for the sake of symmetry.

Unfortunately he expresses himself very briefly in the lines that deal with Peter. The thing particularly regrettable from our standpoint is that the point in which we are especially interested, the place where Peter suffered the many torments, is not named at all. Thus even this single early text which finally gives us a certain reference to the death of Peter seems to fail us. Indeed, it is not even clearly said that the apostle died as a martyr. The text in its actual form only says that some time and somewhere Peter had to endure many torments, that he 'bore witness', and that he then attained to the place of glory.

If one reads these statements apart from the context in which they occur, then indeed, in company with those who contest the Roman stay of Peter, one must deny that the passage gives any information of any kind concerning a Roman martyrdom or even concerning any martyrdom whatever. The sentences regarding Peter theoretically permit the interpretation that in his life he had to suffer manifold trials, that (through preaching) he bore witness, and that then, somewhere and at some time, he died a natural death and finally, as the reward of his endurance, was taken up to the place of glory.

It has been correctly pointed out that the author cites the series of Old Testament examples, beginning with Cain and Abel, in chronological

---

[1] The remark of K. Heussi, in *War Petrus in Rom?*, p. 25, is indeed correct: in ch. 4:9 it is said of Joseph that he was persecuted 'unto death' ($\mu\acute{\epsilon}\chi\rho\iota\ \theta\alpha\nu\acute{\alpha}\tau\sigma\upsilon$), and yet he escaped with his life. Consequently, according to Heussi, neither is the 'struggle unto death' in ch. 5:2 to be interpreted of the martyr death. But in connection with $\dot{\alpha}\theta\lambda\acute{\epsilon}\omega$ ('struggle', 'contend') the words $\acute{\epsilon}\omega\varsigma\ \theta\alpha\nu\acute{\alpha}\tau\sigma\upsilon$ ('unto death') are probably not merely rhetorical emotion as they are in the example of Joseph. In the latter example, moreover, the author makes clear that a real death is not in mind. For he expressly adds, 'unto slavery'. The preceding emotional 'unto death' he put here only in view of the main thesis expressed in ch. 3:4 (9:1).

order. Hence it has been considered necessary to conclude from this fact that Peter died before Paul suffered martyrdom. The fact that the author reports so little concerning Peter, while he says much more about Paul, is said to be explained by the fact that he knows nothing more about Peter than the very vague facts mentioned above.[2]

With reference to the martyr death itself (apart from the question of where it occurred), we must first of all recall that this death, as we have seen, is attested about the time of the writing of First Clement, at least in John 21:18 (13:36 ff.), and perhaps also in I Peter 5:1. Could it be then that Clement knew nothing of such a death? This is indeed improbable.

Furthermore, the context shows that the two items concerning Peter and Paul are constructed in a quite similar way, even if it is true that the one concerning Peter is much shorter. Now it is universally conceded that in any event the notice concerning Paul speaks of his martyr death.[3] But if in that account the expression 'bear witness' is, to say the least, closely connected with the words, 'so . . . he went to the holy place', then it cannot properly be understood otherwise when it is similarly said of Peter: 'and so, after he bore witness, he went to the place of glory that was due him'.[4] In addition, we must also take into account the elsewhere

---

[2] This is *grosso modo* the thesis developed by K. Heussi, *War Petrus in Rom?* H. Dannenbauer, 'Die römische Petruslegende' (*Historische Zeitschrift*, 1932, pp. 246 f.), also asserts that I Clement is completely ignorant concerning the fate of Peter. He explains this ignorance by the fact that the Neronian persecution completely destroyed the Roman church and broke the chain of all living Christian tradition. For the contrary view, see G. Krüger, 'Petrus in Rom' (*ZNW*, 1932, pp. 303 f.). That Clement had no definite knowledge at all concerning Peter is asserted also by Ch. Guignebert, *op. cit.*, p. 275, and K. Holl, *Gesammelte Aufsätze*, Vol. II, 1928, p. 65, note 1. The latter, however, assumes that Peter came to Rome, though only after the death of Paul, and then was there but a short time; he explains in this way the fact that precisely in Rome the church had as few memories of Peter as I Clement, ch. 5, shows us they did (*Gesammelte Aufsätze*, Vol. II, 1928, p. 67). Accordingly, it is quite remarkable when one reads the following in J. Haller, *Das Papsttum*, Vol. I, p. 476: ' . . . who knows how many have protested in silence (against the acceptance by modern scholarship of a Roman stay of Peter), without raising their voice! I know concerning the most learned and acute church historian of the last fifty years, Karl Holl, that he did not share the "prevailing view".'

[3] K. Heussi also assumes this, though here too he still does not understand μαρτυρήσας ('having borne witness') as a reference to martyrdom (*War Petrus in Rom?*, p. 25).

[4] This testimony probably does not resume the preceding 'suffering of manifold torments', but cites the μαρτυρεῖν ('bear witness') as a further point; for οὕτω ('so', 'thus') is best referred to ἐπορεύθη ('went'), just as οὕτως in the notice concerning Paul belongs to ἀπηλλάγη ('was freed'). So H. von Campenhausen, *Die Idee des Martyriums in der alten Kirche*, 1936, p. 54, who shows that what is involved is a 'martyrological' way of speaking, which here is applied to Peter and to Paul, and in Eusebius, *Ecclesiastical History*, II, 23, is used of James. So also H. Lietzmann, *Petrus römischer Martyrer*, 1936. This is in opposition to Heussi, *op. cit.*, p. 24, note 12. In his last book, *Die römische Petrustradition in kritischer Sicht*, 1955, p. 22, note 2, Heussi seeks to refute v. Campenhausen; he reproaches him for inserting an 'and' before 'so' and for incorporating the main clause into the subordinate clause. The objection, correct in itself, does not however invalidate the parallelism established by v. Campenhausen.

attested usage in stories of martyrdom, in which the Greek word *doxa* refers to glory. The word *martyrein* for 'bear witness' is at least already on the way to becoming the technical term for witness by martyrdom.[5]

Not as proof but as confirmation we may also recall that according to the theme stated at the end of ch. 3, it is death that is portrayed as the result of jealousy.[6] To be sure, in most examples of the first group the trial does not lead to death, but doubtless the writer's special concern is with the cases which ended in this way. That is why the first example of the entire section, the story of Cain and Abel, is treated with disproportionately large detail.[7]

If we thus must assume with the greatest probability that Clement here refers to the martyr death of Peter, then—we must repeat—he himself at least knew also the place of the martyrdom, since it is not customary to hand down narratives of martyrdoms without any indication of place. In our passage Clement does not need to mention it, since he can assume that it is known; moreover, he is not giving a report about martyrs but an example of the results of envy and strife.[9]

There is the further fact that examples one, three, and four, and probably also the disputed fifth one,[10] speak of Christians who have suffered death as martyrs. The fourth example is reasonably clear in this respect; the great multitude of the elect here mentioned are, as is *univer-*

[5] So J. B. Lightfoot, *The Apostolic Fathers*, I, 1–2, 2nd ed., 1890, *ad loc.* R. Knopf, *Handbuch zum Neuen Testament, Ergänzungsband*, 1923, p. 51, also interprets μαρτυρήσα ('having borne witness') in the sense of martyr death. So do H. Delehaye, *Sanctus Essai sur le culte des Saints dans l'antiquité*, 1927, p. 79, and H. v. Campenhausen, *op. cit.*, p. 54. On the contrary, E. Günther, *Martys, Geschichte eines Wortes*, 1941, pp. 117 ff. rejects the meaning 'be a martyr', and H. Strathmann, in G. Kittel's *Theologische Wörterbuch zum N. T.*, Vol. IV, p. 511, is very hesitant. L. Sanders, *L'hellénisme de S Clément de Rome et le paulinisme*, 1943, pp. 21 f., wishes to give the word the same meaning it has in Epictetus.

[6] See above, p. 91 f.

[7] This is rightly emphasized also by R. Knopf, *Handbuch zum Neuen Testament Ergänzungsband*, 1923, p. 49.

[8] So H. Lietzmann, *Petrus und Paulus in Rom*, 2nd ed., 1927, pp. 235 f. See above pp. 89 f.

[9] B. Altaner, 'Neues zum Verständnis von 1. Klem. 5, 1–6, 2' (*Historisches Jahrbuch* 1941. p. 25), shows that ch. 9 of the Epistle of Polycarp uses I Clem., ch. 5, almost word for word, and he seeks to show that Polycarp understood the passage to mean that Paul Ignatius, Zosimus, and 'other apostles' suffered martyrdom in Rome.

[10] One usually thinks of cruelties, especially executions, in the form of mythologica presentations (Tertullian, *Apology*, 15). That would correspond also to the *ludibri* attested for the Neronian persecution in Tacitus, *Annals*, XV, 44. Another explanation L. van Liempt, *Handelingen van het veertiende nederlandsche Philologen-Congres t Amsterdam*, 1931, pp. 37 f., whom M. Dibelius follows (*op. cit.*, p. 24), says that th martyr women are here only *named* after the mythical heroines, to express the greatness of their sufferings, not the manner of their punishment: 'They are true Dircae and Danaids.' The most recent, interesting conjecture is by A. Dain, in *Recherches de Scienc religieuse*, 1951–2, pp. 353 ff.: there is here a scribal error for *neanides paidiskai* ('slav maidens').

*sally recognized*, the Christians who suffered the martyr death under Nero, for we know nothing of any other persecution of a 'great multitude'[11] in this period apart from that which Nero instigated. Concerning it, the narrative of Tacitus, *Annals*, XV, 44, speaks exactly as does Clement of a *multitudo ingens*, a 'great multitude'.

But the notice concerning this fourth example contains still another item that is very important for our study: 'they became a glorious example *among us*'.[12] Since Clement writes from Rome, we thus possess, at least for this group of martyrs, the information concerning the place. It is Rome. This confirms the conclusion that we are here dealing with the martyrs of the Neronian persecution.[13] However, the champions of the Roman tradition about Peter are often much too hasty in drawing from this place reference of the fourth example a conclusion concerning the preceding examples, in which, as we have seen, nothing is said concerning the place. If the examples of the second group are actually to be separated from one another and placed, like those of the first group, in a strictly chronological series, then we have so much the less right to say without further evidence that the words 'among us' refer also to Peter and Paul. This is particularly true if the 'pillars' of the first example likewise did not all 'suffer persecution and contend unto death' in Rome.

We dare not be too hasty in adding the words 'in Rome' to the verb in the statement, 'they [the great multitude] *were gathered with*[14] these men [Peter and Paul]', as though there were any necessity to ask at what place they were gathered with them. The assembling here mentioned is not necessarily meant in a geographical sense. Nor is it meant in the sense in which the challengers of the Roman tradition are accustomed to interpret it: 'at the place of glory'. Rather, the question as to the 'where' should not be asked at all in connection with this expression.[15] The probable intent of the verb 'they were gathered with them' is to add to the preceding examples as a simple *fact* the example of the great multitude, which indeed we must seek in Rome on the basis of the other reasons named above. The example is a further illustration, from the quite recent past, of Christian martyrdoms suffered as a result of jealousy.

[11] πολὺ πλῆθος.  [12] ἐν ἡμῖν.
[13] This is recognized also by K. Heussi, *op. cit.*, although on p. 21, note 9, he does not intend to exclude the possibility that ἐν ἡμῖν means 'in the midst of us Christians'.
[14] συνηθροίσθη.
[15] Against K. Heussi, *op. cit.*, p. 22; but also against M. Dibelius, *Rom und die Christen im ersten Jahrhundert*, 1942, p. 23. The latter in connection with his thesis that Clement here follows the pattern that popular philosophy draws from athletic contests and wishes to give examples of Christian 'endurance' and Christian 'athletic prowess', writes: 'the place where the two groups meet is rather the imaginary arena in which the contests of the Christian "athletes" occur'.

Precisely on the basis of this factual connection, however, we must as
whether in examples two to five we are not dealing with the same outwar
circumstances. If so, the division into four particular cases could agai
be connected with the fact that the author was determined to attain th
number of seven for this second group also. Indeed, we have seen that h
added examples six and seven only for this reason. But if that is true, w
must consider the possibility that the sequence of examples two to fiv
need not be understood as a chronological succession.[16]

The possibility thus exists of assigning all four examples to the Neronia
persecution in Rome. It is indeed correct that the expression 'nearest to u
in ch. 5:1[17] is given a temporal sense only to distinguish the second grou
from the first; this conclusion is also indicated by the phrase 'our genera
tion', which stands in the following sentence. But the fact that, at least i
the fourth example, Clement uses the words 'among us' proves that he i
concerned to give in the second group examples that are particularly clos
to him also in place.

We have no right, however, to extend the words 'among us' to th
notice concerning Peter, unless it can be proved that other really importar
features connect examples two to four (and perhaps also five) so closel
together that we must assume that all three or four occurred at the sam
time and at the same place.

Here again we must recall the aim that this entire enumeration serve
What is common to all these examples of both groups, the Old Testamer
as well as the Christian ones? Each of them, with deliberate monotony, i
introduced by the words 'on account of jealousy', or 'on account of jea
lousy and envy', or 'on account of jealousy and strife'. The citation o
each example contains at least one of these words. The connecting lin
between all these very different cases is therefore this: jealousy, envy, an
strife have always caused disaster. At times it is suffered by the righteou
that is, by the victims; at times by the guilty, that is, the authors of envy
jealousy, and strife—as is the case in examples five and six of the firs
group.

This context should be given more careful attention not only in th
general interpretation, but also in the explanation of details. Special em
phasis has recently been laid on the idea that Clement is strongly in
fluenced by *Hellenism* and is concerned to apply to the Bible and to th
history of the beginnings of the Church the literary artistry and concepts o
the Cynic-Stoic philosophy.[18] This is undoubtedly correct. But it wi

---

[16] In that case the argument mentioned above on p. 97 collapses.          [17] ἔγγιστα.
[17] M. Dibelius, 'Rom und die Christen im ersten Jahrhundert' (*Sitzungsbericht d*

ot do to see in this attempt, so to speak, the main aim of the discussions
n our section, as though Clement intended to offer here a moralistic and
hilosophical discussion concerning endurance, and clothed it in the
avourite Cynic and Stoic illustration of the contest in athletic games. No
loubt Clement uses this pattern for the illustrations he introduces to
lescribe the afflictions of the apostles. But it constitutes a misunderstand-
ng of his purpose when it is said that he here desires to show the exem-
lary character of the endurance of the apostles. The central theme of the
ection is not endurance but envy, jealousy, strife.[19]

Thus the brevity of the statement concerning Peter, as compared
vith the much more detailed report concerning Paul, could be con-
ected with the fact that *in this respect* the example of Peter had less to
ffer than that of Paul.[20]

Perhaps, however, the above-mentioned central theme may actually
ermit us to draw indirect conclusions as to the unnamed place of the
vents. Clement is characterizing the vice which is causing such devastat-
ng results in the previously so exemplary church of Corinth that he is

*eidelberger Akademie der Wissenschaften, Philologisch-historische Klasse*, 1942), has
hown this in a thorough study. See above, p. 76, note 36, and p. 97, note 15 (even before
im E. Dubowy, *Klemens von Rom . . . 1914*). Still more comprehensive is the work
vritten independently of M. Dibelius by the Roman Catholic theologian L. Sanders,
*'hellénisme de S. Clément de Rome et le paulinisme*, 1943. On the illustration of the
ontest, much used in popular philosophy, see also P. Wendland, *Die urchristlichen
.iteraturformen*, 1912, p. 357, note.

[19] Even in the often mentioned important essay of K. Aland, 'Petrus in Rom' (*Histori-
che Zeitschrift*, 1957, pp. 510 ff.), this is not sufficiently taken into account. The philo-
ophical pattern used by Clement, to be sure, does not fit the motive of envy. But this
loes not at all change the fact that this and not that is the main theme of the section.
So it is unfortunate that K. Aland also (just like Heussi) takes no position concerning
he interpretation of I Clement 5 which was already proposed by me in the first edition
f this book. Even E. Dinkler passes over it lightly in his remarkably documented re-
earch survey, 'Die Petrus-Rom-Frage' (*Theologische Rundschau*, 1959, pp. 210 f.), in
vhich he only takes note of A. Fridrichsen's supplementary comment on my thesis.

[20] M. Dibelius, *op. cit.*, p. 28, explains this brevity from the fact that Clement did
ot wish to speak more in detail of the martyr death of the two for political reasons;
e did not wish to present the Roman state as the opponent of the Christian athlete.
Rather, in connection with his philosophical scheme of Christian athletic activity, he
referred to limit himself to the πόνοι ('torments', 'troubles') and ἔργα ('works'). Con-
erning that subject, there was much more to tell of Paul than of Peter, who probably
ame to Rome only for execution, perhaps, like Ignatius, as a prisoner. It seems to me
hat almost all previous explanations suffer from the fact that they fail to take as starting-
oint that 'envy' is the main theme. Although Peter also fell a victim to envy, there is
nore to report concerning Paul precisely in this respect. Even the mention of his coming
o the West, if it deserves special attention at all, could be connected with the envy which
'aul himself feared (Rom. 15:20) and which his activity in the Roman Church, which he
ad not founded, threatened to arouse (see above, p. 47). But however that may be, in
o case can we agree with the conclusion of K. Heussi, *Die römische Petrustradition in
ritischer Sicht*, 1955, pp. 28 f.; from the fact that Paul is called 'preacher *in the East
nd in the West*' Heussi concludes that only a work in the East was known of Peter. The
.ast is not named in the notice about Peter, nor does the West receive any emphasis in
he notice about Paul.

addressing. It is the vice which has caused such bad results in the earlier Biblical period as well as in the quite recent Christian past. The word or rather the words that he uses to describe it do not mean simply in a general way, 'hate of the world for the children of God'.[21] This is the meaning some have given, in an attempt to escape the only possible conclusion that results from our text when it says that Peter and Paul suffered on account of jealousy and strife. The three synonymous Greek words mean jealousy, envy, strife. The word that we have translated jealousy[22] appears sixteen times in our section; the one that we have translated envy,[23] four times; the one that we have translated strife,[24] three times.

It is of course correct that the first-named word, that is, the one most often used here, means primarily 'zeal' in a good sense, and so understood it actually appears as a divine quality.[25] But the very change of meaning from the good to the bad quality shows that the vice which finally is characterized by this word is primarily not simply hate in a general sense, but rather jealousy that has sprung from zeal (*aus Eifer entstandene Eifer-Sucht*).[26] To be sure, the word can also take on the more general meaning of 'hate'. But the fact that the three words are here grouped together shows that what is here to be thrown into the foreground is precisely that which is common to all three, and this is not simply hate but specifically envy and jealousy.[27]

[21] So L. Sanders, *op. cit.*, p. 5, note 1, and J. Munck, *op. cit.*, pp. 58 ff., both of whom think they must therefore oppose the thesis that I defended in 'Les causes de la mort de Pierre et de Paul d'après le témoignage de Clément Romain' (*Revue d'Histoire et de Philosophie religieuses*, 1930, pp. 294 ff.). R. Knopf, *Handbuch zum Neuen Testament Ergänzungsband*, p. 47, in his comment on ch. 3:2, quite correctly defines ζῆλος as 'jealousy of the esteem, position, advantages of the other'. With this, however, does not agree the fact that on p. 50 he writes of '*hate*, envy, and jealousy of the world against the children of God'. P. Meinhold, 'Geschehen und Deutung im 1. Clemensbrief' (*Zeitschrift für Kirchengeschichte*, 1939, p. 90), correctly states that 'ζῆλος ("jealousy") and ἔρις ("strife") are used by Clement in a sense similar to that in which they are used by Paul in Rom. 13:13; I Cor. 3:3; II Cor. 12:20; Gal. 5:20. For Clement as well as for Paul they signify those moral weaknesses of *ill will* and *envy* which proceed from the dominance of the passions over the man who is no longer led by the Spirit.' Meinhold, however, does not draw from this the consequences for the explanation of I Clement ch. 5.

[22] ζῆλος.    [23] φθόνος.    [24] ἔρις.

[25] See A. Stumpff in Kittel's *Theologisches Wörterbuch*, Vol. II, pp. 879 f.

[26] Chr. Eggenberger, *Die Quellen der politischen Ethik des 1. Clem.*, 1951, p. 36, thinks here of 'Zealots'. Similarly, but with better arguments, Bo Reicke, *Diakonie, Festfreude und Zelos in Verbindung mit der altchristlichen Agapenfeier*, 1951, pp. 373 ff.

[27] The example that J. Munck, *op. cit.*, pp. 60 f., cites from I Clem. 45:4 would be no counterproof sufficient to outweigh the weighty majority of clear examples where ζῆλος means 'jealousy' in chs. 3 and 4, even if ch. 45:4 were an exception that had in mind only the hate of the world. But, as he himself concedes, jealousy is certainly present in one of the two examples cited in ch. 45:4.; also in the case of the three men in the fiery furnace it is not to be forgotten that the starting-point is a denunciation by some Chaldean against certain Jews who had been entrusted by Nebuchadnezzar with the administration of the province Babylon (Dan. 3:12).

I cannot understand how one can even suggest that the word here means hate in the general sense; this entire section is introduced by Clement only because it is this particular vice of jealousy that threatens to corrupt the whole church to which he writes. He says this quite plainly in the introduction of the Letter, in the three opening chapters which immediately precede our section. In them he does not speak of 'hate in general', but of jealousy, envy, and strife, which have arisen among the members of the Christian church at Corinth (ch. 3:2, 4). It is for this reason, and only for this reason, that Clement speaks in the following chapters of this vice 'through which death entered into the world', as he says with an allusion to the envy of the devil at the very beginning of the world (chs. 3:4 and 9:1).[28]

It is further clear that in the Old Testament examples the author, following his explicit aim, deals with envy and jealousy among *brothers*. According to the passage of Wisdom 2:24 cited in ch. 3:4, it is admittedly the power hostile to God, the death-dealing devil, who is here at work. But among brothers! It is for this reason that the classic example of Cain and Abel, with which the entire series is introduced, takes so disproportionate an amount of space. It is the example that is especially typical. Only one among the Old Testament examples could be considered an exception; it is that of David and the Philistines. But it is connected with the example of David and Saul; it is only mentioned with reference to that example, and for the very purpose of emphasizing that Saul belongs to the same people that David does. Hence Clement writes, 'On account of jealousy David not only had to endure envy from foreigners, but he also was persecuted by Saul, the King of Israel.' The emphasis rests upon the latter fact.

The other examples are quite clear in this respect: the jealousy of Cain for his *brother* Abel; of Esau for his *brother* Jacob; of the sons of Jacob for their younger *brother*. The fourth example is particularly interesting. Here the author explicitly stresses the fact that Moses had to flee from Pharaoh on account of the jealousy of one of *his own people*.[29] The two

---

[28] J. Munck, *op. cit.*, p. 60, note 84, concedes that in this quotation from Wisdom 2:24 the *envy* of the devil is intended; in doing so, he refers to B. Noack, *Satanas und Soteria*, 1948, pp. 43 f. But that which is involved in this passage is *envy*, and *death* as its result; it is not the fact of the hate of the 'powers hostile to God'. There at the beginning envy appears in its clear original form as the power of the devil hostile to God. But it is the special characteristic of this devilish vice that since its entrance into the world it has been at work *among brothers*. This belongs to the very nature of 'jealousy', 'envy', and 'strife'. This is seen in the Corinthian church, and this is what Clement wishes to prove by his examples, at the head of which he puts in detailed form the one of Cain and Abel.

[29] ὁμόφυλος.

remaining examples from the earlier period also have this point in common with the others.

The examples of the second group, with the exception of that of Paul, are not known from other sources, or are too little known to serve to support or undermine this result. Only the quite generally stated example of the married partners readily confirms the previous conclusion. But even with regard to the others, we must assume from the start that Clement chose these particular Christian examples so that they not only harmonize with the Old Testament ones but are convincing for the readers in view of the *aim of the writing*. What meaning would it have in this letter simply to adduce in so general a way examples that illustrate persecutions of Christians and show their endurance? The thing needed here is rather to prove to the Corinthian Christians, divided by jealousy and envy, where these vices lead. We therefore must expect that in this second group also the author is speaking of jealousy among members of *one and the same fellowship*.

From this fact, however, there results an important conclusion for the examples which are here of particular interest to us. When Clement, in this very passage, writes that Peter had to suffer 'on account of unrighteous jealousy', and Paul 'on account of jealousy and strife', and the great multitude of the elect 'on account of jealousy', this in the context of our letter can only mean that they were *victims of jealousy from persons who counted themselves members of the Christian Church*. In saying this we naturally do not mean that they were martyred or perhaps murdered by other Christians, but that the magistrates were encouraged by the attitude of some members of the Christian Church, and perhaps by the fact that they turned informers, to take action against others. In just the same way Moses, in one example of the first group, had to flee from the Egyptian king because of the jealousy of a fellow-countryman.

We are, of course, unable to say anything more definite concerning the nature of this jealousy. It should be remembered, however, that even the examples of the first group would be in part *quite unintelligible if we did not have the Old Testament*. In any case, however, the discussion must deal with the jealousy and envy of other Christians and not, for example, with that of the magistrates. The latter really had no reason at that time to be envious or jealous of the Christians, but they might well have had reasons for taking action against Christians.[30]

We have seen that statements are made concerning the life and the

---

[30] The Jews cannot be meant here as authors of jealousy, for in the time of Clement they were no longer regarded as belonging to the same fellowship.

death of Peter as well as Paul. It has indeed been asserted that the mention of jealousy refers only to the life and not to the death of the two apostles.[31] In the notice concerning Peter, however, the words 'on account of jealousy', which stand at the beginning of the relative clause, must be connected grammatically not only with the first part, 'he endured many torments', but also with the second part, 'he went to the place of glory'. Since this second part of the sentence marks so to speak the climax, we must assume that the words 'on account of jealousy' are to be connected also and particularly with this second part, and we have seen that the entrance into the place of glory' obviously presupposes his death. But in that case Peter attained martyrdom 'on account of jealousy'. Moreover, in the statement concerning Paul, the words 'on account of jealousy and strife' are so placed that they clearly have in view the end. They look to the time when Paul receives the victor's prize, even if the subsequently mentioned sufferings, troubles, and glorious deeds which precede his death are connected with the crowning with the victor's prize and form its presupposition. Grammatically, no doubt, this description is no longer dependent on the words 'on account of jealousy and strife', and since the characterization of Paul's activity here has a greater rhetorical and factual detail, it is possible that we should not ask how far each individual event is conditioned by jealousy. However, it should certainly be emphasized that in II Corinthians 11:26, in the enumeration of his afflictions, Paul names in particular the 'dangers among false brothers!'[32] Apart from this fact, it should also be recalled that Clement, in keeping with the theme announced for the section in ch. 3:4, must necessarily be interested particularly in those cases that have 'led to *death*' (ch. 9:1).

We find a confirmation of this interpretation of our passage in ch. 47, which refers directly to the aim of the writing. Here are mentioned the quarrels which have broken out in the Corinthian church and threaten not only its unity but its very existence. The author reminds the disunited church members that in their own church at Corinth there had once been dissension. He recalls that Paul at that time warned them against divisions, when some had declared that they belonged to the party that used his own name, others that they belonged to that of Cephas, and others that they belonged to that of Apollos. Clement ends this exhortation with the following decisive words, which are really a commentary on ch. 5 and prove that one cannot possibly interpret it in any other way than we have done: 'The news [of your present quarrels] has reached not only us but also *persons of different faith*, so that your folly causes the name of the

---

[31] J. Munck, *op. cit.*, pp. 61 ff.  [32] κίνδυνοι ἐν ψευδαδέλφοις.

Lord to be blasphemed and *brings you yourselves into danger*' (that is, at the hands of those of different faith).

We now understand still better why Clement, the Roman Bishop, reminds the divided Corinthians how, not long before, jealousy and strife among Christians had led to the suffering of martyrdom by the greatest apostles and by a great multitude of elect ones. The situation is the same, in so far as the danger of death threatens from *those outside the Church*, while the occasion for their intervention is given by the jealousy of *Christian brothers*. That, according to ch. 4:10, was exactly the situation of Moses and his fellow-countryman in relation to the king of Egypt.

In all of these cases Clement is content to mention, without giving detailed circumstances, the mere fact of the jealousy; it is the thing with which he is concerned. He could omit details because he could assume that the facts were known. The death of the two apostles, indeed, cannot be dated much more than thirty years before the writing of First Clement. So he can limit himself to references, just as in giving the Old Testament examples he could assume that the detailed circumstances were known in part from the Bible.

It is of course probable that not much was said of the particularly painful circumstances that contributed to those martyrdoms. The Christians who had caused the death of other Christians did not offer an edifying example for others. Moreover, it is possible that the abrupt ending of The Book of Acts may be explained in this way.[33] Did the author, who wishes to show the working of the Holy Spirit in the Church of Christ, perhaps have scruples about speaking of this grievous and momentous jealousy? However that may be, Clement on the contrary had every reason for mentioning it in *his* writing, in order to show what danger threatens the most valuable members of a church at the hands of pagan persecutors, if the church is divided by jealousy.

I find a further confirmation of the correctness of this explanation of our text by comparing the statement of Clement concerning jealousy with what we read on the same subject in the letters of Paul. This comparison will then lead us straight back to our main problem, the question as to the place. Thus far we have learned from the letter of Clement only that Peter, like Paul and others, fell victim to non-Christian persecutors as a result of disunity caused by jealousy. We now ask: *in what place*, according to the sources at our disposal, could *such events* have occurred? Where, in the time of Peter and Paul, did there exist in a local church jealousy which could lead to persecution and the death of martyrs? This

[33] See above, pp. 82 ff.

question, which I raised long ago, should be examined by scholars. In no case can it be settled by reference to the fact, correct in itself, that Clement has here used a philosophical pattern.[34]

We possess a letter of Paul in which the apostle explicitly writes that envy and strife reign in the church where he is at the time of writing; he further says that he is there as a prisoner. This is found in Philippians 1:15–17: 'There are some people here who preach Christ out of *envy and strife*. Others do it out of good will. Some proclaim Christ out of love, for they know that I lie here [in prison] for the defence of the Gospel. Others, however, do it because of *a quarrelsome spirit*, not out of pure motives; they wish to *bring affliction upon me in my imprisonment*.' It is startling that we find here in a letter of Paul, written from a place where the apostle is held prisoner, almost the same words that occur in I Clement, ch. 5: envy, strife.[35]

The place of writing of Philippians is of course uncertain, since it is not definitely named in the letter. Independently of our problem I, like many scholars, have long assumed that it must refer to the imprisonment in Rome.[36] We have seen that the great multitude of elect ones who are mentioned in I Clement 6:1 as having suffered martyrdom on account of jealousy must *certainly* be sought in Rome; 'among us' proves that. Furthermore, we shall see in particular that *Romans* contains features which point to friction between the Jewish Christian and Gentile Christian sections of the Roman church. Without reasoning in a 'vicious circle', we thus may combine these data and conclude that only concerning the *Roman* church do we know (1) that jealousy ruled in it (I Clem. 6:1); (2) that Paul seems to have feared difficulties in it due to the fact that its membership included both Jewish and Gentile Christians (Rom. 15:20); (3) that Paul spent a time in it as a prisoner of the Roman Empire and during his imprisonment had to expect 'affliction'[37] from other members of the church (Phil. 1:15 f.).

We here should recall the vigorous tone which Paul uses in this same

---

[34] See above, pp. 98 f.

[35] φθόνος, ἔρις, ἐριθεία.

[36] So among others A. Jülicher—E. Fascher, *Einleitung ins N. T.*, 7th ed., 1931, pp. 120 f.; K. Holl, *Gesammelte Aufsätze*, Vol. II, p. 67. The necessity of assigning the letter to the doubtful imprisonment at Ephesus, as do P. Feine—Behm, *Einleitung in das N. T.*, 1936, pp. 174 ff., W. Michaelis, *Einleitung ins N. T.*, 1946, pp. 205 ff., and recently also P. Benoit, *La Sainte Bible* (Jerusalem), *Les Epîtres de S. Paul. Aux Philippiens*, 1949, pp. 11 f., and others, I have never really seen, even if it is true that the mention of the 'praetorium' and of the people 'of the house of Caesar' does not *necessarily* refer to Rome. The distance between Rome and Philippi I do not feel to be a difficulty. In content the letter fits much better at the end of the life of Paul.

[37] θλίψιν (Phil. 1:17).

Epistle to the Philippians against the Jewish Christians, who are probably to be sought in the circles of those whom he designates in Galatians 2:4 as 'false brothers'. In Philippians 3:2 he actually goes so far as to call them 'dogs'. These people, who have caused him difficulties everywhere on his journeys, he accordingly encountered also in Rome. *Peter* certainly did not belong to their number. We have seen that he, on the contrary, always stood closer to Paul, and it would be an error to believe that after the episode in Antioch a break occurred between Peter and Paul.[38] According to I Clement, ch. 5, it is rather to be assumed that Peter himself had to suffer at the hands of those people.

— We recall that in the preceding chapter[39] we concluded on other grounds that Peter, as a delegated representative of the Jerusalem church, found himself by reason of his free attitude towards the Law *in an even more difficult situation than Paul* (Gal. 2:11 ff.). In view of this fact, one could very well say that the '*varied* troubles' caused by jealousy (I Clem. 5:4) refer to such difficulties with the Jerusalem leaders who commissioned him and with their over-zealous helpers.[40]

That such conflicts already existed in Rome before Paul arrived there is indicated above all by Paul's *letter to Rome*. Paul must have heard of such things. Only so can we explain the way he opposes Judaism in this letter, which he addresses to a church he has not yet visited. We mentioned above[41] how concerned he is in ch. 15:20 ff. to excuse himself for making an exception this time and coming to a church that he has not founded. We have seen further the reason why this troubles his conscience so much; he thereby is untrue to a principle whose observance he has considered a 'point of honour', because it seems to him to correspond to the spirit of the Jerusalem agreement (Gal. 2:9). The emphasis with which he speaks of this in ch. 15 proves that he does not go without some anxiety to this church which probably was founded and then cared for by the Jewish Christian group. If he already had to contend, in the churches which he had brought into being, against the opposition of the Jerusalem mission, how much more in this church, where he may be treated from the outset as an intruder. That entire section in ch. 15 clearly betrays anxiety. It is possible that this anxiety presupposes in Paul special knowledge of the situation in Rome, which plainly is con-

[38] This is rightly challenged also by M. Dibelius—W. G. Kümmel, *Paulus* (Göschen), 1951, p. 124 (Eng. Tr., *Paul*, 1953, p. 135).
[39] See above, p. 53.
[40] That these difficulties had already begun for Peter at an earlier time is rightly emphasized by W. Grundmann, 'Die Apostel zwischen Jerusalem und Antiochien' (*ZNW*, 1940, p. 128).
[41] See above, p. 47.

trolled by the Jewish Christians. This explains the unusually long and careful description of himself in the opening verses, and also the special content of the letter.[42]

The events in Rome show only too well how justified was Paul's fear.[43] The conflicts there became acute. Even Peter, who as the responsible organizer of the Jewish Christian mission had come at this time to the capital city, perhaps for the very purpose of removing internal difficulties, was apparently singled out for attack and was deserted by some of his own group. This was doubtless the result of the very conciliatory standpoint that he took. As the official leader of the Jerusalem mission he no doubt had everywhere, as we have mentioned, a difficult position. But now he was made the object of unusually strong hostility by the extremists of the Jewish Christian party.

After the writing of Philippians, therefore, the conflicts, which seem to have become more acute after Paul's arrival at Rome, may finally have degenerated into open attacks, and things may even have gone so far that during the time of persecution those people did not shrink from pointing out to the magistrates the leading men, when summoned to do so. This furthermore may find a confirmation in the pagan source which tells of Nero's action against the Christians; in Tacitus, *Annals*, XV, 44, we read: 'The [Christians] first seized who made a confession were convicted, and then upon their evidence a great multitude. . . .'[44] It has been said that such informing during a persecution, when the hearing is accompanied by torture, is nothing abnormal.[45] Nevertheless, Tacitus makes it a special point to mention this fact. Naturally we cannot prove, but can only suppose, that the zealous ones were really to be sought among those 'first seized'. In any case, this would correspond completely

---

[42] We have seen above that one cannot conclude from this fact with H. Lietzmann, *Sitzungsbericht der Berliner Akademie der Wissenschaften*, 1930, No. 8, that Peter came to Rome to agitate against Paul. See p. 79. On this subject see E. Hirsch, 'Petrus und Paulus' (*ZNW*, 1930, pp. 63 ff.).

[43] C. Cecchelli, *Gli Apostoli a Roma*, 1938, p. 101, has actually proposed the hypothesis that Paul, on account of conditions in Rome, asked Peter to come to the capital city. The fact that Peter was so to speak responsible for the Jewish Christian part of the Church could indeed argue for this hypothesis. Moreover, C. Cecchelli also assumes a betrayal of the two apostles by a 'new Judas'. See *op. cit.*, p. 96.

[44] *Igitur primo conrepti qui fatebantur, deinde, indicio eorum, multitudo ingens*. . . . On recent interpretation of this text see H. Fuchs, 'Tacitus über die Christen' (*Vigiliae christianae*, 1950, pp. 65 ff.), and A. Kurfess, 'Tacitus über die Christen' (*Vigiliae christianae*, 1951, pp. 148 f.). According to Chr. Eggenberger, *Die Quellen der politischen Ethik des 1. Klem.*, 1951, pp. 127 f., Clement would be dependent on Tacitus at this point.

[45] J. Munck, *op. cit.*, p. 63.—He further writes that from this passage it follows that the persecution was already going on. That is correct. But I do not understand how this is supposed to argue against my interpretation. After all, it is not necessary to assume that Peter and Paul had been seized at the very beginning.

with the saying of Jesus preserved in Matthew 24:10: 'They will deliver up one another.'[46]

It could also be that the attention of the Empire was turned to the apostles by some other way than by direct report. This much, however, is certain: *according to the opinion of Clement* it happened as a result of the jealousy which separated the members of a church from one another; and since such an assertion, which runs contrary to all later tendencies, could not possibly have been invented, the opinion that Clement here expresses must have corresponded with the reality.

Theoretically, of course, the possibility remains open that what took place in Rome could also happen elsewhere, that therefore disputes in the Church could become the external occasion for executions of other Christians by the Empire, so that we would not have to assume as a certainty that the martyrdom of Peter occurred in the same place as did that of Paul and the great multitude. But this is improbable, and in any case the fact remains that the existence of such jealousy is attested only for Rome, where it is attested by I Clement 6:1, almost certainly by Paul's letter to Philippi, and indirectly also by the letter to the Romans. Therefore the indication of place in ch. 6:1, 'among us', that is, in the church of Bishop Clement of Rome, quite probably refers to all the Christian martyrdoms mentioned by the author and caused by jealousy. Whether Peter and Paul suffered martyrdom simultaneously during the Neronian persecution itself, or (separately) shortly before, cannot be determined with certainty. In any case, however, their deaths belong in this persecution period.

It is likely, moreover, that by way of warning for the disunited Corinthians Clement recalled, in addition to the parties which at an earlier time had split their church (ch. 47), precisely such Christian examples of jealousy and division as he could report from his own Roman church.

Furthermore, it has been suggested that in Mark 15:10 the Evangelist added the remark, 'Pilate knew that the high priests had delivered Jesus up *out of envy*',[47] under the special influence of the events in Rome; Mark indeed wrote his Gospel in Rome, and so was a witness of those events.[48]

---

[46] Of course my interpretation of I Clement 5 does not stand or fall with the adducing of this passage from Tacitus. It is therefore a complete distortion of my argument when K. Heussi, *Die römische Petrustradition in kritischer Sicht*, 1955, p. 23, note 2, reports nothing concerning my exegesis of the section except that it 'starts from the presupposition' that Peter and Paul were caught up in the arson trial of the year 64.     [47] διὰ φθόνον.

[48] This thesis has been defended, in conjunction with my article (see above, p. 75), by A. Fridrichsen, 'Propter invidiam, Note sur 1. Clém. Rom. V' (*Eranos Rudbergianus*, 1946, pp. 161 ff.).

Finally, a further trace of these unhappy events appears to have been preserved in the *later legends* of the Acts of Peter. When we there hear that Peter was executed because he induced prominent Roman ladies to leave their husbands, the element of jealousy may constitute at least the historical kernel of this legend.[49]

Still more striking, however, are two passages of the Acts of Paul.[50] They reproduce legends in which Paul expressly appears as the victim of jealousy. First, in Ephesus, it is said that a certain Diophantos, whose wife was a disciple of Paul and was with him day and night, became jealous and occasioned his battle with wild beasts.[51] It is further told[52] that in Corinth a Spirit-filled man predicted to Paul that he would depart from this world in Rome as a victim of jealousy.[53] Here, no doubt, statements of Paul (I Cor. 15:32) are combined with I Clement, ch. 5. In any case both the Acts of Peter and the Acts of Paul have correctly preserved from I Clement, ch. 5, the fact that the death of the two apostles had been occasioned by jealousy, although they could only conceive this jealousy in the primitive form of the jealousy of a pagan husband with regard to his Christian wife. The idea of jealousy among church members, of a 'danger among false brethren' (II Cor. 11:26) was far from their minds; such a thought contradicted their entire outlook.

We reach the following conclusion. From the investigation of I Clement we conclude, not with absolute certainty but yet with the highest probability, that Peter suffered martyrdom at Rome about the time of the Neronian persecution, while divisions existed in the church there. Peter and Paul, therefore, became martyrs at about the same time, not necessarily on the same day, but probably in the same period of persecution, which may have covered a more or less extended period.[54] Concerning Peter, First Clement does not permit us to say whether he also carried on a real activity in Rome as a missionary or church leader. Just as little can we learn from this text when he came to Rome.[55] The quarrels of which we hear render likely the assumption that this happened shortly before

---

[49] *Actus Vercellenses*, 33 ff.

[50] I owe this reference to my colleague Erik Peterson. See ΠΡΑΞΕΙΣ ΠΑΥΛΟΥ. *Acta Pauli nach dem Papyrus der Hamburger Bibliothek*, edited by C. Schmidt, 1936.

[51] Page 2, line 8 of the Papyrus.

[52] Page 6, line 27 of the Papyrus.        [53] ζηλωθέντα ἐξελθεῖν.

[54] A greater separation in time, such as K. Holl, for example, assumes in *Gesammelte Aufsätze*, Vol. II, 1928, p. 67, note, is naturally not excluded.

[55] J. Munck, *op. cit.*, assumes that they both came thither as condemned men. That both suffered martyrdom *together* he believes it necessary to conclude from the fact that only the common death can have caused the *ancient* tradition to name the two apostles together, although they had worked quite separately; indeed, all the later apocryphal Acts, apart from the Acts of Peter and Paul, which dates only from the fifth century, also tell of them separately. He finds the common martyrdom confirmed also in Rev. 11:3.

the persecution and specifically in connection with his responsibility for
the Jewish Christian part of the Church.

We now come to the last of the early literary witnesses, the *Letter of
Ignatius of Antioch to the Romans*. At the beginning of the second century
this martyr, a prisoner condemned to execution in the Circus at Rome,
writes while *en route* to the Christian church of that city, which soon will
witness his martyrdom.

In ch. 4:3 of this writing we read: 'Not like Peter and Paul do I give
you commands.[56] They [were] apostles, I am a condemned man; they
were free, I am even till now a slave; but when I suffer, I shall become
Jesus Christ's freeman, and I shall arise in him as a free man.' This is
what Ignatius writes to the Roman church. It is to be noted that he recalls
to the mind of this particular church the examples of Peter and Paul.

To be sure, not a word is said to indicate that the two apostles were in
Rome. The sentence could be taken simply to mean that Ignatius wished
to say: 'I do not command you *as if* I were Peter and Paul.' The parallel
passages in the letter of Ignatius to the Ephesians (ch. 3:1) and to the
Trallians (ch. 3:3) could support such an interpretation. There Ignatius
actually does write in very general terms: 'I do not command you as
though I were somebody', 'not as an apostle'.[57] Nevertheless, it is noteworthy that precisely in his letter to the *Romans* he is not content with
such a general way of expressing himself, but refers to Peter and Paul
*by name*. In no case can it be said that the combined mention of Peter and
Paul would *necessarily* force itself upon a writer as soon as he sought for
apostles to name. This might be true in a later time, but not in the time of
Ignatius. One cannot evade the question: How could it happen at that time
that Ignatius named the two together? After all, these two apostles, apart
from their meetings in Jerusalem and their conflict in Antioch, nowhere
worked together. Indeed, according to the Jerusalem agreement of Galatians 2:9, they headed two separate missionary organizations.[58]

The most plausible answer seems to me to be the reference to their
common martyrdom in Rome, especially since it can be shown that in
another passage (ch. 3:1) Ignatius refers to First Clement.[59] Thus the

---

[56] οὐχ ὡς Πέτρος καὶ Παῦλος διατάσσομαι ὑμῖν.

[57] K. Heussi rightly points to these parallels in *War Petrus in Rom?*, pp. 40 ff.

[58] J. Munck, following W. Bauer, *Rechtgläubigkeit und Ketzerei*, 1934, p. 116, rightly
puts this question. In any case, the answer of H. Dannenbauer, 'Die Römische Petruslegende' (*Historische Zeitschrift*, 1932, p. 258), that the two apostles had been together in
Antioch, is insufficient.

[59] O. Perler, 'Ignatius von Antiochien und die römische Christengemeinde' (*Divus
Thomas*, 1944, pp. 442 f.), has demonstrated this.

combined mention of the two in our writing is also best explained by saying that Ignatius cites by name to the Romans those apostles who were with them as martyrs, just as he himself is now coming to them as a martyr. Even if he here emphasizes the difference between them and himself, yet this negative comparison has meaning only if the writer is conscious that he nevertheless has something in common with them. This is not the apostolic office, but probably the martyrdom in Rome. In the parallel passage in the Letter to the Trallians (ch. 3:3) Ignatius gives no names of apostles, precisely because in relation to this church, which no apostle has visited, there is no occasion to do so. In his letter, on the other hand, to the Ephesians, whom *Paul* had visited, he mentions the name of this apostle, even if in a quite different context (ch. 12:2). He calls the Ephesians 'fellow-initiates of Paul', because Paul has been in Ephesus as an apostle. So he mentions Peter and Paul in his letter to the Romans, because they both have been in Rome.[60]

It must be admitted, of course, that even these texts of Ignatius do not give us absolute certainty. However, we again must conclude that Ignatius in all probability knew of a Roman martyrdom of Peter and Paul.

Does this passage also permit the conclusion that the two apostles were active in Rome prior to their martyrdom? The expression 'give commands'[61] appears to make this likely. It has, indeed, been said that his word simply refers to the instructions of Paul's letter to Rome. In that case, however, Peter would then be wrongly linked with Paul. It therefore could be that Ignatius here refers to a missionary and ecclesiastical activity of the two apostles. The connection, however, in which Ignatius here speaks of 'giving commands' makes this unlikely. The chapter at whose end stands the sentence that interests us contains in its first part the famous summons to the Roman Christians not to intervene with the imperial authorities on behalf of Ignatius, since he does not want to be deprived of martyrdom. The mention of the commands of Peter and Paul, therefore, stands in a context in which Ignatius is speaking of his martyrdom and of the attitude of the Roman church towards this martyrdom. Ignatius himself is compelled at the beginning of this chapter to 'give a command' regarding this.[62] So the most natural explanation probably is that the giving of commands by Peter and Paul also was connected with their own martyrdoms. If so, this mention contains no indication concern-

---

[60] This is also emphasized strongly by H. Lietzmann, and recently by K. Aland, 'Petrus in Rome' (*Historische Zeitschrift*, 1957, pp. 509 f.). In connection with this passage the latter shows with particularly convincing clarity the doubtful character of the method by which K. Heussi seeks to invalidate the witness of the texts.   [61] διατάσσεσθαι.
[62] Ch. 4:1: ἐντέλλομαι; this means that he gives a command 'to all churches'.

ing a longer preaching activity of the two apostles, although on the other hand it does not exclude such preaching. It is sufficient, then, to assume that before their death the two apostles had an opportunity to give instructions to the Roman church with reference to their martyrdom.

It is very probable that we can add as a further indirect witness from the first century a passage from the apocryphal writing, the *Ascension of Isaiah*,[63] of which it has been said that it is the first and earliest document that attests the martyrdom of Peter in Rome. The passage in question is ch. 4:2 f., where we read the following prediction: '. . . then will arise Beliar, the great prince, the king of this world, who has ruled it since its origin; and he will descend from his firmament in human form, king of wickedness, murderer of his mother, who himself is king of this world; and he will persecute the plant which the twelve apostles of the Beloved shall have planted; one of the Twelve will be delivered into his hands.' It seems beyond doubt that Nero is here meant by Beliar, who descends in human form and murders his mother. Less clear in the mention of the 'one of the Twelve' who is delivered into his hands. As apostles who were victims of Nero, Peter and Paul are to be considered.[64] Paul, however, cannot be meant here, for according to ch. 3:17 the author uses the phrase 'the Twelve' in the narrower sense.[65] In that case this passage probably refers to Peter. The statement is of course vague, and the mention of the 'delivering up' stands in need of further definition.[66] Above all, the indication of the place is also lacking. Nevertheless, the passage speaks of an apostle who fell into Nero's hands, and so we probably can think only of Rome. The passage has not yet received the attention it deserves in connection with our problem. This is because the dating of the Christian apocalypse, ch. 3:13 to 4:19, to which this passage belongs, has been in dispute. Some have thought it was written in the lifetime of Nero,[67] while others wish to put it later, in the third century.[68] Independently of our question the decision for a date about the year 100 seems the most probable.[69] The conclusion recently established that the Apocalypse of

[63] See R. H. Charles, *The Ascension of Isaiah*, 1900; E. Tisserant, *Ascension d'Isaïe*, 1909; J. Flemming—H. Duensing, *Die Himmelfahrt des Jesaja*, in E. Hennecke, *Neutestamentliche Apokryphen*, 2nd ed., 1924, pp. 303 ff.
[64] According to E. Zeller, *Zeitschrift für wissenschaftliche Theologie*, 1896, pp. 558 ff., what is involved is the exile of the apostle John.
[65] E. Tisserant, *op. cit.*, p. 117, rightly points to this fact.
[66] For this reason A. Harnack, *Geschichte der altchristlichen Literatur, Die Chronologie*, Vol. I, 1897, p. 715, denies that this passage speaks of the martyrdom of Peter.
[67] C. Clemen, 'Die Himmelfahrt des Jesaja, ein ältestes Zeugnis für das römische Martyrium des Petrus' (*Zeitschrift für wissenschaftliche Theologie*, 1896, pp. 388 ff.).
[68] A. Harnack, *op. cit.*, pp. 578 f.
[69] So R. H. Charles, *op. cit.*, and E. Tisserant, *op. cit.*, p. 60.

Peter knows the same tradition confirms the dating at the beginning of the second century.[70] Thus this witness may not be simply ignored, as has usually happened in recent discussions.

\* \* \*

We have reached the end of our study of the early literary documents[71] and can now sum up the results:

*Prior to the second half of the second century no document asserts explicitly the stay and martyrdom of Peter in Rome.* Nevertheless, we have established: 1. As far as the *fact of the martyr death* of Peter is concerned, we possess an ancient tradition concerning it, John 21:18 ff., and this seems presupposed also in other texts. 2. As far as the *stay of Peter in Rome* is concerned, this is excluded for the time at which Paul writes his letter to the Romans. The founding of the Roman church by Peter can neither be proved nor regarded as probable. Since, however, according to Romans 15:20, it was the work of Jewish Christians, there exists a cogent reason for saying that he came to the capital city as the responsible leader of the Jewish Christian mission. The First Epistle of Peter probably presupposes in ch. 5:13 that at some time Peter was in Rome. As far as his *activity* in the Roman church is concerned, no early text compels us to contest it. But on the other hand, neither is it explicitly mentioned by a single text of the ancient period, and in any case it is difficult, for reasons of chronology, to include a very long activity. Of an episcopal office of Peter nothing is ever said. In the form in which this office is first asserted in the fourth century,[72] it is historically impossible. From everything that we know concerning the situation within the Roman church from

---

[70] See E. Peterson, 'Das Martyrium des heiligen Petrus nach der Petrusapokalypse' (*Miscell. G. Belvederi*, 1954/5, pp. 181 ff.). E. Dinkler, 'Die Petrus-Rom-Frage' (*Theologische Rundschau*, 1959, pp. 215 ff.), who rightly attaches high value to our text as a witness, prefers however not to date it before 140, because of its kinship with II Peter.

[71] J. Zeiller, *L'Eglise primitive* (*Histoire de l'Eglise*, 1946, p. 229; Eng. Tr., *History of the Primitive Church*, Vol. I, 1942, p. 235), adds as a further witness from the first half of the second century that of Papias; as reported by Eusebius, *Ecclesiastical History*, III, 39, 15, he tells that Mark wrote his Gospel in accord with the sermons of Peter. But that the Gospel was written in Rome ('composé à Rome') and that the sermons of Peter were preached in that city ('en cette ville'), as J. Zeiller asserts, this text of Papias does not say at all!

[72] *Catalogus Liberianus* (year 354): 'After the resurrection of Christ the blessed Peter received the episcopal office . . . for twenty-five years, one month, and eight days he was (bishop) in the time of Tiberius Caesar, Gaius, Claudius, and Nero, from the consulate of Minucius and Longinus to that of Nerinus and Verus.'—That would be from 30 to 55. Another calculation of the twenty-five years (43–68) is found in Eusebius, *Chronicle* (ed. Helms, pp. 179 ff.). All these statements stand in such flagrant contradiction to The Acts and the letters of Paul that it is unnecessary even to discuss them.

Paul's letters to Rome and Philippi and from First Clement, his activity like that of Paul, may be connected with the relations between the Jewish Christian and Gentile Christian parts of the Church. 3. As far as the *martyr death of Peter in Rome* is concerned, we have concerning it two texts that must be regarded as indirect witnesses: I Clement, ch. 5, and Ignatius, Romans 4:3. Neither of them says explicitly that Peter had been in Rome. In both cases, however, and particularly in First Clement which presupposes in the Church definite circumstances that fit only Rome, we can establish a great probability. It is sufficient to let us *include the martyrdom of Peter in Rome in our final historical picture of the early Church, as a fact which is relatively though not absolutely assured.* We accept it, however, with the self-evident caution that we have to use concerning many other facts of antiquity that are universally accepted as historical. Were we to demand for all facts of ancient history a greater degree of probability, we should have to strike from our history books a large proportion of their contents.

The argument from silence cannot be used as a counterproof against the martyr death of Peter at Rome, especially since the reason for that silence can be explained from the special circumstances of the martyrdom, as we can deduce them from I Clement, ch. 5. Furthermore, from the later silence of the Roman Bishop Anicetus, in the first Passover debate about the middle of the second century, we cannot conclude that at that time nothing was known as yet of a stay of Peter in Rome. In that controversy Polycarp, the Bishop of Smyrna, appeals to John and other apostles with whom he has associated to support the way of celebrating the Passover festival which he defends, while Anicetus only recalls the usage of those who were 'the most ancient ones before him', and says not a word concerning Peter.[73] This, however, could at the most be cited as evidence that Anicetus knew nothing of a leading activity of Peter in Rome; in no case can it be cited to show lack of knowledge concerning his martyrdom.[74]

If it were not imperative to handle with caution all arguments from silence, one could reverse the argument. To support the indications we possess of a martyrdom in Rome one could cite the fact that the entire early Christian literature is *completely* silent concerning the death of Peter

---

[73] Eusebius, *Ecclesiastical History*, V, 24, 16.

[74] Apart from that fact, Anicetus also could not boast, as Polycarp could, of direct relations with the apostles. M. Goguel, *L'Eglise primitive*, 1947, p. 213, explains the failure of Anicetus to appeal to the apostles by the consciousness of the Roman church that the Easter festival had been introduced only a short time before, and so did not reach back into the apostolic age.

We do not have even the slightest trace that points to any *other* place which could be considered as the scene of his death. In favour of Rome there are at least important even if indirect hints, which there are good grounds for so interpreting. Their value as proof, moreover, is increased precisely by their indirect and merely allusive character. It is a further important point that in the second and third centuries, when certain churches were in rivalry with the one in Rome, it never occurred to a single one of them to contest the claim of Rome that it was the scene of the martyrdom of Peter. Indeed, even more can be said; precisely in the east, as is clear from the Pseudo-Clementine writings and the Petrine legends, above all those that deal with Peter's conflict with Simon the magician, the tradition of the Roman residence of Peter had a particularly strong hold.

In the second half of the second century the Roman tradition about Peter begins to be explicitly attested. It can scarcely be proved that this is to be explained as a defence against Marcion, who recognized only Paul as a true apostle.[75] It is sufficient rather to take account of the universal effort, which appears in this period, to prove the apostolic origin of the churches. It will not do, however, to ascribe to such tendencies the *invention* of Peter's stay and martyrdom at Rome; their function can be limited to the emphasizing and development of traditions that already existed independently of them.

On the other hand, the chief value for historical study of these *late* texts, which now in increasing number assert that Peter was in Rome and became a martyr there, concerns only the history of dogma; they attest the *development* of the tradition. In theory the possibility cannot be excluded that perhaps here and there the basis of the tradition is a good earlier source which we no longer possess. Yet even if this is so, we must be fundamentally sceptical towards these later texts, when we see how in this very period the development of Christian legend flourishes and how it seeks to fill out the gaps in the New Testament narrative. Where in addition contradictions between these texts and the early sources appear, their trustworthiness must be challenged from the start. With this reserve, however, it is interesting to get acquainted with at least the earliest of these witnesses, those of the second and third centuries.

\* \* \*

[75] So K. Heussi, *War Petrus in Rom?*, p. 56, according to whom Peter's stay and death in Rome were first invented to meet the necessities of this anti-Marcionite struggle.

First of all, however, we must note the silence of a Christian writer who lived in Rome. This is *Justin Martyr*, from whom we possess extensive writings that date from the middle of the second century. Neither in his Apologies nor in the Dialogue with Trypho is Peter's Roman stay mentioned. This is the more striking in view of the fact that he speaks three times of Simon the magician, who in this period was regarded as the great opponent of Peter.

Among the later texts the chief one is the letter, already mentioned, from the Corinthian Bishop *Dionysius* to the Romans. Its date is about the year 170. Eusebius has preserved some fragments of it for us.[76] We have already spoken of it in connection with the question concerning the stay of Peter in Corinth.[77] Dionysius takes pains to prove the common bond between the two churches of Rome and Corinth. He recalls first the letter of Clement, which, he says, was regularly read in Corinth, and which bound the two churches together. For example, Peter and Paul had 'planted' the church of Corinth and had taught there; in like manner, both had taught together in Italy as well, and had borne witness at the same time. We have already seen[78] that at least *one* historical error occurs here: the assertion that Peter together with Paul *founded* the church of Corinth. This is excluded by I Corinthians 3:6 and 4:15. In addition Dionysius here asserts that they had taught *together*[79] in Italy, which certainly refers to Rome. This *joint* preaching activity is not indeed impossible in view of the early texts, but the statement scarcely goes back to early tradition.

Towards the end of the second century *Irenaeus* writes,[80] chiefly in connection with a description of gospel origins that goes back to Papias, that Peter and Paul had preached in Rome and founded the church, and he repeats this assertion when he speaks of the Roman church as the 'very ancient and universally known church founded and organized by Peter and Paul'. Here, too, occurs at least *one* error: the Roman church in any case was not *founded* by Paul. That is entirely clear from his letter to the Romans. This at once calls in question the historical trustworthiness of the statement. Concerning the martyr death of Peter in Rome, be it noted, nothing is said here. But from this fact no negative conclusion can be

---

[76] Eusebius, *Ecclesiastical History*, II, 25, 8.
[77] See above, p. 56.          [78] See above, p. 56.
[79] It is impossible to defend the assertion that ὁμόσε ('to the same place', 'together') only indicates that they went to the same place, Italy, but not at the same time. For ὁμόσε here as often stands for ὁμοῦ ('together'). See Blass-Debrunner, *Grammatik des neutestamentlichen Griechisch*, 7th ed., 1943, Part II, Supplement, Par. 103, p. 19. See also W. Bauer, *Griechisch-deutsches Wörterbuch*, ὁμόσε.
[80] *Adversus Haereses*, III, 1-3.

drawn, for neither is anything said here concerning the martyr death of Paul.[81]

In contrast to this, *Tertullian*[82] at about the same time congratulates the Roman church because the apostles 'have spread their teaching' in it 'with their shed blood', because in it Peter has suffered a martyrdom 'like the death of the Lord', and Paul in the manner of John the Baptist has attained the 'palm of martyrdom'. When, however, he adds at the same time the legend that the apostle John was dipped in boiling oil at Rome and yet survived uninjured, the value of his statements concerning Peter and Paul is thereby lessened. We must speak later of a further text of Tertullian[83] which probably refers to the *grave* of Peter.

*Clement of Alexandria* reports[84] that Peter wrote his first letter in Rome and 'used a cryptic word in designating the city of Rome by the name Babylon'. This is a notice which at the most need be considered in the history of the interpretation of 1 Peter 5:13.

The statement of *Origen*[85] that Peter was crucified in Rome with his head downward scarcely has historical value, even if the crucifixion as such appears to be attested in John 21:18 f.[86]

The statement of the Roman Presbyter *Gaius*, however, deserves greater respect. Not as though the fact of the stay and martyrdom of Peter in Rome could be based upon it. It dates only from the beginning of the third century. The importance of this account, which comes from Rome itself, consists rather in the fact that here the Roman tradition about Peter is given a definite topographical support, which can serve as a clue in the archaeological search for Peter's grave.

Gaius is here opposing the Montanist Proclus, who in his polemic had appealed to the fact that the church of Hierapolis in Asia Minor possesses the graves of Philip and his daughters.[87] Gaius writes the following words:[88] 'But I can show the trophies[89] of the apostles, for if you go to the Vatican Hill or to the Highway to Ostia, you will find the trophies of those who have founded this church.'

We need not stop to consider the statement concerning the joint *founding* of the Roman church by the two apostles; this statement, in spite of its

---

[81] This is rightly stressed by M. Goguel, *L'Eglise primitive*, 1947, p. 216, in opposition to Ch. Guignebert, 'La sépulture de Pierre' (*Revue historique*, 1931, pp. 225 ff.).

[82] *De praescriptione haereticorum*, 36; *Scorpiace*, 15; *Adversus Marcionem*, IV, 5.

[83] See below, p. 121.

[84] Eusebius, *Ecclesiastical History*, II, 15, 2.    [85] *Idem*, III, 1, 2,

[86] In Christian typology the phrase ἔκτασις τῶν χειρῶν ('stretching out of the hands') refers to the crucifixion. Tertullian, *Scorpiace*, 15, already refers the ζώσει ('he will gird') of John 21:18 to the binding to the cross.

[87] Eusebius, *Ecclesiastical History*, III, 31, 4.

[88] *Idem*, II, 25, 7.    [89] τρόπαια.

historical inaccuracy, had become by this time a fixed tradition. It is important, however, to know that in the time of Gaius the places which were connected with the martyrdoms of Peter and Paul were definitely located.

Whether the word 'trophies' here means graves is disputed. The Greek word can also mean simply 'victory memorials' and need not always designate a definite object. It can be meant quite generally as a place which recalls a victory or an event interpreted as a victory,[90] and in the ancient Christian view martyrdom belongs to this category. The narrower meaning of 'burial place', however, is also clearly attested.[91] Thus there are two possibilities. The two places designated as 'trophies' were regarded either as the burial places of the apostles[92] or as the places where they had been executed.[93]

It is clear in any case that Eusebius understood the word in the sense of 'burial places'. For he introduces the quotation from Gaius with the remark that Gaius, who is speaking against Proclus, speaks of the places 'in which were buried the sacred bodies of the apostles named (Peter and Paul').[94] Furthermore, the mention of the places by Gaius is probably to be considered parallel to the appeal that his Montanist opponent Proclus makes to the graves of Philip and his daughters in Asia Minor, although Eusebius reports this latter point in another part of his book.[95] If the two are parallel, the assumption is still more likely that in the opinion of Gaius the 'trophies' of Peter and Paul meant their graves.

Thus the only certain fact is that about the year 200 there were shown in Rome the places with which was connected the memory of the martyrdoms of Peter and Paul. For it is inconceivable that Gaius only invented these locations to serve the needs of his anti-Montanist polemic. The

---

[90] See F. Lammert, Article on τρόπαιον in Pauly-Wissowa, *Reallexikon der klassischen Altertumswissenschaft*.

[91] See P. Monceaux, 'Enquête sur l'épigraphie chrétienne d'Afrique' (*Mémoires présentés à l'Academie des Inscriptions et Belles-Lettres*, Vol. 88, 1910, p. 260). So also J. Carcopino, *Etudes d'histoire chrétienne*, 1953, pp. 99 ff., 251 ff., and C. Mohrmann, 'A propos de deux mots controversés de la latinité chrétienne: tropaeum-nomen' (*Vigiliae Christianae*, 1954, pp. 154 ff.).

[92] So H. Lietzmann, *Petrus und Paulus in Rom*, p. 210, and also K. Heussi, *War Petrus in Rom?*, p. 64. Likewise, H. Delehaye, *Les origines du cult des martyrs*, 1933, p. 264.

[93] So C. Erbes, 'Das Alter der Gräber und Kirchen des Paulus und Petrus in Rom' (*Zeitschrift für Kirchengeschichte*, 1885, pp. 1 ff.); *Die Todestage der Apostel Paulus und Petrus und ihre römischen Denkmäler*, 1899; 'Die geschichtlichen Verhältnisse der Apostelgräber in Rom' (*ZKG*, 1924, pp. 38 ff.). Likewise Ch. Guignebert, *La primauté de Pierre et la venue de Pierre à Rome*, 1919, pp. 305 ff. See also Th. Klauser, *Jahrbuch für Liturgiewissenschaft*, 1924, p. 296, and now *Die römische Petrustradition im Lichte der neueren Ausgrabungen unter der Peterskirche*, 1956.

[94] Eusebius, *Ecclesiastical History*, II, 25, 6.

[95] Ch. Guignebert, *op. cit.*, believes for this reason that this reference must be denied.

tradition which designated these two place *must therefore have existed before he wrote*.

This still does not prove, however, that the tradition is true as far as the *graves* are concerned. For in any event almost a century and a half lies between the death of the apostles and this earliest testimony as to the place where it occurred. In favour of its correctness it has been argued, as we shall see, that if the tradition were only a later invention, these places would not have been invented in such great geographical distance from one another as are the Vatican Hill and the Highway to Ostia. It has further been argued that in this case the burials would have been located not in pagan cemeteries but rather, in accordance with a later tendency, in Christian catacombs.[96] This argument certainly deserves serious consideration. On the other hand, it still is not completely decisive, for as has already been remarked, the tendency to join the two apostles is not common in the ancient apocryphal literature.[97]

Should the word 'trophies' refer to *graves*, the following argument can be made against the correctness of the tradition that Gaius attests concerning their location. It is hard to conceive that the surviving Roman Christians could have recognized the bodies of the apostles among the many corpses, largely charred as they probably were by fire, and could then have taken them away and have honoured Peter with a grave in the very garden of Nero. This is hardly conceivable if we are dealing with the Neronian persecution, in which we must assume that the remains were thrown into the Tiber.[98] We should also emphasize that in the first century *not the slightest trace of a cult of martyr relics* can be found. The first testimony to that we find only about A.D. 150, in the Martyrdom of Polycarp.[99] In view of the *expectation of the end of the world* in the immediate future, a concern for relics clearly constitutes an anachronism in thinking of the sixth decade of the first century, especially in those terrible days of persecution under Nero. We shall return to this point when we speak of the archaeological results. Finally, should the most recent hypothesis be correct, according to which 'the two witnesses' of Revelation 11:3 ff. are to be identified with the two apostles Peter and Paul, then their bodies were not buried at first and the rise of the tradition of their direct rapture to Heaven would exclude any knowledge of the place of their burial.[1]

In case the 'trophies' mentioned by Gaius, however, are not the ancient

---

[96] So H. Lietzmann, *Petrus und Paulus in Rom*, pp. 246 ff.
[97] See above, p. 109, note 55; p. 110.
[98] See K. Holl, *Gesammelte Aufsätze*, Vol. II, p. 65, note 1.
[99] According to H. Grégoire's thesis (see below, p. 154, note 15), the year is 177.
[1] See above, pp. 89 f.

burial places, there still remains the possibility that the two places were the *places of execution*, which then without further evidence were later regarded, perhaps even by the time of Gaius, as the burial places. On the other hand, it can be assumed that the executed persons, if buried at all, were buried at the place of their execution, or at any rate in the immediate neighbourhood. This being so, the graves would then be at least approximately located, though not precisely identified—this was not possible or even attempted in the earliest period.

We must return to this text of Gaius when we speak of the results of the excavations under the Church of St Peter. At present our chief task is to evaluate the significance of this literary witness as such. Although it dates only from the beginning of the third century, yet greater importance attaches to it than to the previously discussed witnesses of equal antiquity. It is true that a purely topographical tradition is not free from the influence of partisan interests. This is especially clear since, as we know also from the Letter of Polycrates,[2] the possession of graves was regarded at this time as a guarantee of the genuineness of a tradition, and so led also to the making of 'deposition lists'. Yet such a tradition naturally offers a greater guarantee of correctness than does a tradition concerning the events themselves.

The attempt has been made to explain this locating of the graves as a later deduction from the narrative of Tacitus.[3] It locates the place of martyrdom of the persecuted Christians in the gardens and the Circus of Nero, which according to the latest excavations were located not, as one had believed, under the present Cathedral of Peter, but probably quite close to it.[4] It is doubtful, however, whether that sort of scholarly reflection, resting upon the study of pagan sources, could conceivably have been at work at that time in the origin of a Christian tradition about where things happened. Apart from this fact, this assumption in any case does not apply to the 'trophy' of Paul on the highway to Ostia, and if one does not come to our text with the *a priori* presupposition that Peter was not in Rome, it is hard to see why the traditional statement that Gaius attests concerning the place of execution or the grave of Peter deserves less credence than does the tradition concerning that of Paul.

Nevertheless, the only *certain* conclusion that we can retain from the text of Gaius is that about the year 200 not only was it universally accepted in Rome that the martyrdom of Peter and Paul occurred in this city, but

[2] Eusebius, *Ecclesiastical History*, V, 24, 2 ff.
[3] So K. Heussi, *War Petrus in Rom?*, p. 66, and M. Goguel, *L'Eglise primitive*, p. 214.
[4] See below, p. 143.

Christians also *pointed out there the places which were regarded as the places of their execution or perhaps even as their graves.*

In this connection should be mentioned the well-known text of *Tertullian*, which according to the most probable assumption was directed against the Roman Bishop *Callistus*, and specifically against the edict he had issued. According to this edict, and contrary to the early practice of the Church, penance should be granted also for sins of unchastity.[5] On this occasion Tertullian turns against what seems to him the arrogant presumption of this Bishop, who refers to himself, and so to 'every church that is near Peter' (*ad omnem ecclesiam Petri propinquam*), the saying of Jesus to Peter concerning binding and loosing, when in fact this saying was directed to Peter alone. In recent study these quoted words have been explained, and probably correctly, in the sense of a purely local nearness, that is, 'at the grave of Peter'.[6] According to this interpretation, Tertullian reproaches Callistus because he refers Matthew 16:18 to himself, with the argument that he is Bishop of a church that has the grave of Peter near it. In this case we find the view attested here that from the grave of Peter, so to speak, the power to loose and bind which had been given to Peter actually streams forth in physical manner and passes over to the Bishop of the church in whose district the grave is located.

If this explanation is correct, it is here presupposed at the beginning of the third century that Peter was buried at the place of execution or near it. This does not necessarily mean that one possessed relics or that the 'trophy' was connected with an actual grave. But the tradition concerning the place of execution also included a statement concerning the place of burial, in so far as it was the custom for executed persons to be buried in the neighbourhood. Whether one knew the *exact* place of burial thus remains doubtful, even if we accept the above interpretation.

A further document from the second century, the *apocryphal Acts of Peter*, is relevant only for the Peter legend, but in so far as its narrative deals with the legendary burial of Peter in the grave of Marcellus, it does

---

[5] *De Pudicitia*, 21. The passage of interest to us is as follows: 'I now inquire into your opinion, [to see] from what source you usurp this right to "the Church". If, because the Lord has said to Peter, "Upon this rock I will build my Church", "To thee have I given the keys of the Kingdom of Heaven", or "Whatsoever thou shalt have bound or loosed in earth, shall be bound or loosed in heaven", you therefore presume that the power of binding and loosing has derived to you, that is, to every church near to Peter, what sort of man are you, subverting and wholly changing the manifest intention of the Lord, conferring (as that intention did) this [gift] personally upon Peter?' (See *The Ante-Nicene Fathers*, Vol. IV, 1890, p. 99.)

[6] W. Köhler, 'Omnis ecclesia Petri propinqua' (*Sitzungsberichte der Heidelberger Akademie der Wissenschaften, Philosophisch-historische Klasse*, 1938). H. Koch, *Cathedra Petri*, 1930, pp. 5 ff., takes a different view.

prove that the author, writing in the second century, knew nothing of the *grave* on the Vatican Hill. When therefore we deal with the excavations under the Church of St Peter we shall return to this text, which has failed to receive just and deserved attention in the present debate.[7]

Among the later literary witnesses we should mention further the statement of *Macarius Magnus* (III, 22), since it goes back to *Porphyrius*, the Neo-Platonic foe of the Christians. In this passage, evidently with the malicious purpose of setting the great promises to Peter in contrast with his actual insignificant work, it is reported that Peter was 'crucified after he had shepherded the sheep for only a few months'. Although this information dates no earlier than the end of the third century, it still has greater value than the witnesses from the second century, since it goes back to an enemy of the Christians and contradicts the Christian tendencies that aim rather to glorify Peter and so seek to extend as much as possible his Roman activity.[8]

In this text Porphyrius, the foe of the Christians, alludes to the command of the Risen One in John 21:16 f. and wishes to show that the 'feeding of the sheep' there promised was not very extensive, since it only lasted so short a time. To be sure, he does not mention Rome. But in this passage no other place need be considered. This results at once from the simple consideration that Porphyrius, in speaking of the brief 'feeding of the sheep', can only have thought of the same place at which occurred the crucifixion mentioned in the same sentence; the 'few months' would not cover the entire preceding missionary activity of Peter in the rest of the Empire. But we know, on the other hand, that in the time of Porphyrius the tradition concerning the martyrdom of Peter in Rome was already so widespread that he certainly must have said so if he had thought of any other place but Rome.[9] Thus we probably can conclude from this text that Peter came to Rome only a short time before his martyr death.

Thus of the later witnesses discussed in this section which assert, beginning with the second half of the second century, the Roman stay and martyrdom of Peter, at least the statement of Gaius, the text of Tertullian against the edict of Callistus, and also the declaration of Porphyrius,

---

[7] See below, p. 155.

[8] A. Harnack, 'Porphyrius gegen die Christen' (*Abhandlungen der Berliner Akademie der Wissenschaften*, 1916); *Mission und Ausbreitung des Christentums in den ersten drei Jahrhunderten*, 1924, Vol. I, p. 63, note 2, rightly ascribes to this notice the highest value as a source. The older assumption of Carl Schmidt, *Die alten Petrusakten*, 1903, pp. 167 ff., that it was only taken from the *Acts of Peter*, would indeed if correct lessen this value, but his theory is incapable of proof.

[9] I should like to argue this against H. Dannenbauer, 'Die römische Petruslegende' (*Historische Zeitschrift*, 1932, p. 243), and K. Heussi, *War Petrus in Rom?*, p. 61.

must be considered as sources for our study in spite of their later date. They deserve attention in so far as two of them reproduce for the period about the year 200 an exact topographical tradition concerning the places of execution or the graves of the apostles in Rome, while the other one is evidence that Peter worked in Rome but a very short period before he suffered martyrdom.

## 4. *The Liturgical Sources*

We still have to study the *liturgical sources* and then examine the results of the excavations. The two are closely connected with one another. The liturgical texts, on the one hand, contain statements concerning the date and place of the martyrdoms or of the martyr festivals, and so can serve as a clue for archaeological investigation; the excavations, on the other hand, can confirm these statements or even show their lack of historical value.

It might be expected *a priori* that our study could finally gain from such a comparison of liturgical history and archaeology the fully certain result to which none of the previously discussed sources has led us. So one has always approached these studies with great hopes.[10]

The most relevant liturgical texts we find in the calendar prepared for Rome. Furius Dionysius Filocalus, the later secretary of Pope Damasus, issued it in the year 354, probably making use of the episcopal archives.[11] He here unites three collections: 1. The *Depositio Episcoporum*, which contains the days of death and burial of the Roman bishops from Lucius (†254) to Sylvester (†335). 2. The *Depositio Martyrum*, a list of the festivals for the martyrs and of the fixed festivals of the church year. 3. The *Catalogus Liberianus*, a detailed list of popes from Peter to Liberius (352–366), with notes concerning the duration and the special events of their pontificate; from this list there then arose later, in the sixth century, the *Liber Pontificalis*.

Two statements of the *Depositio Martyrum* concern us here. (The already mentioned statement[12] which the *Catalogus Liberianus* contains

[10] H. Lietzmann built his epoch-making work, *Petrus und Paulus in Rom*, entirely upon the connection between the history of liturgy and the study of archaeology.

[11] See Th. Mommsen, *Monumenta Germaniae historica. Auctores antiquissimi* 9, 1892, pp. 15 ff. L. Duchesne, *Le liber Pontificalis I*, 1886, pp. 10 f. C. Kirch, *Encheiridion fontium historiae ecclesiasticae antiquae*, 1923, p. 331. See also H. Lietzmann, *Die drei ältesten Martyrologien (Kleine Texte)*, 3rd ed., 1921, pp. 2 ff. H. Achelis, 'Die Martyrologien, ihre Geschichte und ihr Wert' (*Abhandlungen der Gesellschaft der Wissenschaften in Göttingen, Philologisch-historische Klasse*, New Series, III, 3, 1900, pp. 6 ff.). Recently H. Stern, *Le Calendrier de 354*, 1953.

[12] See above, p. 113.

concerning his twenty-five-year ministry as bishop is completely worth-
less.)

One of the statements refers to February 22 and is as follows:

*VIII cal. Martias natale Petri de cathedra.*

The other refers to June 29 and is as follows:

*III cal. Jul. Petri in catacumbas et Pauli
Ostense, Tusco et Basso consulibus* (=258).

We need not pause very long on the former statement. In its present
form it is a charge to observe the 'anniversary of Peter's entrance upon
office', for that is probably what we should understand by *natale de
cathedra*. The hypothesis is probably correct that a pagan festival of
*cara cognitio* or also *caristia*, in which the Romans held meals at the graves
of their dead, is here simply transferred to Peter. Since this festival was
also designated by the Greek word *cathedra* ('chair', 'seat'), either on
account of the custom of sitting at table or of reserving a seat for the
deceased, it thus is explained how it was connected particularly with the
supposed 'episcopal see' of Peter.[13]

It could also be that before June 29 was regarded as the day of the
death of the two apostles, February 22 was originally considered, in view
of the meaning of the ancient *caristia* celebration, as the *day of their
death*.[14]

We need not concern ourselves with the fact that in the so-called
*Jerome Martyrologium*, in addition to 22 February, there further appears
as *cathedra Petri* January 18, which corresponds to an ancient Celtic
festival. Indeed, February 22 appears as the festival of Peter's episcopal
office in Antioch, January 18 of that in Rome. What we have here is a
later harmonization of two competing dates for the same festival.[15]

From the statements concerning the festival of Peter's entrance upon
office we thus obtain neither directly nor indirectly any addition to our
knowledge concerning the activity of Peter.

More important is the already cited notice of the *Depositio Martyrum*
for June 29: 'Peter in the catacombs, Paul on the Highway to Ostia, in

[13] H. Usener, *Das Weihnachtsfest*, 1911, p. 274; Fedor Schneider, 'Ueber Calendae
Januariae und Martiae im Mittelalter' (*Archiv für Religionswissenschaft*, 1920–1, pp. 386
ff.); H. Lietzmann, *op. cit.*, pp. 19 ff.; L. Duchesne, *Origines du culte*, 5th ed., 1925,
p. 294; Ch. Guignebert, 'La sépulture de Pierre' (*Revue historique*, 1931, pp. 225 ff.).
Against the connection with the pagan *Caristia* see especially P. Batiffol, *Cathedra
Petri*, 1938, pp. 123 ff.

[14] So C. Erbes, *Die Todestage der Apostel Paulus und Petrus*, 1899, p. 44, and M.
Goguel, *L'Eglise primitive*, p. 225.

[15] By rigorous reasoning H. Lietzmann, *op. cit.*, pp. 29 ff., reached this conclusion.

the consulship of Tuscus and Bassus.' Its content stands in direct connection with the archaeological work and discussions, for it mentions the catacombs and the Highway to Ostia. According to it, the celebration for Peter was held only in the catacombs (not on the Vatican Hill), and that for Paul on the Highway to Ostia. The fixing of the date by naming the consulate of Tuscus and Bassus, however, is at first sight obscure. This consulate falls in the year 258, and what we expect is the indication of the year that the apostles died. To identify one of the two consuls, Bassus, with the consul of the same name under Nero is purely hypothetical.[16] But the notice cited from the *Depositio Martyrum* has been compared with a similar one for the same day, June 29, which stands in the late Bern manuscript (eighth century) of the *Jerome Martyrologium*. For this day it runs as follows:

> *III. cal. Jul. Romae, via Aurelia, natale sanctorum Petri et Pault apostolorum, Petri in Vaticano, Pauli vero in via Ostensi, utrumque in Catacumbas, passi sub Nerone, Basso et Tusco consulibus.*
>
> That is, 'June 29, on the Aurelian Way, martyr festival of the holy apostles Peter and Paul, of Peter on the Vatican Hill, of Paul on the Highway to Ostia, both in the catacombs, suffered under Nero, in the consulate of Bassus and Tuscus'=258.

Thus here the burial place of Peter on the Vatican Hill is also mentioned. This notice, which thus connects the martyrdom of Peter with the Vatican Hill and that of Paul with the Highway to Ostia, but then mentions also the catacombs, appears more complete than the one cited above from the *Depositio Martyrum*, whose statement connects Peter and the catacombs on the one hand, and on the other hand Paul and the Highway to Ostia. However, as it stands it too yields no clear meaning. For on the one hand it says that the apostles suffered martyrdom under Nero, while on the other hand the consuls Bassus and Tuscus are named. The consulate of these two, however, is dated, as we have said, in the year 258. Therefore it has been proposed to alter the text by striking out the words *via Aurelia* and *passi sub Nerone* and changing *utrumque* into *utriusque*.[17] The following text then results:

[16] So P. Monceaux, 'L'apostolat de S. Pierre à Rome à propos d'un livre récent' (*Revue d'Histoire et de Littérature religieuses*, 1900, pp. 216 ff.), who expands the text as follows: *passi sub Nerone Basso (et Crasso consulibus; translati in Catacumbas Basso) et Tusco consulibus*, that is, 'suffered under Nero in the consulship of Bassus (and Crassus; transferred to the catacombs in the consulship of Bassus) and Tuscus'. Dom H. Quentin also, in 'Tusco et Basso consulibus' (*Resi conti della Pontificia Accademia di archeologia*, 1926-7, pp. 145-7), traces the mention of the two consuls back to a copyist's error.

[17] So L. Duchesne, *Liber Pontificalis* I, pp. civ ff., and H. Lietzmann, *op. cit.*, pp. 110 ff.

'June 29: Martyr festival of the holy apostles Peter and Paul, of Peter on the Vatican Hill, of Paul on the Highway to Ostia; of both together in the catacombs. In the consulate of Bassus and Tuscus.'[18]

This text presupposes that in the year 258 the memory of *both* apostles was celebrated in the catacombs, and it is now customary to interpret this in the sense that the relics were later *transferred to the catacombs*, and *to this transfer the date of 258 would refer*. The place in question would be the so-called Saint Sebastian Catacomb on the Appian Way, where, as we shall see, the excavations have brought to light a cult room in which, according to the inscriptions it contains, memorial meals, so-called *refrigeria*, were held in the fourth century. In this way it would be explained how the remembrance of Peter was celebrated at two places at the same time, that is, on the Vatican Hill and in the catacombs: his bones were first buried on the Vatican Hill, then in the year 258 were transferred to the catacombs, and finally in the fourth century were brought back to the Basilica that Constantine built on the Vatican Hill at the original place of burial.

Since the persecution of the Christians under Valerian took place in the year 258, the transfer would be explained either by the fear of the Christians that the relics of the apostles might be dishonoured, or—on account of an imperial ban—by the impossibility of assembling for the memorial festivals at the graves located in pagan cemeteries.[19]

Such a transfer, furthermore, could be supported by a whole series of more or less legendary later traditions concerning the graves. In themselves they have scarcely any historical value; nevertheless, they are to be considered in so far as almost all of them, though indeed in different ways, reckon with a removal of the graves occasioned by definite events.[20] Apart from Prudentius (fifth century), who transfers the two graves together into the 'marshland of the Tiber', and the *Acts* of Pseudo-Linus

[18] Similarly J. P. Kirsch, *Der stadtrömische christliche Festkalendar*, 1924.

[19] See H. Lietzmann, 'The Tomb of the Apostles ad Catacumbas' (*Harvard Theological Review*, 1923, p. 157). As a result of his book on *Petrus und Paulus in Rom* the theory of the *Translatio* (the transfer of the bodies) has been widely accepted. It had already been defended by L. Duchesne, *Liber Pontificalis*, 1886, pp. civ ff., and 'La memoria apostolorum de la Via Appia' (*Atti della Pontificia Accademia Romana di Archeologia*, I, i, 1923, pp. 1 ff.). It is also supported by J. P. Kirsch, 'Die neu entdeckte memoria Apostolorum an der Via Appia bei Rom' (*Jahresbericht der Görresgesellschaft*, 1921, p. 27; 'Die "memoria Apostolorum" an der Appischen Strasse zu Rom und die liturgische Festfeier des 29. Juni' (*Jahrbuch für Liturgiewissenschaft*, 1923, pp. 33 ff. See below, p. 128, note 29, for the names of those who oppose this theory).

[20] See Ch. Guignebert, *La sépulture de Pierre*, and M. Goguel, *L'Eglise primitive*, pp. 222 ff.

(sixth century),[21] who names as the place the Naumachia, the material in question is chiefly the *Martyrdom of Peter and Paul* (fifth century). It speaks of the attempt—frustrated by an earthquake—which pious eastern Christians made to steal the sacred relics of the two apostles and take them back to the east. This had as its result that the bodies were buried where the Orientals, when they fled, had left them lying; there they remained until a year and seven months later, when they were transferred back to their original place.[22] According to the *Life* of Pope Cornelius (251–3), which stands in the *Liber Pontificalis*, a certain Lucina, with the consent of the Pope, brought the bodies out of the catacombs and buried Paul near the place of his execution, while Peter was buried by Cornelius on the Vatican Hill in the Temple of Apollo.[23]

Possibly the sole historical kernel in these late traditions is just the memory of a transfer. However, we cannot simply accept this transfer as an assured fact, for in its generally accepted form there is no ancient text that actually mentions it for the year 258. Rather, we are dealing here only with a *hypothesis*; moreover, it rests upon the correction of the text of the *Jerome Martyrologium*, and this correction has not been thoroughly substantiated.[24]

The only solid fact is that the memory of Peter was celebrated on the Appian Way, and as we shall find confirmed by the result of excavations, so was that of Paul. In earlier times the opinion attested by the *Liber Pontificalis*, I, 67, was widely held, that the apostles were buried together here *from the beginning* and only later were transferred to separate graves. In more recent times this view still found occasional defence;[25] it was then

---

[21] A. Lipsius, *Die apokryphen Apostelgeschichten und Apostellegenden*, 1882–90, Vol. II, p. 113.

[22] This story is found in another form in the *Passio* (the story of the suffering) of the Syrian martyr Sharbil (W. Cureton, *Ancient Syriac Documents*, 1864, pp. 61 ff.). Lipsius, *op. cit.*, Vol. II, p. 312, and C. Erbes, 'Die Gräber und Kirchen Pauli und Petri in Rom' (*Zeitschrift für Kirchengeschichte*, 1885, pp. 31 ff.), have proved that the origin of this story is to be sought in a misunderstanding of the Damasus inscription in the Saint Sebastian Catacomb, where it is said that the Orient *sent* the apostles. See below. p. 133.

[23] Duchesne, *Liber Pontificalis*, I, p. 150. C. Erbes, 'Die geschichtlichen Verhältnisse der Apostelgräber' (*ZKG*, 1924, pp. 72 f.), believes that he finds a historical nucleus in the notice regarding Paul.

[24] The later Bern text of the *Jerome Martyrologium* from the eighth century perhaps does not deserve unqualified trust, since we could have here a subsequent attempt at explanation by a copyist, who did not know what to make of the date of the *Depositio Martyrum* (June 29, 258). In any case, the year 258 is not necessarily to be connected with the catacombs.

[25] P. Styger, *Die römischen Katakomben*, 1933, pp. 350 f.; *Römische Märtyrergrüfte*, 1935, I, pp. 15 ff. F. Tolotti, 'Ricerche intorno alla Memoria Apostolorum' (*Rivista di Archeologia Cristiana*, 1946, pp. 7 ff., 1947/8, pp. 13 ff.), and *Memorie degli Apostoli in catacumbas*, 1953, pp. 111 ff.

almost universally abandoned, but seems again to be receiving at least some consideration in connection with the completely unsolved riddles which the latest excavations under the Cathedral of St Peter present.[26] The date 258 proves, however, that the entire notice in the *Depositio* and the *Martyrologium* refers to the time not of burial but of another event, which must be connected with the memory of Peter (and Paul).

Nevertheless, this event need not be the transfer of the bones from their original graves to the Appian Way. Due to the authority of Lietzmann, that assumption has become almost a dogma among scholars today, and in St. Sebastian it is presented as fact by the monks who lead conducted tours. But apart from the fact that it is not really supported by a single text, there is the added fact that other considerations make the assumption of a transfer very difficult *if not impossible*. According to the Roman legislation for the protection of graves, it was a crime punishable by death to remove from the grave the remains of a deceased person. Any infraction of this law by the Christians, moreover, would have been extremely dangerous at the time of Valerian's persecution of the Christians, since Christian meetings at cemeteries were then forbidden and these places therefore were probably closely watched to enforce the ban.[27] Furthermore, it recently has been correctly pointed out that the transfer to the Appian Way in particular is quite improbable; it was one of the busiest streets, and a few hundred yards away, at the tomb of Caecilia Metella, there was an imperial police station.[28] In addition, it is impossible to see how the Christians could have feared injury to the graves, since such a thing was contrary to Roman feelings, and moreover the cult of relics was not yet so developed at that time that the Christians would need to reckon with imperial action against the graves of martyrs. In reality that persecution was directed against the leaders of the church. For these reasons a line of scholars for many years back have completely refused to believe in a transfer of the remains of the two apostles.[29] The

[26] See the report by A. Ferrua concerning the latest excavations: 'A la recherche du tombeau de S. Pierre' (*Etudes*, 1952, pp. 35 ff.). A. Ferrua here recalls this ancient tradition in a very involved sentence; in an article that appeared at about the same time, 'La Storia del sepolcro di san Pietro' (*La civiltà cattolica*, 1952, pp. 15 ff.), he merely explains that this theory has been given up by scholars.

[27] In opposition to this objection J. Ruysschaert, 'Réflexions sur les fouilles vaticanes le rapport officiel et la critique. Données archéologiques' (*Revue d'Histoire ecclésiastique* 1953, pp. 573 ff.), makes the point that this law, like every other one, could be broken (pp. 626 f.).

[28] I owe this reference to the article by Alfons Maria Schneider, 'Die Memoria Apostolorum an der Via Appia' (*Nachrichten der Akademie der Wissenschaften in Göttingen, Philologisch-Historische Klasse*, 1951, p. 5).

[29] So J. Wilpert, 'Domus Petri' (*Römische Quartalschrift*, 1912, p. 121); G. La Piana 'The Tombs of Peter and Paul ad Catacumbas' (*Harvard Theological Review*, 1921

proponents of the thesis of a transfer have recently taken account of the objections stated, to the extent that they assume only a *partial* transfer, possibly of the head.[30] The difficulties mentioned would thereby be lessened, but by no means removed.

This transfer is the more questionable since the excavations under the Basilica of St Sebastian, of which we still must speak, also prove only that a *cult* of the apostles was practised at that place; they do not prove that the relics were to be found there.

But why, then, was this specific day June 29, 258 connected with this cult? As far as this day is concerned, we should consider first of all the insufficiently noticed fact that June 29 was celebrated as the day of the foundation of Rome by Romulus. To the festival for the founder of the city corresponded the festival for the founder of the Church.[31] We may note further that it was also the day on which was deposed the rival pope Novatian, who died about this time. This fact, in connection with other observations, suggests interesting hypotheses, which could solve many difficulties.[32] For the time being, the following explanation gives the most

pp. 81 ff.); C. Erbes in *Zeitschrift für Kirchengeschichte*, 1924, p. 38; especially H. Delehaye, 'Hagiographie et archéologie romaines, II, Le Sanctuaire des apôtres sur la voie Appienne' (*Analecta Bollandiana*, 1927, pp. 297 ff.), and *Les origines du culte des martyrs*, 2nd ed., 1933, pp. 264 ff. A. von Gerkan, in the report he adds to the second edition of H. Lietzmann's *Petrus und Paulus in Rom*, pp. 248 ff., also takes a sceptical attitude towards the acceptance of the *Translatio*. (But he now takes a positive position; see 'Basso et Tusco consulibus', *Bonner Jahrbuch*, 1958, pp. 89 ff.). E. Schäfer, 'Das Petrusgrab' (*Evangelische Theologie*, 1951, pp. 477 f.), makes the point that there would have been no reason for a transfer, since Valerian's prohibition against entering Christian cemeteries dates not from the year 258 but from 257. Moreover, the grave of Peter was located not in a Christian cemetery at all, but in a pagan one; fear that the grave would be violated would have been groundless, since indeed nothing is known of violations of Christian graves in times of persecution. Most recently, A. M. Schneider, *op. cit.*; see the preceding note. For further orientation on this entire question see also: H. Leclercq, Article on 'St. Pierre' in *Dictionnaire d'archéologie chrétienne et de liturgie*, 1939, columns 822 ff., and L. Hertling—E. Kirschbaum, *Die römischen Katakomben und ihre Märtyrer*, 1950, pp. 102 ff.

[30] So J. Ruysschaert, in the article cited (*Revue d'Histoire ecclésiastique*, 1953, pp. 627 f.); J. Toynbee and J. W. Perkins, *The Shrine of St. Peter and the Vatican Excavations*, 1956, p. 182; and especially E. Kirschbaum, *Die Gräber der Apostelfürsten*, 1957, pp. 141 ff. and 201 ff. (Eng. Tr., *The Tombs of St. Peter and St. Paul*, 1959, pp. 142 f., 199 ff.). The latter leans especially on an article of E. Josi, 'Conferenze della Società dei cultori di archeologia cristiana' (*Rivista di Archeologia Cristiana*, 1953, pp. 94 f.), which maintains that according to a text of the Roman jurist Julius Paulus (third century) the grave by law is located where the head is.

[31] See C. Erbes, *Die Todestage der Apostel Paulus und Petrus und ihre römischen Denkmäler*, 1899, pp. 39 f.: 'The festival for the founder of the city of Rome was best suited for the festive celebration of the founder or founders of the Roman Church.' Pope Leo the Great, in Sermon 82 on June 29, points out: 'The apostles founded the city better than did those who built the walls and sullied them by fratricide.'

[32] *Martyrologium Hieronymianum*, in the text on June 29 as contained in the entire textual tradition. See H. Delehaye—H. Quentin, *Acta Sanctorum Novembris*, Vol. I, 1931, p. 342. Concerning the grave of Novatian, found in 1932, and its historical

I

light. We have seen that the naming of the year 258 cannot refer to the
original graves of the apostles, and probably also cannot refer to the more
than doubtful transfer of the bones. It is rather concerned only with the
rise of a cult dedicated to the apostles. Whether the cult arose at the same
time at the three places named—the Vatican Hill, the Highway to Ostia,
and the Appian Way—or at first only at the two former places, or only on
the Appian Way, cannot be determined from the liturgical sources. Only
excavations could throw further light on this point. The need of a cult
veneration and of a cult place appeared just at that time, about the middle
of the third century, and so at the time when a catacomb for the Roman
bishops was laid out, the Callistus Catacomb. So it is intelligible that
especially at that time Christians desired to honour the memory of the
two apostles who had long been regarded as the founders of the church.
In this connection it is very interesting that they still *desired to distinguish
clearly the founders from the bishops*; they did not choose for the founders
simply the Bishop's Vault. Moreover, the same veneration was still paid
to Paul that was given to Peter. The theory of the exclusive episcopal
office of the Prince of Apostles thus did not yet exist, or at least had not
yet fully triumphed.

The two notices cited from the *Depositio Martyrum* concerning June 29
refer to the cult veneration. But if that is true, we can leave as it is the far
earlier notice of the two, that is, the brief one; we do not need to change
its text.[33] We then understand why Peter is mentioned here only in connection with the catacombs, and why he alone is mentioned. At the time
when the Roman calendar originated, that is, in the year 354, the Basilica
which Constantine had begun to build for Peter at the place of the Vatican
'trophy' was not yet complete.[34] So for a time the only cult site at which
Peter was venerated was still the place in the catacombs, while in the case
of Paul the Basilica of St. Paul Outside the Walls, which was much smaller
and therefore required less time for completion, was already dedicated
to the cult.[35]

On the basis of the liturgical sources, therefore, we can only say the
following: The remembrance of Peter in Rome was attached to different
places, to the Vatican Hill and to the catacombs. June 29 is not the day
of the death of the two apostles.[36] It has a connection—probably by

connections, see L. C. Mohlberg, 'Osservazioni storicocritiche sulla Iscrizione tombale de
Novaziano' (*Ephemerides liturgicae*, 1937, pp. 242 ff.). On the possibility of a heretical
cult see below, pp. 135 and 153.      [33] See above, p. 125.      [34] See below, p. 141.
[35] This convincing line of argument is used by E. Kirschbaum, 'Petri in Catacumbas'
(*Miscellanea liturgica in honorem L. Cuniberti Mohlberg*, 1948, pp. 221 ff.).
[36] So also P. Batiffol, *Cathedra Petri*, 1938, p. 174: 'The festival of the two apostles will
be celebrated the same day, June 29, not because this date is the anniversary of their

association with the memorial day of the founder of the city of Rome—
with a Christian celebration of the year 258. This year became decisive for
the origin of the cult dedicated to the two apostles. According to the usual
thesis, indeed, this was because at that time the transfer of the bones to
the Appian Way took place. But according to the more probable view, it
was because a cult of both apostles began here without such a transfer
and perhaps without the physical presence of the remains.

The liturgical sources, taken by themselves, thus yield little help in
solving our problem. Indeed, in view of the disharmony in the liturgical
tradition, which connects the Vatican Hill on the one hand and the catacombs on the other with the memory of Peter, the problem has long since
become greatly complicated. This fact has created among scholars as well
as among churchmen an embarrassment, which become noticeable today
as soon as anyone speaks of this double tradition. This may also explain
the fact that even in the fifteenth and sixteenth centuries there obviously
was no certainty concerning the place of burial of the apostles. This is clear
from the following rarely noted *passage in Luther*:[37] 'But this I can cheer-
fully say, because I have seen it and heard it at Rome, that at Rome they
do not know where the bodies of St. Peter and St. Paul lie and whether
they lie there. The pope and cardinals know quite well that they do not
know these things.'

## 5. *The Excavations*

Do the results of the excavations carry us further? It corresponds fully
to the statements of the literary and liturgical sources if a burial took place
at two places: on the Vatican Hill, under the present cathedral of St. Peter,
and on the Appian Way, in the catacombs under the present Basilica of
St. Sebastian. A third task still awaits fulfilment by archaeological investigation; systematic excavations should also be carried out under the Church
of St. Paul Outside the Walls. It is true that various archaeological observations have already been made there, following the fire of the year 1823
and in connection with the rebuilding. But a systematic archaeological
examination of the place has not been made in recent times.[38]

martyrdom, but because it is the anniversary of the institution of a joint observance in
their honour.'
    [37] M. Luther, *Wider das Papsttum vom Teufel gestiftet*, 1545 (Weimar edition, 54),
cited from E. Mülhaupt, *Luthers Evangelien-Auslegung*, Vol. II, p. 551.
    [38] Concerning the grave of Paul see C. Cecchelli, 'La Tomba de S. Paolo' (*Capitolium*,
1950, pp. 115 ff.).—Excavations under Saint Paul's would be especially instructive, inasmuch as less mediaeval plundering would be expected here than under the Basilica of
Peter.

We speak first of the excavations which were undertaken in 1915 and have been continued ever since on the Appian Way, in the catacombs under the Basilica of St. Sebastian.[39] In earlier times this basilica was called the 'Basilica of the Apostles'; only later did it serve as the grave of Saint Sebastian, from whom it then received its present name.[40]

According to the *Liber Pontificalis*, Pope Damasus erected a church there, at the place 'where the bodies of the holy Apostles Peter and Paul had rested'. They had lain there under the *platonia* (*platoma*, marble slab). The excavations, however, have not confirmed this assertion. They have shown, however, that in the first century there was at this place a Roman villa, columbaria, and graves, and at a still earlier time a pit from which volcanic soil was dug. More important for our question was the discovery of a *triclia*, that is, a cult room; according to the inscriptions, which invoke Peter and Paul,[41] it served for the veneration of the two apostles.

According to the most recent studies of the graffiti, and above all the confirmation of the consular date 260 on one of them,[42] this room must have originated shortly before this date, probably in the year 258, already mentioned in connection with the liturgical sources. Its inner arrangement, with stone benches encircling the room, as well as some of the inscriptions, permit us to see that here were celebrated so-called *refrigeria*, meals for the dead, in honour of Peter and Paul. We read, for example, in one of the graffiti: 'For Peter and Paul I, Tomius Caelius, have held a

[39] See on that point the already mentioned fifty-page report by A. von Gerkan, published in the second edition of H. Lietzmann, *Petrus und Paulus in Rom*, 1927, pp. 248 ff. See also J. P. Kirsch, 'Das neuentdeckte Denkmal der Apostel Petrus und Paulus "in Catacumbas" an der Appischen Strasse in Rom' (*Römische Quartalschrift*, 1916-22, pp. 5 ff.); G. Mancini—O. Marucchi, 'Scavi sotto la basilica di S. Sebastiano sulla Appia antica' (*Notizie degli Scavi*, 1923); R. Chéramy, *Saint-Sébastien-hors-les-murs*, 1925; F. Fornari, *S. Sebastiano 'extra moenia'*, 1934; P. Styger, *Römische Märtyrergrüfte*, 1935; A. Prandi, 'La memoria Apostolorum in Catacumbas' (*Romana sotterranea Cristiana*, 2, 1936); Alfons Maria Schneider, 'Die Memoria Apostolorum an der Via Appia' (*Nachrichten der Akademie der Wissenschaften in Göttingen, Philologisch-historische Klasse*, 1951, pp. 1 ff.); concerning the most recent excavations: F. Tolotti, *Memorie degli Apostoli in Catacumbas*, 1953.

[40] See on that point F. W. Deichmann, *Frühchristliche Kirchen in Rom*, 1948, pp. 22 f.

[41] 191 graffiti have been discovered, 33 of them in Greek. They are in part written in low Latin and invoke the intercession of the apostles; for example, *Paule et Petre petite pro Victore* ('Paul and Peter, pray for Victor'). We certainly have here a popular cult. It is conceivable that the pilgrims who came to Rome from abroad stopped here on the Appian Way before their entrance into the city. See concerning the graffiti: E. Diehl, *Inscriptiones latinae christianae veteres*, 1924; H. Lietzmann, *op. cit.*, pp. 163 ff.; A. M. Schneider, *Refrigeria nach literarischen Quellen und Inschriften*, 1928; P. Styger, *Die römischen Katakomben*, 1933, pp. 341 ff. These works are now partly outdated by R. Marichal's discovery of a graffito with the consular date 260; see his study, 'Les dates des graffiti de St. Sébastien', *C. R. Ac. Inscr. et B. L.*, 1953, pp. 60 ff.

[42] R. Marichal, *op. cit.*, pp. 60 ff.

*refrigerium.*'[43] The meal eaten in honour of the apostles was naturally considered a meritorious work. This abuse appears to have been especially widespread in the continuation of the pagan religious meals; these could not be uprooted and were given a Christian framework in the Church by being connected with the martyr cult. Augustine later denounced the abuses to which this bad custom gave occasion.[44] In his time such meals had already been banned for several decades, but they continued to be celebrated in secret.

It cannot be disputed that such 'meals for the dead' presuppose in theory the presence of the relics of the martyrs venerated.[45] This has been made the chief support for the assertion that the apostles were actually buried for a time in the catacombs.[46] But in view of the fact that the Church prohibited these *refrigeria*, it is possible that in exceptional cases *refrigeria* were held in spite of the absence of relics.[47]

That the cult in memory of the apostles could arise here, even if their bones were not present, becomes explicable from an inscription which has been found near the crypt of the Basilica of St. Sebastian. It is a thirteenth-century copy of an inscription that goes back to Damasus. Its text is probably to be translated as follows:[48] 'Whoever you may be who searches for the names of Peter and Paul, you should know that here the holy ones once dwelt. The Orient has sent us the disciples—that we concede without argument; but on account of the merit of the (shed) blood—for indeed they have followed Christ beyond the stars and have reached the heavenly bosom and the kingdom of the pious—Rome has the greater right to claim them as its citizens. Damasus desires to sing this to your praise, ye new stars.'

The statement concerning the 'dwelling' of Peter and Paul is usually explained to mean that their remains once rested in St. Sebastian.[49] To be sure, there are other possible interpretations of this word. One could think, for example, of a tradition according to which the apostles had

---

[43] *Petro et Paulo Tomius Caelius refrigerium feci XIV kal. Apriles.*

[44] Augustine, Epistle XXIX *ad Aurelium.*

[45] See Th. Klauser, *Die Kathedra im Totenkult der heidnischen und christlichen Antike,* 1927; A. M. Schneider, *Refrigerium,* 1928.

[46] For H. Lietzmann this is one of the decisive arguments that favour acceptance of the theory of the transfer of the bones in the year 258 ('The Tomb of the Apostles ad Catacumbas', *Harvard Theological Review,* 1923, pp. 147 ff.).

[47] So G. La Piana, 'The Tombs of Peter and Paul ad Catacumbas' (*Harvard Theological Review,* 1921, pp. 81 ff.).

[48] *His habitasse prius sanctos cognoscere debes, nomina quisque Petri pariter Paulique requiris. Discipulos Oriens misit, quod sponte fatemur. Sanguinis ob meritum—Christumque per astra secuti aetherios petiere sinus regnaque piorum—Roma suos potius meruit defendere cives. Haec Damasus vestras referat, nova sidera, laudes.*

[49] See above, p. 132.

actually lived here during their lifetime. With this would agree the fact that this place was in a Jewish quarter.[50] One could even assume that the inscription had in mind a cult presence of the two apostles. It is of course doubtful whether Damasus, when in the fourth century he used the word 'dwelling', thought only of a cult presence. But in any case the most natural thing is to explain the origin of the cult on the Appian Way in the third century not by the presence of relics, but by the need of venerating the memory of the two founders of the Roman church at a place where such veneration was possible, even if the bones were not there. This view is the more probable since we can point out in St. Sebastian, though not indeed in the *triclia*, possible traces of a double cenotaph, that is, a fictitious grave, such as one often set up in ancient times when one wished to celebrate the memory of a deceased person at a place other than the site of the actual grave.[51] The choice of the Appian Way as a cult site can be explained by the fact that in the immediate vicinity the Callistus Catacomb had been laid out, from the time of Pontianus (A.D. 235), for the burial of the Roman bishops; Christians wished to assemble in the vicinity of the later bishops for the cult veneration of the founding apostles.

Without the use of hypothesis we cannot hope to explain the fact that there was in the catacombs a common memorial place for the two apostles, which still served this purpose even when Christians definitely fixed the location of the graves not here, but on the Vatican Hill and on the Highway to Ostia. Quite improbable is the supposition that in the catacombs we have the *original* grave of the apostles.[52] Another hypothesis is that in the third century the remains were *transferred* to the catacombs for a limited time. As we have seen, this hypothesis, in spite of its wide popularity, which it owes chiefly to Lietzmann's book and recently to the official report concerning the excavations, offers so many difficulties that the tendency exists, and no doubt rightly, to give it up.[53] It is theoretically possible to assume that in the third century Christians sought out relics of the apostles that up to then they had not possessed, and so in the year 258 there occurred the so-called discovery, *inventio*, of the (genuine or spurious) remains, objects such as we find were held to be martyr relics

[50] According to Juvenal, *Satire* III, 12 ff., the sacred grove of Egeria is leased to the Jews. See G. La Piana, 'Foreign Groups in Rome during the First Centuries of the Empire' (*Harvard Theological Review*, 1927, pp. 341 ff.); further, J. B. Frey, 'Les communautés juives à Rome aux premiers temps de l'Eglise' (*Recherches de Science religieuse*, pp. 275 ff.). Actual dwelling here was first assumed by J. Wilpert, *Römische Quartalschrift*, 1912, pp. 117 ff.; now F. Tolotti, *Memorie degli Apostoli in Catacumbas*, 1953, who assumes that Peter lived here and baptized in a pool of water found in that lowland, and then was also buried here immediately after the martyrdom.

[51] H. Delehaye, *Les origines du culte des martyrs*, 1933, p. 267, also assumes a cenotaph.
[52] See above, p. 127.                          [53] See above, p. 128.

in the fourth and fifth centuries.[54] This, however, is nothing more than an unproved and unprovable possibility.

Thus concerning the place at the Sebastian catacombs we conclude that even if one did not have the bones at this place, there arose here in the third century a cult in honour of the two apostles.[55] Did this happen because at the site of the 'trophies' of Peter and Paul on the Vatican Hill and on the Highway to Ostia, which *as places* certainly had been venerated in earlier times, assemblies for worship became difficult since they were located in pagan cemeteries? Or was it one of the schismatic churches of the third century which first of all created the cult site on the Appian Way, before the great Church took it over at the beginning of the fourth century? In favour of the second possibility weighty reasons have recently been presented.[56] Or is a third assumption correct which sees a popular private cult arise on the Appian Way in connection with a discovery of relics on June 29, 258?[57]

\* \* \*

Even before the rise of a *cult* of the apostles the *memorial places* for the apostles already existed on the Vatican Hill and on the Highway to Ostia. For even before the year 258, probably for more than half a century before, efforts were being made to possess the relics or at least the burial places of the apostles. In the East, this need had made itself felt much earlier than in Rome, where, as we shall see, there was no interest at all in relics or burial places, not even in those of the great martyrs of Rome, prior to the end of the second century.[58] In the Martyrdom of Polycarp we hear for the first time of a cult of relics, devoted to the memory of the great Bishop of Smyrna. Towards the end of the second century Polycrates, the Bishop of Ephesus, writes to the Roman Bishop Victor concerning the Easter celebration. In this connection he appeals explicitly

[54] See H. Achelis, *Die Martyrologien, ihre Geschichte und ihr Wert*, 1900, pp. 74 ff.; E. Schäfer, *Die Epigramme des Papstes Damasus I. als Quelle für die Geschichte der Heiligenverehrung*, 1932, pp. 101 ff.; also E. Schäfer, 'Das Petrusgrab' (*Evangelische Theologie*, 1950, pp. 474 f.).

[55] So H. Delehaye, *Les origines du culte des martyrs*, 1933, pp. 267 f., and Alfons Maria Schneider, *op. cit.* (see p. 128, note 28), pp. 1 ff. The latter does not believe that this happened as early as the year 258; rather, this year saw the origin of the cult on the Vatican Hill and the Highway to Ostia. But since Marichal found the consular date 260 among the graffiti of the Triclia (see above, p. 132), the year 258 is to be regarded as assured.

[56] See above, pp. 129 f. This thesis, advocated and supported by A. M. Schneider and C. Mohlberg, is now championed with unusual emphasis by E. Dinkler in his series of articles, often mentioned in this book, on 'Die Petrus-Rom-Frage', *Theologische Rundschau*, 1959/60.

[57] See H. Chadwick, 'St. Peter and St. Paul in Rome; the Problem of the Memoria Apostolorum ad Catacumbas' (*Journal of Theological Studies*, 1957, pp. 31 ff.).

[58] See below, pp. 154 f.

to the fact that 'in Asia great stars, who will arise on the last day when Christ returns, have found their resting place',[59] and he enumerates them. The more the time receded when Christians could still see on the basis of living tradition the connection of a church with apostles, so much the greater need did the East feel of proving apostolicity in another way, namely by the possession of apostolic burial places. We have every reason to assume that this tendency arose in the East, where, in the debates over the claims of Rome, which were presented with ever increasing vigour, this argument was not overlooked.

In order not to leave this claim to fame to the eastern churches alone, there arose in Rome at the very end of the second century the effort to make a similar appeal to the possession of apostolic 'trophies'. To this effort we owe that statement of Gaius concerning the 'trophies' on the Vatican Hill and on the Highway to Ostia; it comes from precisely this time. With this also agrees quite well the view that we have found attested for this same period, according to a likely interpretation, in the text of Tertullian.[60] It declares that from the grave of the apostle Peter the power committed to Peter streams forth upon the Roman Bishop. Hence there was created—again about that same time—a burial place for the Roman bishops.

We thus establish the fact that the church in Rome, in the decades that immediately precede the origin of the cult of the apostles in the year 258, also became interested in possessing apostolic 'trophies'. But just for this reason it is improbable that Christians would have transferred these trophies away from the Vatican Hill and the Highway to Ostia, after having appealed to them, as the Gaius reference proves, for a period of limited duration. Those places remained unmolested. If an additional cult centre was also created on the Appian Way, those ancient 'victory sites' retained their power to attest and prove the apostolicity of the church. But what now is the situation with reference to these 'trophies', in particular the 'trophy' of Peter on the Vatican Hill?

\*　　\*　　\*

We thus come to the actual question concerning the *excavations* under the Church of St. Peter. In the year 1939 work highly important for archaeology was here undertaken. In an unusually clear manner it gives us information concerning the nature of the terrain lying under the present Church of St. Peter and the use made of it in ancient Christian times. If

[59] Eusebius, *Ecclesiastical History*, III, 31, 3.　　[60] See above, pp. 121 f.

archaeology is in any position to throw light upon the question concerning Peter, it could be expected that it would do so here, and many probably cherished the hope that here, at one stroke, a final solution would be found for the much debated historical question whether Peter died in Rome as a martyr.

It was not the first time that excavations had been made there. As early as the year 1615, when the present *Confessio* of the Cathedral of St. Peter was built, and especially in 1626, when the foundations were laid under the dome for the four spiral bronze pillars of the Bernini Canopy, discoveries were made concerning the secrets concealed underneath. It was discovered that the place at which one locates the grave of Peter contains clearly pagan graves and burial chambers. They date from the years 150 to 300, and are at different depths; several more were later found. The seventeenth-century reports of these first diggings have been carefully studied in recent times.[61] But only the systematic work of 1939 has finally clarified the topography under the Church of St. Peter. It also has put an end to erroneous earlier assumptions that rested on false reports. Although it had been undertaken in a way that excluded broad participation by scholars, its results, thanks to a series of articles by competent writers, were made known as early as the years 1941–50,[62] except for the archaeological details concerning the simple ancient monument, whose remains are located under the present altar, and three graves found under it, which probably incorrectly, as we shall see, were dated as early as the first century. In a radio broadcast in the year 1942 Pope Pius XII referred quite briefly to this monument, and identified it with that 'trophy' of Peter which Gaius mentioned.

In his Christmas message on December 23 1950, he definitely asserted that 'the grave of the Prince of Apostles has been found'. At the same time he conceded in all honesty that the remains of human bones found in the region of the grave cannot be identified with certainty as the mortal remains of the apostle.

The categorical assertion that the grave itself had been found could first be tested by archaeologists when a year later, at the Christmas season of

---

[61] See H. Lietzmann, *Petrus und Paulus in Rom*, 1927, pp. 191 ff.

[62] Among the works which appeared before the official excavation report should be named: C. Respighi, 'La tomba apostolica del Vaticano' (*Rivista di Archeologia Cristiana*, 1942, pp. 5 ff.); E. Josi, *Gli scavi nelle sacre Grotte Vaticane: Il Vaticano nel 1944*, pp. 189 ff.; *Le Sacre Grotte: Vaticano*, edited by G. Fallani and M. Escobar, 1946; E. Kirschbaum, 'Die Ausgrabungen unter der Petruskirche in Rom' (*Stimmen der Zeit*, 1949, pp. 292 ff.); 'Gli scavi sotto la basilica di S. Pietro' (*Gregorianum*, 1948, pp. 544 ff.); P. Lemerle, 'Les fouilles de St-Pierre de Rome' (*La Nouvelle Clio*, 1950, pp. 393 ff.); E. Schäfer, 'Das Petrusgrab' (*Evangelische Theologie*, 1951, p. 459).

1951, the long-announced official publication concerning this part of the excavation appeared. It had been impatiently awaited by the scholarly world, and appeared after a noteworthy delay.[63] The impatience was the more intelligible since, except for the excavation leaders appointed by the Vatican, almost no archaeologist was permitted to see that place under the altar, while the remaining part of the excavations was already accessible, at least to scholars. Since then many archaeologists from all camps have attempted to form their own judgment not only by use of the comprehensive publication, splendidly illustrated in the second volume,[64] but also at the site itself. A vigorous discussion has developed concerning the results of the excavations, which, as we shall see, permit quite different interpretations. In this discussion it is noteworthy that the supporters and opponents of the conclusions are not divided in such a way that the opponents belong only to the camp of scholars independent of Rome while the supporters belong to the camp of Roman Catholic scholars. On the contrary, a large number of renowned Roman Catholic scholars, including theologians, reject decisively the positive conclusions of the official report, while independent archaeologists, though only singly and in most cases with reservations, embrace them.[65] But with all the criticism

[63] B. M. Apollonj-Ghetti, A. Ferrua, E. Kirschbaum, E. Josi (Foreword by L. Kaas), *Esplorazioni sotto la Confessione di S. Pietro in Vaticano*, 2 vols. (one volume of text and one of illustrations), 1951 (cited hereafter as *Espl. Vat.*, 1951).

[64] Unfortunately the plans contained in it do not have a uniform scale, and cross-sections of the strata are lacking; this makes use of the work difficult.

[65] Almost simultaneously with the joint excavation report one of the four directors, A. Ferrua, published individually two articles: 'La storia del sepolcro di San Pietro' (*La Civiltà cattolica*, 1952, pp. 15 ff.) and 'A la recherche du tombeau de S. Pierre' (*Etudes*, 1952, pp. 35 ff.). It is noteworthy that already in these two works the conclusions of A. Ferrua diverge *in essentials* from those of the official publication in which he shared (see below, pp. 151 f.). Even this shows that the archaeological data are not unequivocal. There are even differences in nuances between the two articles here named.—Among those who express themselves as in agreement with the conclusions of the report is J. Carcopino, 'Les fouilles de S. Pierre' (*Revue des deux mondes*, 1952, pp. 588 ff.) and *Etudes d'histoire chrétienne. Le christianisme secret du carré magique. Les fouilles de Saint-Pierre et la tradition*, 1953. To be sure, he also proposes original solutions which show essential divergences in details. See below, pp. 148, 150 ff.; V. Capocci, 'Gli scavi del Vaticano' (*Studia et Documenta Historiae et Juris*, 1952, pp. 199 ff.); J. Ruysschaert, 'Réflexions sur les fouilles Vaticanes, le rapport officiel et la critique. Données archéologiques. Données épigraphiques et littéraires' (*Revue d'Histoire ecclésiastique*, 1953, pp. 573 ff.; 1954, pp. 5 ff.), investigates the excavation report in an independent way and with clear presentation. Although in single points he goes his own way, he defends the report against its critics, whose arguments he considers with integrity and thoroughness.—J. Toynbee and J. W. Perkins, in *The Shrine of St. Peter and the Vatican Excavations*, 1956 (beautifully illustrated; on it see O. Cullmann's review in *Journal of Ecclesiastical History*, 1956, pp. 238 ff.), concede that we cannot be certain whether the grave of Peter has been found, since the actual archaeological data do not reach back beyond the end of the second century. But in agreement with the excavation report they emphasize very strongly that the hypothesis which assumes the existence of an older grave at the place in question explains much that otherwise remains dark, while nothing

that must be expressed—one of the excavation conductors quite honestly concedes errors in details[66]—it must in any case be recognized that the report of the excavation strives for objectivity, and unlike later publications is distinguished by a heartening reserve wherever what was discovered so dictates. By the use of epigraphy the attempt has recently been made to obtain more tangible results.[67] Since the publication of the official

contradicts the identification with the grave of Peter. In general they proceed in a cautious and deliberative manner, and they form a sceptical judgment of the interpretations which M. Guarducci, *Cristo e San Pietro in un documento preconstantiniano della necropoli vaticana*, 1953, gives of the scribblings on the walls of the Valerian Mausoleum (portrait and invocation of Peter?). Yet in the positive evaluation of the bones found under the red wall they show themselves less reserved than the official report. To the open opponents of the conclusions of the four archaeologists originally commissioned by the Vatican belong above all the already often mentioned but now deceased Roman Catholic theologian A. M. Schneider, who in his article, 'Das Petrusgrab im Vatikan' (*Theologische Literaturzeitung*, 1952, columns 321 ff.), firmly denies that the grave has been discovered; A. v. Gerkan, whose earlier works we mentioned above on p. 129 and who among other things accuses the excavation directors of insufficient consideration of the terrain: 'Die Forschung nach dem Grab Petri' (*Evangelisch-Lutherische Kirchenzeitung*, 1952, pp. 379 ff.); 'Kritische Studien zu den Ausgrabungen unter der Peterskirche in Rom' (*Trierer Zeitschrift*, 1954, pp. 26 ff.); 'Zu den Problemen des Petrusgrabes' (*Jahrbuch für Antike und Christentum*, 1958, pp. 79 ff.); P. Lemerle, 'La publication des fouilles de la Basilique Vaticane et la question du tombeau de Saint-Pierre' (*Revue historique*, 1952, pp. 205 ff.), who also denies the discovery of the 'trophy' of Caius and thinks it impossible to identify any ancient Christian remains under the *Confessio*; Erik Peterson, 'Uber das Petrusgrab' (*Schweizerische Rundschau*, 1952, pp. 328 ff.), who regards the 'trophy' as a cenotaph; H. I. Marrou, 'Les fouilles du Vatican' (*Dictionnaire d'archéologie chrétienne et de liturgie*, 1953, columns 3291 ff., 3310 ff.), who denies, as Peterson and I do, the discovery of the grave, and assumes rather that the 'trophy' of Caius which has been found had been erected over the place of execution of Peter; H. Torp, 'The Vatican Excavations and the Cult of Saint Peter' (*Acta archaeologica*, 1953, pp. 27 ff.), who ascribes a pagan origin to the monument which has been identified as the 'trophy' of Caius; likewise E. Schäfer, 'Das Apostelgrab unter Sankt Peter in Rom' (*Evangelische Theologie*, 1953, pp. 304 ff.); especially Th. Klauser, *Die römische Petrustradition im Lichte der neuen Ausgrabungen unter der Peterskirche Arbeitsgemeinschaft für Forschung des Landes Nordrhein-Westfalen*, 1956), and the study of A. v. Gerkan, probably the most thorough attack to date on the official thesis.—In addition to the already mentioned work of A. Ruysschaert (see above, p. 138), an answer to leading critics is contained especially in E. Kirschbaum's new book, *Die Gräber der Apostelfürsten*, 1957 (Eng. Tr., *The Tombs of St. Peter and St. Paul*, 1959); it is generally accessible and beautifully illustrated, and clearly summarizes the content of the two official volumes. Kirschbaum defends the research report by seeking to show that the opponents make an erroneous reconstruction of the terrain. At the same time he here discreetly opposes the works of Guarducci's new scholarly supporter, Prandi (see below, p. 140), who by using other presuppositions strives to further the search for the grave of Peter. To E. Dinkler we owe the most complete critical report on the excavations; it includes the most recent excavations. With regard to the grave of Peter he himself reaches negative conclusions. He is also sceptical concerning the identification of the memorial monument as the 'trophy' (*Theologische Rundschau*, 1959, pp. 289 ff.).

[66] E. Kirschbaum, *op. cit.*, p. 93 (Eng. Tr., pp. 95 f.).

[67] M. Guarducci, *Cristo e San Pietro in un documento preconstantiniano della necropoli vaticana*, 1953 (see above, note 65); especially the latest publication of the same authoress: *I graffiti sotto la confessione le San Pietro in Vatiano*, 3 vols., 1959, in which she studies the graffiti, no thorough study of which had been undertaken previously, and by assuming the use of cryptography among Christians tries to show that the name of Peter occurs several times. See below, p. 147.

archaeological report—more exactly, since 1953—new excavations also have been undertaken, without the participation of the original leaders who wrote that report.[68] Manifestly there exists in Vatican circles the opinion that one can make further advance only on the basis of entirely new foundations. In reality, the continuation of the excavations thus far has only confirmed what was assured by that report, while it serves to warn us to exercise a still greater caution and reserve towards the report's uncertain features and conclusions. In dealing with the question about Peter's grave, only indirect significance attaches to the discoveries recently made during the building of a garage north of the Vatican, at a point about 400 metres distant in a straight line from the Church of St. Peter. Graves of palace personnel from Neronian or perhaps still more ancient times were found here. None of these were Christian. This cemetery was distant enough to lie outside the Neronian gardens.[69]

The most recent investigation of the region has not yet been concluded, and so the discussion likewise continues. Nevertheless all the previous work permits us even now to judge whether the excavations under the Church of St. Peter can solve one way or the other the question concerning the Roman stay of Peter. Even here, however, I note explicitly that even if this question should be answered in the negative, this does not mean at all that Peter was never in Rome. *The question concerning the grave of Peter and the question concerning his stay in Rome are to be kept strictly separate.*

Let us now begin with that part of the new excavations concerning which a rather detailed documentation has already been published. We must first recall that under the present Church of St. Peter was the ancient basilica which Constantine erected in the fourth century in honour of Peter. It was completely torn down at the building of the present Church of St. Peter, which was begun in the year 1506 and completed about 150 years later. Unfortunately there is no ancient text which tells of its origin. However, we possess an early description of its form from Canon Tiberius Alfaranus of the sixteenth century;[70] we also possess ancient engravings. Various extensive studies have been carried on recently to sift this

---

[68] A. Prandi was entrusted with the new excavations, carried out since 1953, which were intended also to support from the archaeological side the epigraphic results of M. Guarducci; see *La zona archeologica della Confessione vaticana. I monumenti del II. secolo*, 1957. However, in opposition to the excavation report of his predecessors, he ascribes the older graves (see below, pp. 149 f.) not to the first, but to the second century. Thereby one of the chief supports of that report becomes untenable.

[69] See F. Magi, 'Ritrovamenti archeologici nell' area dell' autoparco vaticana' (*Triplice omaggio a S. Santità Pio XII*, Vol. II, 1958, pp. 87 ff.).

[70] Tiberius Alfaranus, 'De Basilicae Vaticanae antiquissima et nova structura' (*Studi e testi*, 1914).

material.[71] It appears that this building was begun under Constantine about the year 333;[72] it perhaps was completed under Constantius.[73] It lay about three metres under the level of the present church, and so upon the level of the present grottoes of the Vatican, in which many popes, even in recent times, have been buried.

The excavations undertaken in 1939 had at first no scientific purpose whatever. They were intended simply to enlarge these grottoes and at the same time to lower their floor level about eighty centimetres. This had become necessary in connection with the burial of Pope Pius XI, who died in 1939. He had left behind the direction that his remains should rest in the grottoes of the Vatican. During the work Roman walls were laid bare, and this gave occasion for a systematic uncovering of the terrain situated beneath the grottoes.

The chief thing that the workmen encountered was an unusually thick wall of considerable size. It was believed at first that this could be identified with the wall of the Circus of Nero, since, according to a misleading report from the beginning of the seventeenth century,[74] the southern

---

[71] H. Grisar, 'Die alte Petruskirche zu Rom und ihre frühesten Ansichten' (*Römische Quartalschrift*, 1895, pp. 237 ff.).

[72] Of the older datings, the most favoured fixed upon the year 324 (Lietzmann, Nicolosi, Marucchi). More recent ones have preferred the year 325 (Th. Klauser, 'Vom Heroon zur Märtyrerbasilika', *Kriegsvorträge der Universität Bonn*, 62, p. 22, and Fr. W. Deichmann, *Frühchristliche Kirchen in Rom*, 1948) or the year 326 (H. von Schoenbeck, *Beiträge zur Religionspolitik des Maxentius und Constantin*, Supplementary volume to *Clio*, 1939, p. 89). In opposition to these views, a promising hypothesis has been proposed, in connection with the latest excavations under the Church of St. Peter, by W. Seston, 'Hypothèse sur la date de la Basilique constantinienne de Saint-Pierre de Rome' (*Cahiers archéologiques*, 1946, pp. 153 ff.). This theory is that the law which Constans promulgated on 28 March 349 allows us to fix the beginning of the construction under Constantine in the year 333. That law fixes the amount of the punishments for all who have removed parts of tombs, and the act is made retroactive to the year 333. We shall see that Constantine was compelled to dig up an entire necropolis in order to erect the basilica for Peter. It is intelligible that this act, which Constantine was forced to take in his capacity as *Pontifex Maximus*, gave occasion for more and more violations of graves, which were justified by appeal to what Constantine had done. This hypothesis could find confirmation in the fact that precisely in the year 333 paganism quite obviously recedes in Constantine's region. See A. Piganiol, *L'empereur Constantin*, 1932, p. 185. A similar date, only a few years earlier (about 330), is suggested in E. Kirschbaum, *Die Gräber der Apostelfürsten*, 1957, pp. 151 f. (Eng. Tr., *The Tombs of St. Peter and St. Paul*, 1959, pp. 151 f.; see also H. I. Marrou, *Dictionnaire d'archéologie chrétienne*, 1953, column 3327). This suggestion is confirmed especially by the latest excavations; the graffiti at the *Tropaion* show the monogram (see below, p. 146).

[73] See the inscription on the apse in Diehl, *Inscriptiones latinae veteres*, No. 1753.— If the assumption is correct (see above, p. 130), according to which at the time of the composition of the *Depositio Martyrum* the basilica for Paul was completed, but that of Peter was not yet dedicated to the cult, the completion of the latter must have taken place after 354. See E. Kirschbaum, 'Petri in Catacumbas' (*Miscellanea Liturgica in honorem L. C. Mohlberg*, 1948, pp. 221 ff.).

[74] Giacomo Grimaldi, *Codex Ambros. A. 178*, edited by Ch. Huelsen (*Miscellanea*, 1910, pp. 257 ff.). *Cod. Barb. lat. 2732, 2733*, Bibl. Vat. H. Lietzmann, *op. cit.*, pp. 311 ff.

walls of the Basilica of Constantine stood upon the northern walls of the Circus of Nero, so that the Church of St. Peter would be situated over the Circus. As early as 1895 a futile effort was made to find traces of the Circus. Now for the first time, however, it has become clear what was the real purpose of this thick Roman wall, which had evidently been seen when the present church was being built in the sixteenth and seventeenth centuries. It did not belong to the Circus of Nero; it simply served to make level the sloping hillside under the present church, in order to serve as a substructure for the Basilica of Constantine. The result was that the emperor erected his church directly above this slope. The summit of the hill lies north of the church, approximately where the Vatican buildings stand today. The hill slopes away in two directions: in a gradual slope towards the east, and so in the direction from the altar to the entrance of the church, to the Piazza of St. Peter and on to the Tiber; and in a much steeper abrupt drop to the south, and so on the left side of the present basilica when viewed from the Piazza of St. Peter.

It was on this steep slope that Constantine erected his Basilica of Peter. The terrain was thus extremely unfavourable; in order to level it off, it was necessary to erect, on the south, high walls, which at the deepest point of the valley reach a height of thirteen metres. On the north, the surface of the hill had to be partly removed, and it required great quantities of soil to make a level site. These extensive labours could have been avoided if the church had been built either above on the hill-top or below in the valley. We therefore must assume that there was *a special reason* for building it right over the steep slope, and this reason can only be that in the time of Constantine it was not simply the Vatican Hill in general but rather this very slope, and probably a particular spot on this slope, that was regarded as the place where Peter was executed or buried.

This is further confirmed by another difficulty that the builders had to accept and overcome when they built the church at this place. The most important discovery that came to light in the course of these excavations is an entire cemetery, situated on this very slope. It consists of two rows of well-preserved mausoleums, separated by a narrow passageway.

Thus while previously one knew only of separate graves under the Church of St. Peter, there has been discovered here an extensive necropolis. The graves date from the second and third centuries after Christ. The first two rows run along the slope, about eight metres under the present church, in the direction of the longitudinal axis of the church; indeed they are so situated that they run slightly uphill towards the west, and so to the place beneath the altar.

The fact that Constantine had to destroy this entire site, in which actual works of art were found, shows anew that there must have been a special reason for him to build the church right at this point. This is especially clear since destruction of cemeteries was regarded in antiquity as especially serious, and he doubtless could permit himself to do this only in his capacity as *Pontifex Maximus*.[75]

How distant the cemetery was from the famous Via Cornelia, on which the grave of Peter is supposed to have been situated,[76] cannot be said with certainty, since no trace of this street has been found where it has been customary to look for it, on the longitudinal axis of the church. Probably it ran to the north, and so above the northern row of graves; the mausoleums of this row are in most cases provided with steps which lead up the hill, so that in addition to the lower entrance on the south they had also an entrance from the upper slope of the hill. It is possible therefore that the Via Cornelia passed by on that side. North of this street, and so outside the Neronian enclosure, lay that other already mentioned[77] Neronian cemetery, quite recently discovered, where imperial palace personnel were buried.

We have already mentioned that the Circus of Nero, contrary to the earlier view, was not situated under the Church of St. Peter. But it doubtless was in the vicinity. For in the mausoleum of a certain C. Popilius Heracla, located on the extreme east, an inscription mentions the wish of this deceased pagan that he may rest on the Vatican Hill at the Circus, *in vaticano ad circum*.[78]

Those buried in the cemetery located under the Church of St. Peter belonged to the most varied pagan cults. Some few Christians of this period also were buried in these pagan mausoleums with their relatives of other faiths, and a complete Christian mausoleum, that of the Julians, adorned with Christian mosaic motifs and dating back for its construction to about the third century, is found among the pagan graves. It is of the greatest importance for the beginnings of Christian art.[79] For our question, the important thing in this connection is that this room is found in this vicinity, that is, only a few metres east of the *Confessio*. Did the Christian who had this mausoleum built at this place wish to be buried

[75] See W. Seston, *op. cit.*, p. 156.

[76] H. Lietzmann, *Petrus und Paulus in Rom*, 1927, pp. 178 f.

[77] See above, p. 140.

[78] That the Circus lay on the Vatican Hill is attested by Tacitus, *Annals*, XIV, 4, and *Historia Augusta*, Elagabalus, 23, and further by Pliny, *Natural History*, XXXVI, 11, 74.

[79] H. Speier, 'Die neuen Ausgrabungen unter der Petruskirche in Rom' (in R. Herbig, *Vermächtnis der antiken Kunst*, 1950, pp. 199 ff.); O. Perler, *Die Mosaiken der Julier-gruft im Vatikan*, 1953.

as near as possible to the place which was held to be the place where the apostle Peter was buried or executed? In this period, indeed, the tendency was already widespread to have oneself buried by the graves of the martyrs. It is a striking fact, however, that in the mausoleums of the Vatican cemetery there is no mention of the name of Peter.[80]

But what is the truth about the grave of Peter itself? Is it really true, as Pius XII explicitly announced in his Christmas message of 23 December 1950, that a grave has been found in which Peter had been buried? We have seen that at the time of Constantine there must have existed a fixed tradition which in some way must have connected with Peter the place where the altar was erected in the Basilica of Constantine. Otherwise, we could not explain the choice of so unsuitable a terrain and especially of a cemetery.

We take the following information from the official publication. First of all, those conducting the excavations were forced to conclude that the sixth-century statement of the *Liber Pontificalis*, I, 176, according to which Constantine surrounded the entire grave of Peter with huge bronze slabs and erected over it a *Confessio* with a golden cross, belongs in the realm of legend. The excavations, at any rate, failed to bring to light anything of that sort; but above all, no traces were discovered to suggest the possibility that such an adornment was present.

In the area under the altar, on the contrary, traces were found lower down of a small columnar monument. It may be reconstructed (see p. 145), although but little of its original form is preserved. Its west wall is formed by the middle part of a strong wall, more than seven metres long and about two and a half metres high; it runs from north to south. To this wall a multiple purpose is ascribed. On the one hand, the so-called *Memoria* is supported by it; on the other hand, it is intended to support a stairway that leads up the hill and is built parallel to it on the back side, that is, on the west. Under these steps ran a small water channel covered over with bricks. On the front side, that is, on the east of the wall, is found a shallow niche, 72 centimetres wide and about 1·40 metres high. On both sides of the niche the wall is painted red. About 74 centimetres in front of the niche two small pillars were erected. These supported a slab of travertine, which was fitted into the wall. Above this slab is found a wider and

---

[80] W. Seston, *op. cit.*, p. 155, emphasizes this point. The interpretation by which M. Guarducci, *Cristo e San Pietro in un documento preconstantiniano della necropoli vaticana,* 1952, finds in the wall scribbling in the mausoleum of the Valerians an inscription about Peter is not assured. See on this J. Toynbee and J. W. Perkins, *The Shrine of St. Peter and the Vatican Excavations,* 1956, and E. Kirschbaum, *Gräber der Apostelfürsten,* p. 23 (Eng. Tr., *The Tombs of St. Peter and St. Paul,* 1959, p. 29).

Reconstruction of the monument located under the Church of St. Peter

It should be explicitly noted that we have here only a conjectural reconstruction on the basis of the excavation report. Only little of the monument can still be seen. See *Espl. Vat.*, 1951, I, Plate G (where there is also given an attempted reconstruction of the upper storey), and the photographs in J. Toynbee—J. W. Perkins, *The Shrine of St. Peter and the Vatican Excavations*, 1956, and E. Kirschbaum, *Die Gräber der Apostelfürsten*, 1957 (Eng. Tr., *The Tombs of St. Peter and St. Paul*, 1959). It is to be noted that the flat slab was located no higher than 1.40 metres; it thus stood only as high as a man's chest.

deeper niche—a sort of second storey. It, however, can no longer be exactly reconstructed. Since several bricks of the channel bear the stamp of Marcus Aurelius Caesar, this small monument can be dated in the second half of the second century, *if it actually was built at the same time as the channel.* This would agree well with the statement in which Gaius reports that he can show the 'trophy' of Peter on the Vatican Hill. In this connection, to be sure, we must not forget that this text *by itself* does not permit us to decide whether the 'trophy' is the place only of the martyrdom, or of a grave, or even merely of a memorial.[81] Since Constantine obviously oriented his entire basilica with reference to this place, it may be assumed with some probability, from the conclusions reached above concerning the unsuitable terrain, that we really are dealing with that 'trophy' of Gaius.[82] This presupposes, of course, that the channel and the monument can both be dated in the same year (*Espl. Vat.*, 1951, I, pp. 103 f.).[83]

Later, towards the end of the third century, a grey wall was erected on the north side of the monument. This occurred in connection with the extension of the cemetery and the building of numerous mausoleums in the vicinity. On this wall a large number of pilgrim inscriptions have been written. They date from a relatively late period, give the name of Christ in the form of the monogram, and express the wish that the deceased may 'live in Christ'.[84] It is remarkable that if we disregard the assumption, to be mentioned later, that cryptic writing was used, the name of Peter is never found, whereas Peter and Paul are invoked in the graffiti on the Appian Way. The advocates of identifying the edifice with the 'trophy' of Peter mentioned by Gaius have previously explained this fact by saying that the relation of the consecrated place to Peter is presupposed as self-evident, while the inscriptions concerning Peter and Paul in the

[81] This is not sufficiently taken into account in *present-day* discussion. The excavations can perhaps settle that controversial question, but may not *start* from it, as though the text of Gaius *in itself* rendered certain one or the other interpretation of the word *tropaion.*

[82] This is assumed also by Th. Klauser, *Die römische Petrustradition*, 1956, who gives as date '165 at the latest'; likewise by A. v. Gerkan, *Zu den Problemen des Petrusgrabes*, 1958, who decides for the time about 180. The report of the *Liber Pontificalis*, according to which Pope Anacletus had already erected a *Memoria* for Peter in the first century, has thus finally been proved false. K. Heussi, ' "Papst" Anacletus I. und die Memoria auf dem Vatikan' (*Deutsches Pfarrerblatt*, 1949, pp. 301 ff.), has already emphasized that this statement cannot be trusted.

[83] P. Lemerle, H. Torp, and E. Schäfer (see above, p. 139, note 65) hold the view that what is involved is a purely pagan construction which has nothing to do with the 'trophy' of Gaius. Also inclined to scepticism are H. Last, 'St. Peter, the Excavations under his Basilica in Rome and the Beginnings of Western Christendom' (*Proceedings of the Classical Association*, 1954, pp. 50 f.), and especially E. Dinkler, *Theologische Rundschau*, 1959, pp. 315 f.

[84] *Victor cum sui(s), Gaudentia vibatis in Christo. Paulina vivas, Nicasi vibas in Christo,* etc. (*Espl. Vat.*, 1951, I, p. 129; II, Plate LVII, a, b; LVIII, a, b).

*triclia* on the Appian Way, where the *refrigeria* took place,[85] were not written directly on a consecrated place, and so a mention of the names was necessary there. In any case, the presence of the Christian graffiti on this grey north wall shows that *at the time when they were written* the holiness of the place must have been specifically recognized. To be sure, the date of the graffiti would have to be determined precisely. In no case do they reach back into very ancient times; the very monogram of Christ shows that.

In the official report these graffiti are not sufficiently studied. It is therefore to be welcomed that in the already mentioned second and most recent phase of the study concerning Peter's grave, the examination of these graffiti takes the prominent place. They are made accessible and discussed in a large and beautiful work which provides clear photographs.[86] In it the authoress undertakes to prove that the Christians here made use of a secret symbol writing, as they did at times elsewhere. At the lower end of the Greek letter Rho, which is contained in the monogram for Christ, there are two small horizontal lines. Since the Rho is identical with the Latin P, this would give the reading 'Pe', and so the first letters of the name of Peter. If this interpretation, which needs to be tested by competent scholars, should prove correct,[87] it would prove nothing as to the actual presence of the grave of Peter, but would only show what the Roman Christians believed on this point at the time they wrote the graffiti —a time still to be determined but in any case later.

The same thing holds true of the graffito on the *red* wall. In the excavation report it still plays no role, since that fragment of the wall fell down during the excavation work and only later was found in the debris by one of the directors. Moreover, the interpretation of the letters contained on it is not certain. Even if the upper line can be read as Peter,[88] yet for the letters written beneath it ($\epsilon$, $\nu$, $\iota$) two different and directly contradictory explanations have been proposed ('Peter is here' or 'Peter is away'—i.e., on the Appian Way); the second of these explanations adds a fourth letter.[89] Whatever was written there can be considered an important witness only for the *faith* which appealed to this small monument after its

---

[85] See above, pp. 132 f.

[86] M. Guarducci, *I graffiti sotto la confessione di S. Pietro in Vaticano*, 1959.

[87] It is rejected by J. Toynbee in *The Dublin Review*, 1959, pp. 234 ff.

[88] A. Ferrua, 'La storia del sepolcro di S. Pietro' (*La civiltà cattolica*, 1952, p. 25), and E. Kirschbaum, *Die Gräber der Apostelfürsten*, 1957, p. 68 (Eng. Tr., *The Tombs of St. Peter and St. Paul*, 1959, p. 70).

[89] M. Guarducci reads ἐνι and interprets it in the sense of ἔνεστι ('he is present'). This is philologically possible. J. Carcopino reads a δ between ν and ι and interprets it as ἐνδεῖ, 'he is away'. This, however, is an unusual expression.

erection, and it was quite misleading when telegraph agencies sent out the message that the graffito on this section of the wall had provided the proof that Peter was buried here.

Provisionally, however, though not with final certainty, we may assert, for the reasons given, that the 'trophy' of Gaius appears to have been found. If this is true, it is the single positive result of the excavations as far as they concern Peter; the result is thus a confirmation of the literary testimony of Gaius, which, however, takes us back only to the end of the second century. Even apart from the meaning of the word 'trophy', however, there was no reason to doubt the correctness of his testimony. Previously, to be sure, it was disputed whether by the word 'trophy' Gaius understood only the place of execution or a monument or a grave. If the identification of the 'trophy' with the columnar monument should finally prove correct, then by 'trophy' we should understand not only a place but also a building found there; even if not the grave, it is a memorial monument. It must further be assumed, then, that a similar monument is located under the Church of St. Paul; this, however, must be confirmed by excavation.

What was *under* this 'trophy' of Peter, however, and whether in particular it concealed a real grave, is another question. It is not answered even by the identification of the 'trophy', although reports in newspapers and illustrated magazines flatly assert that it has been. It is true that before the niche is a cavity 80 centimetres wide and 80 centimetres long; it was covered with a thick slab. Is this square place, which H. Grisar saw more than fifty years ago, to be called 'the grave of Peter'? The dimensions could lead one at first to suppose that at a *later* time his relics had been brought here, possibly in an urn.[90] I really cannot understand how anyone can speak without qualification of a 'discovered grave of Peter', since in any case *no remains of a grave survive*. The most that one could say would be that one may *conjecture* the earlier existence of a normal grave at a much greater depth, *if that grave was really crossed over later by the red wall* (*Espl. Vat.*, I, p. 139). Thus even one of the four excavation directors, in his later separate publication, concedes that what we have here is not the laying bare of a grave but a 'laborious circumstantial proof'.[91]

But what are the reasons cited to support this assumption? Around the empty square space are found a row of graves in the ground. Three of them lie at a moderate depth. In the deepest one (designated by γ in

[90] According to J. Carcopino, *Etudes d'histoire chrétienne*, 1953, pp. 179 ff., the bones of Peter from the beginning had merely been collected in an urn.
[91] E. Kirschbaum, *Die Gräber der Apostelfürsten*, 1957, p. 9 (Eng. Tr., *The Tombs of St. Peter and St. Paul*, 1959, pp. 16 f.).

the report) was buried a small boy whose skeleton is extant. This grave was crossed over and damaged in the building of the red wall. The libation tube found above it indicates that it most probably is Neronian.[92] On the other hand, it belongs in the middle of the second Christian century, as is shown by a brick which dates from about the year A.D. 123.[93] In that case a Neronian grave, if such was present here, would have to lie much deeper. The other, particularly poor grave (designated by $\theta$ in the report) is covered by six bricks. One of them bears the stamp of Vespasian and so was used at the earliest in the year 70, but in view of the age of the grave $\gamma$, which dates no earlier than the second century, this brick must be regarded rather as having been re-used at a later time.[94] Thus we see that in any case none of these graves of the environs reaches back into the Neronian time; indeed, they scarcely can belong in the first century.[95] Therefore it is not proved that in Nero's time this place was already used as a burial ground. To be sure, one points to the divergence of the orientation of the threshold before the niche from that of the wall; to the remains of a wall which could have served to protect the side wall of the supposed grave; to the finding of an oil lamp; but particularly to the fact that the foundation of the red wall runs on a higher level at the spot where the grave is supposed to be.[96] All these indications, so it is said, prove that

[92] The reference to the use of a libation tube by Christians in San Sebastiano in the fourth century, which is supposed to make probable the Christian character of this grave, is deprived of validity by the demonstration of A. v. Gerkan that in the first century there were no libation tubes even in pagan graves ('Zu den Problemen des Petrusgrabes', op. cit., 1958). Toynbee and Perkins, op. cit., pp. 148 ff., also speak in favour of a pagan grave.

[93] Thanks for this demonstration are due to A. Prandi, La zona archeologica della Confessione Vaticana, 1957.

[94] E. Kirschbaum, Die Gräber der Apostelfürsten, 1957, pp. 85 f. (Eng. Tr., The Tombs of St. Peter and St. Paul, 1959, p. 88), argues against this that even the poorest man could have procured six new bricks. In this case the grave would belong in the years between 69 and 79, and thus still not in the Neronian period.

[95] That they date from the first century is denied by A. v. Gerkan, on the basis of the reconstruction of the terrain, in 'Kritische Studien zu den Ausgrabungen unter der Peterskirche in Rom' (Trierer Zeitschrift, 1954, pp. 26 ff.); 'Zu den Problemen des Petrusgrabes', op. cit., pp. 79 ff., and Th. Klauser, Die römische Petrustradition im Lichte der neuen Ausgrabungen unter der Peterskirche, 1956. Against their objections see E. Kirschbaum, Die Gräber der Apostelfürsten, 1957, pp. 98 ff. (Eng. Tr., The Tombs of St. Peter and St. Paul, 1959, pp. 100 ff.). A. Prandi, La zona archeologica della Confessione Vaticana. I monumenti del II. secolo, 1957, also denies that any grave dates from the first century.

[96] This is emphasized by J. Ruysschaert, 'Réflexions sur les fouilles Vaticanes' (Revue d'Histoire ecclésiastique, 1953, p. 597), and with special emphasis by E. Kirschbaum, Die Gräber der Apostelfürsten, 1957, p. 87 (Eng. Tr., The Tombs of St. Peter and St. Paul, 1959, p. 90). A. Prandi also (see preceding footnote) refers on p. 218 to the fact of this elevation. In opposition to this, Th. Klauser, 'Die römische Petrustradition', 1956, op. cit., pp. 55 ff., and A. von Gerkan, 'Zu den Problemen des Petrusgrabes', 1958, op. cit., pp. 89 f., assume that the wall cavity existing at this place is the result not of a deliberate elevation but of a destruction.

at one time the grave of Peter was here and that already in the first century Christians had themselves buried here around this grave. But neither the Christian character nor the suggested age of the graves in question has been proved.

In the extension of the niche beneath the ground some *bones* were admittedly found (*Espl. Vat.*, I, p. 121, Fig. 87). But the desire to base an additional proof upon them can hardly be approved; Pius XII himself, as already mentioned, has candidly conceded this. For it is not astonishing to find bones in a plot containing graves. Moreover, a grave of the Neronian time would have to lie much deeper than the place at which the bones were found.[97] In the generally accessible publications which have appeared in addition to the official report, these bones unfortunately play a much greater role than in the report itself.[98] They have subsequently been studied, and the result is reported to be, first, that they are the bones of a man, and second, of a vigorous man (therefore Peter?).[99] On tours in the Church of St. Peter one can also hear that investigation proves that these bones and the skull preserved in the Lateran as the head of Peter must belong together. The presence of these few bones under the red wall is said to be explained by the fact that they were put there in haste when the wall was built. But that there are only a few is connected with the transfer to the Appian Way in the year 258. That is, what was involved in that transfer was not a complete but only a partial transfer of relics. This transformation of the classical transfer-thesis is intended likewise to meet the objection that a legal removal of the skeleton from the Vatican Hill to the Appian Way is unthinkable.[1] In connection with Roman legal usage, according to which the place of a grave is determined by the presence of the head,[2] as well as with the separate preservation in the Lateran of a relic regarded as Peter's head, it has been thought that the partial removal may have taken the form of a transfer of the skull.[3]

[97] This is conceded by E. Kirschbaum, *Die Gräber der Apostelfürsten*, p. 88 (Eng. Tr., *The Tombs of St. Peter and St. Paul*, p. 91).

[98] So already in J. Ruysschaert, *op. cit.*, *R. H. E.*, 1953, pp. 624 ff.; later especially by J. Toynbee and J. W. Perkins, *The Shrine of St. Peter and the Vatican Excavations*, 1956, and E. Kirschbaum, *Die Gräber der Apostelfürsten*, 1957, pp. 198 ff. (Eng. Tr., *The Tombs of St. Peter and St. Paul*, 1959, pp. 195 ff.). On the other hand, J. Carcopino, *Etudes d'histoire chrétienne*, 1953, pp. 229 f., in spite of his positive position on the question of Peter's grave, proves very sceptical regarding the genuineness of the bones found. Acceptance of their genuineness cannot be reconciled with his thesis that only an urn had been buried.

[99] E. Kirschbaum, 'Das Petrusgrab' (*Stimmen der Zeit*, 1952, p. 406), and *Die Gräber der Apostelfürsten*, 1957, p. 198 (Eng. Tr., *The Tombs of St. Peter and St. Paul*, 1959, p. 195).      [1] See above, pp. 128 f.      [2] See above, p. 129, note 30.

[3] See especially E. Kirschbaum, *Die Gräber der Apostelfürsten*, 1957, pp. 199 ff. (Eng. Tr., *The Tombs of St. Peter and St. Paul*, 1959, pp. 196 ff.).

Attention is further called to the fact that later, in the time of Constantine, a small marble box, 77 centimetres long and 30 centimetres in breadth and depth, was embedded in the graffiti-covered north wall. This box was discovered in the excavations. When brought to light it contained an unidentifiable mass of earth and all sorts of remains.[4] The assertion that it once contained bones of the apostle and at a certain time was emptied is a hypothesis that cannot be demonstrated. The presence of this box has in fact given rise to every possible theoretical construction. According to the most widespread one, Constantine had the remains, especially the head, brought back from the Appian Way and placed in this box.[5] The fact that today it no longer contains any bones is explained either by the plundering of the place by the Saracens in the year 846[6] or by the placing of the head in the Lateran about this time.[7]

Probably even Roman Catholic scholars had originally little expectation that one would find genuine relics of Peter, although the pious Roman Catholic from the common people, who like many others has believed for centuries that he kneels above the bones of the Prince of Apostles in the present Church of St. Peter, was able to cherish this illusory hope. From the scientific point of view it can only be asked whether at the time of Constantine Peter's bones were still really there. Concerning that we know absolutely nothing.

He who reads without prejudice the reports concerning the most recent excavations must concede that if one assumes that the bones of Peter had rested under the monument discovered, the entire archaeological question concerning the grave of Peter becomes only more complicated than it already was. Prompt witness of this is the fact that one of the leaders of the excavations, in an essay published soon after the appearance of the

[4] For an exact description see *Espl. Vat.*, 1951, Vol. I, p. 162; Vol. II, Plate LVIIb.
[5] So A. Ferrua, 'A la recherche du tombeau de S. Pierre' (*Etudes*, 1952, pp. 44 f.); E. Kirschbaum, *Die Gräber der Apostelfürsten*, 1957, p. 203 (Eng. Tr., *The Tombs of St. Peter and St. Paul*, 1959, pp. 199 f.); somewhat differently J. Carcopino, *op. cit.*, pp. 230 ff., who thinks first of a burial in the mausoleum of the Julians, in which the portrayal of Christ-Helios is found; only in the time of Gregory the Great were the bones so to speak hidden in this box, to protect them from plundering, which however they did not escape.
[6] *Ann. Bertiniani, anni 846.*—The graves of the apostles were spared by the Goths in the year 410 and by the Vandals in 455. On the other hand, it must be asked whether the elephants which, according to Aelius Lampsidius (ch. 22), Elagabalus brought to the Vatican had not already destroyed the place.
[7] So E. Kirschbaum, 'Die Reliquien der Apostelfürsten und ihre Teilung. Zur Geschichte einer alten Überlieferung' (*Xenia Piana*, 1943, pp. 51 ff.), and *Die Gräber der Apostelfürsten*, 1957, pp. 204 ff. (Eng. Tr., *The Tombs of St. Peter and St. Paul*, 1959, pp. 200 ff.). On this see H. Grisar, 'Le teste dei S. S. Apostoli Pietro e Paolo', *Civiltà Cattolica*, 1907, pp. 444 ff. J. Ruysschaert expresses scepticism on this in 'Réflexions sur les fouilles vaticanes', *R. H. E.*, 1953, p. 625.

official report, actually discusses the assumption—with the most extreme caution, to be sure, and only as a query—that the bones had already been transferred once from the Appian Way to the Vatican Hill. (On account of the small dimensions of the square cavity before the wall, he says), there forces itself upon one the memory of the ancient tradition according to which Peter, after his martyrdom, was first buried not here, but on the Appian Way together with Paul.[8] He thus suggests the old thesis that has been rather generally rejected.[9] Be that as it may, the author goes on to say that in the second half of the second century the relics of Peter were deposited on the Vatican Hill in a small urn. There they supposedly remained until 258, when they were (again) transferred to the Appian Way, and finally, under Constantine, were brought back a second time.

These and similar complicated hypotheses—recently it has also been assumed that already under Anacletus (76–88) the bones of Peter were buried in an urn on the Vatican Hill[10]—show clearly what difficulties result when one assumes that the bones of Peter had rested at the place so constituted as the report describes.

On the assumption that Peter had been buried here, the most recent excavations raise more new questions than they answer old ones. Did the wall painted red really *cross over* the supposed 'grave of Peter' as well as that of the boy? *Is such a site of the 'trophy' conceivable?*

We have seen how difficult it is to defend the theory of the (even partial) transfer to the Appian Way about the year 258. Even more difficult is the theory of an original burial on the Appian Way.

Therefore I ask whether everything is not explained much more simply if we assume that perhaps the pillar monument was the 'trophy' of Gaius, but was so regarded at first only in the sense of a memorial monument erected at *the place of the martyrdom*. With this idea, to be sure, the thought of the grave may have been connected very early, even if one had no relics. For somewhere on the Vatican Hill—possibly in a common grave—the victims of the Neronian persecution will have been buried. Is it not possible that in the cavity under the 'trophy' we are dealing only with a *cenotaph*, in much the same way, perhaps, as we must assume there was one on the Appian Way?[11] In that case the three memorial sites, on the Vatican Hill,

---

[8] A. Ferrua, *op. cit.* (*Etudes*, 1952, p. 43). But in the above-mentioned article in *La Civiltà cattolica*, p. 17, he seems rather to approve the rejection of this theory.

[9] See above, pp. 127 f. In other points the articles of Ferrua, especially the one in *Etudes*, are more reserved than the official publication.

[10] So J. Carcopino, *Etudes d'histoire Chrétienne*, 1953, p. 179.

[11] For the designation *sepulchrum* for cenotaph, see Tacitus, *Annals*, II, 83. The following also think of a cenotaph: A. M. Schneider, *op. cit.*, *Theologische Literaturzeitung*, 1952, p. 332; E. Peterson, 'Über das Petrusgrab' (*Schweizerische Rundschau*, 1952, pp.

on the Highway to Ostia, and on the Appian Way, were all three not burial places but memorial or cult sites, at which Christians celebrated the memory of the apostles, since they did not possess a real grave. The fact that in addition to the separate cult sites there also arose the common one on the Appian Way *could* be explained, as said, by the fact that in the pagan cemeteries on the Vatican Hill and on the Highway to Ostia assemblies were hindered and the need was felt of holding a celebration for both apostles at *one* place. Or it *could* even be that at first one of the schismatic churches of the third century had honoured here the memory of the apostles. In such a case we might be driven to think of the Novatian group, who likewise appealed to the primacy of Peter; this suggests itself especially since the liturgical sources possibly point in this direction.[12] The memorial site would then have been taken over by the great Church at a later time.

These, we grant, are only hypotheses; but without hypotheses we can reach no conclusions in this question. They seem to me, however, to do more justice to the archaeological evidence, in so far as they take into account only such objects as have actually been found.

In order to prove that the bones of Peter really rested in the supposed grave under the present dome, we would need more certain indications than have been produced by the most recent excavations. Indeed, we actually must say that in this case particularly convincing and absolutely irrefutable arguments would have to be presented, since *the reasons which speak* a priori *against the possibility that Christians buried Peter in the immediate neighbourhood of Nero's garden are almost overwhelming*. How could the Christians undertake an interment in this very spot in the terrible days of the Neronian persecution?[13] Did any possibility exist of

328 f.); H. I. Marrou, *Dictionnaire d'archéologie chrétienne et de lit.*, column 3344. The fact that people later sought here the never known and never found grave is explained by Th. Klauser, *Die römische Petrustradition im Lichte der neuen Ausgrabungen unter der Peterskirche*, 1956, pp. 71 f., by the Roman Christians' assumption, probably circulated very early, that somewhere in the nearer or more distant surroundings the remains of Peter must rest, because he had been executed here. The objections of J. Carcopino, *op. cit.*, pp. 174 f., J. Ruysschaert, *op. cit.*, p. 593, J. Toynbee–J. W. Perkins, *op. cit.*, 1956, and E. Kirschbaum, *Die Gräber der Apostelfürsten*, 1957, pp. 87 and 112 (Eng. Tr., *The Tombs of St. Peter and St. Paul*, 1959, pp. 90 and 113 f.), are not valid; they say it is inconceivable that a mere memorial marker was erected at this precise place, that is, in a field of graves, rather than in another place on the Vatican Hill, or alternatively that it is inconceivable that Christian burials were made later at a memorial place without the presence of the bones. To the first objection the answer is that the place of *martyrdom* can have been precisely fixed by a tradition; to the second, that the desire of Christians to be buried here is sufficiently explained by the fact that from a certain time the place of martyrdom was identified as the place of burial.    [12] See above, pp. 129 and 135.
[13] So rightly K. Heussi, 'Das Grab des Petrus' (*Deutsches Pfarrerblatt*, 1949, pp. 82 ff.). E. Kirschbaum, *Die Gräber der Apostelfürsten*, 1957, pp. 120 f. (Eng. Tr., *The Tombs of St. Peter and St. Paul*, 1959, pp. 121 f.), argues among other points that Peter was not

distinguishing the body of Peter from the others? Is it not to be assumed that the bones of those executed, in case their ashes were not scattered on the Tiber, were thrown into a common grave?[14]

Furthermore, how can Christians in Rome have had any interest in *relics* in the first century? In the time of Nero the Christians expected the world to end soon. In any case, we do not have even the slightest trace of a cult of relics before the martyrdom of Polycarp, and so at the earliest the middle of the second century, and then we still are not dealing with Rome but with Smyrna.[15] In *Rome* no one took an interest in the graves of the martyrs in the first two centuries. Indeed, prior to the third century there was no interest whatever in the graves; even the graves of the Bishops of Rome exist only from the beginning of the third century, and then in the Catacomb of Callistus.[16] If prior to this time emphasis was already placed in Rome on the possession of the mortal remains of martyrs and bishops, how then does it happen that we hear nothing of a grave either of Ignatius of Antioch, whose desire to be *completely* consumed by the wild beasts (Rom. 4:2) can scarcely have been fulfilled,[17] or of the martyr bishop Telesphorus, or of Justin, who nevertheless suffered the martyr death in Rome and were highly honoured there?[18]

The assertion that the cult of graves must be older than the cult of martyrs, since even Jews as well as Romans honoured the physical remains of their relatives, proves nothing, because in this very point the Christians of the earliest time were manifestly different from both their

---

executed at the Neronian garden festival. But we have seen that the interpretation of I Clem. 5 ff. favours the view that he was. Th. Klauser, *Die römische Petrustradition*, 1956, pp. 11 ff., on the basis of I Clem. 6:1 ff., similarly places the death of Peter at the time of that festival.—Even if it is correct that we do not know the exact limits of the Neronian garden (E. Kirschbaum, *op. cit.*, p. 43 (Eng. Tr., p. 48); also J. Ruysschaert, *op. cit.*, p. 614), it is at least clear that it was located in the *immediate* neighbourhood. Completely improbable is the assumption that the Christians would have asked for the body of Peter to bury it! The parallel of Joseph of Arimathaea can in no case be adduced here, as is done by E. Kirschbaum, *op. cit.*, p. 121 (Eng. Tr., p. 122), for what was there involved was to the Romans an individual criminal, and the petitioner did not belong to a fellowship branded as a band of criminals.

[14] So Th. Klauser, *op. cit.*, p. 70.

[15] According to the most recent theory (H. Grégoire, 'La véritable date du martyre de S. Polycarpe, 23 févr. 177', in *Analecta Bollandiana*, 1951, pp. 1 ff.; *Les persécutions dans l'empire romain*, 1951, pp. 28, 106 f.), the martyrdom of Polycarp should be dated later, in the year 177.

[16] See above, p. 134.

[17] The fact that in the fourth century (Chrysostom, *Homily on the Martyr St. Ignatius*, Migne, *P. G.*, Vol. 50, pp. 587 ff., and Jerome, *De viribus illustribus*, Migne, *P. L.*, Vol. 23, pp. 632 ff.) we hear that his remains were brought to Antioch only proves that in a time when the cult of relics was flourishing the question as to the remains of Ignatius was raised.

[18] This point, which seems to me decisive, is rightly stressed also by E. Schäfer 'Das Petrusgrab' (*Evangelische Theologie*, 1951, pp. 472 f.).

Jewish and their pagan environment. This is proved by the data just stated, and with this agrees the fact that in the first century and probably also in at least the first half of the second century no knowledge at all of the grave of Peter can be demonstrated,[19] because the first Christians were completely indifferent concerning the burial place of those related to them.[20] Someone should make an intensive study of how this indifference is to be explained. It is connected with the expectation that the end was near, but also with the particular Christian conceptions of the resurrection; they were different even from those of the Jews.[21]

Against the assertion that even before the end of the second century a grave of Peter was known on the Vatican Hill, one fact, it seems to me, is of the greatest importance. I have already referred to it,[22] but in all the discussion thus far it has received too little attention. The apocryphal Acts of Peter, it is true, contain no historical narratives but rather only legendary stories of Peter's martyrdom and burial. They doubtless permit us, however, to determine what was told concerning Peter at the time of the origin of these Acts, and therefore in the second century. It is thus of the utmost importance that the legend *knows nothing of a burial of Peter in a poor grave in the Neronian gardens*; it rather reports (in dependence on Jesus' burial by Joseph of Arimathaea) that the converted senator Marcellus, after careful preparation of the body, buried Peter in his own grave, for which act however the apostle, who appeared to him at night, reproved him (ch. 40), referring to the saying of Jesus that it is only the 'dead' who bury their dead (Matt. 8:22; Luke 9:60). This, quite apart from the different location of the burial, proves that still at that time the Christians were not only indifferent towards the cult of graves but actually rejected it.

In reality the Christian interest in graves first arose in Rome about the time when Gaius wrote to Proclus, when Callistus apealed to the nearness of Peter's grave, and when Bishop Fabian created in the Catacomb of Callistus a resting-place for the bishops. This, then, occurred in the first half of the third century. It occurred in connection with the necessity of

[19] It does not agree with the facts when E. Kirschbaum, *Die Gräber der Apostelfürsten*, 1957, p. 121 (Eng. Tr., *The Tombs of St. Peter and St. Paul*, 1959, p. 122), writes 'that from the earliest time his [Peter's] grave was known on the Vatican Hill in the neighbourhood of the Neronian gardens'.

[20] Although the problem is not quite the same, we nevertheless must refer in this connection to the fact that even the place of the grave of Jesus was not venerated.

[21] It is not excluded that the saying of Jesus, 'Let the dead bury their dead' (Matt. 8:22; Luke 9:60), also exercised an influence. In any case, the apocryphal Acts of Peter, on the basis of the resurrection faith, interpret the saying as a condemnation of interest in the dead body. He who troubles himself about a corpse is himself a dead man.

[22] *Journal of Ecclesiastical History*, 1956, pp. 238 ff.

proving the apostolicity of the Roman tradition, after this tendency had arisen somewhat earlier in the east.[23]

This, however, concerns only the question of the grave. Regarding the location of the *places of execution*, the question stands otherwise. It is clear without further argument that the memory of the place of execution long continued, especially when it concerned victims of the terrible Neronian persecution. Even this memory would perhaps have been lost in the course of time, if in the third century there had not been an interest in finding the very graves of Peter and Paul, who had long been regarded as the founders of the church. Naturally one looked for them where the *execution* was located by the tradition, which still remained alive and for a part of the Neronian victims was fixed in writing by Tacitus.[24] Now at this time, that is, in the *third Christian century*, a pagan cemetery had existed at this place or in its vicinity for at least a hundred years. This we know from the latest excavations. Thus there was so much the more occasion to *connect the place of execution and the later cemetery* as the place of burial.[25]

The same development is probably to be assumed for the tradition as to Paul's grave, which also was located in a pagan cemetery, situated in the direction of the place of execution at the Three Fountains. For St. Paul's Church also is situated in the area of a pagan necropolis. Paul as a Roman citizen probably was not executed at the same place as Peter and the other victims.

We come accordingly to the following result, which can also be regarded as the conclusion of this entire section concerning Peter the Martyr: The archaeological investigations do not permit us to answer in either a negative or an affirmative way the question as to the stay of Peter in Rome. The grave of Peter cannot be identified. The real proofs for the martyrdom of Peter in Rome must still be derived from the indirect literary witnesses, and from them we have reached the conclusion that probably Peter actually was in Rome and suffered execution under Nero. The excavations speak in favour of the report that *the execution of Peter took place in the Vatican district.*

\* \* \*

[23] Therefore the lists of the bishops of Rome, the *Depositio Martyrum*, and the *Depositio Episcoporum*, begin in the first half of the third century.

[24] *Annals*, XV, 44.

[25] Quite hypothetical and not very likely is the assumption of H. Gregoire, 'Le Tombeau de Valerius Herma [Hermas] et l'inscription relative à S. Pierre' (*La nouvelle Clio*, 1952, pp. 399 f.), that the Christians, searching for the grave of Peter, localized it in the mausoleum of the Valerians.

In summary of our entire historical section, to the end of which we now have come, we must say that during the lifetime of Peter he held a pre-eminent position among the disciples; that after Christ's death he presided over the church at Jerusalem in the first years; that he then became the leader of the Jewish Christian mission; that in this capacity, at a time which cannot be more closely determined but probably occurred at the end of his life, he came to Rome and there, after a very short work, died as a martyr under Nero.

We must keep in mind these historical results as we now turn to the theological question of the primacy of Peter and his significance for the later Church.

PART TWO

The Exegetical
and Theological Question

# The Problem

WE SHALL start here with the exegesis of the saying of Jesus in Matthew 16:17 ff.: 'You are Rock, and upon this Rock I will build my Church...' In a first chapter we deliberately limit ourselves to the *strictly exegetical question*: What place do these words occupy in the framework of the Synoptic tradition? Are they really genuine words of Jesus or were they only ascribed to him by the Church? In the former case, what did Jesus intend to say by them? In that connection a special problem results from the fact that in the Greek the statement of Matthew 16:18 refers to the future: I *will* build my Church. Moreover, the imperative in the two parallel sayings most closely related to ours, the command in Luke 22:31 f.: 'Strengthen your brothers', and the commission of the Risen One in John 21:16: 'Feed my lambs', refer to the time after the death of Jesus. Does this mean to say that in the promise of Matthew 16:18 Jesus reckons with centuries, with the Church of *all* generations? Or does it mean that he has in mind only the Church which was then to be built in the Apostolic Age, that is, in the lifetime of Peter after Christ's death? This question also is first of all a purely exegetical and historical one.

After answering this question, however, we must examine in a second *doctrinal and theological chapter* the question whether, even if the exegesis should conclude that Jesus thought only of the time of Peter, there is a legitimate possibility of extending that promise and that commission beyond the period of the foundation that Jesus had in view and applying it to the entire period of the later Church down to the present day.

Here in this quite concrete application arises the problem of the New Testament conception of time, which I have discussed elsewhere.[1] Is the period when the foundation was laid normative for the later period, in such a way that it represents the permanent unique foundation upon which the entire later structure rests once for all? Or is it normative in the sense that what happened at the beginning is continually repeated in an analo-

---

[1] O. Cullmann, *Christus und die Zeit. Die urchristliche Zeit- und Geschichteauffassung*, 2nd ed., 1948 (Eng. Tr., *Christ and Time*, 1950).

gous way during the entire period of the Church, so that the promises and commissions which Jesus gave for the period of the apostolic foundation should be handed on, without hesitation or change, as commissions valid for Christians who live in later years?

I note in advance that we must not make the matter all too easy for ourselves by answering too hastily with a clear-cut Yes or No. For in reality the problem is too complex to permit a solution in this simple manner. It is impossible for us to say in advance, in a generalizing way, that everything which Jesus said may be referred only to his time and the time of his immediate disciples, and so can have no validity for later generations. But on the other hand, it is also much too simple when it is declared that everything which Jesus said to an apostle concerning the Church can only be understood as said also to a whole chain of bishops, who can be designated as successors of *this specific apostle*. An application to the future is conceivable which respects the historical uniqueness of the situation in which the Church was founded. In reality, therefore, the problem presents itself in the following way: *How is the unique element to be marked off from that which is constantly repeated?*

This means, however, that we must raise the fundamental question concerning the essential difference between the apostolic office and the office of bishop. Can the uniqueness and unrepeatable quality which belong to the apostolic office in the New Testament be reconciled with an extension of a specifically apostolic commission to later bishops? Here, too, we propose to be on our guard against thinking that the question is already solved in advance.

In conclusion, however, we have to discuss also the very important problem whether it is justified for a saying addressed to an apostle to be limited to a *particular* line of bishops. In other words, can that utterance be extended chronologically on the one hand, while at the same time it is limited in its spatial application to a single chain of succession? Is it actually to be held that the *principle of succession* tied to such a line is the only possible view? Or is this view legitimate at all? From the viewpoint of exegesis this question would scarcely be asked if the Roman Catholic Church did not proclaim as a dogma that Peter as the Prince of Apostles handed on his succession to the chain of *Roman* bishops. Can *such* a dogmatic extension of the saying of Jesus be reconciled with the results of exegesis and with what we know of the history of Primitive Christianity? Can that saying of Jesus legitimately be limited to the future bishops of a particular episcopal see, when the Scripture says not a word on this point, and does not even consider it necessary to mention the stay of the apostle in this city, and when in addition the historical tradition concerning a Roman episcopal office of Peter is of such a character as we have shown it to be?

To what extent, finally, does the actual *historical role* that the Roman church and its bishops played in the second and third centuries justify the Bishop of Rome in making a theological and indeed exclusive claim to the saying that Jesus addressed to Peter? Is it legitimate to give such absolute validity to a situation which only appears during the course of ancient church history, but is neither present nor hinted at when the apostles are founding the Church? In other words, the Roman church does not play a leading role at all during the lifetime of the apostles. At the earliest it begins to play such a role in Christendom at the turn from the first to the second century. Even then this role is not yet given a theological foundation. Is it possible to derive from the fact of this later role the standard that in all subsequent times, even down to the end of the period of the Church, only the bishop who stands in this particular chain of succession may lead the entire Church? Is it permissible to take this position and then interpret the saying of Jesus to intend the limitation just described, as though there were no other possible way of applying it to the present? Is the saying of Jesus really to be so understood that it can only be fulfilled where a church head, appealing to so one-sidedly conceived a Petrine chain of succession, has for a time exercised an actual primacy? Is it to be so understood that in all the future the only way it can be fulfilled is to establish in the same one-sided way the connection with this primacy that has once been realized in history?

As a marginal issue, the purely theological question may also arise whether the appeal to a *dogma* is sufficient here. In this case of the primacy of the Roman bishop, it is not just any dogma that is involved, but the one that *gives the basis of the claim of the Roman Catholic Church* that it alone is justified in proclaiming any dogmas whatever.

These questions are intended to state the problem and to show how the theological problem is connected with the exegetical one.

Usually the only possible fulfilment of the saying to Peter that is even considered is the Roman Catholic one. With a certain unquestioning confidence that the issue is self-evident, some give an affirmative and some a negative answer. We, however, shall study whether exegesis does not lead to another solution, so that the apostle Peter actually has for the Church of all times a 'fundamental' importance in the etymological sense, but in a way that corresponds with the meaning and purpose of that saying as well as with the basic New Testament view.

# I

# The Exegetical Question: the Meaning of Matthew 16:17–19

THE INTERPRETATION of Matthew 16:17 ff., like the discussion of the historical question concerning the stay of Peter in Rome, has been blurred all too often by confessional prejudices. Just as it is not permissible, in dealing with the question whether Peter was in Rome, to solve it in one way or the other on the basis of one's attitude towards the papacy, even so the discussion of the question as to what Christ meant by his words to Peter concerning the Church must not be burdened in advance by one s judgment regarding the later papal claim. As in the former question, so also here one must react against the conscious or unconscious popular view—as though, for example, one who recognizes the genuineness of that saying somehow makes a concession to this papal claim, or as though one who challenges its genuineness deals a particularly effective blow to this claim to power.[1]

The history of interpretation which we prefix to the study of our passage teaches us that the confessional standpoint has quite often coloured the exegesis, and that usually the result is fixed in advance and then subsequently read into the text.

## 1. The History of the Leading Interpretations

We lack a detailed history of the way in which our section has been interpreted throughout the centuries, from the ancient Church Fathers down to our own day. Such a work would be of the greatest value not only for exegetes but also for the historians of doctrine and of the Church. To be sure, we find, in the older commentaries and also in books on church history, references to the interpretations that the Church Fathers and the

---

[1] In most recent times the 'genuineness' of Matt. 16:17 ff. has been limited to a remarkable extent even by some Roman Catholic exegetes. See below, p. 174. This is possible on the basis of the tradition principle.

Reformers gave. Apart from a study of the most ancient period,[2] however, there is lacking a complete and connected presentation of interpretations of the saying. As far as more recent study is concerned, the various contributions which the last fifty years have made to the understanding of our passage receive in part at least a systematic presentation in new commentaries and also in journal articles.[3]

We cannot pretend to give here even an approximately complete survey of the history of the exegesis of Matthew 16:17 ff. Of the older explanations I shall mention only those which are particularly typical. I shall speak somewhat more in detail of the more recent ones, but at first will report only their conclusions. In our interpretation of the text we shall come back to individual arguments of earlier exegetes.

The first attempts at explanation are still free from the ecclesiastical and political tendency to use the saying for or against the claim of the Roman Bishop. Only at the beginning of the third century, in the west, does this interest in the saying of Jesus become prominent.

In the first two centuries we find very few traces of any use of Matthew 16:17 ff. The first certain evidence of such a use occurs in *Justin's Dialogue* (100,4; 106,3), though only for vs. 17,[4] and further in the *Pseudo-Clementina*. *Origen* starts from his distinction between letter and spirit in order to explain that the letter directs this saying concerning the Rock to Peter, while the Spirit has in mind everyone who becomes such as Peter was.[5]

*Irenaeus* (*Against Heresies*, III, 18) gives an explanation of the passage, but speaks only of vs. 17. He does not mention the saying about the keys, but cites next vss. 21 f.[6]

When we come to the explanation of *Tertullian* mentioned above,[7] we already find ourselves in the area of exegesis influenced by ecclesiastical

---

[2] J. Ludwig, *Die Primatworte Mt. 16:18, 19 in der altkirchlichen Exegese*, 1952.

[3] See. J. R. Geiselmann, *Der petrinische Primat (Mt. 16, 17), seine neueste Bekämpfung und Rechtfertigung*, 1927, and especially K. L. Schmidt, Article on ἐκκλησία in G. Kittel's *Theologisches Wörterbuch zum N. T.* (this article has appeared spearately in English translation under the title, *The Church*, 1950, in the series, *Bible Key Words* from Gerhard Kittel's *Theologisches Wörterbuch zum N. T.*). On the latest literature see R. Bultmann, 'Die Frage nach der Echtheit von Mt. 16, 17–19' (*Theologische Blätter*, 1941, pp. 265 ff.), and A. Oepke, 'Der Herrenspruch über die Kirche: Mt. 16, 17–19 in der neuesten Forschung' (*Studia Theologica*, Lund, 1948–50, pp. 110 ff.).

[4] See E. Massaux, *Influence l'Evangile de de S. Matthieu sur la littérature chrétienne avant S. Irénée*, 1950. The possibility of use he accepts for Ignatius and the Odes of Solomon.

[5] Origen on Matt 16:18: 'For rock means every disciple of Christ.'

[6] W. L. Dulière, 'La péricope sur le pouvoir des clefs. Son absence dans le texte de Matthieu aux mains d'Irénée' (*La nouvelle Clio*, 1954, pp. 73 ff.), concludes from this that the text of Matthew which Irenæus had before him did not contain vss. 18–19. He tries to show that it made its way into the canon from Antioch about 190.

[7] *De pudicitia*, 21. See above, p. 121.

politics. In his struggle against the author of that edict concerning the extension of penance, whom we may identify with the highest probability as the Roman Bishop Callistus,[8] he explicitly rejects the interpretation that 'the power to bind and loose has passed on to this bishop, that is, to the entire Church that is near to Peter'.[9] This, he says, would 'twist the obvious purpose of the Lord, who committed this to Peter *personally*'.[10] And Tertullian proceeds: 'What does all that have to do with the Church, and particularly with you, psychic one? According to the person of Peter this authority belongs to spiritual men. . .' From this we probably may conclude that Callistus (217-22) had already referred Matthew 16:17 to himself,[11] perhaps indeed with special appeal to Peter's grave.[12] Tertullian completely rejects that application of the saying to later bishops, and indeed not only to those of Rome but to bishops generally.

In doing so he stands in opposition to *Cyprian*; the latter also is unwilling to see any ground for the primacy of the Roman Bishop over the re-

[8] The expressions *pontifex maximus* and *episcopus episcoporum*, which Tertullian uses in the same passage to designate the author of the edict, which he calls an *edictum peremptorium*, are best suited, even though they are ironical, to Callistus, whom Hippolytus also reproaches in his *Philosophoumena* for his lax exercise of penance. This in any case is more natural than it is to follow P. Galtier ('Le véritable édit de Calliste', *Revue d'Histoire ecclésiastique*, 1927, pp. 465 ff.; 'Ecclesia Petri propinqua, A propos de Tertullien et de Calliste', *Revue d'Histoire ecclésiastique*, 1928, pp. 40 ff.; *L'Eglise et la rémission des péchés aux premiers siècles*, 1932, pp. 139 ff.) in ascribing the edict to a Carthaginian bishop Agrippinus (see also G. Bardy, 'L'édit d'Agrippinus', *Revue des Sciences religieuses*, 1924, pp. 1 ff.). The great majority of scholars identify the bishop addressed with Callistus; so P. Batiffol, *L'Eglise naissante et le Catholicisme*, 1927, p. 350; *Cathedra Petri*, 1938, pp. 175 ff.; H. Koch, *Kallist und Tertullian*, 1920; *Cathedra Petri*, 1930, p. 6; E. Caspar, *Geschichte des Papsttums von den Anfängen bis zur Höhe der Weltherrschaft*, Vol. I, 1930, p. 26, and especially A. Harnack, 'Ecclesia Petri propinqua' (*Sitzungsbericht der Berliner Akademie der Wissenschaften*, 1927). M. Goguel, *L'Eglise primitive*, 1947, p. 194, holds on the contrary that the theory of P. Galtier is possible, but he does not make a definite decision.

[9] On the expression *ad omnem ecclesiam Petri propinquam* see above, p. 121, the hypothesis of W. Köhler, 'Omnis ecclesia Petri propinqua, Versuch einer religionsgeschichtlichen Deutung' (*Sitzungsbericht der Heidelberg Akademie der Wissenschaften*, 1937-8). Harnack's proposal (*op. cit.* in the preceding note) to take *omnem* as a scribal error for *romanam* is purely hypothetical, and is rejected even by most Roman Catholic scholars. See Batiffol, *Cathedra Petri*, 1938, p. 178. Contrariwise K. Adam, 'Neue Untersuchungen über den Ursprung der kirchlichen Primatslehre' (*Tübinger Theologische Quartalschrift*, 1928, pp. 169 ff.).

[10] For the Latin text of this passage see above, p. 121, note 5.

[11] A different view is taken by K. Heussi, 'Die Nachfolge des Petrus' (*Deutsches Pfarrerblatt*, 1949, pp. 420 f.). According to him Callistus appealed to Matt., ch. 16, only to prove the right of *all* bishops to forgive sins.

[12] According to E. Caspar, 'Primatus Petri' (*Zeitschrift der Savigny-Stiftung für Rechtsgeschichte*, 1927, pp. 253 ff.), Callistus did not appeal to Matt. 16:17 ff. Tertullian first did so, to oppose Callistus; but he did not suspect what spirits he was conjuring up. In this way, much as Cyprian later did without intending to do so, he gave the Roman episcopal see the weapons with which it would henceforth defend its primacy. Against this theory M. Goguel, *L'Eglise primitive*, 1947, pp. 195 f., makes the point that on this view it would be remarkable that this effect of the argument of Tertullian and Cyprian does not show itself until so much later.

maining bishops derived from the saying of Jesus, but he does consider that the whole body of bishops is addressed in Peter. When Jesus says only to Peter that he is the Rock, he thereby points simply to the necessity of the unity of the Church.[13] Cyprian developed his view, which he already had championed at an earlier time, mainly in connection with his dispute with the Bishop Stephan (254–7).[14] The latter, therefore, evidently appealed, as Callistus did, to Matthew 16:17 ff.; he as Bishop of Rome proposed to derive from it his primacy over the entire Church. *Firmilian*, Bishop of Caesarea in Cappadocia, in a letter to Cyprian, opposes this interpretation of Stephan in which the Roman Bishop claims that he is entitled by succession to the *cathedra* of Peter.[15]

These explanations are burdened with tendencies drawn from ecclesiastical politics. For a time, the saying of Jesus to Peter plays scarcely any role in grounding the papal claim. Then, from the beginning of the Middle Ages, it is regularly used by the popes, as though no other understanding of it were possible.[16] Yet it is noteworthy that the outstanding ancient commentators who concerned themselves with Matthew 16:17 ff. without discussing questions directly related to church politics considered other possibilities of interpretation. Thus *Chrysostom* explains that the rock on which Christ will build his Church means the faith of confession.[17] According to *Augustine*, Jesus meant by the rock not Peter but himself, an explanation which Luther will follow.[18] In his *Retractationes*,[19] Augustine writes that earlier, under the influence of Ambrose, he referred the word

---

[13] *De catholicae ecclesiae unitate*, cap. 4–5; *Epistolae* 33, 59, 73, 75, 76, 81, etc. Concerning Cyprian's exegesis, see J. Chapman, *Revue Bénédictine*, 1902–3; *ibid.*, 1910; and K. Adam, 'Cyprians Kommentar zu Mtth. 16, 18–19 in dogmengeschichtlicher Beleuchtung' (*Tübinger Theologische Quartalschrift*, 1912); H. Koch, *Cyprian und der römische Primat*, 1910: *Cyprianische Untersuchung*, 1926; especially *Cathedra Petri*, 1930.

[14] By using all of the writings of Cyprian a unified interpretation of the saying to Peter can be made, in so far as he always recognizes the primacy of Peter as a sign of unity, but on the other hand always refuses to derive from it for the later Bishops of Rome a pre-eminent position over the other bishops, who are all successors of Peter. However, it is not quite clear how he connects with this view the 'pre-eminence' (*principalitas*) he recognizes for Rome (*Epistola* 59, 14). P. Batiffol, *Cathedra Petri*, 1938, emphasizes in all parts of his book this idea, that according to Cyprian Rome is 'the chief church, whence the sacerdotal unity has arisen' (*ecclesia principalis, unde unitas sacerdotalis exorta est*). (See on this point H. Koch, *Cyprian und der römische Primat*, 1910; *Cathedra Petri*, 1930.) If *principalis* were really to be thus understood, that Jesus with the words 'you are Peter' founded *this* church, then Cyprian's exposition could scarcely be regarded as *entirely* consistent and unified.

[15] In connection with Cyprian, *Epistola* 75, 17.

[16] The mediaeval exegesis of the passage, to be sure, has not yet been studied. A thorough study now in preparation will show that it exhibits a greater variety than we suppose.

[17] See J. Chapman, *Early Papacy*, pp. 72 ff.

[18] Augustine, *Sermons* 76, 147, 149, 232, 245, 270, 295.

[19] I, 21, 1.

'rock' to Simon. However, he goes on, it does not say, 'You are the rock', but 'you are Peter'; the rock is mentioned only in the following sentence, and there it seems best to refer the word to Christ. He leaves the decision to his readers. A similar embarrassment is to be observed in other writers, for example *Cyril of Alexandria*. We thus see that the exegesis that the Reformers gave—though, as we shall see, it is questionable—was not first invented for their struggle against the papacy; it rests upon an older patristic tradition.

We mentioned earlier the striking fact that the Reformers attach little significance to the question whether Peter was in Rome or not, even though Luther had doubts about the matter. We find among them rather an intensive concern with the saying of Jesus in Matthew 16:17 ff., and their specific interest is in polemic against the Pope. *Luther*, on the one hand, like Augustine, interprets the rock to mean Christ himself: 'Thus this rock is the Son of God, Jesus Christ himself and no one else.'[20] From this basis he establishes the connection with Peter; he emphasizes that the word directed to Peter has in view (not his person but) only his faith in Jesus the Rock: 'You are . . . the rock man, for you have recognized the true man who is the true Rock, and you have named him as the Scripture names him, that is, Christ.'[21] 'Not upon the rock . . . of the Roman Church is the Church founded, as some decrees explain it, but upon the faith which Peter confessed for the entire Church.'[22] *Calvin* argues quite similarly; the words which the Roman Catholic teaching refers to the person of a man were in reality spoken only of Peter's faith in Christ. Hence the designation 'rock' is addressed both to Simon and to the other believers. The bond of faith in Christ is the basis on which the Church grows.[23] Likewise for *Zwingli* Peter is only the type of him who believes in Christ as the sole Rock.[24] It is only a variation of all these interpretations when *Melanchthon* refers the saying to preaching and the preaching office.[25] Thus in the final analysis all the Reformers agree that Peter was named 'Rock' by Jesus not as a person but only as a believer. The true Rock of the Church, they hold, is Jesus Christ.

[20] *Wider Das Papsttum vom Teufel gestiftet* (Weimar edition, 54; E. Mülhaupt, *Luthers Evangelien-Auslegung*, Vol. 2, pp. 545 f.).
[21] *Ibid.*, Mülhaupt, p. 548.
[22] 'Resolution Lutheriana super propositione XIII de potestate papae 1519' (Weimar edition, 2; E. Mülhaupt, *op. cit.*, Vol. 2, p. 525). Further passages in Mülhaupt, *op. cit.*, Vol. 2.
[23] See Calvin, *Commentaire, ad loc.*
[24] Among other places, his sermon on providence (Zwingli, *Hauptschriften*, Vol. II, p. 195); 'Concerning the True and the False Religion' (Zwingli, *Hauptschriften*, Vol. ix, pp. 158 ff.).
[25] *De potestate et principatu Papae*, chs. 22 ff.

We pass over the following centuries and come to recent times. We speak first of two typical interpretations which are rather closely connected with the Reformation view, but seek to give it a more solid exegetical basis. First of all, there is the interpretation of *Th. Zahn*. Like the Reformers, he emphasizes the faith of Peter, but on the other hand he also takes account of the fact that Peter was the *first* confessor and so occupies a special position in the foundation of the Church.[26] The commentary of *Strack-Billerbeck* connects more closely with the Reformers. It starts from the assumption that the Greek text was a mistranslation from an Aramaic original text. The correct English translation of the original would be as follows: 'I say to you, yes to you, Peter: On this rock I will build my Church.'[27] The word 'rock' in this passage, therefore, would not mean Peter. Jesus did not say: 'You are the rock', but rather: 'I say to you, Peter', etc. When he then proceeds: 'On this rock I will build my Church', he speaks of his own Messianic dignity, his own divine sonship, in which men must believe.

Towards the end of the nineteenth and at the beginning of the twentieth century, however, another interpretation dominated in Protestant scholarship. The saying, it was held, was not spoken by Jesus at all. It was ascribed to him later, and this was done at a time and place where one had an interest in glorifying Peter. The more recent discussion of our passage often revolves around this question of 'genuineness' or 'spuriousness'. Can this saying have been spoken by Jesus, or was it only created by the Church after his death? This question, as already noted, should be independent of that concerning the justification of the papal claim. As a matter of fact, even today the battle lines are not so drawn in this matter that the genuineness is recognized only by Roman Catholic scholars, while Protestant scholars contest it. Rather the discussion on this issue—as on the question of Peter's stay in Rome—takes place among Protestant exegetes themselves. Indeed, even in the area of Protestant exegesis it is not true that only the exegetes who rightly or wrongly are called 'conservative' defend the genuineness of the saying, while the interpreters who rightly or wrongly are given the liberal label oppose it. On this point we should recall above all that even such radical critics as *D. F. Strauss* and

---

[26] See Th. Zahn, *Das Evangelium des Matthäus*, 4th ed., 1922, *ad loc.*

[27] *Kommentar zum N. T. aus Talmud und Midrasch*, Vol. I, pp. 732 ff. Jesus, on this view, said: גם אני אמר לך אתה פטרוס. The translator by mistake understood אתה as the subject of a new sentence, when it was only the repeating of the second person singular pronoun already contained in לך. This is also the view of G. Gloege, *Reich Gottes und Kirche*, 1929, pp. 274 f.

*F. Ch. Baur* regarded the genuineness as quite obvious. On the other side there have been Roman Catholic exegetes recently who have greatly limited the genuineness.

It was New Testament scholars, and above all *H. J. Holtzmann*, who towards the end of the nineteenth century first denied vigorously that Jesus uttered the saying; he could not possibly have so spoken, because he had no intention of founding a Church. The passage, on this view, appears to have received its present form only in the second century. The church consciousness which comes to expression in it is already basically Catholic in character. Indeed, Holtzmann actually goes so far as to explain that we here have to do with a first stirring of the Roman self-consciousness.[28] The entire course of critical study at the beginning of the twentieth century is then dominated by this conception, and it would take too long to cite here the names of all those who regard the saying as irreconcilable with the teaching of Jesus. The chief reason for denying that Jesus said it is always said to be the mention of the 'Church'. How can Jesus have spoken of the Church? After all, he preached only the Kingdom of God. It was only after his death that something quite different, that is, the Church, appeared. According to the famous word of A. Loisy: 'Jesus announced the Kingdom of God, but what appeared was the Church.'[29] It was to justify subsequently this unexpected development that this saying was ascribed to Jesus. So we hear from *Johannes Weiss* and *E. Klostermann* to *M. Dibelius, B. S. Easton, M. Goguel*, and many other representatives of New Testament scholarship, and from historians of this generation,[30] that the saying cannot come from Jesus. The only exception, apart from such conservative scholars as *Th. Zahn*[31] and *A. Schlatter*,[32] is *A. Schweitzer*, who recognizes the genuineness of Matthew 16:18; he takes his starting-point, it is true, from the same contrast between an earthly Church and the Kingdom of God, but identifies the Church here with the Kingdom of God and interprets the passage in a purely eschatological way.[33] Among opponents of the genuineness, the representatives of the school of comparative religion, for example, *A. Dell*,[34] *H. Gressmann*, and *R. Reitzenstein*, attempt to explain the statement of Matthew 16:17 ff. not only from the

[28] *Handkommentar*, I, *ad loc.*

[29] *L'Evangile et l'Église*, 1902, p. 111. See also *Les évangiles synoptiques*, 1908.

[30] See also J. Grill, *Der Primat des Petrus*, 1904, p. 79; J. Schnitzer, *Hat Jesus das Papsttum gestiftet?*, 1910, p. 82; F. Heiler, *Der Katholizismus. Seine Idee und seine Erscheinung*, 1923, pp. 39 ff.

[31] See above, p. 169.

[32] *Der Evangelist Matthäus*, 1929.

[33] *Geschichte der Leben-Jesu-Forschung*, 4th ed., 1926, p. 416 (cf. Eng. Tr., *The Quest of the Historical Jesus*, 2nd ed., 1911, p. 369, note).

[34] *ZNW*, 1914, pp. 1 ff. See above, p. 21.

tendency to legitimitize the later Church, but also from motifs found in comparative religion.

*A. Harnack* takes a somewhat less radical attitude. To be sure, he too holds that Jesus cannot have spoken the promise with reference to the Church. This saying rather was coined at a later time, and probably in Rome, as it strove for the primacy. But in contrast to his predecessors Harnack denies to Jesus, in the entire section, only this one sentence concerning the Church; the remaining parts of the utterance addressed to Peter he regards as genuine. With these words Jesus assured Peter of immortality: 'You are Peter, and death will not conquer you.' This is how the words concerning the gates of hell are to be understood. Jesus said nothing to Peter, however, concerning the building of the Church. This part was rather inserted later into the original promise.[35] Since Harnack did not intend to put forth his explanation as a mere conjecture, he attempted to determine an original text in which those words concerning the Church, and only those words, had actually been lacking. This text, he held, was the Diatessaron of Tatian. This latter assertion, however, was refuted from the Roman Catholic side as early as 1922.[36]

We thus have seen that it is mainly the mention of the Church that has caused scholars to declare the passage spurious. So also it is precisely on this point that a change of opinion occurred in the period between the two world wars; the attempt was made to prove that in reality Jesus could very well have spoken of a Church, on the condition that in this connection one does not think of the Church in the modern sense, but of what the Aramaic equivalent meant to a Jew of that time. Here it is chiefly two scholars who must be named: *F. Kattenbusch*, who in his work on the place of origin of the Church proposes the thesis that the Son of Man idea leads to that of a 'People of the Saints';[37] and then *K. L. Schmidt*, who in two decisive articles[38] seeks to determine the Aramaic expression

[35] 'Der Spruch über Petrus als den Felsen der Kirche' (*Sitzungsbericht der Berliner Akademie der Wissenschaften*, 1918, pp. 637 ff.).

[36] See especially S. Euringer, 'Der locus classicus des Primates (Mt. 16, 18) und der Diatessarontext des heiligen Ephraim' (*Festgabe für A. Ehrhard*, 1922, pp. 141 ff.); also, A. Kneller, *Innsbrucker Zeitschrift für katholische Theologie*, 1920, pp. 147 ff.; J. Sickenberger, 'Eine neue Deutung der Primatstelle (Matt. 16, 18)' (*Théologique Revue*, 1920, pp. 1 ff.); and against A. Harnack also Ed. Meyer, *Ursprung und Anfänge des Christentums*, Vol. I, p. 112.

[37] *Festgabe für A. Harnack*, 1921, pp. 143 ff. The collective meaning of the Son of Man concept is also emphasized by T. W. Manson, *The Teaching of Jesus*, 1931, p. 211, and R. Newton Flew, *Jesus and his Church*, 1938. See also H. Odeberg, *The Fourth Gospel*, 1929, pp. 39 f.; N. A. Dahl, *Das Volk Gottes*, 1941, p. 90.

[38] 'Das Kirchenproblem im Urchristentum' (*Theologische Blätter*, 1927, columns 293 ff.); 'Die Kirche des Urchristentums' (*Festgabe für Ad. Deissmann*, 1927, p. 259). See also especially *Theologisches Wörterbuch zum N. T.*, Vol. III, Article on ἐκκλησία, 1936 (English translation, *The Church*; see note 3 of this chapter).

which lies behind the Greek word for Church, and on this basis shows
that the word fits perfectly as an utterance of Jesus, since it refers to the
idea of the People of God, the remnant or the separate synagogue.

In this way the chief argument against genuineness seemed to be removed. At the same time, interesting studies by *J. Jeremias*[39] emphasized
by other arguments the Semitic character of the word and its roots in
Jewish conceptions of the cosmic rock. Hence there now occurred a swing
back to an extensive agreement among Protestant exegetes in favour of
accepting the genuineness. It finds expression, for example, in the book
of *O. Linton* concerning 'The Problem of the Primitive Church in Recent
Study'.[40] The late Roman Catholic New Testament scholar from Fribourg, *F. M. Braun*, O.P., in his exceedingly instructive book, 'New Light
on the Church', also confirms this new consensus among Protestant
scholars.[41] So it might seem that the question as to genuineness has finally
been settled along this line.

In the year 1941, however, a reaction again occurred. It came from *R.
Bultmann*, in connection with my remark in my monograph on 'The
Kingship of Christ and the Church'.[42] I had said that the challenge to the
genuineness of Matthew 16:17 ff. cannot be justified on scholarly grounds.
In a rather long essay in *Theologischen Blätter*,[43] Bultmann seeks to under-
mine this statement; he defends anew the assertion of spuriousness that
he had championed earlier. He seeks to refute F. Kattenbusch and K. L.
Schmidt; he points to the absence of the word 'Church' in the teaching
of Jesus, and above all tries to demonstrate that Jesus spoke only of a
Kingdom to come in the future, not of a Church that is now being realized.
In so doing, he, like his earlier predecessors, believes that in the last analysis he must think in terms of a modern understanding of the word
'Church'. Even Bultmann, however, had already conceded in previous
studies that the saying must have been coined and ascribed to Jesus at a
very early time, since its character is entirely Semitic and so it comes from
the period of debates in Palestine concerning the law.

Thus the question was raised anew by R. Bultmann. In the subsequent

---

[39] *Golgotha*, 1926, pp. 68 ff.; *Angelos*, 1926, p. 109.

[40] *Das Problem der Urkirche in der neuern Forschung*, 1932.

[41] *Neues Licht auf die Kirche*, 1946 (German translation of *Aspects Nouveaux du
problème de l'Eglise*, 1942, enlarged and revised by the author). On p. 85 Braun names as
representatives of this consensus: F. Kattenbush, K. L. Schmidt, H. D. Wendland,
G. Gloege, W. Michaelis, J. Schniewind, F. Leenhardt, R. Otto, A. Fridrichsen, R.
Newton Flew, O. Cullmann. The list could easily be extended, for example by those
whom Braun often cites: O. Linton, J. Jeremias, etc.

[42] *Königsherrschaft Christi und Kirche*, 1941, p. 22.

[43] 'Die Frage nach der Echtheit von Matth. XVI, 17-19' (*Theologische Blätter*, 1941,
pp. 265 ff.).

debate *W. G. Kümmel* took a prominent role with his much discussed essay on 'The Church Concept and the Consciousness of History in the Primitive Church and in the Mind of Jesus'.[44] He likewise comes to the conclusion that the saying was not uttered by Jesus but was only ascribed to him later by the Church. His arguments, however, are essentially different from the earlier ones. His starting-point is that in Primitive Christianity, as with Jesus, there was a tension between the eschatological future and the present, but that the tension was solved in a different way in each case. In the case of Primitive Christianity, the Church was regarded as the already present fulfilment; for Jesus, on the contrary, the already present fulfilment was connected only with his person. The two solutions, according to Kümmel, could not have stood side by side in the mind of Jesus.

Others have challenged the genuineness with still other arguments. For example, *Emanuel Hirsch* does so after the manner of the older critics and without considering the recent statement of the problem.[45] *J. Haller* completely rejects the recent studies and discards the saying without offering any real exegetical foundation.[46] *H. Strathmann*[47] regards the saying, in connection with his somewhat schematic geographical division of the roles of the evangelists, as the creation of the church at Antioch.[48] *E. Stauffer* takes a special position; while he regards the utterance as a saying of the Lord, he assigns it not to the Incarnate Jesus, but to the Risen One, who spoke the words on the occasion of his first appearance, which was granted to Peter.[49] *H. v. Campenhausen* considers that 'a statement of Jesus founding the Church on Peter' is 'inconceivable'; he is of the opinion that 'there should be no doubt about this, in spite of recent attempts to salvage that view'.[50]

*N. A. Dahl*[51] and *O. Michel*[52] do not deny the genuineness categorically, but take an extremely cautious attitude. *R. Liechtenhan*, on the contrary,

---

[44] *Kirchenbegriff und Geschichtsbewusstsein in der Urgemeinde und bei Jesus (Symbolae Biblicae Upsalienses)*, 1943. Even earlier W. G. Kümmel had opposed the genuineness, in *Die Eschatologie der Evangelien*, 1936, p. 16.

[45] *Frühgeschichte des Evangeliums*, II, 1941, pp. 306 ff.

[46] *Das Papsttum*, 2nd ed., 1951, pp. 4 f., 473 f. The saying, he contends, could only have originated after the year 70, when events proved that the temple rock had no permanence. This unexpected conclusion J. Haller draws from the above-mentioned work of J. Jeremias.

[47] 'Die Stellung des Petrus in der Urkirche. Zur Frühgeschichte des Wortes an Petrus Mt. 16, 17–19' (*Zeitschrift für systematische Theologie*, 1943, pp. 223 ff.).

[48] See above, p. 27, note 39.

[49] 'Zur Vor- und Frühgeschichte des Primatus Petri' (*ZKG*, 1943–4, pp. 1 ff.).

[50] *Kirchliches Amt und geistliche Vollmacht in den ersten drei Jahrhunderten*, 1953, pp. 140 f.

[51] *Das Volk Gottes. Eine Untersuchung zum Kirchenbewusstsein des Urchristentums*, 1941, p. 165.

[52] *Das Zeugnis des Neuen Testaments von der Gemeinde*, 1941, pp. 9 f., 22 f.

while he carries on a debate with R. Bultmann and continues the ideas of Kümmel, nevertheless uses these ideas in a different way. He represents the view that Jesus' eschatological expectation concerning the future included the foundation of his Church; towards the setting and form of the saying, however, he takes a critical attitude.[53] Especially does the larger work of A. Oepke[54] offer anew a full defence of the genuineness. In doing so, it emphasizes mainly the idea of the People of God, an idea solidly rooted in Jewish conceptions; on the other hand, by showing the rhythm in which these verses are constructed, it seeks to ascribe the saying to the Logia Source and at the same time to show its organic attachment to the narrative framework as it appears also in Mark. On this point, however, the younger generation of New Testament scholars who stand under the influence of R. Bultmann follow their master in firm rejection of the genuineness.

Thus at the present time the question is once more in flux, and we can scarcely speak any longer of a consensus of opinion. A statistical study made in 1950, in which the position of thirty-four modern authors on this problem was studied, showed that they divide into two approximately equal groups.[55] Since then, in connection with the just described tendency of New Testament scholarship in Germany, the proportion opposed to genuineness may have increased.

Up to this point we have mentioned only Protestant scholars. Quite recently there have been occasional instances when even Roman Catholic exegetes have restricted to some extent the genuineness of the passage in its present form. This is done chiefly by A. Vögtle in his two Biblische Zeitschrift articles (1957/8), which rest on thorough and cautious literary analysis.[56] In general, however, the modern Roman Catholic expositors are usually content to offer a searching detailed exegesis. It is noteworthy that we find very little concerning the point which one would gladly find discussed by precisely these scholars—concerning the question, that is, whether and how it accords with the purpose of Jesus to refer these words to bishops as successors, whether and how, indeed, the promise of Jesus contains any idea whatever of a succession. F. M. Braun, in debate with K. L. Schmidt in the above-mentioned work,[57] is the only one who even takes up the question. He does not, indeed, discuss it in an exegetical way;

[53] Die urchristliche Mission, 1946 (Abhandlungen zur Theologie des Alten und Neuen Testaments).

[54] 'Der Herrnspruch über die Kirche, Mt. 16, 17–19, in der neuesten Forschung' (Studia Theologica, 1948–50, pp. 110 ff.).

[55] See A. Oepke, op. cit., p. 111, note 1.

[56] A. Vögtle, 'Messiasbekenntnis und Petrusverheissung. Zur Komposition Mt. 16, 13–23 Par.' (Biblische Zeitschrift, 1957, pp. 252 ff.; 1958, pp. 85 ff.).

[57] See note 41 in this chapter.

this the scope of his book scarcely permitted. In the Roman Catholic commentaries the presence of the idea of succession is for the most part not examined; it is rather presupposed as an undiscussed fact. And yet this should be proved, for it certainly is not at all self-evident, and he who reads the saying without prejudice will never by himself get the idea that Jesus here speaks—in a sort of prophetic way—to successors of Peter. The Roman Catholic exegetes really owe a more thorough explanation on this point than one usually reads in their commentaries. The discussion of the first edition of the present book called forth for the first time and in a gratifying way a more intensive grappling with this question.[58]

I choose as examples of the too long prevailing neglect of the problem two recent Catholic commentators who have dealt with the Gospel of Matthew; they are P. Dausch and M. J. Lagrange. In *Dausch*[59] we read but a single sentence concerning the specific question that here interests us: 'since, according to the second half of verse 18, the Church founded upon Peter is to be unshakable in its stability and in its duration, and since it is almost universally conceded that Peter came to Rome and died there, the primacy is already assured on this basis alone'. *M. J. Lagrange*, however, deals with this question somewhat more in detail.[60] After a detailed criticism of Harnack, he mentions the objection of the 'Anglicans' that the passage speaks only of Peter, not of any possible successors. Why this objection is ascribed only to the Anglicans is not clear. In reality we are dealing here with a question which Protestants of all denominations have raised long since and repeatedly in opposition to the Roman Catholic presupposition. Lagrange replies that in this saying Jesus did not limit the duration of the Church. As long as there is a Church, it will have the same foundation, even if the head and the members change. There thus exists, he claims, a 'successive unity' in the leadership of the Church. Jesus will see to it that in order to provide the foundation for the Church there will be at all times shepherds of the quality of Peter, that is, of the same faith. History proves that this has been the case, and this confirms the trustworthiness of the Lord's saying.[61] Concerning this retreat from exegesis to later history, which we find almost universally among Roman Catholic scholars,[62] we shall speak in the closing chapter. For in any case it can

[58] See my booklet, to appear later, on *Peter and the Pope*.
[59] *Kommentar zum Matthäusevangelium*, 1936, *ad loc.*
[60] *Evangile selon S. Matthieu*, 5th ed., 1941, *ad loc.*
[61] J. Sickenberger also omits any discussion of successors in his explanation of Matt. 16:17 ff. in *Biblische Zeitfragen*, 1929, pp. 16 ff.
[62] See for example K. Pieper, *Jesus und die Kirche*, 1932, and K. Adam, *Wesen des Katholizismus*, 1934; more recently, the Roman Catholic reviews of the first edition of my book.

be considered only as a confirmation and not as a justification of the exegesis.

## 2. The Narrative Framework of Matthew 16:17-19

We now undertake, on the basis of a careful examination of the text, to explain the verses under discussion. First of all we must give close attention to the context in which they stand. This very context raises questions, especially since Mark and Luke have the same narrative framework, but without the crucial verses which here concern us. These momentous words concerning the rock on which Jesus will build his Church thus stand in but one of our four Gospels, the Gospel of Matthew. For many this fact still constitutes what we may call the first external occasion for challenging the genuineness. This argument, however, should certainly be discarded. The fact that a saying belongs to the so-called special material of Matthew is no justification at all for even raising the question of genuineness. How many pearls we would have to discard as spurious from Jesus' Sermon on the Mount—to name only this one example—if we were to let ourselves be guided by this principle![63]

The point has been made that the historical framework, which is found also in Mark and Luke though without these verses, is interrupted by this section in Matthew in a rather unfortunate way. We therefore propose to begin by studying this argument. Do the verses fit the narrative framework or not? On this point one thing must be noted in advance; even if it should prove true that the section with which we are concerned breaks the narrative framework, or in chronological respects is actually irreconcilable with it, we still could not draw from that fact the conclusion that the words are spurious, that is, that they were not spoken by Jesus. This conclusion would rather warrant only the preliminary conclusion that a unit of tradition, handed down separately, has been inserted here by Matthew in a setting in which it did not originally belong.

First, however, we must look more closely at this historical framework. It deals with the so-called confession of Jesus by Peter at Caesarea Philippi, and we propose to read this narrative in the form in which it stands in the Gospel of Mark. On the whole, Matthew gives it, apart from variations in detail, in the same form that Mark has; only he introduces in this framework the promises of Jesus to Peter.

---

[63] It therefore seems to me unnecessary to follow the explanation that Eusebius gives in his *Demonstratio evangelica*, 3, 5. He explains the silence of the Gospel of Mark, which goes back to Peter, by the humility and modesty of the apostle. This is the interpretation given by Roman Catholic exegetes such as P. Dausch, *Kirche und Papsttum—eine Stiftung Jesu*, 1911.

The narrative, common to all three Synoptics, is probably presented most vividly and in most effective simplicity in Mark. Precisely in this Gospel, moreover, it has a quite central position. One is inclined to trace the story back to a direct participant, that is, to the chief participant, to Peter himself, in case the notice of Papias is correct, according to which the evangelist Mark was the interpreter of Peter, and in his Gospel reported the stories from the life of Jesus which Peter cited in his sermons as illustrative examples.[64] In any case, Matthew and Luke, in the parallel passages, do not possess the same freshness as does Mark, in whose Gospel a certain animation marks this entire narrative. This animation permits us in a way to share in the excitement of those who were present at the event itself.

Mark is conscious of the fact that in this moment something of special importance must have happened. Even the beginning of the conversation must have been an impressive moment. Previously Jesus had commanded silence and had done everything to prevent any discussion of his Messianic calling from arising. Now on his own initiative, though in the narrow circle of disciples, he starts a conversation concerning this question to which previously he had carefully avoided making so much as the merest allusion. Now he is the very one who asks: 'Who do the people say that I am?' Then he asks further—and here we note how both the questioner and the persons questioned are inwardly moved—'And you, who do you say that I am?' Then comes the answer of Peter, which again in its modest brevity embodies the emotion of the disciple: 'You are the Christ.' Matthew, because he gives the answer a fuller form, weakens the effect: 'You are the Christ, the Son of the Living God.' This expansion appears to be in fact a weakening of the Marcan text. But we shall see that the addition, 'the Son of the Living God', is not merely an edifying liturgical paraphrase, such as we often find in Matthew, but that the Evangelist, by joining two quite different Christological titles (Messiah and Son of God), betrays that throughout in Matthew 16 he has joined two entirely different narratives. In one Peter says to Jesus: 'You are the Messiah.' This narrative, located at Caesarea Philippi, is given also by Mark and Luke. In the other Peter says to Jesus: 'You are the Son of God.' This is reported only by Matthew (vss. 17–19). In the narrative framework of the event at Caesarea Philippi, which Matthew has in common with Mark and Luke, the answer of Peter consists of the simple and in this case more forceful statement, 'You are the Messiah', as we read in Mark.[65] What the demon-

[64] Eusebius, *Ecclesiastical History*, III, 39, 15 f.

[65] As compared with this, it is probable that the fuller Lucan wording, 'the Christ of God', is also secondary.

M

possessed man had already said to Jesus in Capernaum: 'Jesus the
Messiah', this we now hear from the mouth of the disciple who is the
representative and spokesman of the others. In the name of all he utters
the great word that up to this time no disciple had dared to speak in the
presence of Jesus. Among themselves the disciples may have discussed it
when Jesus was absent, and what Peter here says will have rested upon
their firm conviction.[66]

They knew that they were not mere disciples of a rabbi, as were all other
disciples. They were certain that their teacher was more than a rabbi, and
they had the proud consciousness, which emerges in other passages, that
they formed the following of the Messiah. One speaks a great deal of the
self-consciousness of Jesus. We could also speak of the self-consciousness of the disciples.

According to Mark, Jesus at first answers nothing in response to
this declaration, and this is very significant. The disciples still do not
know in what way he conceives this Messianic calling. Jesus says neither
Yes nor No. He simply commands the disciples not to tell this to anyone
that is, not to tell anyone that he is the Christ. Only when he shall suffer
will the people recognize in him the Messiah. The disciples, however
must now be the first ones to be taught in what sense he is the Messiah
This instruction follows in verses 31 f. It is attached to the command
ment to say nothing to anyone concerning his Messianic calling, and it
likewise explains this command. This is *the entirely natural continuation of
the narrative*. In view of the importance of the occasion the passion pre
diction necessarily followed here, and it explains all the commands to be
silent. This prediction and the protest of Peter by no means form a new
narrative. Neither are they a sort of epilogue. Rather, they give *the point
of the entire event at Caesarea Philippi*.[67] Now that the word 'Messiah' has

[66] W. Michaelis, *Das Evangelium nach Matthäus* (*Prophezei*), Part II, 1949, p. 339
assumes on the contrary that Peter previously had suspected nothing of this kind; Jesus
words presuppose a sudden disclosure. This may hold good only for the other tradition
which Matthew has here inserted (Son of God).

[67] This must be emphasized in opposition to R. Bultmann, 'Die Frage nach der
messianischen Bewusstsein Jesu und das Petrus-Bekenntnis' (*ZNW*, 1919-20, pp. 165
ff.), and *Geschichte der synoptischen Tradition*, 2nd ed., 1931, *ad loc.*, whose view is that
the Marcan narrative of the event at Caesarea Philippi closes with the command of
silence (in this point, but only in this point, he agrees with K. L. Schmidt, *Der Rahmen
der Geschichte Jesu*, 1919, pp. 217 ff.). He then further asserts that the report in Mark is a
torso; the original narrative, which to be sure was only created by the Church, demand
as continuation not something like the reprimand of Peter (vs. 31 f.), but what we read in
Matt. 16:17 ff. Mark shortened the account here due to his 'anti-Petrine' attitude
(see on this point above, pp. 26 f.), and so robbed the story of its conclusion. Quite sim
lar, though with acceptance of the genuineness of the Matthean narrative, is the judgmen
of W. Michaelis, *Das Evangelium nach Matthäus*, Part II, p. 339. A. Schlatter, *D
Evangelist Matthäus*, 1929, *ad loc.*, actually goes so far as to explain the Marcan omission

been uttered, and Jesus has not rejected this title but also has not accepted it, he must inform the disciples of the restricted sense in which alone he applies the word to himself: Messiah—yes, but in a quite different way from what you think; Messiah, but as a suffering, rejected, executed one. Mark adds that Jesus now spoke openly—he 'said everything'.[68]

And then follows—not at all a new narrative or an appendix but— the *real point* of the story, in which the protest of Peter proves that even the innermost group of disciples had not grasped the real meaning that the Messianic calling had for Jesus. Peter, too, shared completely the dia- bolical political conception of the Messianic calling, as the devil had represented it in person in the temptation story, when he offered to Jesus the kingdoms of the world. We know that at every step Jesus had to define his task in opposition to Zealotism and its Messianic ideal, and yet he himself was finally nailed to the cross as a Zealot.[69] The idea of a suffering Messiah was entirely foreign to Peter, and *according to Mark it was en- tirely foreign to him when he uttered that confession, 'You are the Messiah.'* This fact must be emphasized, that even when he spoke that confession, according to Mark, he still had not grasped *its essential meaning*. And even now he does not grasp it. He reacts against this idea of the suffering of the Messiah, and so great is his astonishment and his emotion that he dares to 'rebuke' Jesus. Nowhere else do we hear that a disciple did this. But this shows how great the astonishment of Peter must have been; it was so much the greater since Jesus has finally for once spoken with his disciples concerning his Messianic calling and evoked the confession of his Mes- sianic role. Peter's position as a disciple, indeed, will also be affected if Jesus is a suffering Messiah; in that case he, like the others, is the dis- ciple of a suffering and rejected Messiah, and for them, too, everything is quite different from what they have conceived it to be.

Jesus, however, turns around, and Mark now notes very acutely that in the words he addresses to Peter, he also has in view the other disciples,

---

of Jesus' words of Matt. 16:17–19 as an effort to make a belated connection of the passion prediction with the confession of Peter. In reality the final verses offer the key to the understanding not only of what happened at Caesarea Philippi but also of the so-called 'messianic secret'. Hence the central position of our section in the Synoptic Gospels. Only in Matthew do the verses which contain the passion prediction and the protest of Peter seem a sort of afterpiece, more or less separated from the preceding narrative by the words ἀπὸ τότε ('from that time'). This very fact speaks in favour of the originality of the Marcan narrative.—To be sure, A. Vögtle, *Messiasbekenntnis und Petrusverheissung*, 1957, p. 256, holds as I do that Matt. 16:17 ff. is an insertion into the Marcan narrative, and he agrees with me on the whole in his judgment as to its basic purpose, but he finds it too 'far-reaching' to see the real 'point' of the Marcan story in the 'Get behind me, Satan!'

[68] παρρησίᾳ ('freely', 'openly', 'plainly').
[69] See O. Cullmann, *Der Staat im Neuen Testament*, 1956, pp. 5 ff. (Eng. Tr., *The State in the New Testament*, 1956, pp. 8 ff.).

for what he says applies also to them. Jesus knows that they, too, share that false conception of his Messianic role and consequently of their discipleship. The example of the sons of Zebedee, for example, proves that.

And then Jesus utters the unusually strong words: 'Depart from me, Satan!'[70] Thus he uses the word that he had hurled at the devil himself at the time of the temptation (Matt. 4:10). The devil is now making use of Jesus' own disciple, Peter; that is his greatest trick. Nevertheless, Jesus recognizes it, and here too Mark portrays with special vividness how he accompanies this harsh word to Peter with the simultaneous look at the other disciples. He who tries to force upon Jesus another Messianic task than the one he has received from God, he who thereby seeks to turn him from this task he has received from God, is a tool of Satan!

The originality of this Marcan narrative, in comparison with the parallels in Luke and Matthew, appears not only in its unclouded clearness, which really is striking, but also in various points of detail. Thus this entire story does not play in Matthew the dominating role that it has in Mark. In Matthew, that is, the disciples have already at an earlier time confessed before Jesus his majesty, at the time of the walking upon the sea (Matt. 14:33). Matthew thereby reduces in advance the importance of the story here reported.[71] In Mark its unique significance rests upon the very fact that here for the *first* time the disciples speak with Jesus with regard to what he is in their eyes. Here it is seen that the arrangement of material, which of course is due to the evangelists, can become important in giving significance to the individual narrative. It is, so to say, a commentary on the part of the evangelist.

Details within the narrative itself also seem to point to the conclusion that Matthew had a shallower grasp than Mark of the bearing of the event. For example, Matthew formulates the opening question of Jesus in a way that already contains an answer: 'Who do the people say that *the Son of Man* is?' In Mark this is put in a form that is certainly more original, 'Who do the people say that *I* am?'[72]

---

[70] We may leave undiscussed the question whether ὕπαγε ὀπίσω μου is to be understood literally, that is, (depart) 'after me', in the sense of a summons to follow him as a disciple. I do not believe that it has a meaning essentially different from the simple ὕπαγε ('depart') in Matt. 4:10.

[71] W. Michaelis, *Das Evangelium nach Matthäus* (*Prophezei*), p. 338, seeks to minimize the significance of this fact by writing that at this point Matthew was conscious that he was anticipating.

[72] Too far-fetched is the explanation of R. Graber, *Petrus der Fels*, 1949, p. 31. He takes the contrary position and gives Matthew the preference here. He holds that Mark and Luke here replaced the expression 'Son of Man' by the first person singular, because the mention of the Son of Man, which points to Daniel and alludes to the people of God who will defeat the world powers, seemed to them too dangerous in this passage.

By this, we do not mean to say in any *a priori* way that verses 17-19, which concern us and are found only in Matthew, are a later creation of the Primitive Church. Nevertheless, the point just made must also be considered when we now put the question that was our chief objective in making a closer examination of this narrative framework: Does Jesus' saying to Peter, which only in Matthew follows Peter's statement concerning Jesus, fit harmoniously into *this framework*? Do these verses 17-19 really belong to this event, and were they spoken on this occasion, or on the contrary did they originally belong in another context and were they first inserted in this passage by Matthew? Even in the latter case, as we have said, they may be fully genuine, that is, spoken by Jesus but on another occasion.

We must consider, at least theoretically, the second possibility, that it was Matthew who inserted into the framework of the Marcan narrative these words of Jesus to Peter. This necessity is made clear by the entire manner in which the evangelists, and Matthew in particular, have arranged the material transmitted to them by the oral or already written tradition. It is the lasting merit of the works on 'Form Criticism' to have proved that the oral gospel tradition, like all oral tradition, contained only single units, without any chronological or geographical connections between them. The work of the evangelists, who assembled these single units of the tradition, consists in the fact that they combined them each in his own way. Thus they are not only collectors but also arrangers. In this connection it can be shown that each one proceeded to arrange the material in his own way, and it is particularly instructive to compare Matthew and Luke in this regard. Matthew in grouping his material follows a plan based on considerations of content and theology; that is, he connects with one another the stories which seem to him to belong together in their theological significance: miracle stories, sayings concerning the Law (Sermon on the Mount), sayings concerning John the Baptist (Matt., ch. 11), parables (Matt., ch. 13), sayings against the Pharisees (Matt., ch. 23), etc. It is of no primary concern to Matthew whether he thereby preserves the chronological sequence; from the start he has written his Gospel from this other point of view. The evangelist Luke, on the contrary, strives, as he himself says in his prologue, to report the events in their chronological sequence.

Hence it is not only justified but actually imperative to ask first not whether the words are genuine, that is, spoken by Jesus, but whether Matthew, who alone includes them, has put them in their chronological setting, or whether here too he has simply connected this section with

Peter's declaration concerning Jesus at Caesarea Philippi because *in its content* it seemed to him to fit here, since both times Peter makes a statement concerning Jesus: the one time a statement for which he must be reprimanded by Jesus as the devil's instrument ('Messiah' in the political sense), but the other time a statement for which he is praised by Jesus as the instrument of direct divine revelation ('Son of God').

First of all, we must recall that in Matthew the giving of the name Cephas—Rock seems first to occur at this point. In Mark, on the contrary, Jesus, as we have seen,[73] gives this name to Simon at an earlier time, when he forms the group of the Twelve (ch. 3:16); and in the Gospel of John he actually gives it at the very first meeting (ch. 1:42). One may say, of course, that in Matthew 16:17 Peter does not *receive* this name for the first time, but that here it is only *explained* to him, after being given to him at an earlier time.[74] In that case there would be no direct chronological conflict between Mark and John. It is noteworthy, however, that Matthew has not reported the giving of the name on any earlier occasion. He thus appears to be of the opinion that this did not take place until the moment when Jesus also explained the name by telling of his purpose to build his Church upon this rock.[75] Then we should assume that although it was accepted as unquestioned fact that Jesus gave to Peter the title Cephas, there was no definitely fixed tradition concerning the time at which he did this.[76]

But however that may be, Matthew seems to have known a tradition according to which the giving and the explanation of the name was the answer of Jesus to a statement of Peter concerning Jesus. This, however, cannot have happened at the same time as the reprimand of Peter at Caesarea Philippi. For we have seen that in Mark and Luke the narrative concerning that event did not produce this reaction, that Jesus rather kept silent concerning it and commanded silence. Peter's utterance of the diabolical conception of the Messiah could not possibly have gained for him the title of honour, 'Rock'. But we understand well that another perception concerning Jesus, given to Peter by God and expressed on a quite different occasion, could have as its result that for it he was named

---

[73] See above, p. 23.

[74] This is stressed especially by Th. Zahn, *Das Evangelium des Matthäus*, 4th ed., 1922, *ad loc*. He points to the fact that the Matthew passage lacks the formula customary in *giving* names (Gen. 17: 5, 15; 32:28; Matt. 1:21, 25; 2:23; Luke 1:13, 31, 59–63; 2:21).

[75] W. Michaelis, *op. cit.*, pp. 340 f., is also of the opinion that Matthew here intends to tell of the *giving* of the name. He thinks that John 1:42 and Mark 3:16 are intended only as a reference to this later time.

[76] See M. J. Lagrange, *L'Evangile selon S. Matthieu*, 5th ed., 1941, p. 324: 'the tradition of the change of name was attested by all, but there was less certainty concerning the occasion'. See also Lagrange's judgment concerning the originality of the setting that Mark presupposes for the giving of the name. See above, p. 23, note 22.

Rock' by Jesus. Only Matthew 16:17 ff. preserves the memory of this revelation given to Peter, which found its expression not in the Messiah title but in the title Son of God. Now Matthew, true to his harmonizing tendency, has joined together the two different narratives and so has combined Peter's two statements concerning Jesus, 'Messiah' (in the political sense) and 'Son of God' ('you are Christ, the Son of the living God'). He has located both at Caesarea Philippi, where Peter, on account of his false conception of the Messiah, had had to be reprimanded as Satan's tool. But the words in which Peter is praised and which are intelligible only in the second narrative will not fit into this framework as an echo or answer to Peter's Satanic conception of the Messiah.

We have seen, in fact, that in the narrative framework Peter plays the role of one who does not understand the Messianic role of Jesus. He rather shares that very conception of the Messiah which Jesus regards as a temptation from Satan. To be sure, he utters the words: 'You are the Messiah.' But the continuation of this story makes clear how abysmally deep is the misunderstanding that separates Peter from Jesus even here. Indeed, we must actually say that the entire story leads on to this continuation; *this is its point*: 'Depart from me, Satan!' We have seen that the parallel to the temptation story is clear. In both cases the devil seeks to persuade Jesus to fulfil a Messianic role radically different from the one with which he knows he is entrusted.

Thus the conclusion of the narrative framework shows that he who spoke those words: 'You are the Christ', was a tool of Satan, not indeed in uttering the confession of the Messiah but rather *in his conception of these words*. This time Satan comes to Jesus in the person of Peter. Therefore Jesus says to his disciple: 'You are not thinking of the things of God but of the things of men.'

When one considers the meaning of this narrative framework, it becomes difficult indeed *a priori* to assume that *in this very context* Jesus said to Peter: 'You are inspired by the Father in Heaven; he has given you a special revelation.' But this is what we read in verse 17. This certainly does not fit well with what we have just established to be the intent in the narrative about Peter's statement. Precisely at this point the quite vivid portrayal of Mark seems to be interrupted and also twisted, if it is followed by the saying of Jesus concerning Peter the rock. For the fact that in the narrative of Mark Jesus at first says nothing at all in reply to this declaration of Peter, and so does not take any position with regard to it, corresponds completely to the attitude he maintains towards the title of Messiah in the entire Synoptic tradition; he always manifests a notable *reserve* towards this title, without explicitly rejecting it.[77] One can trace this in the hearing before the High Priest. He knows that the title of Messiah, used without qualification and addition, can give rise to grave misunderstandings. Thus the silence of Jesus, as Mark presupposes it in our passage, can scarcely be explained as an accidental or deliberate omission of a saying of Jesus; it rather has theological significance.[78]

I therefore consider it exegetically very probable (1) that Matthew found in an ancient oral tradition the words with which Jesus explains the title Cephas, or at least the early portion of them (vss. 17-18 and perhaps 19a);[79] (2) that he found them as an answer to an actual confession of Peter to the Son of God (not to the Messiah); and (3) that in accord with his entire method of arranging material he sought for this separately transmitted fragment of tradition a suitable place from the standpoint of *content*, and thought he had found it in the story of the reprimand of Peter at Caesarea Philippi. The assumption actually forces itself on us that by putting together these two traditions Matthew wanted to show that the image of Peter as the instrument of the devil must be corrected by that of Peter as the instrument of the divine revelation.[80]

[77] Jean Héring, *Le Royaume de Dieu et sa venue*, 1937, pp. 111 ff., goes further in saying that he rejected the title. The irreconcilability of Matt. 16:17 ff. with the narrative framework of Mark 8: 27 ff. he also emphasizes strongly (p. 127, note 2).

[78] This is in opposition to Héring, *op. cit.*, p. 125, who takes account of this possibility. Mark, he says, already interpreted the silence in the sense of an unqualified acceptance of the Messianic title; I on the contrary believe that Mark correctly understood the meaning of this silence, that is, he also regarded it not directly as a sharp rejection, such as J. Héring ascribes to Jesus, but as an attitude of *reserve*. This reserve is in full harmony with the 'Back, Satan'; nevertheless, there exists in our narrative a heightening, which leads from this silence to that climax. See on this question O. Cullmann, *Die Christologie des Neuen Testaments*, 2nd ed., 1958, pp. 118 ff. (Eng. Tr., *The Christology of the New Testament*, 1959, pp. 117 ff.).

[79] On vs. 19b see below, p. 210. These words concerning binding and loosing, and possibly also the saying concerning the keys (see below, p. 209), perhaps do not belong to the same item of tradition as vss. 17-18. It is only with regard to these sayings that I cannot agree with A. Vögtle, *op. cit.*, when he denies the unity of the section vss. 17-19.

[80] E. L. Allen, 'On This Rock' (*Journal of Theological Studies*, 1954, pp. 59 ff.), has rightly raised the question concerning the purpose for which Matthew introduced the section here. His answer, that Matthew saw in the words of Jesus a means of legitimizing a situation which *after the death of Peter* had arisen in a local church (Antioch?), which appealed to Peter, does not absolutely contradict my answer to this question given here and in greater detail in my essay, 'L'apôtre Pierre instrument du diable et instrument de Dieu' (*New Testament Essays* for T. W. Manson, 1959, p. 94). But to Allen's assumption that on this view *Matthew* understood Jesus to have in view a *succession* to Peter the leader of the Church—a view combatted in John, ch. 21—I shall state my position in my projected book, *Peter and the Pope*; the assumption belongs in the circle of problems there to be treated, and a similar objection has often been made against me by Roman Catholic critics. See below, pp. 213f., and in another way above, p. 31, note 54. An essentially different explanation of the purpose of Matthew is given by G. Bornkamm, 'Enderwartung und Kirche im Matthäusevangelium', in the volume of essays in honour of C. H. Dodd, *The Background of the New Testament and its Eschatology*, 1956, pp. 256 ff., and now in *Ueberlieferung und Auslegung im Matthäus-Evangelium*, 1960, pp. 13 ff.

Peter was inspired by the Father not at Caesarea Philippi, where he rather represented the devilish conception of the 'Christ', but on another occasion, where he recognized in Jesus the 'Son of God'. According to the saying in Matthew 11 : 27, which in content belongs to this second tradition, no one knows the Son except the Father, so that a revelation by him is necessary.[81]

A further trace of the fact that originally the two traditions were not connected could be found in the fact that in vs. 17 the object is lacking. It does not say in that verse: '*This* [namely, that I am the Christ] has been revealed to you not by flesh and blood but by my heavenly Father.' The demonstrative pronoun 'this', which we usually add in the translation, is lacking in the Greek text. In the original tradition also some object certainly must have stood here; it cannot have been lacking even in a separate unit of tradition. However, one can ask whether the fact that it is lacking in Matthew is not to be explained by saying that the unit originally had another introduction.

The very reverse has been asserted—that verses 17–19, as far as geographical location is concerned, stand in a setting entirely suitable to them.[82] Indeed, it has actually been asserted that the Marcan narrative is a torso in its present form, that is, without the verses that Matthew alone contains. It is said to require just such an answer as the explanation of Jesus which we read in Matthew. Since Jesus himself evoked the Messianic confession of his disciples, the narrative cannot have ended with the mere command not to tell about it. Matthew 16:17 ff. would thus present the original and natural conclusion.[83] This view, however, overlooks the fact that the conclusion of the Marcan narrative is *not* the command to keep silent. It is rather those words of Jesus to Peter: 'Depart from me, Satan!'—and they are also taken over by Matthew. The attempt has also been made to show that the answer of Jesus has been constructed

---

[81] A. Vögtle, *op. cit.*, *Biblische Zeitschrift*, 1958, pp. 96 ff., who refuses to connect the promises to Peter with the scene at Caesarea Philippi or even with another ancient tradition concerning a *confession of Peter*, regards this beatitude as an editorial item simply created by Matthew on the basis of the saying in Matt. 11 :25 ff. By means of it the Evangelist has inserted the promise to Peter, which derives from another tradition, into the Marcan narrative concerning the event at Caesarea Philippi.

[82] The Matthew context of the verses is regarded as original by O. Immisch, 'Matthäus 16, 18' (*ZNW*, 1916, p. 18; he appeals to the geographical references in the words), and also, with rejection of my thesis as already presented in the first edition of this book, by M. Overney, 'Le cadre historique des paroles de Jésus sur la primauté de Pierre' (*Nova et Vetera*, 1953, pp. 206 ff.); B. Willaert, 'La connexion littéraire entre la première prédiction de la passion et la confession de Pierre chez les Synoptiques' (*Etudes Lov.*, 1956, pp. 24 ff.).

[83] So R. Bultmann, W. Michaelis, A. Schlatter (see above, p. 178, note 67), and also Th. Zahn, *ad loc.*

in exact parallelism to Peter's confession. Just as in that confession it says: 'You are the Christ', so here: 'You are Peter.' As we have seen, however, the words 'You are Peter' really cannot be connected directly with the diabolically meant statement 'You are the Messiah'; they can only be related to the confession, 'You are the Son of God.'

In view of what has been said, it must at least be assumed with great probability that the disputed verses originally did not belong in the context in which Matthew has placed them. This decision says nothing concerning genuineness or spuriousness.

It is entirely false to describe as 'Peter's confession' the narrative framework of the Caesarea Philippi event as we read it in Mark. Only the verses in Matt. 16:17 ff., which Matthew has inserted from another tradition, offer a 'confession of Peter', that is, to Jesus as the Son of God. The narrative framework, on the contrary, should be given the heading, 'Reprimand of Peter's Satanic Conception of the Christ'.[84]

If the event of Caesarea Philippi is not really the original framework of these traditional words, then the question arises whether, if we provisionally assume their genuineness, it still is possible to discern their setting. The most favoured theory in this case is that while the saying was indeed spoken by Jesus, it was spoken not by the Incarnate Jesus, but rather by *the Risen One*, on the occasion of an appearance to Peter alone. On this view, the entire incident was transferred back into the life of the Incarnate One at a later time.[85] Many things favour this possibility. It really is striking that the very first and so possibly the most important appearance of Jesus, that is, the one to Peter, is nowhere narrated in the New Testament. And yet it is clearly presupposed—for example, in the

[84] On this point see the detailed argument in my article, 'L'apôtre instrument du diable et instrument de Dieu' (*New Testament Essays* for T. W. Manson, 1959, p. 94). My conclusion that vss. 17-19 do not belong in the context of the narrative about Caesarea Philippi is followed, though with strong variations in other respects, by A. Vögtle, 'Messiasbekenntnis und Petrusverheissung' (*Biblische Zeitschrift*, 1957, pp. 252 ff.; 1959, pp. 85 ff.), who by a careful analysis tests whether on literary grounds the Marcan or the Matthean conception is secondary. Even before he wrote, agreement with me on this point was expressed (for the most part in reviews of my book) by P. Benoit (*Revue Biblique*, 1953, p. 571); C. Spicq (*Revue des Sciences Phil. et Theol.*, 1953, pp. 180 ff.); and M. E. Boismard (*Divus Thomas*, 1953, p. 236). Without approving my definite insertion of the verses in the Passion Story, H. Lehmann, 'Du bist Petrus . . . Zum Problem von Matthäus 16, 13-26' (*Evangelische Theologie*, 1953, pp. 46 ff.), also agrees with me in concluding that vss. 17-19 do not fit in the framework of the Caesarea story; similarly, G. Bornkamm, *op. cit.* (*The Background of the New Testament and its Eschatology: Studies in Honour of C. H. Dodd*, 1956, pp. 256 f.).

[85] So chiefly E. Stauffer, 'Zur Vor- und Frühgeschichte des Primatus Petri' (*ZKG*, 1943-4, pp. 1 ff.); R. Bultmann, *Theologie des Neuen Testaments*, 1948, p. 46 (Eng. Tr., *Theology of the N. T.*, I, p. 45). See above, p. 62, and also H. Lehmann, *op. cit.*, p. 64; G. Bornkamm, *op. cit.*, p. 260; A. Vögtle, *op. cit.*, 1958, p. 103: 'possibly therefore first as the Risen One'.

oldest text that we possess, in the earliest summary of the Christian faith, in I Corinthians 15:5. We have seen that in this passage the appearance to Peter stands first in a chronological enumeration of those who have seen the risen Lord. Furthermore, we have found in Luke 24:34 the mention of the fact that the Lord appeared to Simon; indeed, the way in which it is mentioned shows that here too we must be dealing with the first of the appearances. We have noted that the significance of this fact for the position of Peter in the Primitive Church simply cannot be overestimated, and we have also attempted to find an explanation of the fact that no narrative account of this most important of all appearances has been preserved.[86]

A trace of such a narrative could indeed exist in ch. 21 of the Gospel of John. To be sure, we have here an appearance before *several* disciples in Galilee. But the dialogue that begins in verse 15 takes place essentially between the Risen One and Peter. The beloved disciple comes in, so to speak, quite incidentally. Therefore it may justifiably be asked whether, although the missing narrative of this appearance of Jesus to Peter alone is not reproduced, it is not at least utilized. For the dialogue refers in its first part only to the relationship between Christ and Peter, and to the commission which is given to Peter. We have spoken of the hypothesis that the lost conclusion of Mark lies behind this passage.[87]

Was it not this narrative, taken up into John, ch. 21, which Matthew found in a somewhat different version, transferred back into the life of the Incarnate One, and so connected with the event at Caesarea Philippi? The very content of the dialogue between Jesus and Peter in John 21:15 ff. might favour this hypothesis. It deals indeed with the same question as Matthew 16:17 ff.; that which in Matthew is a promise appears here in the imperative, as a commission of the Risen One to Peter: 'Feed my lambs.'

It must be conceded that this hypothesis is attractive. At the least, we may reckon with the possibility that it is correct. Yet after all it is only a hypothesis. For we possess no conclusion of Mark which narrates the appearance to Peter alone, and John, ch. 21, does not say that its account deals with such an appearance.[88]

On the other hand, it is improbable to me that Jesus never *during his lifetime* explained the title 'Rock'. For it must be assumed that it was during his lifetime that he gave the title to Peter. It is true that 'Sons of Thunder', the title of the sons of Zebedee, is also nowhere explained. But that may be connected with the fact that the gospel tradition naturally had less interest in them. In reality, Jesus must have explained their title

[86] See above, pp. 63 f.      [87] See above, pp. 61 f.      [88] See above, pp. 61 f.

also. On this ground I cannot agree with the above-mentioned hypothesis without further evidence.

But must we not consider another occasion *within* the lifetime of Jesus when the explanation of the title could have been given? It has been supposed that there might have been a situation *similar* to that at Caesarea Philippi.[89] On that other occasion, however, Peter did not express the political Messianic image, but uttered the confession of Jesus' divine sonship, so that vs. 17 is in place as the answer of Jesus. In dealing with this verse we should think above all of John 6:66 ff.,[90] where we actually have a confession of Peter which gives a direct parallel to the verses in Matthew 16:17 ff. and so to the special tradition of Matthew concerning Peter's confession. To the question whether the disciples also want to leave Jesus, Peter here answers: 'We have come to the faith and the knowledge that you are the "Holy One of God".' Since the expression 'Holy One of God' is synonymous with 'Son of God',[91] the parallelism with Matthew 16:17 ff. is clear. From the Gospel of John we can derive no direct indication, but only an indirect one, concerning the occasion on which Peter spoke these words. They follow the narrative of the miraculous feeding. But in the Gospel of John this narrative is viewed in connection with that other miracle of bread which occurs in the Eucharist. This points us to the possibility that the Fourth Evangelist knew a tradition in which Peter made the confession at the Last Supper. This is suggested also by the fact that the Gospel of John in this very context speaks of the treason of Judas Iscariot, which Jesus, according to the Synoptics, predicted on that very occasion.

In this case, however, we are not restricted to a pure hypothesis. Rather, we have in one of the Synoptic Gospels a parallel text. To be sure, it does not contain the Christological confession, but it does contain a confession of Peter to Jesus and above all an exact parallel to the second part of the tradition utilized in Matthew 16:17 ff. This parallel is in the form of a commission to Peter to strengthen the brethren and it is given in this very framework, that is, the framework of the Last Supper. It is the already often mentioned passage Luke 22:31, which resembles Matthew 16:17 ff., not indeed in its literal wording, but in its meaning. It is embedded in the prediction of Peter's denial: 'Simon, Simon, Behold, Satan has asked for you in order to sift you in the sieve like wheat. But I have prayed

[89] So K. L. Schmidt, 'Die Kirche des Urchristentums' (*Festgabe für Ad. Deissmann*, 1927, p. 283).
[90] Similarly Bernard Weiss (*Meyer's Kommentar*, 10th ed., 1910), *ad loc.*
[91] See O. Cullmann, *Die Christologie des Neuen Testaments*, 2nd ed., 1958, pp. 287, 292 (Eng. Tr., *The Christology of the New Testament*, 1959, pp. 280, 295).

or you that your faith may not waver, and do you, when you have
urned, strengthen your brethren.' Peter then said to him: 'Lord, with
ou I am ready to go even to prison and death.' Jesus replied: 'I tell you,
Peter, the cock will not crow today until you have denied me three
imes.' Peter's readiness for martyrdom is also presupposed by the parallel
n John 6:66, where the confession to the 'Holy One of God' is the
answer to Jesus' question: 'Do you also want to go away?'

The dialogue in Luke thus contains three things: (1) The vow of Peter
that he will go with his Lord to prison and to death. (2) The prediction of
Peter's denial. (3) The command of Jesus to Peter to strengthen his
brothers after his conversion.

Was not this the true context also of our saying in Matthew 16:17 ff.?[92]
If so, we could easily understand how Matthew could hit upon the idea of
connecting it with the event at Caesarea Philippi. There, too, the thing
first reported in Mark is a—falsely conceived—confession of Peter, even
though it is of another kind than in this passage, where it takes the form of
a declaration that he is ready to stand courageously for his Lord. In addition, however, John 6:66 shows that the tradition underlying all three
texts has joined together the Christological confession and the vow of
loyalty. On this view Matthew could have had a further reason for intro-
ducing the saying in the place where we now read it. In Luke Simon,
together with the other disciples, is brought into connection with *Satan*
and this occurs specifically with reference to the suffering of Christ, which
is indirectly in view also in the prediction of the denial. The parallel in
John 6:66 seems also to have known a mention of the devil in this connection: 'One of you is a devil.' But there it is definitely not Peter but
Judas. Was this, perhaps, also a contributing factor in the choice of the
scene of Caesarea Philippi, where Peter is addressed at the end as Satan?
Did not Matthew desire by joining the two traditions to supplement the
one portrait of Peter by the other?

I am inclined to presuppose that the framework of the Passion story
as Luke gives it was the setting also for the saying reproduced by Matthew.
My reason is that ch. 21 of the Gospel of John, which in many respects
appears to be a still more direct parallel to Matthew 16:17 ff. ('feed my
sheep'), seems consciously to refer to a tradition according to which there
occurred during the lifetime of Jesus a scene such as Luke 22:31-4
portrays. The dialogue between the Risen One and Peter, in John 21:15 ff.,
presents a direct replica of that dialogue in Luke 22:31-4 between the

[92] A similar yet somewhat different position is taken by R. Liechtenhan, *op. cit.*,
pp. 9 ff.

Incarnate One and Peter, and probably can only be understood in the light of the latter passage.[93] It is striking that we find here exactly the same connection between vow, prediction, and command that we have in Luke 22:31-4, except that in John these words correspond to the post-resurrection situation. For the first time since the prediction of the denial Peter again stands before his Lord, but now he stands before the Risen One. In place of the threefold denial by Peter comes now his threefold assurance: 'Yes, Lord, you know that I love you.' To the vow of Peter that he will go with the Lord to prison and to death corresponds the prophecy of the martyrdom. In place of the command to strengthen his brothers there comes here the command to feed the sheep of Christ, which shows the common possession of the same tradition that we find in Matthew 16:17 ff. The picture of the 'sheep' he is to 'feed' implies that of the 'flock', and this concept, as we shall show,[94] is closely related to that of the 'church' in Matthew 16:18.

Some scholars, as we have seen above, assume that the basis for Matthew 16:17 ff. was a resurrection appearance to Peter which has been used in John 21:15 ff.[95] On the basis of the inner and formal relationship between Matthew 16:17 ff., Luke 22:31 ff., John 6:66, and John 21:15 ff., I also assume a relationship between John 21:15 ff. and Matthew 16:17 ff. But I do so in the reverse sense; John 21:15 ff. attests a knowledge of a narrative from the passion story of the Incarnate One; according to this narrative Jesus, after the Last Supper, on the evening before the crucifixion, and on the occasion of Peter's assurance that he will follow his Lord to death, predicts the denial, but at the same time predicts also Peter's conversion and the founding of his flock on Peter as the rock. This connection is present in Luke 22:31-4.

We thus confirm the following three-cornered relationship: Matthew 16 and Luke 22 agree in predicting the leading role of Peter in the future fellowship of the disciples; Matthew 16 and John 6 agree in the confession of Peter: 'You are the Son [the Holy One] of God'; John 6 and Luke 22 agree both in the vow of Peter that he will follow Jesus and in the framework of the Last Supper in which the scene takes place. We may make in addition the following observation: John 21, with its reference to the denial of Peter, presupposes the same framework as do John 6 and Luke 22; John 21, like Matthew 16 and Luke 22, presup-

---

[93] This is contested by M. Goguel in *L'Eglise primitive*, 1947, p. 192, and *Jésus*, 1950, p. 390 (see above, p. 62), probably in connection with his unconvincing thesis that the denial of Jesus by Peter is unhistorical ('Did Peter Deny his Lord? A Conjecture', *Harvard Theological Review*, 1932, pp. 1 ff.).

[94] See below, p. 203.     [95] See above, pp. 186 f.

poses the prediction or the commission of the leading role of Peter in the Church. We are driven to the conclusion that behind the three narratives, Matthew 16:17 ff., Luke 22:31 ff., and John 6:66 ff., there lies as *common source* a narrative which belongs to an older tradition and must have been known also to the author of John 21. We can reconstruct its main content: At the Last Supper (or immediately thereafter) Peter says to Jesus: 'You are the Son of God', and he promises to follow him even to death. Jesus answers that God has given Peter this revelation concerning him, and he foretells Peter's denial, but at the same time he adds that Peter will have to fulfil a special task towards the company of disciples, which will fall into the same temptation he is to meet.

He who considers without prejudice these complex relationships between the relevant passages in Matthew 16, Luke 22, and John 21 will have to concede that the transfer of the promise to Peter into the framework of the Last Supper is no arbitrary hypothesis; indeed, he must concede that it has better textual support than the popular hypothesis, which in itself is not impossible, that the setting of the words was a resurrection appearance.[96]

We conclude: the saying in Matthew 16:17 ff. most probably belongs to the Passion story; it was originally transmitted in connection with the prediction of Peter's denial, but was placed by Matthew in another setting. We shall see later[97] that the immediate nearness of the death of Jesus, and above all the connection with the Last Supper, make the saying concerning the 'Church' particularly intelligible. We are dealing here with a very strong exegetical probability. Nevertheless, I note expressly that *the interpretation as a whole that is given in what follows does not stand or fall with the acceptance of this theory concerning the original setting.*

[96] I venture to hope that my critics will re-examine my thesis in the form I have given it both in the above-cited essay in the T. W. Manson memorial volume (see above, p. 186, note 84) and with less detail in the above discussion. When A. Vögtle, *op. cit.*, *Biblische Zeitschrift*, 1958, p. 92, rejected it, he knew only the discussion in the first edition and the intimations in my *Christology of the New Testament*. H. Lehmann, *op. cit.*, p. 63, likewise considered only the parallel in Luke 22:31 ff. when he felt forced to reject the transfer of the scene into the Passion Story. Critical expressions concerning my thesis come also from P. Gaechter (*Zeitschrift für katholische Theologie*, 1953, pp. 331 ff.), F. M. Braun (*Revue Thomiste*, 1953, pp. 395 f.), Y. Congar (*La vie intellectuelle*, 1953, p. 20), and J. Dejaifre (*Nouv. Revue theol.*, 1953, pp. 220 f.); some of them are quite willing to leave verses 17-19 in the framework of the Caesarea scene.

[97] See below, p. 197. The theological relation to the Passion is emphasized very strongly, though to be sure on the basis of the narrative framework, by Karl Barth, *Kirchliche Dogmatik*, II, 2, 1942, pp. 482 ff.

### 3. *Genuineness and Meaning of the Saying*

We must first test whether the reasons that have been urged against the genuineness are valid. The assumption of earlier opponents of the genuineness, that the verses were lacking originally even in Matthew and were inserted into the text only later under the influence of Roman claims, we seldom find today in this form.[98] Recently, however, the observation that possibly Irenaeus did not have the saying about the keys in his text of Matthew has led to the renewal of this hypothesis in the form that starting from Antioch this promise entered the text about 190.[99] For the most part, however, the thesis of spuriousness is defended today in the form that Matthew has reproduced here a saying that was not uttered by Jesus but created by the Church. In that case, however, it must be demanded at the start that the defenders of this thesis make clear the circumstances and reasons that led the Church to create such a saying as early as the days before Matthew was written.

This demand is the more urgent since the great antiquity and the Palestinian origin of the section may today be considered beyond question. This is shown by the quite Semitic linguistic character of this section. On this point, in fact, almost all scholars are united, whether they accept or reject the genuineness.[1] We have observed that even Bultmann, who is particularly emphatic in denying that Jesus spoke these words, has always claimed that the Palestinian church must have created the saying. Above all it is emphasized here, and probably correctly, that the saying could hardly have arisen first in the Greek Dispersion, because in the Greek, and so in the gospel text as we have it, the word play here plainly intended is not contained at all. Only in the German translation is it restored: 'You are rock (Fels), and upon this rock (Felsen) I will build my Church.' In Greek Simon's title reads *Petros*, with the masculine ending. We have seen that the name *Kepha* was reproduced in Greek by Petr*os*. But Jesus says that he will build his Church upon this Petr*a*. The words that should correspond do not really correspond here. In the Aramaic, however, we

---

[98] However, see O. J. F. Seitz, 'Upon This Book' (*JBL*, 1950, pp. 329 ff.) and W. E. Bundy, *Jesus and the First Three Gospels*, 1955, pp. 293 ff. K. L. Schmidt, *Die Kirche des Urchristentums*, p. 281, rightly calls it 'too clumsy to be taken seriously'.

[99] So W. L. Dulière, 'La péricope sur le pouvoir des clefs. Son absence dans le Texte de Matthieu aux mains d'Irénée' (*La nouvelle Clio*, 1954, pp. 73 ff.). Yet even he shows that Irenaeus knew vs. 17. (See above, p. 165.)

[1] So also A. Harnack, 'Der Spruch über Petrus als den Felsen der Kirche: Matt. XVI, 17 f.' (*Sitzungsbericht der Berliner Akademie der Wissenschaften*, 1918, pp. 637 ff.). W. Dulière, *op. cit.*, believes that this after all is sufficiently explained by the origin at Antioch.

have both times the same word *Kepha*: 'You are *Kepha* and upon this *Kepha* I will build my Church.' Thus here the name and the thing are exactly identical. Therefore we must assume that the saying was originally coined in Aramaic.[2]

The Semitic character is confirmed by various other observations: the designation of the father of Peter in *bar-yônâ*,[3] the expression 'flesh and blood' for 'men';[4] the word pair 'bind and loose';[5] then also the strophic rhythm—three strophes of three lines each—which is found similarly in other sayings of Jesus, for example, Matthew 11:7–9 and 11:25–30;[6] and further the illustration of the rock as foundation, to which there is an exact parallel in the rabbinical literature, where Abraham is mentioned as the rock of the world.[7]

The fact that only Matthew gives the saying also points to the Palestinian origin of the tradition.[8] Still another consideration can be cited to show that the tradition is very early. The story would scarcely have been handed on at a time when Peter no longer stood at the head of the Jerusalem church and James was already the leader there. The saying must thus have been transmitted at a time when Peter was still in Jerusalem.[9] The very early character of the tradition, which is vouched for by the Palestinian character of the verses, naturally does not prove beyond question that the utterance must come from Jesus, but it nevertheless is an important *presupposition* for that conclusion.

We have seen that the *chief objection* to its genuineness concerns the

[2] M. Goguel, *L'Eglise primitive*, 1947, p. 189, note 4, finds this argument indecisive, since in a play on words the correspondence need not be complete.

[3] See above, p. 23, on the thesis of R. Eisler in *Jesous basileus ou basileusas*, p. 67.

[4] In the N. T. in I Cor. 15:50; Gal. 1:16; Eph. 6:12; Heb. 2:14. Frequent in Jewish literature (Sirach 14:18), but not yet in the O. T.

[5] אסר and שרא. See below, pp. 210 ff.

[6] See J. Jeremias, *Angelos*, 1926, pp. 107 ff., and especially A. Oepke, *op. cit.*, pp. 150 f.

[7] See the rabbinical explanation of Isaiah, ch. 51:1, in Strack-Billerbeck, *Kommentar zum N. T. aus Talmud und Midrasch*, Vol. I, p. 733; J. Jeremias, *Golgotha*, p. 73: 'When God looked upon Abraham, who was to appear, he said: Behold, I have found a rock on which I can build and base the world. Therefore he called Abraham a rock.'

[8] H. Strathmann, 'Die Stellung des Petrus in der Urkirche' (*Zeitschrift für systematische Theologie*, 1943, pp. 255 ff.; see above, p. 27), in connection with his view of the geographical origin of each Gospel, assigns this saying to the Antiochene tradition. In opposition to this, W. Michaelis, *op. cit.*, p. 353, makes the point that in Antioch Greek was spoken.

[9] W. Michaelis, *Das Evangelium nach Matthäus*, p. 350, actually thinks that the reason Luke did not include this saying was that it found its fulfilment only in the earliest period. Others, however, are of the opinion that it was precisely later Palestinian disputes between Peter and James (relatives of Jesus) that could have given occasion to the creation of the saying. (So K. Goetz; R. Bultmann thinks of debates in Palestine over the Law; M. Goguel of discussions that took place after 70.) But we know too little of such disputes to explain on this basis the origin of the saying. According to J. Jeremias, the early character of the saying is clear also from the fact that we find such early traces of its use, in the N. T. itself: Gal. 1:16–18 and 2:9.

N

mention of the '*Church*'. Jesus, it is said, cannot have spoken of the Church, since he proclaimed only the coming Kingdom of God.

The first thing to note, in reply to this claim, is that it is correct that the word for 'Church' (*ekklesia*) occurs in the Gospels only *one* other time. This, too, is in the Gospel of Matthew, ch. 18:17: 'If (the brother who has sinned) does not listen to them, tell it to the Church.' The genuineness of this passage also is vigorously disputed; in addition, the meaning here is not the same.

These statistics concerning the use of the word, however, cannot be decisive. The issue in question is rather whether not only the word but also the thing that the word designates is lacking. That is how we must put the question. In this connection it has justly been recalled[10] how striking it is that in the entire letter of Paul to Rome the word 'cross' does not occur a single time, although the letter treats of the atoning death of Christ from beginning to end. It has further been pointed out that in the Gospel of John also the Greek word for Church (*ekklesia*) is nowhere found, and yet it cannot be doubted that this Gospel speaks of the Church; indeed, the peculiar character of this Gospel consists precisely in the fact that it connects the historical Jesus with the Church.[11]

The problem lies elsewhere. First of all we must be on our guard against falling into the mistake of most exegetes, who think that they must oppose the genuineness of the utterance because it mentions the 'Church'. They assume it to be self-evident that the word for 'Church' can only designate an organized Church in the later sense. Then they seek to show that Jesus cannot have held this anachronistic view of the Church. Such a procedure, however, must be rejected.

We first must emphasize that the Greek word for Church, *ekklesia, does not designate anything like a Christian creation*, but belongs to the Jewish sphere.[12] We still find the word in this original meaning in the New Testament, in Acts 7:38: 'It is this (Moses) who was in the *ekklesia* in the wilderness with the angel . . .' In this passage *ekklesia* means the people of Israel whom Moses led through the wilderness. In the Greek translation of the Old Testament, the Septuagint, *ekklesia* occurs about a

---

[10] See A. Oepke, *op. cit.*, p. 114.

[11] See O. Cullmann, *Urchristentum und Gottesdienst*, 2nd ed., 1950, pp. 39 ff. (Eng. Tr., *Early Christian Worship*, 1953, pp. 38 ff.; cf. *Les sacrements dans l'Évangile johannique*, 1951, pp. 9 ff.). On the question of the Church in the Gospel of John, see also E. Gaugler, 'Die Bedeutung der Kirche in den johanneischen Schriften' (*Internationale kirchliche Zeitschrift*, 1924, pp. 97 ff.).

[12] See L. Rost, *Die Vorstufen von Kirche und Synagoge im Alten Testament*, 1938; further, O. Michel, *Das Zeugnis des Neuen Testaments von der Gemeinde*, 1941, pp. 5 ff.; J. Y. Campbell, *Journal of Theological Studies*, 1948, pp. 130 ff.

hundred times, and in these cases it usually translates the Hebrew *qahal*,
which, when connected with the genitive *Yahweh*, 'of God', always designates the people of Israel with a reference to redemptive history. There is a
series of still other Hebrew and Aramaic words that can be rendered in
Greek by *ekklesia*.[13] All of these expressions, of which some can also be
translated into Greek by *synagoge*, refer to Israel as the people of God; one
of them (*kᵉnishta*) can also mean 'separate synagogue'.

We must start from the meaning 'people of God' when we ask the question whether or not Jesus can have spoken of the Church. Let us then put
in place of the all too modern word 'Church' the expression 'people of
God': 'on this rock I will build my people of God'. In this sense Jesus
did not have to create anew the concept used. It already existed; indeed,
it was *quite common* in Jewish thinking. Every Jew was certain that he was
a member of this *ekklesia*. As soon as a group within late Judaism became
conscious that the role of the people of God, to which Israel as a whole
had proved disloyal, was being realized in them and through them, the
concept of the *ekklesia* in its Semitic form necessarily moved into the foreground. This was especially true in the Jewish 'congregation of the New
Covenant', which has become so well known through the recent discoveries
near the Dead Sea.[14] The ancient prophetic idea of the 'remnant' of Israel
(Isa. 7:3; 10:21) leads directly to such a revitalization of the people of God
consciousness in small separate communities.

Above all, the Jewish Messianic expectation includes the conception of
a Messianic community and is inconceivable without it.[15] Here we should

[13] Hebrew equivalents: *qahal*, *edhah*, *ṣibbur*, *kᵉneseth*; Aramaic: *qᵉhala*, *ṣibbura*, and
most frequently *kᵉnishta*. On all lexicographical questions it is sufficient to refer to
K. L. Schmidt's basic article on ἐκκλησία in G. Kittel's *Theologisches Wörterbuch
zum N. T.*; it carries further the older but helpfully orienting compilation of H. Cremer,
in H. Cremer-Kögel, *Biblisch-theologisches Wörterbuch des neutestamentlichen Griechischen*,
11th ed., 1923. There is much in favour of *kᵉnishta* as the basic word (K. L. Schmidt).
Whether, however, it is to be preferred because it likewise designates the building I would
assert with less confidence, since indeed the figure of the building is included in the
general idea of the people of God, and so is also implied by the phrase *qehal Yahweh*.
(See on this point Ph. Vielhauer, *Oikodome, das Bild vom Bau in der christlichen Literatur
vom Neuen Testament bis Clemens Alexandrinus*, 1939.) I would prefer, with M. J. Lagrange,
*Commentaire, ad loc.*, to leave open the question as to which Aramaic word should be
considered most likely. Indeed, it is not of basic importance, for the important thing is that
all of these words belong to the thought world of the people of God. Lagrange considers
both *qᵉhala* and *kᵉnishta* as possible Aramaic equivalents, Zahn *kᵉnishta*, Bultmann
and Michaelis *qᵉhala*. Schlatter points to the Hebrew words *qahal* and *edhah*.

[14] Examples taken from the earlier discovery (see L. Rost, *Die Damaskusschrift*, in
*Kleine Texte*, 1933): *edhah* in vii, 20; x, 4, 8; xiii, 13; *qahal* in vii, 17; xi, 22 (S. Schechter's edition). See also O. Michel, *Das Zeugnis des Neuen Testaments von der Gemeinde*,
1941, pp. 17 ff. With regard to the new discovery see among others K. G. Kuhn, 'Die
in Palästina gefundenen hebräischen Texte und das Neue Testament' (*Zeitschrift für
Theologie und Kirche*, 1950, pp. 194 ff.). See above, p. 65.

[15] Enoch, 38:1; 53:6; 62:8; 83:8; 84:5.

recall the Son of Man designation; in the Book of Daniel (ch. 7:9-28) it refers to 'the people of the saints', and on the basis of the idea of representation is applied to a single personality. But an eschatological community is the essential possession also of the Messiah of the official Jewish hope.

In so far as we, in agreement with the entire gospel tradition, ascribe to Jesus the Messianic consciousness in any form whatsoever, we should have to assume, even if we had no text on the subject, that his thinking included the idea of the eschatological people of God that belonged to him. If he considered himself to be the Danielic Son of Man (Mark 14:62 and parallels), he also knew that according to Daniel 7:18, 27 the Son of Man represents the 'people of the saints'.[16] The concept of representation, which is indispensable for the understanding of the Old Testament redemptive history, is fundamental for Jesus' knowledge of his own redemptive work. When he speaks of the people of God that he is founding, he certainly thinks of the 'remnant of Israel', which will represent this people in its entirety and about which the Gentiles will be gathered.[17]

Compared with the ancient Jewish idea of the people of God, the new feature which Jesus brought is that this *ekklesia*, this people of God, is reconstituted in view of the end. It is reconstituted on the basis of what he conceives to be his special Messianic deed, the suffering of the Servant of God. In the creation of this new people of God built upon this basis consists his specific work on earth.

In this *Jewish* sense there is an 'ecclesiology' even in the thinking of Jesus, and it is solidly anchored in his 'Christology'. Therefore we can understand it when a scholar such as Bultmann, who denies that Jesus had any Messianic consciousness, also challenges the genuineness of the word concerning the *ekklesia*. He who, on the contrary, is of the opinion that Jesus regarded himself as the Messiah, even if in the special sense of the Son of Man and the Suffering Servant of God, should refrain even on this basis from rejecting too quickly the genuine-

---

[16] To have centred attention on this idea is the lasting merit of F. Kattenbusch, 'Der Quellort der Kirchenidee' (*Festgabe für Harnack*, 1921, pp. 142 ff.). T. W. Manson and R. Newton Flew hold the same idea; see above, p. 171, note 37

[17] K. L. Schmidt and F. Kattenbusch also assume that the 'remnant', the 'separate congregation', represents Israel in its entirety. For this reason I consider unjustified the criticism that Oepke, *op. cit.*, pp. 114 ff., 140, who here agrees with R. Bultmann, makes against K. L. Schmidt and F. Kattenbusch. The idea of a Pharisaic separation is not at all essential to the idea of the remnant; the former only presents the danger to which the latter *can* lead. The fact that the group of Jesus comprises precisely the *lost* sheep excludes all Pharisaism. See below, p. 197.

ness of Matthew 16:17 ff.; as Messiah Jesus must have had in view a community.[18]

Connected with this special way in which Jesus conceived his Messianic work is the fact that the people of God is no longer simply identical with the Jewish nation. Even the prophetic idea of the remnant and the preaching of John the Baptist had already purified the conception of the people of God in this sense. Jesus knew himself to be sent to the 'lost sheep of the house of Israel' (Matt. 10:6; 15:24), but this very limitation to the *lost* sheep finally breaks through every national restriction and likewise excludes every Pharisaic-sectarian separation. It is true that the redemptive road to the founding of the people of God goes by way of Israel. But the very reduction to this fellowship within Israel creates the presupposition for the realization of the people of God that is to include all mankind.

The Messianic reconstitution of the people of God aims at the 'new *covenant*', which Jesus announces and likewise establishes *at the Last Supper*, on the evening before his death. Covenant and people of God belong together.[19] If my theory is correct that Jesus gave the promise of Matthew 16:17 ff. in the setting indicated by Luke 22:31 f., and so in connection with the Last Supper and the words spoken there, then *in this context* the prediction of the building of the *ekklesia* stands out in unusually bold relief. The connecting of the new building with Jesus' Messianic work of suffering unto death then becomes particularly clear. But it also is clear on other grounds.

Jesus speaks of *his ekklesia*. To me this does not seem, as has been claimed, irreconcilable with the fact that in Judaism the concept involved was the people *of God*, the $q^e hal Yahweh$, the *ekklesia* of the Lord (Num. 16:3; Deut. 7:6). It is possible, in fact, for the Messiah-Son of Man to speak of *his ekklesia*.[20] In this capacity he also can say that he will 'build' this people. There is no contradiction here with the fact that this building is the work of God.[21]

If one reads the words of Matthew 16:17 in the light of this essentially Jewish idea and takes account of the fact that in the time of Jesus *qahal*—

[18] See P. Volz, *Die Eschatologie der jüdischen Gemeinde im neutestamentlichen Zeitalter*, 1934, p. 49. This is very strongly stressed also by F. J. Leenhardt, *Etudes sur l'Eglise dans le Nouveau Testament*, 1940, p. 16. See also O. Linton, *Das Problem der Urkirche in der neuern Forschung*, 1932, p. 148: 'The Messiah is not a private person. Essential to his rule is a Church.'

[19] See L. Rost, *Die Vorstufen von Kirche und Synagoge im Alten Testament*, 1938, pp. 18 ff. On the Church and the Last Supper see F. Kattenbusch, *op. cit.*

[20] Matt. 13:41 speaks of the 'Kingdom of the Son of Man'.

[21] The difficulty seen here by K. L. Schmidt, *Die Kirche des Urchristentums*, p. 288, I do not feel. Yet E. Klostermann, *Das Matthäusevangelium*, p. 140, also finds it objectionable that Jesus says 'my' Church.

*ekklesia* was a quite common concept, firmly rooted in Jewish thinking, one really cannot *on that basis* deny the genuineness of the saying. I therefore maintain my statement, which Bultmann took as the starting-point of his recent denial of this genuineness; I hold that there is no scientific justification for this denial. For sound scientific method requires that we explain the concepts first of all according to the sense that they have in the environment to which the writing belongs whose text is to be explained. It is not right to start from a later concept of the *ekklesia* and then conclude that it cannot possibly be ascribed to Jesus. It must first of all be asked whether there is not an *ekklesia* concept that corresponds to the Jewish thinking whose categories Jesus took over.

Furthermore, it can be shown that this very image of the *rock* is connected in Judaism with the idea of the community. Reference has properly been made to the conception of the holy rock. But we can discern a still more precise context if we recall that in the *Book of Daniel*, which Jesus must have known, the Son of Man concept, so central for him, is connected with the conception of the Messianic 'people of the saints', which brings to an end the world empires. In the same Book of Daniel (ch. 2:34 f., 44 f.) we read of a block of stone which is *interpreted to mean an empire* that will shatter all empires.[22] This block of stone separates from the mountain, smashes the statue of Nebuchadnezzar, and then grows into a great mountain, which fills the entire world. Already in Judaism this stone had been referred to the Messiah.[23] Still more important for our study, however, is the fact that the saying of Jesus in Luke 20:17 f. certainly has in mind this passage of Daniel: 'What means this saying of Scripture: The stone which the builders rejected has become the cornerstone? He who falls on this stone will be shattered; on whomsoever it falls, it crushes him.'[24]—In the designation of Abraham as the rock we have already found a Jewish preparation for the view that Jesus, and later the apostles,[25] become the rock, the foundation.[26]

---

[22] To have shown these connections is the merit of Joachim Jeremias; see his book, *Golgotha*, pp. 77 ff.

[23] Strack-Billerbeck, *Kommentar zum N. T. aus Talmud und Midrasch*, Vol. I, p. 877.

[24] The verb λικμᾶν is explained only by Dan. 2:34 f., 44 f. R. Graber, *Petrus der Fels*, 1948, p. 29, shows that the relation to the Daniel passage is much closer when seen from Matthew 21:42 ff. than it is from the parallel Lucan passage, from which J. Jeremias starts. This, however, is the case only if vs. 44, which is lacking in good textual witnesses, is original. The discussions of R. Graber are perhaps particularly fitted to prove this originality. R. Bohren, *Das Problem der Kirchenzucht im Neuen Testament*, 1952, pp. 32 ff., believes that he sees another connection, which however has in view only the prophet. This is Jer. 1:18 f.: 'I make you today an iron pillar and a bronze wall . . . they will fight against you, but will not overcome you.'

[25] See below, pp. 222 f.

[26] See above, p. 193.

Moreover, the image of the *building* of a community is fully intelligible from the Jewish manner of thinking and expression.[27] The Old Testament speaks of the *House* of Israel (Num. 12:7; Ruth 4:11; Amos 9:11; etc.). Jesus also uses this expression in Matthew 10:6 and 15:24. Therefore the illustration, in its application to the Church, is quite common with the writers of the New Testament books, particularly in I Timothy 3:15, which speaks of the house of God, which is the *ekklesia* of the living God, and further in I Peter 2:5 (the spiritual house), Ephesians 2:22, Hebrews 3:2 ff.; 10:21. We must further recall that the idea of 'edifying'[28] is common in application to the fellowship (Amos 9:11 f.; in the New Testament particularly Acts 9:31). Paul also uses it, originally not in the specific individualistic and pietistic sense, but in the meaning that the illustration contains of the building up of the Church.[29] Of especial importance for our question, however, is the fact that Jesus himself, as we shall see,[30] speaks in another saying concerning the fellowship founded by him; he here uses the analogous illustration of the *temple* that he will rebuild.

\* \* \*

In our passage it is presupposed that the people of God will be formed while the present age still lasts. The future 'I will build' could perhaps mislead us to identify its realization with that of the purely future Kingdom of God which comes at the end. But what follows, the saying concerning 'binding and loosing', and particularly the contrast between earth and heaven, shows that Jesus means a people that already appears in this age.

This very fact, however, leads many to deny that Jesus spoke this saying. Is it possible that Jesus, who certainly announced the Kingdom which comes at the end, actually expected the realization of the people of God *in this present age*? In the last analysis this problem of time stands in the background of the entire debate. In considering it, we wish to distinguish from one another the following limited questions: 1. Did Jesus lay the foundation of a Messianic fellowship even in his lifetime? 2. Did he expect that even after his death this age would still continue, and that then especially this fellowship would be built up, before the end would come?

As we begin to consider the first question, we should note at the outset that it is given a false perspective if it is placed in the form of an alter-

[27] For all details I refer to the careful study of Ph. Vielhauer, *Oikodome, das Bild vom Bau in der christlichen Literatur vom N. T. bis Clemens Alexandrinus*, 1939.
[28] οἰκοδομεῖν.
[29] I Cor. 8:1–10; Rom. 14:19; 15:2, 20.
[30] See below, pp. 204 f.

native: present *or* future Messianic community. The Jewish idea of the people of God—*qahal*—*ekklesia* cannot be forced into this alternative. Rather it includes both present and future. Particularly, however, it must be considered that for Jesus, in view of his Messianic self-consciousness, present and future, promise and fulfilment, even if distinguished, nevertheless do not represent opposites; on the contrary, in his person the fulfilment has already been anticipated. Particularly in reference to the Messianic community we must not say; present *or* future, promise *or* fulfilment.[31]

Perhaps the quite one-sided view of Albert Schweitzer is responsible for the fact that many are still unable to see the problem except in the form of an either-or alternative. Before Schweitzer the scholars, in their presentation of the teaching of Jesus, were all too quick to push eschatology into the background or completely discard it. They described it by using the slogan: 'a concession conditioned by contemporary Jewish ideas'. Thus they held that the essential thing in it was only the relation to the contemporary situation. For this reason the reaction of Albert Schweitzer was entirely necessary. But it in turn succumbed again to the temptation to survey the entire teaching of Jesus in a false time perspective; it presented his teaching as though Jesus expected everything from the future. In reality it is the very tension between 'already fulfilled' and 'not yet fulfilled' that is characteristic of the New Testament conception of time.[32] This conception, indeed, runs through the entire New Testament; it already marks the attitude of Jesus in the Synoptic Gospels.[33] Even in Jesus' own preaching the Kingdom of God is on the one hand still not present, for it comes only at the end; and yet in the presence of Jesus it has already broken in: 'If I cast out demons by the Spirit of God, then the Kingdom has already come to you' (Matt. 12:28). 'Tell John what you hear and see: the blind see again, the lame walk, lepers are cleansed, the deaf hear, the dead rise, and to the poor the good news is preached' (Matt. 11:4 f.).

Thus there can be no doubt that Jesus himself reckons with such an anticipation of the Kingdom of God; in his person the decision has already occurred, even if the completion is expected only in the final time. It would curtail the preaching of Jesus to accept as valid only the one or the

---

[31] On what follows see my book, to appear later, on the *Eschatology of the New Testament*. In it I shall investigate more intensively this aspect of the problem.

[32] See O. Cullmann, *Christus und die Zeit*, 1948, pp. 72 ff. (Eng. Tr., *Christ and Time*, 1950, pp. 84 ff.).

[33] See W. G. Kümmel, *Verheissung und Erfüllung* (*Abhandlungen zur Theologie des Alten und Neuen Testaments*), 2nd ed., 1953 (Eng. Tr., *Promise and Fulfilment*, 1957).

other aspect. He who regards as decisive only the sayings concerning the future should ask himself what it is then that really distinguishes Jesus at all from other prophets. Promise was uttered by all prophets, even promise for a near future. But the new thing with Jesus is the very fact that even now there is a fulfilment.

It is doubtless universally conceded that after the death of Jesus, in *Primitive Christianity* and for *Paul*, this tension between present and future, promise and fulfilment, really exists. But in Primitive Christianity this does not mean, as the adherents of Albert Schweitzer in particular assert, a reinterpretation or falling away from the position of Jesus, who had spoken only of the future; rather, this tension is *already present for him*. There does exist on this point a certain difference between Jesus and the Primitive Church; Jesus is conscious that the fulfilment is present *in his person*, while the Primitive Church sees the fulfilment *in the Church*. But there is no conflict here at all. Rather, the fulfilment in the person of Jesus leads directly to the fulfilment in the Church, and the fulfilment in the Church points back in turn to the fulfilment in the person of Jesus.[34] Therefore it is not merely possible that Jesus also sees the people of God already beginning to be constituted in his day; we would almost have to postulate this even if we had no clear texts to prove it.

A direct contradiction between the future Kingdom of God and the already realized people of God is only a construction built on the basis of modern thinking. For Jesus the two aspects certainly do not coincide, but they do not form opposites, as we are inclined to believe on the basis of a modern thought pattern. The higher concept that even in Judaism unites both aspects, present and future, is this very idea of the 'people of God'. It is used here equally with reference to its present and its future realization, and as soon as the conviction is present that the end has already been anticipated, even if the completion is still to come, the distinction practically loses its importance.

Thus the foundation of the earthly people of God dates back in the time of the Incarnate One, even if it is really 'built up' only after his death. Jesus created the foundation for this people of God even in his lifetime. In order to prove this by texts, we again must refuse to be misled into regarding as decisive only the occurrence of the word *ekklesia*. We must

---

[34] This must be given unqualified emphasis in opposition to W. G. Kümmel's much esteemed essay, *Kirchenbegriff und Geschichtsbewusstsein in der Urgemeinde und bei Jesus*, 1943 (see above, p. 173). The point to note is that he sees here an irreconcilable parallelism of two related forms of the historical consciousness, and draws from this the conclusion that Matt. 16:17 ff. is spurious. The conclusions which W. G. Kümmel here draws seem to me in reality to contradict his own premises.

investigate whether the thing is not actually present in passages where the word is lacking. In this connection particular reference has properly been made to the forming of the group of the Twelve. The attempt has indeed been made to deny that Jesus did this and to transfer its origin into the later time of the Primitive Church.[35] But there really exists no necessity for doing this, and what is more, it is quite impossible to see how this group could have arisen as late as the time of the Primitive Church; on the contrary, it was necessary rather to take pains to re-establish it after the defection of Judas. But what could the establishing of this group mean if not the founding of the people of God which is to prepare for the Kingdom of God? The reference to the Jewish idea of the people of God is here quite plainly present. The number Twelve, indeed, must be connected with the number of the twelve tribes of Israel.

The most important thing, however, is not merely the *choice* of the twelve disciples; it is above all the *mission* they received from Jesus, that is, the role that he gives to this fellowship. It cannot be sufficiently emphasized that the command he gives in sending them forth refers to the identical *Messianic* functions that *Jesus himself* fulfils in his role of the 'Coming One'. Here it is confirmed that even in the present age the Messiah needs for his preparatory work a community, and that the group of the Twelve represents at least the start of the future Messianic *ekklesia*. We have seen that in his answer to the Baptist Jesus cites these facts as a sign that with his coming *the time of redemption has already broken in*: 'the blind see, the lame walk, lepers are cleansed, the dead rise, to the poor the good news is preached'. In a strikingly parallel manner Jesus commands his disciples when he sends them forth: 'Go to the lost sheep of the house of Israel and proclaim that the Kingdom of Heaven has come near . . . heal the sick, raise the dead, cleanse the lepers, cast out demons' (Matt. 11:4 f.; 10:7 f.). The analogy between this command and the answer to the Baptist deserves further consideration. For here it becomes clear that for Jesus not only his own coming but *also the existence and the work of the group of disciples is already the fulfilment and inbreaking of the time of redemption*. The same deeds that he himself does they also are to accomplish, as proof that the prophecy has already been fulfilled in him.[36]

---

[35] So, following many others, R. Bultmann, 'Die Frage nach der Echtheit . . .' (*Theologische Blätter*, 1941). On the contrary, the significance of the Twelve as a preliminary stage of the Church is emphasized with special force by G. Gloege, *Reich Gottes und Kirche im N. T.*, 1929, and also by H. D. Wendland, *Die Eschatologie des Reiches Gottes bei Jesus*, 1931.

[36] It is connected with this, as H. Riesenfeld points out in *Ämbetet i Nya Testamentet*, n.d., pp. 17 ff., that the metaphors with which Jesus' functions are described are transferred to the apostles.

Thus the forming and the sending forth of the group of disciples is quite closely connected with his Messianic conviction. When he also says, on the other hand, that they will not have completed visiting the cities of Israel before the Son of Man comes (Matt. 10:23)—a saying which moreover permits various interpretations[37]—it still remains true that the work of the group of disciples is a Messianic work, and that thus, even in the lifetime of Jesus, the fulfilment does not occur only in his person; rather, in these men the people of God has already begun to be realized.[38] We should understand in this way the saying concerning the fishers of men (Mark 1:17 and parallels) and that concerning the work in the harvest (Matt. 9:37 f.); and the parable of the fishnet (Matt. 13:47 ff.) confirms the provisional and yet anticipatory character of the catch of fish.

Where such things happen as Jesus enumerates in his answer to the Baptist (Matt. 11:4 f.), the question whether the Kingdom of God is future or present loses all point.[39] The anticipation of the Kingdom of God thus occurs here even in the lifetime of Jesus; the foundation of the people of God is laid, even if it also remains true that the real building is only carried out after the death of Jesus, on the basis of the new covenant. This *ekklesia* that is 'built' after the death of Jesus will be an anticipation of the Kingdom of God, but the group of disciples in the lifetime of Jesus is on its part an anticipation of that *ekklesia*.

Jesus regards the narrower and the wider group of disciples as a fellowship with a particular task. As such it already represents a realization. This is clear also from other passages; it appears, for example, when he speaks of his true family (Mark 3:33 ff. and parallels), and especially when he addresses the disciples as a 'flock', as he does in Luke 12:32: 'Fear not, little flock, for it has pleased your Father to give you the Kingdom'; and further in Matthew 26:31: 'I will smite the shepherd and the sheep of the flock will be scattered.' With this agrees also the already mentioned 'lost sheep of the house of Israel' (see also Matt. 9:36). We know from the Damascus Document that also in the Jewish 'community of the New Covenant', which has now become better known, the concept of the shepherd was common, and that the *ekklesia* concept is in reality expressed by this image.[40] In the remaining writings of the New Testament the desig-

[37] See O. Cullmann, *Le retour du Christ, Espérance de l'Eglise selon le Nouveau Testament*, 1943, pp. 23 f., and especially my *Eschatology of the New Testament*, which is in preparation.
[38] This should be stressed against A. Loisy, *L'Evangiles synoptiques*, p. 9, with whom R. Bultmann, *op. cit.*, column 275, allies himself when he writes that the fact that Jesus gathered disciples has nothing to do with the Church.
[39] Wherever the Kingdom of God is *a living reality*, this is the case. Think of Blumhardt. [40] See above, pp. 65 f., 195.

nations flock, shepherd, sheep, and feeding almost always refer to the
Church. We should think here above all of the Gospel of John: John 10:1
ff.; 21:16 ff., but also of I Corinthians 9:7 and Acts 20:28.[41]

\*  \*  \*

The fellowship that Jesus founded even in his lifetime does of course
point to the *future*. Only after his death will it develop, will it be 'built up'
in the real sense. We have seen that the Messianic consciousness must lead
to the founding of the Church. For Jesus, however, this consciousness
involves the necessity of his death. Therefore his death is the real starting-
point of the new people of God. The establishing of the Lord's Supper[42]
can only mean that the new fellowship is founded by his death. But here
the question arises whether for Jesus the time immediately after his
death is the time of the complete fulfilment or whether, before the end
comes, the time of anticipation begun by his earthly work will still continue for a while, and continue as the period of the Church. Matthew
16:17 ff. implies this second assumption. Before we deal with the question
whether this agrees with the general expectation of Jesus as we are able
to deduce it from the Synoptic Gospels, we still must study a very important utterance of Jesus. It seems to me to be an exact parallel to
Matthew 16:17 ff., and it also refers to the time after the death of Jesus.
I refer to the saying that Jesus spoke concerning the *temple* and that
obviously played a decisive role in his so-called trial.[43] To be sure, it was
—at least according to Mark 14:57 f.—false witnesses who accused Jesus
of having said: 'I will destroy this temple made by hands and in three
days build up another not made by hands.' Later also, however, at the
cross, a similar saying is ascribed to him by the passers-by. Moreover, it is
possible to explain wherein the *false* witness probably consisted, if we

[41] R. Bultmann, *op. cit.*, column 268, denies that in the Synoptic passages the idea of a
group is present: in the Gospel of John, he claims, the words have a quite different
meaning.

[42] See above, p. 197.

[43] M. Goguel, *Jésus*, 2nd ed., 1950, pp. 330 ff. (Eng. Tr., *The Life of Jesus*, 1933, pp.
507 ff.), speaks in support of the genuineness of this saying, but does not connect it
with Matt. 16:17 ff. (He relates it, on the contrary, to the parable of the vinedressers;
extension to the Gentiles.) As arguments in favour of genuineness he points out that the
prediction of the destruction of the Temple cannot be a prophecy '*ex eventu*', since indeed the temple was destroyed in 70 by fire, not by earthquake, as the saying of Jesus
presupposes ('there will not remain one stone upon another'); he further cites the fact
that to Stephen also a similar saying is ascribed (Acts 6:10 ff.). M. Goguel assumes that
Judas informed the Jewish magistrates of this utterance of Jesus. A high estimate of the
saying about the temple and its significance for Primitive Christian thinking is found in
Marcel Simon, 'Retour du Christ et reconstruction du Temple dans *la* pensée chrétienne primitive' (*Aux sources de la tradition chrétienne, Mélanges M. Goguel*, 1950,
pp. 249 ff.).

take into account another saying of Jesus, which stands in Mark 13:2. A disciple there says to Jesus: 'Behold what great stones and what great buildings!' Jesus answers him: 'There will not remain one stone upon the other which will not be destroyed.' He thus clearly predicts here the destruction of the temple. It therefore is probably true that what Jesus really said was worded in the way that the Gospel of John (ch. 2:19) actually puts it into his mouth on the occasion of the cleansing of the temple: '*Destroy this temple, and in three days I will build it up.*' The falsified feature in this saying, accordingly, as it is ascribed to the false witnesses in Mark, would be only the change of person in the first half of the sentence. Jesus would not have said: '*I* will destroy', but 'the temple will be destroyed'. In the second half of the sentence, on the contrary, the first person seems quite in place: 'I will rebuild it.'

Only in the Gospel of Mark do we read 'another not made by hands', after it has been said previously of the temple at Jerusalem that it 'was made by hands'. But whether this precision is original or not—there is no real reason why it should not be so—in any case Jesus had in view a fellowship when he announced that he would again erect the destroyed temple. We have already seen, indeed, that it was already common in Jewish terminology to apply to the people the image of the building. In the New Testament area this usage is quite common; the Church is the temple or the 'spiritual house', as it is called in First Peter (ch. 2:5 ff.).[44] It is possible that the author of the Gospel of John, when he went on to apply the saying about the temple to the body of Christ, likewise thought of the Church.[45]

In any case, however, it must be assumed, in keeping with the Synoptic tradition, that Jesus proclaimed the building of a temple not made by human hands. By this he can only have meant the new people of God that he intended to found.[46] For our study this saying about the temple is the more important since here, exactly as in Matthew 16:18, the illustration of the building occurs. *We thus have here a direct parallel to the saying concerning the ekklesia*, and if it plays so small a role in discussions of our question, this results only from the fact that scholars let themselves be misled by statistics of word usage, and so no longer pay attention to the essential idea.

\*          \*          \*

[44] See above, p. 199.

[45] See O. Cullmann, *Urchristentum und Gottesdienst*, 2nd ed., pp. 72 ff. (Eng. Tr., *Early Christian Worship*, pp. 71 ff.).

[46] Concerning the Jewish Messiah and the rebuilding of the temple see Enoch 90:28 ff. On this point see J. Engnell, *Studies in Divine Kingship*, 1943; E. G. Kraeling, 'The Real Religion of Ancient Israel' (*Journal of Biblical Literature*, 1928, p. 138); H. Riesenfeld, *Jésus transfiguré*, 1947, p. 59.

By his saying concerning the temple, as well as by the words of institution of the Lord's Supper, Jesus announces a new fellowship for the time *after his death*. With this agrees the fact that in Matthew 16:17 ff. he speaks in the future tense: 'I *will* build my *ekklesia*.' We have seen that according to this saying this future must still fall in this age, since otherwise the contrast between heaven and earth would have no meaning. This very fact, however, gives occasion for the final objection which is raised against the genuineness of the passage. It is claimed that if Jesus spoke of a future realization of the people of God, to follow after his death, he can only have meant its final realization in the Kingdom of God. Those other promises, such as the saying concerning the temple, must in such a case be understood to mean that with the death of Jesus the consummation of the Kingdom of God already occurs. Since, however, in Matthew 16:17 ff. the *ekklesia* is already realized in the present age, it is alleged that there exists here a contradiction, and therefore this saying cannot come from Jesus.[47]

The question thus arises: Did Jesus then expect any intermediate period—even if short—between his death or resurrection and his return? If it is really true, as Albert Schweitzer asserts, that Jesus expected the Kingdom of God to come at the moment of his death, then indeed there would no longer be any place for a period of the Church. The people of God would pass over directly into the final Kingdom of God. We cannot discuss this problem in its full extent, and I limit myself to mention of a few outstanding points. First of all, we have no text which really supports Schweitzer's hypothesis. For Jesus his own death undoubtedly constitutes the central event in the redemptive process that leads to the Kingdom of God. But he sees the tension between present and future; it is already present in his lifetime, and he knows that by his death it is not yet removed.[48]

After the death of Jesus, various events must still occur before the end: destruction of Jerusalem and persecution of the disciples. One may also recall the often emphasized necessity of the Gentile mission, which is to be carried out only after Jesus' death, before the end comes (Mark 14:62). That may be the specific task of the little flock in the period after his death and before the end; it is to build up the people of God in such a way that the Gentiles find acceptance in it. What Jesus has already revealed as

[47] So R. Bultmann, 'Die Frage nach der Echtheit von Mtth. 16, 17–19', *Theologische Blätter*, 1941.
[48] See on this point W. Michaelis, *Der Herr verzieht nicht die Verheissung*, 1942, W. G. Kümmel, *Verheissung und Erfüllung*, 2nd ed., 1953, pp. 58 ff. (Eng. Tr., *Promise and Fulfilment*, 1957, pp. 64 ff.); O. Cullmann, *Christus und die Zeit*, pp. 131 f. (Eng. Tr., *Christ and Time*, pp. 149 f.).

proclamation, the inclusion of the Gentiles in the people of God, is to become reality after his death. Therefore the redemptive history must still continue for a period after his death, because the command given at the sending forth of the disciples is not yet fully carried out; it can only be fully carried out when Jesus has died and arisen.[49] The establishing of the new covenant at *the Last Supper* probably presupposes, even if the explicit command to repeat the rite should not be original, a continuation of the Messianic time of preparation that has begun in the earthly work of Jesus.

Moreover, the promise of Mark 14:28, whose genuineness usually is not contested, is probably only correctly understood by assuming that in it Jesus did not consider that his death was identical with the consummation: 'but after I have risen I will go before you into Galilee'. Here belong further the words concerning fasting (Mark 2:18 ff.): 'When the bridegroom is taken from them, then they may fast.' Also in his answer to the high priest (Mark 14:62 and parallels), Jesus distinguishes between the moment when the Son of Man will sit at the right hand of God and the one when he will come again on the clouds of Heaven. To be sure, Jesus does not reckon with a duration of millennia, but he does assume that there will be a rather brief period of time between his resurrection and return, as becomes clear from what he says in expectation of the approaching end. That, however, does not concern us in our study.[50] The important thing here is that he anticipates after his death also some period within which the Kingdom of God is prepared, and if it has already been anticipated, it is nevertheless not yet completed. In this period of time falls the building of the *ekklesia* of which Jesus speaks in Matthew 16:17 ff.

\* \* \*

Now that we have thus established from every angle that Jesus spoke of a building of the new people of God, and have seen in what sense he did so, we still have to explain the further sayings connected with this subject. The question as to who is meant by the rock we postpone until we have discussed the remaining points, since it will lead us directly to the doctrinal question.

[49] E. Peterson, in his highly regarded essay, 'Die Kirche', 1929 (now printed in the collection, *Theologische Traktate*, 1951), is right when he sees in this the real essence of the Church. So also O. Cullmann, *Christus und die Zeit*, 2nd ed., 1948, pp. 138 ff. (Eng. Tr., *Christ and Time*, pp. 157 f.); in this matter I stress strongly the retention of the eschatology, while in the view of E. Peterson it is, so to speak, dissolved in the Church.

[50] See O. Cullmann, 'Das wahre, durch das Ausbleiben der Parusie gestellte Problem' (*Theologische Zeitschrift*, 1947, pp. 177 ff.), and my *Eschatology of the New Testament*, which is in preparation.

In the saying we first hear that the gates of Hades will not prevail against this *ekklesia* which Jesus will build upon the rock. By Hades is meant the realm of the dead[51]—and not chiefly the realm of sin and damnation.[52] This is the truth in the thesis according to which this passage speaks of the triumph that the resurrection brings over death.[53] Whether a translation error for 'porter' is present here may remain undiscussed.[54] It is possible. Nevertheless, the image of the gates of the realm of the dead is already found in Israelite and Jewish writings: Isaiah 38:10; Psalms 9:13; 107:18; Job 38:17;[55] Wisdom of Solomon 16:13; III Maccabees 5:51; Psalm of Solomon 16:2. The idea is that the gates of the realm of the dead, which close behind all men, will no more be opened, that the realm of the dead will no more permit its dead to escape. Matthew 16:18 states, probably with the same figure and in dependence on it, that before the attack of the Church the gates which otherwise stand firm against every attempt, however strong, to storm them, lose their previously unconquerable power; before the Church they must open. If this is the case, the *ekklesia* is here thought of as the attacker. One could indeed seek also to regard the gates as the attackers.[56] When we think that the *ekklesia* is conceived in this illustration as a building, this might seem almost more likely. But the question whether the *ekklesia* or the

---

[51] So also E. Klostermann, *Das Matthäusevangelium*, *ad loc.*, and A. Schlatter, *Der Evangelist Matthäus*, *ad loc.*

[52] R. Bohren, *Das Problem der Kirchenzucht im Neuen Testament*, 1952, pp. 63 f., assumes rather that from the gates of hell stream forth spirit hosts who fight to prevent the building of the Church. W. Vischer, *Die evangelische Gemeindeordnung*, 1946, p. 21 sees both united. So does M. Meinertz, *Theologie des Neuen Testaments*, Vol. I, 1950, p. 75. On the entire subject see especially W. Bieder, *Die Vorstellung von der Höllenfahrt Jesu Christi*, 1949, pp. 43 ff.

[53] A. Harnack, 'Der Spruch über Petrus als den Felsen der Kirche, Matth. XVI, 17 f.' (*Sitzungsbericht der Berliner Akademie der Wissenschaften*, 1918, pp. 637 ff.), deletes the saying concerning the Church. He prefers to see here only a prediction of the resurrection of *Peter*; he replaces αὐτῆς ('it') by σου ('you'). (See above, p. 171.) This, however, is impossible, because the explanation of the name Peter requires the figure of the building. (So rightly M. J. Lagrange, commentary on Matthew, p. 324.) Whether αὐτῆς ('it') is to be connected with ἐκκλησία ('church') or with πέτρα ('rock') was already considered by the Church Fathers (Origen); πέτρα is too far removed, and on the basis of content also ἐκκλησία must be the word meant here. (See M. J. Lagrange, commentary on Matthew, p. 327.)

[54] R. Eppel, *Aux sources de la tradition chrétienne*, *Mélanges offerts à M. Goguel*, pp. 71 ff., holds that πύλαι ('gates') would represent שַׁעֲרֵי, while πυλωροί ('gate-keepers', 'porters') would represent שֹׁעֲרֵי (reference to Job 38:17, LXX). In another way Ed. Bruston, *Les promesses de Jésus à l'apôtre Pierre*, 1945, pp. 10 ff., assumes here a translation error for 'assaults of the abyss'.

[55] The LXX, to be sure, reads πυλωροί ('gatekeepers', 'porters') here. See the preceding note.

[56] R. Eppel, *op. cit.*, p. 72, appeals to J. Dutlin, 'The Gates of Hades' (*Expository Times*, 1916, pp. 401 ff.), in pointing out that the verb κατισχύω ('prevail') fits an attack rather than a defence.

world of the dead is thought of as the attacker can hardly be answered with certainty.[57]

It is clear, on the contrary, that according to this saying *the ekklesia is included in the function of Jesus*, which consists of his victory over death by his death and resurrection. The task that was given to the disciples during Jesus' lifetime as a Messianic function,[58] the conflict with death, whether in the form of healings of the sick or raisings of the dead (Matt. 10:7 f.), is here promised to the entire *ekklesia*. The foundation that is laid in Peter thus has to support a building that means victory over death. It is predicted that the *ekklesia* founded upon Peter as the rock will indeed exist in the time when death still rules, and so will exist in the present age,[59] but it will nevertheless share already in the resurrection power that marks the Kingdom of God. We shall remind ourselves, when we discuss and reach a conclusion concerning the essential nature of an apostle, that in the New Testament the apostles are first of all witnesses of the resurrection who are entrusted with a commission.

The illustration of the building, and likewise that of the door, give occasion to use that of the *keys* of the Kingdom of God. It is possible that the following words *did not belong originally in this context* and that Matthew first placed them in this framework. Indeed, we know his tendency to bring together all items that deal with the same theme. Thus in ch. 11 he has assembled the various sayings concerning the Baptist. But in the present case the saying concerning the keys connects well with the one concerning the building. Mention has just been made of the gates of Hades; now the doors of the Kingdom of Heaven are in mind. Just as Hades is the realm of the dead, so the Kingdom of Heaven is that of life in the resurrection. This illustration of the keys seems to have been common. In Revelation 1:18 it is said of the Son of Man that he has the keys of death and of Hades, manifestly in order to open them for those imprisoned within. In Revelation 3:7 it is said, with a reference to Isaiah 22:22, that the Holy One has the 'keys of David', with which he irrevocably opens and closes (see also Rev. 21:25). In Matthew 16:19 it is presupposed that Christ is the master of the house, who has the keys to the Kingdom of Heaven, with which to open to those who come in. Just as in Isaiah 22:22 the Lord lays the keys of the house of David on the shoulders of his servant Eliakim, so Jesus commits to Peter the keys of his house, the

---

[57] For the conception of the gates as the attacking force, see Th. Zahn, commentary on Matthew, p. 542, and M. J. Lagrange, commentary on Matthew, p. 326.

[58] See above, pp. 202 f.

[59] This confirms the view that it is not simply the coming Kingdom of God that is meant here.

Kingdom of Heaven, and thereby installs him as administrator of the house.[60] There exists a relation between the house of the *ekklesia*—whose building was mentioned just before, and whose foundation is Peter—and the heavenly house whose keys he receives. The connecting element here too is the idea of the people of God.

Here again Peter is connected with the resurrection. The so-called power of the keys makes him, so to speak, the human instrument of the resurrection. He is to lead the people of God into the resurrection Kingdom. That is the task which he will have to carry out on earth after the death and resurrection of Jesus. In this connection we must think of that other saying of Jesus which rests upon the very same illustration; it is his saying to the Pharisees: 'you close the door to the Kingdom of Heaven' (Matt. 23:13). The Pharisees might indeed boast that they on the contrary open the door to the Kingdom of Heaven. But it is not they, it is rather he called rock, Peter, who has this office. In connection with Matthew 23:13, the saying against the Pharisees, Matthew may have had in mind here too the *mission* that Peter will carry out by his preaching, and by which he will open access to the Kingdom of Heaven, while the Pharisees 'rush over sea and land to make a single proselyte, and when he has become one, they make of him a son of Hell who is twice as bad as they are' (Matt. 23:15).[61] It is characteristic that in Matthew this utterance follows right after the one on the opening of the Kingdom of Heaven, and this justifies us in assuming that in Matthew 16:19 the giving of the 'keys of the Kingdom of Heaven' was connected with the apostolic mission by Jesus himself.

Furthermore, it is not certain whether the saying that now follows, concerning 'binding and loosing', originally belonged in this same context. Indeed, Matthew uses it a second time in Matthew 18:18 as directed to all the disciples. He may also have known a tradition according to which Jesus spoke it to Peter alone, and when one takes account of the tendency of the evangelist to connect sayings on the same theme, it is quite probable that it was he who first placed here this saying, which had been spoken in another connection, and united it with his special tradition concerning the dialogue at the Last Supper.

What do the expressions 'bind' and 'loose' signify? According to Rab-

---

[60] On the illustration of the steward of the household see Mark 13:34; Luke 12:42; 16:1 ff.; I Cor. 4:1; I Pet. 4:10. Th. Zahn, *Das Evangelium nach Matthäus, ad loc.*, is hardly right when he thinks here not of admission but only of authority over secret chambers.

[61] The connection with Matthew, ch. 23, has been pointed out by J. Schniewind, *Das Evangelium nach Matthäus (Das N. T. Deutsch)*, 1927, *ad loc.*, and also by W. Vischer, *Die evangelische Gemeindeordnung*, 1946, pp. 24 f.

binical usage[62] two explanations are equally possible: 'prohibit' and 'permit', that is, 'establish rules';[63] or 'put under the ban' and 'acquit'.[64] Since for Jesus entrance into the Kingdom of Heaven is closely connected with forgiveness of sins (Matt. 18:18 and John 20:23), the latter meaning is doubtless chiefly in mind here, but without excluding the other, which is equally well attested by Rabbinical texts.[65] Indeed, the power to teach and to discipline cannot be sharply separated. Peter thus receives a share in the authority of Christ to forgive sins. To the functions that had been committed to the disciples even in the lifetime of Jesus, the same ones, as we have seen,[66] that Jesus himself exercises (Matt. 11:4 ff.; 10:7 f.), there is now added this highest office of forgiving sins, an office that Christ alone controls but commits also to Peter with a view to establishing the earthly people of God. In case the binding is meant to refer also to the demonic powers, there would be a further connection with the preceding illustration.[67]

We now recall that this promise was given not only to Peter, but in almost the same words to the other disciples as well: 'Truly I tell you, all that you shall bind on earth will be bound in heaven, and all that you shall loose on earth will be loosed in heaven' (Matt. 18:18); 'If you forgive the sins of any, they will be forgiven; if you retain the sins of any, they will be retained' (John 20:23). This is important for the question as to the character of the pre-eminence with which Peter is certainly distinguished here. The 'binding' and 'loosing' he shares with the other disciples. This corresponds completely with what we have established in the historical section, in our chapter concerning the disciple Peter and his position among the Twelve. He is to be sure the first among them, but nevertheless is their representative in all things; he always speaks in the name of the others, and people turn to him in order to speak at the same time to all the disciples. This unique position comes to expression also in the fact that the promise of the effectiveness of his 'binding' and 'loosing' is given not only to him but also to the other disciples, but it is given to him

---

[62] אסר and שרא.

[63] So G. Dalman, *Worte Jesu*, I, p. 175 (Eng. Tr., *The Words of Jesus*, 1909, p. 214); E. Klostermann, *Das Matthäusevangelium, ad loc.*; likewise Th. Zahn, *Das Evangelium nach Matthäus, ad loc.* (he denies any connection with John 20:23); and W. Michaelis, commentary on Matthew, *ad loc.*

[64] So A. Schlatter, *Der Evangelist Matthäus, ad loc.*; J. Schniewind, *Das Evangelium nach Matthäus, ad loc.*

[65] See Strack-Billerbeck, *op. cit.*, Vol. I, p. 738, on Matthew, *ad loc.*

[66] See above, pp. 202 f.

[67] So R. Bohren, *Das Problem der Kirchenzucht im Neuen Testament*, 1952, pp. 52 ff., who agrees with F. Heiler, *Urkirche und Ostkirche*, 1937, p. 59. With a somewhat different turn, A. Dell, *op. cit.* (*ZNW*, 1914, pp. 138 ff.).

in a special way, and only for him, according to Matthew, is it connected with the announcement that upon him as the rock the *ekklesia* is to be built. This corresponds with the historical fact which, as we have established, occurred after the death of Jesus; Peter, in the earliest period, stands at the head of the Primitive Church in Jerusalem, but soon gives up this position to act in dependence on James in organizing the Jewish Christian missionary work; this work he does in company with other apostles, but as its leader.

\*     \*     \*

This, however, leads us to the final exegetical question we must ask; it will also form the transition to the discussion of the doctrinal problem: Whom does Jesus mean when he says that upon the rock the new people of God will be built? The question could seem superfluous were it not that the really self-evident reference to the person of Peter has been contested, and often is still contested, from the Protestant as well as from the Catholic side.

The solution of the Reformers, that the rock is only the faith of Peter,[68] does not satisfy. The text offers no real support for this interpretation. Rather, the parallelism of the two statements: 'you are rock, and upon this rock I will build . . .' shows that the second rock refers to nothing different from the first one.[69] This is more clearly expressed in the Aramaic, where the same word *kepha* occurs both times, than it is in the Greek. The explanation that Jesus did not say at all: 'You are Peter', but: 'I say to you, yes to you, Peter',[70] is purely hypothetical, in spite of the fact that it refers back to the Aramaic. There may indeed be some truth in the view that in the last analysis the rock means Christ himself (as in Matt. 21:42). But that is not what is said here; this passage says that Jesus' role as rock is transferred to a disciple.[71] So there remains only the one possibility, that by this saying Jesus actually meant the person whom he characterized by the name 'rock'. Indeed, if the saying were referred to the faith of Peter, one could no longer directly discern the connection with the giving of the name, and the saying certainly intends to point to this and even to explain it. The giving of the name, which is an established

---

[68] See above, pp. 168 f.

[69] For this reason we must also pronounce unsatisfactory the thesis that G. Gander represents in his article '*ΠΕΤΡΟΣ-ΠΕΤΡΑ*' (*Revue de Théologie et de Philosophie*, 1941, pp. 5 f.). He holds that *Kepha*, in Syriac *Kipha*, is a name of both persons and things, so that it refers to Peter only in the first but not in the second part of the sentence.

[70] Strack-Billerbeck, *op. cit.*, see above, p. 169.

[71] H. Riesenfeld, *Ämbetet i Nya Testamentet*, n.d., pp. 17 ff., shows how the metaphors which designate Jesus' own functions are transferred to the apostles.

fact even apart from Matthew 16:17 ff., deals with the person of Peter, and not merely with his faith, just as the person of the sons of Zebedee is in view when Jesus gives them the title 'Sons of Thunder'.

For this reason all Protestant interpretations that seek in one way or another to explain away the reference to Peter seem to me unsatisfactory. No, the fact remains that when Jesus says that he will build his *ekklesia* upon this rock, he really means the person of Simon. Upon this disciple, who in the lifetime of Jesus possessed the specific advantages and the specific weaknesses of which the Gospels speak, upon him who was then their spokesman, their representative in good as well as in bad, and in this sense was the rock of the group of disciples—upon him is to be founded the Church, which after the death of Jesus will continue his work upon earth.

The Roman Catholic exegesis must be regarded as correct when it rejects those other attempts at explanation.[72] On its part, however, it proceeds in an even more arbitrary way when it tries to find in this text a reference to 'successors'. He who proceeds without prejudice, on the basis of exegesis and only on this basis, cannot seriously conclude that Jesus here had in mind successors of Peter; this was not his meaning when he said to Peter that he was the rock on which was to be built the fellowship of the people of God that leads to the Kingdom of God. We shall speak later concerning the doctrinal problem; we shall ask whether it cannot be said subsequently, in the light of church history, that the saying may be referred to certain successors. But at first we propose to keep this question clearly separate from the exegetical one, as all serious exegetes, including Roman Catholic ones, are accustomed to do when they deal with other Biblical passages.

On exegetical grounds we must say that the passage does not contain a single word concerning successors of Peter. It speaks on the one hand of *Peter* and on the other hand of the *Church*.[73] Of these two words one, the *ekklesia*, refers to a fellowship which is to be built in the future, without any time limit being given. The other word, Peter, refers to a human person, whose earthly activity will necessarily be limited by his death. Accordingly it could be said that a single human person, who will die at a certain time, cannot be the foundation of a fellowship which is to continue for an indefinite period.

[72] M. Meinertz, *Theologie des Neuen Testaments*, Vol. I, 1950, p. 74, does indeed make one concession to the Protestant interpretation when he writes, 'the confession [that Peter makes] in faith is the presupposition'. But naturally he nevertheless considers that it is the *person* of the confessing one that is addressed.

[73] J. Jeremias rightly calls to my attention in a letter that even where in the rabbinical tradition Abraham or the twelve patriarchs are spoken of as cosmic rock (see J. Jeremias, *Golgotha*, 1926, p. 74), all thought of successors is excluded.

It is true that the duration of the Church is not limited in Jesus' words. However, neither is it *explicitly* extended to the period after the death of Peter, and this also must be noted in a saying addressed to the historical Peter. The question of duration is not considered at all; it is left open. Jesus' expectation concerning the end includes, to be sure, a short intermediate period between his death and the end, but this period does not extend over several generations. In no case, therefore, is it justified to proceed as Roman Catholic scholars usually do. Since the period of building is not limited, they conclude too hastily that in the entire promise to Peter Jesus must have spoken also of the period after Peter's death, and therefore successors of Peter must also be addressed here.[74] *Peter's feeding of the lambs in John 21:16 ff. is certainly limited by his martyrdom!*[75] So the statement 'I will build my *ekklesia*' need not be extended beyond the lifetime of Peter. It could be that *at the moment* when he gave a promise to *Peter* in particular, Jesus limited himself to speaking concerning the initial building to follow immediately after his resurrection.

But if we nevertheless assume that *in this first statement* Jesus thought of a period embracing many generations[76]—his expectation that the end was near speaks against this[77]—this would not mean at all that the rock— Cephas—Peter mentioned in this sentence includes also successors of Peter. In this sentence it is *only the work of building* which belongs to an unlimited future, *not the laying of the foundation of the rock* on which is built! In the future Jesus will build upon a foundation which is laid in the time of his earthly career and in the time and person of the historical apostle, Peter. We shall see[78] that in the entire New Testament the illus-

---

[74] Even in so thorough and cautious an exegete as F. M. Braun, *Neues Licht auf die Kirche*, 1946, we read on p. 165: 'Since . . . the apostles appear endowed with special and complete authority and since the operation of the Church, which is to continue to the fulfilment of the times, extends over an intermediate period of indeterminate duration, it would only be consistent even apart from other considerations, if the "new consensus" [see above, pp. 172 f.] would concede that the succession corresponds to Jesus' intention and that the apostles, after exercising their power for some years, transferred to others their authority as church leaders.' In opposition to K. L. Schmidt, whom F. M. Braun cites on the same page, I prefer to avoid playing off a 'prophetic succession' against the 'apostolic succession'. That an apostolic succession is directly or indirectly present in *other* passages of the New Testament, but in a sense still to be defined (see below, pp. 224 f.), I freely recognize. But I deny the more emphatically that Jesus spoke of such a succession in Matt. 16:17 ff. W. Michaelis, *Das Evangelium nach Matthäus*, p. 354, actually makes an argument for genuineness out of the failure to mention the succession; had the saying been invented later, the succession would have been mentioned.

[75] But we should of course consider whether *the author* of John 21 is not already opposing an extension of the application to include his own time, in which Peter is already dead but many are appealing to him to support their claim to the leadership. So E. L. Allen; see above, p. 184, note 80.

[76] W. Michaelis, *op. cit.*, p. 346, believes it necessary to conclude from the illustration of the 'building' that Jesus must have 'had in mind a longer development'.

[77] On this point see my *Eschatology of the New Testament*, which will appear shortly.

[78] See below, pp. 222 f., and H. Riesenfeld, *Ämbetet i Nya Testamentet*, n.d., pp. 17ff.

tration of the foundation, which indeed is identical in meaning with that of the rock, always designates the unique apostolic function, which is chronologically possible only at the beginning of the building; see Ephesians 2:20; Romans 15:20; I Corinthians 3:10; Galatians 2:9; Revelation 21:14, 19. In Matthew 16:18 Peter is addressed in his unrepeatable apostolic capacity.

Everything that is said of Peter in this entire promise really concerns the Peter who then lived; this is true even if the period of building that continues after Peter is explicitly in mind, which however can scarcely be assumed in view of Jesus' expectation that the end was near. The content of *the next sentence*, the giving to Peter of the keys, the power to bind and loose, also refers to the future. In this case, however, the reference certainly is not to an unlimited future, but to the life of Peter following the death *of Jesus*. Here Jesus certainly speaks no longer of building during an unlimited period; he speaks rather of the specific rock itself, the apostolic foundation—represented by Peter—of the Church that is to be built. The preceding saying concerning building, which is not explicitly limited as to time, gives no exegetical justification for assuming an unlimited duration of time for the entrusting with the keys, the binding and loosing, which is given explicitly to Peter, the rock of the building. Whether and in what way these words directed to Peter may also be legitimately applied *subsequently* to the *later* Church we shall not discuss until the final chapter. On exegetical grounds it must be said that we have no right to see successors addressed in Peter. That would have to be indicated in some way. Wherever Jesus speaks elsewhere of the functions his disciples are to exercise, he plainly means only the disciples themselves and not their successors. And if in the first sentence, which deals with the building, Jesus really included also the period after Peter, which is not probable, this would mean only that the *unique* mission as rock which the historical Peter fulfils *in the redemptive history* is of such a character that its unique effectiveness continues even beyond his death, so that the historical Peter—and not any successors—would be and remain the foundation even in this unlimited further building. When the Johannine Christ, in the high priestly prayer (John 17:20), speaks concerning the coming generations who will believe 'through the word of the apostles', he does not speak also of successors to the apostles. He speaks of the *apostles themselves*, of what their once-given preaching signifies for the future Church.

That successors are not addressed is clear also from the Lucan parallel to Matthew 16:17 ff. We have seen that in that passage the command to strengthen the brothers is quite closely connected with the prediction of the denial. Peter must first be converted. Here it is certainly clear that in this section, which implicitly speaks of the future Church, Jesus did not include in his outlook any successors. What is said here is directed only to the historical Peter who denied Jesus.

To be sure, the sentence concerning the keys, concerning loosing and binding, speaks of functions of the historical Peter that continue in the Church. They refer to church leadership, and this indeed must continue to exist. That, however, does not mean that in this saying in Matthew 16:17 ff. Jesus is speaking of the leadership that *later* leaders will give. On the contrary, all that is said here deals with the leadership of him who, according to the preceding sentence, has also the unique mission, absolutely decisive for the Church and *not to be repeated*, of being the *rock*, of presiding as apostle over the Church immediately after the death and resurrection of Jesus.

As soon as any saying Jesus spoke to the disciples refers to a continued effect of the deeds of the apostles, the Roman Catholic exegetes speak of *successors*. It must be said with all emphasis, however, that continued effect need not mean continued effect *in 'successors'*.

In what he says Jesus certainly does not exclude the activity of other church leaders in later times. But in this *saying concerning the foundation* he does not speak of them; he speaks of Peter. Concerning men who are installed as leaders by apostles the New Testament actually does speak elsewhere, and we shall mention the passages later.[79] Here, however, in what Jesus says to Peter in Matthew 16:17 ff., nothing of the sort is said.

It therefore will not do to argue in the following way: The time of building that Jesus mentions in the first sentence is not limited. But the historical Peter will die. Consequently he cannot be the rock of a Church that continues to exist after him. Therefore Jesus must have successors in mind along with Peter.

It is also impossible to start from the second sentence to give an exegetical defence for the reference to successors, and so to say something like the following: The power of the keys, and further the binding and loosing, which are entrusted to Peter, must be exercised also in the Church later built by Jesus. Consequently, together with Peter, successors also must be addressed who will carry out this binding and loosing and administer the keys. This also is exegetically too hasty a conclusion. Jesus will build not upon the keys, nor upon the binding and loosing, but *upon*

---

[79] See below, pp. 223 ff.

*the apostle Peter*, to whom Jesus *at that time* committed the keys and the binding and loosing.

It must again be explicitly noted that the exegetical conclusion, that this passage speaks only of Peter, still says nothing concerning the possible application of the saying. It may be proper, however, for us to indicate a crucial point which stands *on the borderline of exegetical study*. The Roman Catholic position concludes, from the continuance of the Church and from the continued necessity of church leadership, that successors are included in the person of the rock addressed, Peter. This conclusion appears to me connected with a failure to grasp the basic attitude of all New Testament thought. In opposition to Hellenism, it is characteristic of the thinking of Jesus as of all Biblical thinking that *what continues has its roots in the once-for-all unique event*. A historically unique event is the redemptive event; that is, it definitely cannot be repeated but is the *foundation* of a continuing situation whose ongoing life derives from this never-to-be-repeated event. This paradox lies at the basis of Jesus' sayings about the future, and finds a classic expression in the illustration of the rock and the *subsequent* building. In this sense we must also regard all the apostolic action, including the loosing and binding promised to Peter, as *the basic event*. It belongs to what happened once for all; it belongs, one may say, to the incarnation of Christ.[80]

But in saying this we have already stepped outside the field of exegesis. Our exegetical study has led us to the following result: There is no need to deny that the saying in Matthew 16:17 ff. is genuine, spoken by Jesus. It very probably does not belong to the event at Caesarea Philippi, but in another setting, that of the passion story. Jesus promises Peter that he will build upon him the earthly people of God that will lead to the Kingdom of God; he promises that in this people Peter will have the leadership, both in missionary work and in organization. His immediate thought, just as in John 21:16 ff., probably deals only with the time of Peter. But even if he explicitly had in view the period following Peter's death as the time of the building of the Church, what is said of Peter as the Rock would refer only to him, the historical apostle; he represents once for all the earthly foundation, the beginning who supports the whole structure of the *ekklesia* that is to be built in the future.

[80] To use the illustration I gave in *Christus und die Zeit* (Eng. Tr., *Christ and Time*): the Apostolic Age belongs to the midpoint, to the *centre*, by which as norm we must measure everything else that occurs in the redemptive process on the time line.

## 2

# The Doctrinal and Theological Question: The Application of Matthew 16:17 ff. to the Later Church

WE NOW leave the exegetical standpoint and ask the doctrinal question. We connect the exegetical result with our knowledge both of the actual course of the history of the Christian Church and of the fact that there still exists today a Christian Church. On this basis we ask: Are we now justified in going further? In the light of these facts can we attribute to the saying a significance that is at least a legitimate *extension* of the promise of Jesus? Roman Catholic theologians, indeed, are accustomed to concede explicitly that the Roman primacy cannot be based upon the exegesis of Matthew 16:17 ff. alone. They grant that this is possible only when this passage is connected with later history.

At the outset we must make a basic statement. It is our right and duty to apply to later generations and to our situation even those sayings of Jesus which deal directly with a unique situation and with specific persons of his time. This, of course, is no longer exegesis in the strict sense; but it may be called application of the exegesis. Preachers do this, and no one thinks of reproaching them with the *a priori* charge that in so doing they are untrue to the text. What Jesus says concerning prayer and almsgiving, for example, in the Sermon on the Mount is of course directed to the disciples who lived in his time; no one, however, will consider it unjustified or contrary to the mind of Jesus to apply his teachings on these subjects to all later Christians. Nevertheless, it must be added that this application must really extend in a straight line the basic idea contained in the saying. That is, it must agree with the exegesis and be grounded in the total witness of the New Testament.[1]

When, as is the case in Matthew 16:17 ff., the saying of Jesus does not have a content addressed simply to the wider circle of disciples, as are,

[1] Here a synthetic combination of the theological views of the various writings of the New Testament is both justified and imperative.

for example, the instructions of the Sermon on the Mount, but refers rather to *quite specific functions*, then in the application the special character of these functions must be respected. This must be done in a twofold way: on the one hand, the significance of the saying for the present may not be seen in the *repetition* of a function, if this is *basically* unique; and on the other hand, the application may not be arbitrarily *restricted*.

With regard to the former point, a role that Jesus promises to an apostle may not be transferred to men of later times, if it belongs to the very *meaning and nature* of the designated function that it can only be exercised by such men as have lived with the Incarnate One *during the earthly life of Jesus*. Indeed, this limitation in time must be taken into account even when —and indeed precisely when—the saying of Jesus in question assigns to this function a lasting significance for the later Church even down to the present time. We shall have to ask whether this is not the case for at least *one* aspect of the saying in Matthew 16:17 ff.

With regard to the latter point, a promise of Jesus may not be limited to one fixed category of later Christians; for example, it may not be strictly limited to one line of bishops tied to a specific see, if the function in question is one that can and must be taken over by men of the post-apostolic period down to the present time, but according to Jesus' saying is neither explicitly nor by suggestion limited to one see which is to be determined according to a particular *principle of succession*. We have to ask whether that sort of narrowing can be justified by the role in church history that the Christian church of one city has played and still plays for the entire Church.

Both of the viewpoints just named must be considered in the application of Matthew 16:17 ff. For we have seen that two things are promised to Peter: 1. He is the rock for the coming Church that is being built. 2. He holds the leadership in the Church whose building is begun. To this corresponds the fact that Peter plays in Primitive Christianity a double role: the unique one as apostle, and the one that is continued in the Church, as leader of the Church. Although the two promises are closely connected with one another, yet for their *application* they must be treated separately. This is because the previously posed question, whether too wide an extension or too narrow a limitation is being made, presents itself differently for each of them.

## 1. *The Laying of the Foundation of the Church*

Even in the course of the exegesis we established the fact that the laying of the foundation is to be understood in the temporal sense. As we now go beyond exegesis, we first must say that this saying, as far as it concerns the rock on which the structure is to be built, is directed to an apostle, not to a bishop. At the moment when Peter receives the promise of being the rock of the coming Church, he is addressed as one of the Twelve. According to the united witness of the New Testament, however, the apostolic office, particularly that of the Twelve, is a unique office not to be repeated. In the post-apostolic period there must always be church leaders, bishops, and missionaries in the Church of Christ, but never again can there be apostles. In the next paragraph we shall speak of the fact that often in the earliest period an apostle himself can be a community leader, at least for a certain time; indeed, Peter himself as apostle led the Primitive Church until he dedicated himself entirely to the mission. But even this will never exist again: there will never again be bishops who, like Peter, lead churches as *apostles*. The functions of leading and doing missionary work do indeed continue; they must continue in the Church. But the function of leading and doing missionary work as an apostle cannot continue. The saying concerning building the Church on Peter as the rock, however, designates an apostle as the basis of the Church that is to be built. When, as in the case of Peter, we are dealing with a church head and missionary who is likewise an apostle, the apostolic concept is necessarily the dominant concept.

We here must ask what the nature of the apostolic office is in the New Testament.[2] The apostle is given a special commission by Jesus as the Incarnate One or when he appeared after his resurrection; so, according to the rule in late Judaism, he is like Jesus himself, and is bound to give accounting to him. Upon the fulfilment of his commission, he returns it to Jesus and cannot hand it on to another.

During Jesus' lifetime the content of the commission is the fulfilment of the Messianic function that Jesus himself exercised, the function of

---

[2] See K. H. Rengstorf, Article on ἀπόστολος in G. Kittel's *Theologisches Wörterbuch zum N. T.*, Vol. I, 1933, pp. 397 ff. (Eng. Tr., in *Bible Key Words*, Vol. II, 1958), and the essay by H. von Campenhausen cited above, p. 59, note 73, as well as his book, *Kirchliches Amt und geistliche Vollmacht in den ersten drei Jahrhunderten*, 1953, pp. 24 ff. Further: Ed. Schweizer, *Gemeinde und Gemeindeordnung im Neuen Testament*, 1959, pp. 176 ff. (Eng. Tr., *Church Order in the New Testament*, 1961, pp. 195 ff.), and T. W. Manson, *The Church's Ministry*, 1948, pp. 31 ff.

preaching and healing the sick.[3] Since after the death of Christ the preaching is first of all witness to the resurrection of Christ, the apostle from then
on must be a personal 'witness of the resurrection of Christ' (Acts 1:22),
and indeed an eyewitness. We all should be witnesses to the resurrection
of Jesus; only the apostles could be eyewitnesses.

The necessity for an apostle to be a witness of the resurrection is clear
from I Corinthians 9:1. In that passage Paul has to defend his apostolic
office. He does it by pointing to the fact that he also, like the other apostles,
has seen the Risen One. In Acts 10:41 Peter says: 'Christ appeared to us
who after his resurrection ate and drank with him.' Thus after the death
of Jesus there were more apostles than the Twelve. This follows clearly
from the enumeration in I Corinthians 15:5 ff., which speaks on the one
hand of the Twelve, and on the other hand of *all the apostles*.

But the 'having seen' must always be connected with a commission.[4]
Concerning Paul we know this (Gal. 1:16). The Eleven also receive such
a commission from the Risen One (Matt. 28:19), and so does Peter in
particular (John 21:16 ff.). In the case of the Twelve, however, a further
special condition must be fulfilled: they must in addition have lived with
the historical incarnate Jesus. That is clearly said in Acts 1:21, where the
substitute for Judas is chosen. The conditions that he must fulfil to belong to the circle of the Twelve are there clearly given; first of all, he, like
all apostles, must be a 'witness of the resurrection of Christ'; in the second
place, he must have 'gone in and out' with Jesus during his lifetime. In
other words, the Twelve have the additional function of guaranteeing the
continuity between the risen and the historical Jesus. Therein consists
their unique function. They twice receive the apostolic commission, first
from the Incarnate One, then from the Risen One. Among them Peter is
the most important. Only at that time could one be an eyewitness of the
historical Jesus, an eyewitness of the resurrection. *There never will be such
a witness again.* Upon one of these eyewitnesses Christ intends to build
his Church.

From the men of his time Jesus chose those who were to be his witnesses, and among them Peter, to whose witnessing he attached a particular value. We shall see that Peter, precisely on the basis of the *apostolic
concept* just established, is actually the first among the apostles. It must be
said at once, however, that according to the united testimony of the New
Testament he shares this 'fundamental' function with the other apostles.

[3] In the lifetime of Jesus there are the smaller group of the Twelve and the larger one
of the Seventy (Luke 10:1 ff.).
[4] See A. Fridrichsen, 'The Apostle and his Message' (*Uppsala Universitete Arsskrift*,
1947). See above, pp. 58, 64.

Thus in Ephesians 2:20, where exactly *the same illustration of the building* is used as in Matthew 16:18, Paul writes that the Church 'is built upon the foundation of the apostles and prophets'. So also Revelation 21:14 speaks of the 'twelve foundations of the walls of the Holy City, on which the twelve names of the twelve apostles of the Lamb are written', and with the same illustration Paul mentions the 'pillars' in Galatians 2:9.[5]

From this it follows that the first Christians actually considered the apostles as such to be the foundation of the Church. Hence also, in the light of the total conception of the New Testament, which we have to consider in this doctrinal section, it is not at all arbitrary when in Matthew 16:17 ff. we see Peter addressed in his *apostolic capacity* and hence emphasize so strongly the apostolic concept. In any case, the illustration of the building in Ephesians 2:20 and Revelation 21:14 is connected with the apostolic function, and this is important. So also in Romans 15:20 the illustration of the foundation occurs to Paul: 'that I may not build upon another foundation'. (See also I Corinthians 3:10.) Perhaps the New Testament passages named actually refer to Jesus' saying concerning the rock in Matthew 16:17 ff. In that case we might say that we have here the oldest commentary on it.

In I Corinthians 3:11; 10:4; Matthew 21:42; and I Peter 2:4 ff. it is said that Jesus himself is the foundation stone or cornerstone. This is doubtless the silent presupposition in all the other passages. But this does not prevent the apostles from being the foundation composed of human instruments of God and resting in turn upon Christ; nor does it prevent Peter from having the prominent role among them and for the Church of all later time.

*Just as in Ephesians 2:20 and in Romans 15:20 the foundation is to be understood in a chronological way, so also in Matthew 16:17 ff.* In Ephesians 2:20 and Romans 15:20, as well as in Revelation 21:14, it nevertheless is impossible, even as a later application, to think of successors of the apostles. Indeed, a recent study has actually proved that in contrast to other New Testament metaphors that were transferred from Jesus to the apostles and from them to the later offices, the illustration of the Rock, of the foundation, is used solely for the apostles. In this fact the uniqueness and unrepeatable character of the apostolate comes clearly to expression.[6]

In the foundation that *all* the apostles form Peter is the specially visible rock. Here again our earlier historical conclusion is confirmed; he does

---

[5] James, although not belonging to the Twelve, very probably was regarded as an apostle. See below, p. 235, note 34.

[6] See H. Riesenfeld, *Ämbetet i Nya Testamentet*, n.d., pp. 17 ff.

indeed share his dignity with the other disciples, but within the group he is particularly representative. Precisely in connection with the concept of the apostle as the specially commissioned witness of the resurrection it is also confirmed that Peter, with the other apostles, forms the foundation and yet at the same time constitutes the rock within this foundation. Peter, that is to say, was the *first* who saw the Risen One on Easter Day. Probably he also received then confirmation of the apostolic commission,[7] and this is the more important since he was the one who had denied Jesus. He accordingly is the apostle *par excellence*. In this essential relation as the outstanding one, he is in a particular way what all the other apostles are. It is interesting to note that here too his position as leader within the apostolic circle rests upon a chronological distinction; *he is the first one who saw the Risen One*, and according to John 21:15 ff. the special apostolic commission given him by the Incarnate One is renewed by the Risen One. We recall that Matthew, in his list of the apostles, gives to Peter the title of honour, 'first'. Thus this also is a part of *the essential role of the apostle* Peter. He is particularly qualified to hand on the news that Jesus, who lived and died on earth, died and rose for the salvation of the world.

Thus the events immediately after the death of Jesus confirm the saying concerning the rock, and if one seeks in the happenings of this period a *confirmation and illumination of Jesus' saying*, he should seek it in the fact that Peter is the first witness of the resurrection, and that his apostolic commission is renewed by the Risen One. This is closely connected with the result of the exegetical interpretation of the statement: 'the gates of the realm of the dead will not overpower the Church'.[8] In the light of the Easter events this interpretation, connected with the promise that the Church is founded on Peter as the rock, receives a particularly strong confirmation in the fact that it is he who is the most important witness of the resurrection of Christ. We have seen that it is not the faith of Peter that is meant by the rock, as the Reformers taught, but rather his person. We now add that it is his person in so far as he had been chosen by the incarnate Christ and in so far as the Risen One appeared to him first of all.

Thus it is absolutely irreconcilable with the New Testament concept of apostleship when a saying on the founding of the Church that was addressed to an apostle is simply referred to future bishops. Elders and

---

[7] So especially if the hypothesis is correct that a report concerning the first appearance of Jesus to Peter, such as perhaps was given in the lost ending of Mark, is used in John 21:15 ff. See above, pp. 61 f., 187 f.

[8] See above, p. 208, note 53. Only in this form may we recognize a grain of truth in the interpretation of A. Harnack—rejected above—that the promise of Peter's resurrection is here given him.

bishops certainly do take the place of the apostles, and one may call them successors, even if this expression opens the way to misunderstandings. But in any case it must not be forgotten for a moment that they occupy a completely different position, and they must not be regarded as successors in the sense of 'continuers of the apostolic function'. They are successors in the chronological sense, but not in their nature. *Their function follows that of the apostles, but as a fundamentally different one.*[9]

So we hear indeed in the New Testament that apostles installed church officers. Paul and Barnabas appointed elders in the cities of Lystra, Iconium, and Antioch (Acts 14:23); moreover, Paul, in his farewell to the elders of Ephesus, commits to them the 'flock', especially in anticipation of false teachers (Acts 20:17 ff.). Tendencies towards a so-called 'apostolic succession'—if we choose to use this ambiguous expression— are thus actually to be found in the New Testament,[10] but with the explicit reservation that this succession, as far as it concerns the essence of the apostolate, is not to be understood in the sense of a continuation. The apostles give over to those men the leadership, *but not their own apostolic office.* For they knew quite well that they could not hand this on at all, since it could only be given by Jesus himself directly and *without mediation* (Gal. 1:12 ff.!). Therefore they did not install any 'apostles' as successors in leadership, but rather 'bishops' and 'elders'. In what way the latter in turn are to follow one another, the New Testament does not say at all, and since the authority of the bishop may not be identified with that of the apostle, the above-named New Testament passages that speak of the installing of local church leaders by the apostles permit no deductions as to how bishops are to follow bishops in the future.[11] In the high-priestly prayer the Johannine Christ speaks of what will follow the apostles. After

---

[9] Against the Roman Catholic theologian M. Meinertz, *Die Theologie des Neuen Testaments*, Vol. I, 1950, p. 79: '. . . thus the apostolate requires a continuing present'.

[10] This is quite strongly stressed by W. Mundle, 'Das Apostelbild der Apostelgeschichte' (*ZNW*, 1928, pp. 36 ff.), an article to which Erik Peterson attaches special importance. See E. Peterson, *Theologische Traktate*, 1951, p. 296 (letter to A. Harnack) and p. 411 ('Die Kirche'). On the question of apostolic succession see also K. H. Rengstorf, 'Das Wort Gottes und die apostolische Sukzession' (*Die Kirche Jesu Christi und das Wort Gottes*, edited by W. Zoellner and W. Stählin, 1937, pp. 187 ff.); A. M. Ramsey, 'The Word of God and Apostolic Succession' (*Lutherische Kirche in Bewegung, Für Fr. Ulmer zum 60. Geburtstag*, 1937, pp. 179 ff.). See Ed. Schweizer, *Gemeinde und Gemeindeordnung im Neuen Testament*, 1959, pp. 192 ff. (Eng. Tr., *Church Order in the New Testament*, 1961, pp. 211 ff.); T. W. Manson, *op. cit.* (note 2 of this section), pp. 52, 54. The Anglican standpoint is represented by K. E. Kirk, *The Apostolic Ministry*, 1946 (especially the essay by G. Dix, 'The Ministry in the Early Church').

[11] This does not intend to say that the Scripture condemns the principle of succession. It does not express itself as to the How of determining the succession of bishops. Only this is certain, that the Holy Spirit operative in the Church is to be at work in the process. So rightly K. H. Rengstorf in p. 202 of the essay cited in the preceding note.

the petition for the apostles he goes on to speak of those who 'believe through the word' (of the apostles; John 17:20). Thus the apostles are followed by the entire Church of the believers. Accordingly the Church has the power of control over the episcopal office, and it is to exercise it as the Holy Spirit guides it (Acts 20:28).

Foundation and building may not be interchanged. Elders and bishops are only *watchmen* who are to see to it that further building is really done on the foundation of the apostles; they are not themselves the foundation. A confusion of foundation and building is present, however, when one appeals to the fact that the apostles installed elders and bishops in order to claim for a bishop Jesus' saying to the rock apostle. Although Roman Catholic theology itself emphasizes very strongly the uniqueness of the apostolic office, it devaluates that office in this decisive point of the appli-cation of Matthew 16:17 ff. There will be no more men who, like Peter, have eaten and drunk with Jesus the Incarnate One, have seen his suffering and his death, and to whom, after the denial, Jesus has appeared as the Risen One three days after his death. Later we shall speak also of the fact that there also will be no more men who, like Peter, are leaders of the *first* Church of Christ, the original church at Jerusalem.

Therefore, in the light also of *the total New Testament witness concern-ing the apostolic office*, and in the light of *the events of the Primitive Church*, that part of the promise of Jesus that speaks of building on the rock Peter may receive subsequent interpretation and application to the later Church only in such a way that this later Church rests once for all and in every generation upon the foundation that was laid *once*; it was laid, that is, at the beginning, at the midpoint of the times, in the time of revelation, when Christ lived on earth, died, and rose.

And now we ask further: But how can the foundation, understood in this chronological way, continue to play this role for the Church of all later times? How can every generation understand that for the Church Peter—and this really means Peter, not pretended successors—is 'actually' Peter in the etymological sense? How can the Church today still be founded upon the historical person of the apostle Peter?

This is only possible if this very temporal uniqueness of the founda-tion formed by the apostles is respected, that is, if the historically unique effect of their person and their work continues to exist in our present as a concrete gift from the time of revelation. This unique gift, which con-stitutes the continuance of the apostles in the period of the Church, is not the person of the bishop who at any given time is the living link in an unbroken chain of succession, but rather the Apostolic Scripture. It is not

P

confessional prejudice, but simply the Primitive Christian apostolic concept, that leads me to affirm this. Here in these writings we today, in the midst of the twentieth century, meet the person of the apostles, the person of the first among the apostles, Peter; in this way they continue to support, he continues to support, the structure of the Church. In the only New Testament text that explicitly speaks of the relation of the apostles to the Church that follows them—I refer to the already mentioned section of the high-priestly prayer in John 17:20—the further working of the apostles is connected not with the succession principle but rather with the *word of the apostles*: 'those who believe through their word'.

Without apostles we would have no New Testament, no knowledge at all of Jesus the Risen One. Everything that we know of him we owe to them. And this—we repeat—is true of Peter in a special way. Papias tells that the Gospel of Mark was written according to the sermons of the apostle Peter, and so rests upon his testimony. If this report is correct, then it is also historical to say that the oral tradition lying behind the written Gospels goes back in the first instance to the apostle Peter, especially if we, in agreement with recent study, regard the Gospel of Mark as the oldest Gospel.

When we read the Gospels, we are thus in contact with the person of the apostles and the rock apostle. We today are no longer in the situation to hear for ourselves the eyewitnesses of the historical life of Jesus and of his resurrection. We can no longer go to Jerusalem, as Paul did, to 'make the acquaintance of Peter' (Gal. 1:18). Nor shall we meet the eyewitness Peter in any other city, even in a bishop who stands in a 'Petrine' chain of succession. But he does remain for us the rock, the foundation; he remains such in the Gospels and in a derived way in the Book of Acts and the letters, which rest entirely upon the first apostolic witness. Here the historical apostolic foundation of the revelation, on which Christ in every generation builds his Church anew, takes concrete form for us also, and *yet retains its unique and never repeated form*. Here the apostles continue to live, and so all Christian Churches, not only the Roman Catholic Church, should write upon their church buildings: 'You are Peter, upon this Rock I will build my Church.' 'Built upon the foundation of the apostles and prophets.' 'I pray for those who believe through the word of the apostles.' Every Christian Church should be '*ecclesia catholica et apostolica*', a catholic and apostolic Church. A Church that is not apostolic is no longer a Christian Church. But it is perverse to wish to be content, for example, with the apostle Paul, as often happens in Protestant churches. It has become the custom to connect the apostle Peter only with the

Roman Catholic Church, and the apostle Paul with the Protestant Church.[12] In reality every Church needs also the apostle Peter, because he as 'first' among the twelve apostles has to guarantee the continuity with the incarnate Jesus.[13]

The application of the saying concerning the rock to the later period can thus be made in this sense, in full agreement with the exegesis, but also with the history of the beginnings of the Church.

The question that is asked from the Roman Catholic side is: Who guarantees in the present the scriptural link that leads back to the apostles? This question is justified in itself. But it may not be answered *on the basis of the saying concerning the rock*, on the basis of Matthew 16:17 ff., which is a 'foundation saying'; for the rock is and remains the once-for-all foundation. To be sure, there must be guarantors, watchmen, shepherds, interpreters in the Church. But they are quite false to this their role if they refer to themselves the saying concerning the rock. They are indispensable materials of which Christ makes use in the further building of his Church. Their specific task is to take care that this rock remains unshaken in the place where Christ has put it, and that it remains just as he has put it. Thus watchmen, shepherds, bishops are instruments of the promise Jesus made to build his Church on Peter.[14]

According to Roman Catholic teaching the connection with Peter can only be guaranteed by the chain of succession of the popes, not by the Scripture. The question about Peter therefore implies the problem of 'Scripture and Tradition', which I treat in detail in another place.[15] It is

[12] This is the usual and particularly favoured procedure at ecumenical conferences. In such a connection the eastern churches hold to the apostle John as their Patron.

[13] I wish to make this reservation also in regard to the book of J. L. Leuba, *L'Institution et l'evénement*, 1950, which otherwise offers a good historical basis for interdenominational conversations.

[14] Richard Baumann, *Das Petrus Bekenntnis und Schlüssel*, 1950, in general formulates the problems correctly, but solves them too quickly along the lines of Roman Catholic teaching. In doing so he is concerned to base his argument entirely on the Scripture. On p. 49 he formulates the following objection against the conception according to which the Church of all time builds *further* on the foundation laid *once*, that is, at the beginning, so that in this building one 'layer' or 'storey' rises on the other to the end of time. He says that in this case 'that which is present in the first layer at the first Pentecost would be something unfinished, scarcely begun'; and that is 'no house and no temple'. This argument, however, is incorrect to this extent, that here the word 'unfinished' is understood in the sense of 'qualitatively uncompleted'. It is not the case, however, that further building takes place because the building without the upper storeys would be incomplete and would represent nothing finished. It is 'unfinished' before the end of time simply in the chronological sense. A qualitative judgment is never included when reference is made to the end, to the fulfilment of the times. The building is already a complete whole in the lowest storey of the church structure; the number of storeys has only chronological significance. The foundation remains the same; it is so firm that it bears the uppermost storeys as well as the lowest ones.

[15] It therefore is no accident that out of the discussion of the first edition of my book

sufficient here to refer to the fact that the principle of a chain of succession is *not* present in Matthew 16. Furthermore, the question must be put: Is a chain of succession, which *unavoidably* is also a source of distortion, really a better guarantee than the Scriptural principle, even if the possibility of mistakes in interpretation must be conceded?

## 2. *The Leadership of the Church*

It is a frequent error of Protestant theologians that they do not sufficiently consider in their theological application the continuation of the saying, in which Jesus clearly speaks of the leadership of the Church. Even if the power of the keys concerns primarily the missionary leadership,[16] yet the power to bind and loose, in both of its possible meanings,[17] definitely presupposes church leadership.

We have said already that the leadership of the Church by Peter is also *apostolic* leadership, and so belongs to the never-to-be-repeated Rock role, the laying of the foundation. For although it is possible, as we have assumed, that Jesus did not utter the saying about the Rock on the same occasion as he did the saying to Peter about the keys, yet in the *present* connection of the words in Matthew the *entire* promise is dominated by the saying about the Rock; it indeed, in connection with the giving of the name, forms the point of departure. But on the other hand, we have pointed out many times that in contrast to the office of the apostle, that of the leader in the Church continues. Thus we here must pay attention to two things; on the one hand, to the non-transferable character of the leadership of the Primitive Church by Peter; on the other hand, to the fact that there must also be leadership later in the Church, so that Peter is in a certain respect the archetype and example for all future church leadership.[18]

Since we are dealing here with application, it is permitted and required that we connect Matthew 16:17 ff. with what we have learned from The Acts and the Letters concerning the actual role that Peter played in the Primitive Church. When we read the promise of Jesus in the light of

---

on Peter issued a discussion of Scripture and tradition such as I carried on in 1953 and the following years with Père J. Daniélou in *Le Dieu vivant*. It found its outcome in my writing, *Die Tradition als exegetisches, historisches und theologisches Problem*, 1954 (out of print). It is to be regarded as the necessary supplement to the preceding discussions and will soon appear again in a volume which will present my collected essays.

[16] See above, pp. 209 f.          [17] See above, pp. 210 ff.

[18] Ph. Menoud, *L'Eglise et les ministères selon le Nouveau Testament*, 1949, pp. 25 ff., rightly distinguishes in the entire New Testament between the unique never to be repeated witnessing office of the apostle and his functions that continue to be exercised in the Church. On this see Ed. Schweizer, *Geist und Gemeinde im N. T. und heute* (*Theologische Existenz heute*, 1952).

the history of the Apostolic Age, it must be said that it was fulfilled in the sense that Peter actually is the head of the Primitive Church. As we have seen, he stands at the head of the Primitive Church of Jerusalem, though to be sure only in the very earliest time. For James will soon take over the leadership in Jerusalem. Nevertheless, Peter retains for all time the unique greatness and dignity of having been *in the first days of the Church of Jesus Christ* the leader of the Primitive Church and thereby of the entire Church of that time. This must stand first of all as a fixed fact in the redemptive history at the beginning. In agreement with this is the result of the exegesis of Matthew 16:17 ff., according to which Jesus, when he promises to Peter the power of the keys, of binding and loosing, thinks of the lifetime of Peter. What Peter will do belongs to the period of revelation, to the time of the apostles, and so to the foundation. For this reason, his exercise of the power of the keys, the power to bind and loose, is so important.

Only the original Church was led by this apostle, and he led it only in its earliest period. For as soon as the foundation for this leadership is laid, Peter will give it up. Another, James, will take it over in Jerusalem, while Peter will concentrate entirely on his missionary work and will do so, indeed, in a *subordinate role under James*.

This later subordination of Peter under James is a fact important in every respect. It confirms first of all that the leadership of the Church by Peter also has its significance for us chiefly as a *starting-point*. James is the actual head of the Church from the moment that Peter dedicates himself completely to missionary work. The memory of *this fact*, which is *attested by the entire New Testament*, was steadily retained in the whole of Jewish Christianity, which took an interest in the ancient traditions.[19] According to Hegesippus, 'The brother of the Lord, James, takes over the leadership of the Church with the apostles.'[20] Particularly important is the fact that the *Pseudo-Clementina*, which are friendly to Peter, clearly subordinate Peter to James.[21] Peter has to 'give an accounting' to James, 'the bishop of the holy Church'. To him Peter sends his public addresses,[22] and

[19] Once more I emphasize that it is on the witness of Paul and The Acts that I support the assertion that James held the leadership of the Church very early, while Peter was still living. I introduce the later Jewish Christian sources only as a secondary confirmation. (See above, pp. 44 f., note 33.)

[20] Eusebius, *Ecclesiastical History*, II, 23, 4. According to Eusebius, *Eccles. Hist.*, II, 23, 1, he receives it 'from the Apostles'.

[21] See C. Schmidt, *Studien zu den Pseudo-Clementinen*, 1929, pp. 108 ff., 322 ff.; O. Cullmann, *Le problème littéraire et historique du roman pseudo-clémentin*, 1930, pp. 250 ff.; H. J. Schoeps, *Theologie und Geschichte des Judenchristentums*, 1949, pp. 122 ff.; G. Strecker, *Das Judenchristentum in den Pseudoclementinen*, 1958, pp. 58 ff.

[22] *Recognitions*, I, 17; *Homilies*, I, 20; *Epistle of Peter*, 1.

Clement calls him 'Bishop of Bishops', 'leader of the holy church of the Hebrews and of the churches *founded everywhere* by God's providence'.[23] Clement traces Peter's commission to him back to a commission that James gave to Peter.[24] These late reports thus agree with what we can learn concerning James from the Letters of Paul and The Book of Acts.[25]

It will not do, however, to make some such objection as that Peter went by way of Antioch to Rome at just that time in order to '*transfer*' the primacy in his own person from Jerusalem to that place. In reality Peter does not leave Jerusalem in order to transfer the primacy elsewhere; he leaves rather to spread the gospel. But the significant thing, as said, is that in relation to the new leadership at Jerusalem he does not continue in some superior position, as though James were only his substitute, or were only Bishop of the church at Jerusalem, already sunk to the position of a local church. He rather subordinates himself to the authority of James as the central government. In a time, therefore, *when Jerusalem continues to hold the leading position* and all other churches—even those founded by Paul, as the collection shows—still look to Jerusalem, Peter himself is dependent on the new leadership in Jerusalem; in Antioch he has to 'fear the people who come from James' (Gal. 2:12)!

One certainly must not exaggerate the importance of the clash between Peter and Paul at Antioch.[26] Nevertheless, it clearly proves something else that seems to me much more important than the rebuke that Paul gave Peter. It proves that *in relation to James*, whose representatives he fears, Peter does not take a leading role. Therefore one cannot speak of a transfer of the leadership by Peter to another place.

The Roman Catholic tradition asserts that Peter was *bishop also in Antioch*.[27] But Galatians 2:12 proves that even if this is correct, he does not in any case lead the entire Church from this centre. It thus proves that he did not transfer the leadership from Jerusalem to Antioch and then

[23] *Epistle of Clement*.

[24] *Recognitions*, I, 17; *Homily*, I, 20. See also Logion 12 of the Gnostic Gospel of Thomas (edition by Brill and Harper and Brothers), which goes back to Jewish Christian Gnostic circles. On this see O. Cullmann, *Theologische Literaturzeitung*, 1960, columns 321 ff.

[25] According to Clement of Alexandria, who likewise stresses particularly Peter's special position among the disciples (*Quis dives salvetur*, ch. 21), Peter, James, and John, after the ascension of Jesus, renounced the pre-eminent position and chose James the Just as the Bishop of Jerusalem. (*Hypotyposeis*, in Eusebius, *Eccles. Hist.*, II, 1, 3. See Jerome, *De viribus illustribus*, ch. 2.) Here, however, the fact is obscured that Peter had the leadership in the *earliest* period. So also among recent scholars we find the opinion represented that James had the highest leadership *from the beginning* (see H. Koch, *Cathedri Petri*, 1930, pp. 171 ff.). But to say that is to transfer back into the earliest period a situation that only emerged after some time. Correctly H. v. Campenhausen, *ZKG*, 1951-2, pp. 136 f.

[26] See above, pp. 48 f.

[27] See above, pp. 54 f., and below, p. 235.

from Antioch to Rome. He exercised leadership over the entire Church only at the beginning of the Jerusalem church and thereby at the beginning of the whole Church. Then he carries out the missionary phase of his apostolic office, and does so in the service of the Jewish Christian church of Jerusalem, whose leadership is in other hands.

As far then as the church leadership by Peter is concerned, we must take seriously the fact that the rock apostle led the *entire* Church only at *one* time. That was when, in the days immediately after Christ's resurrection and in the days of the giving of the Spirit to the Mother Church in Jerusalem, he stood at its head and exercised the work of binding and loosing, the memory of which the narrative about Ananias and Sapphira has preserved (Acts 5:1 ff.). When, therefore, the history of the Primitive Church is invoked to give present significance to the primacy of Peter in relation to leadership over the entire Church, this can happen only in the following way: The Church of today recognizes the redemptive plan of God in the fact that at its initial stage—this really was true at its initial stage—stands the apostle to whom Jesus gave the name 'Rock', and to whom he announced that on him he would build the Church.

\* \* \*

But in addition to the honoured place in redemptive history that our present Church should give to Peter as the first and indeed the apostolic head of the earliest Church, one may go further in applying to the later period Jesus' promise to Peter. We have seen that there must be leadership in the Church, even after the apostolic period when the foundation is laid and down to the present day. In this respect the leadership of the first head of the Church may be example and pattern, but nothing more than this. The leader or leaders of the future Church are given an example in the leadership that is committed to Peter. But Peter himself cannot so to speak arise in every new generation. Never again will the *kepha*, the Rock, himself exercise the leadership. But all leadership of the later Church built upon the apostle should know that the keys are given to it and that it has the task of binding and loosing.

It is a fact that in the beginning a single person stood at the head of the Church as a 'rock' among the 'pillars'. But it is not necessary to conclude from this that also in all later times a single person must stand at the head of the entire Church. *The entire Church is no longer identical, as it was in the first days, with one local church.*

The question as to what principle is to determine the leadership of the whole in the following period cannot be answered on the basis of an almost automatically operating mechanism. With a certain blindness to the problems involved, the Roman Catholic Church regards it as self-evident that *no other principle can here be considered except that of succession tied to an unbroken chain*. It claims as decisive—in connection with its view that Matthew 16:17 ff. has in mind successors—first, the fact that Peter was bishop of a specific church, that is, Rome, and second, that this very church has actually 'led' in the history of the Church.

If, in accord with all that has been said, the leadership of the Church by Peter is to be considered only as a pattern, this means that such an exclusive application to the Roman bishops standing in a line of succession to Peter is really impossible from the start. If in what follows we nevertheless investigate the question of the realization of the primacy in history, this occurs only because on the Roman Catholic side the history is always introduced to answer the question as to where, in connection with Matthew 16, the succession to Peter is to be sought.

We first of all must return to the principle of apostolic succession, of which we already have spoken in connection with Peter's role as the Rock. In doing so, we now have to focus particularly on the relation of the succession principle to Rome as the historical seat of the *leadership of the entire Church*. We have seen[28] that the idea of succession in its later form cannot be derived from Matthew 16:17 ff., even if we add to it the New Testament passages that speak of the appointment of local church heads by the apostles. No indication is present in Matthew 16:17 ff. that the centre of the Church is located where one finds the bishop whose office is validated by a chronological chain of succession which leads back to Peter.[29] This, to be sure, is admitted by the defenders of the Roman claim to primacy, and they never support their argument upon this saying alone, without adding those other theological considerations of which we shall speak later. But we still must ask here whether, even if one does not hold the Scripture alone to be authoritative, it is not at least noteworthy that in the entire apostolic record, that is, the entire New Testament, not a single passage so much as mentions the name of Rome *in connection with Peter*, and therefore it is not only in Matthew 16:17 ff. that reference to a 'transfer' of the centre is completely lacking. This latter fact should cause serious thought when the reading of the succession

[28] See above, pp. 213 ff., 223 f.

[29] The objection has been made that John 21:16 ff. presupposes an understanding of the words to Peter which though of subsequent origin nevertheless reaches back into an ancient time; this understanding, since it must here be rectified by the Risen One, would envision a succession. Concerning this objection I shall state my position later in my book on *Peter and the Pope*. See above, p. 184, note 80, and p. 214, note 75 (cf. p. 31, note 54).

principle into Matthew 16:17 ff. is supposed to be legitimized by a historical development in which Rome moves into the central place as the 'holy city'.

From the historical point of view, as we have seen, we can indeed explain the *silence* of the entire New Testament concerning any relation of Peter to Rome. *Theologically*, however, we hardly can do so *if* this relation is to justify the exclusive claim that the Roman bishops make to this saying of Jesus.[30] In our historical study we have concluded, on the basis of all sorts of indirect arguments, that Peter very probably came to Rome at the end of his life and there became a martyr. But does this suffice as the starting-point for an assertion that takes so uniquely important a theological role in the picture of redemptive history, the assertion, that is, that only *this* church whose leadership passes in continuous succession through the Roman bishops may appeal to Peter and that it is the only 'catholic and apostolic Church'? In particular, should not the silence of the Scripture concerning Peter's episcopal office in Rome stimulate us to consider whether it is really true that for all time to come the Church is to be led only on the basis of this succession principle?

We now go on, however, beyond the Scriptural witness. What is the truth in general concerning the presupposition, assumed without any discussion, that the leadership of the entire Church in the post-apostolic period is to be determined by a designated episcopal see by the chain of succession of the occupants of this see? Of certain *individual churches* we can say that by instituting local church heads[31] the apostles, in their unique capacity as apostles, thus created the first bishops of these churches. This, to be sure, says nothing at all as to who after them is to choose the subsequent bishops.[32]

The apostle Peter, on the other hand, never established a bishop as the leader of the *entire Church*, and above all he himself never gave distinction to *any* Church *except Jerusalem* as the seat of his own leadership of the entire Church. *For even if, after his leadership of the Jerusalem*

---

[30] M. Meinertz, *Theologie des Neuen Testaments*, Vol. I, 1950, p. 79, concedes: 'With regard to the succession to Peter, there naturally is still no supporting proof for that in the New Testament.' My opposition to this statement is directly against the word 'naturally'. For this does not seem to me at all natural, if salvation is really to depend on this succession.

[31] See above, pp. 223 f.

[32] Ed. Schweizer, *Gemeinde und Gemeindeordnung im Neuen Testament*, 1959, pp. 192 ff. (Eng. Tr., *Church Order in the New Testament*, 1961, pp. 211 ff.), emphasizes here that in the Pastoral Epistles even this installation by the apostles did not take place without the presence of the congregation, and in *Geist und Gemeinde im N. T. und Heute*, 1952, he stresses that in I Tim. 1:18 the installation occurs only after 'preceding prophetic direction'.

*church, he temporarily as apostolic missionary was the leader of still other churches, yet so much at least is definite, that when he was there he was only the leader of those single churches, and in no case leader of the entire Church. Peter was the leader of the entire Church only at Jerusalem.*

Thus if *one* church wished to claim a special position in this respect and if the very principle of fixing the succession to Peter by a formal line of succession were not completely arbitrary, it could only be the church of Jerusalem. In the New Testament this is the only church of which we hear that Peter stood at its head. Of other episcopates of Peter we know nothing certain. Concerning Antioch, indeed, as we shall see—and we shall return to this point—there is a tradition, first appearing in the course of the second century, according to which Peter was its bishop. The assertion that he was Bishop of Rome we first find at a much later time. From the second half of the second century we do possess texts that mention the apostolic *foundation* of Rome, and at this time, which is indeed rather late, this foundation is traced back to *Peter and Paul*, an assertion that cannot be supported historically.[33] Even here, however, nothing is said as yet of an episcopal office of Peter. But even if Peter did occupy in Rome an episcopal position, this could hold good at the most for the *local* church in Rome, for it is a fixed fact that *at that time*, in the sixth decade of the first century, Rome still played no leading role in the Church at large, and Peter did not rule the entire Church from Rome. In our present discussion, however, we are concerned with the question as to how the succession was determined, and this concerns the leadership of *the Church at large*. In that connection we only wish to show, in an anticipatory way, that not only in the Scriptures, but also *in the history of Primitive Christianity*, *there is no trace at all* that the succession to Peter in the leadership at large was to be determined by the fact that he was bishop in this or that city. In the life of Peter there is no starting-point for a *chain of succession* in the leadership of the Church at large.

The fact that Peter most probably suffered his martyrdom in Rome cannot give to this church the dignity that belongs solely to the Mother Church in Jerusalem, the dignity of having once represented the entire Church and of having been led as such by the apostle Peter *in the apostolic period of revelation*.

But even Jerusalem naturally is not to be considered as permanent bearer of succession in the universal leadership of the Church. The authority of James, moreover, is not derived from Peter but from his direct relations to Jesus. He probably was regarded as an apostle who was

[33] See above, pp. 117 f., 47, 80 f.

instituted as such by Jesus himself. This is the view of Paul,[34] and the later tradition also was still able to report that he was appointed bishop by Jesus himself.[35] A chain of succession in the leadership of the *entire Church*, going back to Peter and to Matthew 16:17 ff., thus does not exist. Concerning Clement of Rome, who is so eagerly designated as the Roman Pope appointed by Peter, it cannot be proved from reliable sources either that he received his office from Peter or that he was the leader of the Church at large; to exhort a divided sister church to harmony in a letter is not enough to establish one as the pope. Peter at the beginning led the entire Church in Jerusalem. But which bishop after him is to play the leading role in each case cannot be decided by the principle of a succession. There is no succession in leadership of the entire Church that leads from Jerusalem to another city. This must be stated as a basic proposition.

Moreover, there are other churches besides Jerusalem and Rome,[36] above all *Antioch*, which regard Peter as their first bishop. We have seen[37] that the tradition of the episcopate at Antioch is exceedingly hard to defend on historical grounds, even if the letters of Ignatius suggest the assumption that the monarchical episcopate developed relatively early at Antioch. It must nevertheless be emphasized that this tradition is much older and better attested than is that of the Roman episcopate. In the time of Peter the Roman church had no more significance, and perhaps even less, than did the one at Antioch. They were both local churches, and as such they were led by Peter, if the traditions in question are correct.

If one were determined to maintain the completely arbitrary principle according to which Peter's episcopal office in a church could aid in giving to its later bishops the exclusive claim to Matthew 16:17 ff., then on this basis Antioch could establish a greater claim to the primacy than Rome. Nevertheless, we have already mentioned and shall again speak of the fact that according to the judgment of most Roman Catholic theologians, even the episcopate of Peter is by no means sufficient of itself. Just as

[34] This conclusion, moreover, seems to follow from the fact that Paul reckons him among the 'pillars' (Gal. 2:9), and especially from Gal. 1:19 (ἕτερον δὲ τῶν ἀποστόλων οὐκ εἶδον εἰ μὴ 'Ιάκωβον: 'but other of the Apostles I did not see except Peter'). H. Koch, however, in 'Zur Jakobus-frage, Gal. 1, 19' (*ZNW*, 1934, pp. 264 ff.), thinks he can explain the passage otherwise: Paul saw no other apostle but Cephas, but did indeed see James. He is regarded as an apostle also by K. Holl, 'Der Kirchenbegriff des Paulus, in seinem Verhältnis zu dem der Urgemeinde' (*Gesammelte Aufsätze*, Vol. II, 1928, p. 49); H. v. Campenhausen, *ZKG*, 1950–1, p. 137.

[35] According to the Pseudo-Clementine Epistle of Peter to James, V, and *Recognitions*, I, 43, James was installed by the Lord; so also according to Epiphanius, *Heresies*, 78, 7, and Chrysostom, in *Homily on First Corinthians*, 38, 5.

[36] The Pseudo-Clementine *Homily* 3, 53, presupposes that there is in Caesarea a *Cathedra Petri* (an episcopal 'chair of Peter').

[37] See above, pp. 54 f.

little does the interpretation of Matthew 16:18 suffice. Rather, to both arguments there must be added as the decisive criterion of the primacy the effective role that a church has played and plays in the further history. Since, however, the episcopate of the apostle and the relation of Jerusalem to Rome are regularly cited as arguments in connection with the history of Peter, we had to examine this question on all sides. We come to the conclusion: There is no basis whatever in any ancient text for the assertion that in connection with the episcopal office of Peter, Rome inherited the legal succession from Jerusalem. Even if Antioch should be inserted as an intermediate stage, such a theory would not be any better supported. *For Peter ruled the Church at large in that period neither from Antioch nor from Rome, but only in Jerusalem and for a short time.* The history of Primitive Christianity gives no warrant of any kind for the assumption that Peter came to Rome to transfer the primacy to that place.

There are some well-known Roman Catholic theologians who, in view of the lack of any basis for such an assertion, do not make the primacy of Rome depend at all on the *stay of Peter in Rome*. Indeed, they believe that in their theological statement they can actually in principle forgo this basis, since it is only *the fact* that the bishops of Rome are successors of Peter—not the How—that is decisive, and since the transfer of the succession to Peter to the bishops of Rome is even conceivable without Peter himself having been in the city of this later episcopal see.[38] This view completely surrenders the appeal to the history of the historical Peter. However, the Roman Catholic teaching seems not completely consistent on this point, and one can ask whether this surrender can really be reconciled with the wording of the Vatican pronouncement.[39]

[38] See R. Graber, *Petrus der Fels*, 1949, p. 37, and Ch. Journet, *L'Eglise du verbe incarné*, 1941, pp. 522 ff. R. Graber cites Dunin-Borkowski, 'Die Kirche als Stiftung Jesu' (*Religion, Christentum und Kirche*, 1923, pp. 45 f.): 'It is a widespread error that the Catholic apologetic must necessarily make the papacy, as the continuation of the rule of Peter, dependent on the stay of the Prince of Apostles in Rome and on his episcopal office there. This is not the case. Certainly one can give such a proof, but it is by no means necessary... As soon as it ... is established that Christ not merely fixed the primacy of Saint Peter but spoke of this primacy as a lasting institution, there is lacking only the proof that the Roman bishops alone claimed the special rights of the Rock man.' Further, L. Kösters, *War Petrus in Rom?*, 1938, pp. 50 f.: 'It would be entirely conceivable that Peter had appointed the chief of the Roman Church as his successor in the primacy received from Christ, even if he himself had never been in Rome.'

[39] *Vaticanum*, fourth session, 18 July 1870, ch. 2: ... *qui [Peter] ad hoc usque tempus et semper in suis successoribus episcopis sanctae Romanae Sedis, ab ipso fundatae eiusque consecratae sanguine, vivit et praesidet et iudicium exercet* ('who even unto this time and always lives and governs and exercises judgment in his successors, the bishops of the holy Roman see, *which was founded by him and consecrated by his blood*'). From the significance, moreover, which is attached in Roman circles to the discovery of the grave of Peter, it seems proved that the opinion held by those named in the preceding footnote and by many eminent Roman Catholic theologians is not generally shared.

But in any case it is true that the stay of Peter in Rome has never been the only decisive argument for the primacy of Rome. All Roman Catholic theologians argue rather that later, from the beginning of the second century on, *Rome effectively played an outstanding and leading role in the Christendom of that time.* One thus can say, they contend, that the historical *development of church history* proves that after the destruction of Jerusalem the primacy passed from Jerusalem to Rome.

To this, however, it must be replied that from the effective historical role which a church plays in *post-apostolic times* no divine right can be derived for *all* time if, as we have just established, this role *lacks any connection with the Apostolic Age,* and if nothing at all is said in Matthew 16 concerning how to apply to the later period of the Church what Jesus said to Peter. It will not do to appeal to tradition as a source of revelation to justify this flight into later history; the sole justification for the Roman Catholic tradition rests on this very assertion of the primacy of Rome. It simply is not true that every development in church history is to be accepted without question as legitimate tradition. And one cannot prove the *foundation* of the Roman tradition by use of this tradition itself. The problem is to show that the tradition of the primacy of Rome, on which all remaining Roman Catholic tradition depends, is valid.

The flight into later history could only assure the primacy to a certain episcopal see if, in the first place, Matthew 16:17 ff. justified us in seeking successors in the sense of a tie with one episcopal chain of succession, and if, secondly, the line could be drawn backwards from the later effectively exercised primacy of one church to the apostolic period and so to the historical Peter. *Neither of these things, however, is true.* That being the case, the effective role that the bishops of the Roman church have played and now play does not prove that they are to exercise the *same* primacy that Peter exercised in Jerusalem after it was promised to him by Jesus.

The Roman church, it is true, gradually attained a pre-eminent position in the course of the second and third centuries. No historian or theologian will dispute this. The question, however, is whether the primacy promised to Peter in Matthew 16:17 ff. and actually exercised by him in Jerusalem in the beginning is therefore to be transferred exclusively to the bishops of the Roman church. That a church occupies a pre-eminent position still does not prove that it stands in such a relation to Matthew 16:17 ff. as to give it a divine right for all time to come. The secular historian, indeed, explains that pre-eminent position by the purely 'immanent' consideration that Rome was the chief city of the Roman Empire, so that the Christian church located there naturally and necessarily attained a special dignity. This reason certainly did play a strongly contributory role. In addition, the theologian will discover factors within the Church, grounded in the situation of that time, and with Ignatius of Antioch he may recognize that the Roman church of that time has also a 'pre-eminence in love'.[40] But even if we wish to speak here of a divinely intended *development* in the history of the Church of Christ, it does not follow from this that this historical role is a sign that it is a divinely intended *norm* for the leadership of the Church of all time. For we say once more: Matthew 16:17 ff. does not say a word as to how the succession to Peter in the leadership of the Church at large is to be determined. It is arbitrary to take into account *a priori* only this *one* possibility that the successor of Peter is to be determined by the line of bishops in one church which stands out among the other churches not in the apostolic period of revelation, but only later. The fact that the bishops of this church in later times *make the claim* that they alone are intended in the promise of Jesus in Matthew 16:17 ff. cannot prove the legitimacy of this claim.

Moreover, *until the beginning of the third century* it never occurred to a single Bishop of Rome to refer the saying in Matthew 16:17 ff. to himself in the sense of the leadership of the entire Church. It was probably Callistus (217–22), though according to others it was actually Stephanus (254–7),[41] who first applied to himself the words 'You are Peter', and this did not pass without contradiction. Tertullian protests: he is determined to refer the saying only to the person of Peter and not to the bishops at all; Cyprian, on the contrary, refers it to *all* later bishops and not to the Bishop of Rome alone.[42] The appeal that the Roman bishops made to Matthew 16:17 ff., moreover, fell far short of general acceptance even in the third century, and only much later does the exclusive reference to Rome become a self-evident axiom.

Irenaeus, to be sure, apparently speaks even in the second century of the oft-cited 'more powerful and pre-eminent position of Rome' (*potentior principalitas*).[43] But the reference of these words to Rome is not at all assured. According to the most recent explanation, which philologically is very convincingly grounded,[44] what is here meant as *the* Church, to which every church must adhere, is not at all the Roman church, but the 'universal' Church in general. Even if Irenaeus had Rome in mind, he would in

[40] Ignatius, *To the Romans* 1:1: προκαθημένη τῆς ἀγάπης.

[41] So, for example, recently also K. Heussi. See above, p. 166, note 11.

[42] See E. Caspar, *Geschichte des Papsttums von den Anfängen bis zur Höhe der Weltherrschaft*, Vol. I, 1938. On this subject, see above, pp. 166 f.

[43] *Against Heresies*, III, 3, 2.

[44] See the distinguished article by P. Nautin, 'Irénée, *Adv. Haer.* III, 3, 2, église de Rome ou église universelle?' (*Revue de l'Histoire des Religions*, 1957, pp. 37 ff.).

any case not be appealing here to Matthew 16:17 ff.[45] Rather, in accordance with the tradition principle of the rabbis and the philosophical schools which Hegesippus, following the Gnostics, seems to have naturalized in the ancient Church,[46] he would be pointing to the particularly well-preserved apostolic tradition. This would be connected only with the *foundation* of the Roman church, by both Peter *and* Paul; it would not be connected with the primacy of Peter.

Moreover, the entire controversy as to whether in Rome appeal was first made to Matthew 16:17 ff. at a somewhat earlier or later time does not have for our question as much significance as is attached to it.[47] In any case, more than one hundred years passed before the primacy of Rome was connected with the promise of Jesus to Peter. The fact that, in a time when the Roman church already had a certain consciousness of pre-eminence, it still did not justify its consciousness by reference to Matthew 16:17 ff., should certainly cause one to think. There is, indeed, a chain of succession of Roman bishops, which may have its value for the Roman church. *There is no chain of succession of leaders of the Church at large*, even though the local Roman chain was later made for this purpose. In the period after James there is a great gap. In the hortatory writing of Clement which is called the First Epistle of Clement, a bishop speaks in a brotherly way to a sister church, just as also happened elsewhere without any conclusion being drawn that such an act justifies a claim to primacy.

It is arguing in a *circle*, a *petitio principii*, to assert that since on the one hand the promise of Jesus to Peter exists, and on the other hand the fact exists that Rome exercised a primacy from a relatively early date, we therefore must conclude that this primacy rests on that promise, in such a way that it is the norm for all time. That this relation exists between Matthew 16:17 ff. and the pre-eminent position that Rome later occupied is precisely the thing it is necessary to prove.

In answer to these and other objections the Roman Catholic theologians are accustomed to point out that the promise to Peter had to become *visible* in history, since the Church is a visible Church and

---

[45] P. Batiffol, 'Cathedra Petri' (*Etudes d'Histoire ancienne*, 1938, p. 14), thinks that in the word *principalitas*, which is to be understood chronologically, the 'You are Peter' is implied. His interpretation, however, does not seem to me to be sufficiently grounded. —We have seen above (pp. 165 f.) that Irenaeus never quotes the saying about the keys. See on this point the above-named thesis of W. L. Dulière (*La nouvelle Clio*, 1954, pp. 73 ff.) that his copy of Matthew contained only vs. 17, not vss. 18–19.

[46] H. von Campenhausen, *Lehrerreihen und Bischofreihen im 2. Jahrhundert. In Memoriam Ernst Lohmeyer*, 1951, pp. 240 ff.

[47] It was chiefly A. Harnack, P. Batiffol, H. Koch, and E. Caspar who took part in this controversy.

continues on earth the work of Christ. The idea of the continuation of the work of Christ in the visible earthly Church I affirm, since I find it especially in the entire Gospel of John as a central declaration. Therefore, as far as I am concerned—I do not speak here at all in the name of official 'Protestant theology'—it is not true that on this point the common basis for discussion is lacking. It should be sufficiently clear from my previous writings that I really take seriously the fact that the present in which we stand, the period of the Church, is not itself redemptive history, but is a prolongation of the redemptive history; this history, to be sure, must continually find its norm in the apostolic period of revelation as the central point of time.[48] The promise of Jesus to Peter was visibly fulfilled in Jerusalem in the days following the resurrection. But from this it does not result that the Roman claim to be henceforth the only *legitimate* visible Church is justified on the ground that, from a certain time on, Rome actually occupied a pre-eminent position in Christendom. It occupied such a position only in the post-apostolic period, which as such is not normative, and even then only during a certain number of centuries. It should not be disputed that this temporary pre-eminent position has some significance for the development of the gospel line of redemptive history in the period of the Church. But this position does not necessarily rest upon the promise of Jesus to Peter, in the sense that therefore for all time to come only the occupant of this episcopal see can be the leader of the true Church; such a conclusion does not follow from faith in the visibility of the Church in which Christ continues his work.

There have been and there are today, outside of the Roman Church, visible churches in other centres also, and it would be arguing again in a circle to reply that such a church is not a real church because it does not stand in succession to Peter. From Matthew 16:17 ff. and the rest of the New Testament come other criteria, in addition to the narrow criterion connected with an episcopal see, which permit us to recognize that Church *which Christ builds upon Peter the Rock*. We cannot discuss here the entire involved question of the criterion of the Church and of tradition.[49] But it should be emphasized that it is arbitrary to assert that Christ built his Church upon Peter only at the place where, at a certain date, a certain episcopal see, whose occupants appealed to Matthew 16, led Christendom.

Developments of the *post-apostolic* period of church history, important as they may be for the development of redemptive history in the period

---

[48] In my book concerning eschatology I shall show that redemptive history and church history are thus as little to be identified as are redemptive history and secular history.

[49] See O. Cullmann, *Die Tradition als exegetisches, historisches und theologisches Problem*, 1954. See above, p. 227, note 15.

of the Church, cannot give an exclusively *normative* position to any of those leading places. For one thing, the intent of Jesus leaves us no possibility of understanding Matthew 16:17 ff. in the sense of a succession determined by a line of bishops. Moreover, the history of Peter knows nothing of a transfer of the ruling seat (*cathedra*) of the Church at large from Jerusalem to another city. In the apostolic period Rome was not the centre of the Church at large. There at the midpoint of the times, the point decisive for the Christian, no hint is anywhere given that the Roman or any other bishop's seat is to be decisive for the further determination of the leadership of the Church at large. In addition to Rome there were, in the post-apostolic period as previously, other centres of the visible Church; there are now other centres and there probably will be still others, whether their name is Antioch, Corinth or Ephesus, Alexandria or Constantinople, Wittenberg, Canterbury or Geneva, Stockholm or Amsterdam.

The actual power that these centres have exercised or now exercise proves nothing as to the legality of any claim they may make that they *alone* stand in succession to the first leader, Peter, whom Christ established over the Church at large. Even the fact that only one of these outstanding places has asserted and now asserts such a claim proves nothing.

The apostolic quality, the connection with Peter, can be preserved in another way. Neither from Scripture nor from the history of the ancient Church can a divine right for the primacy of Rome be derived.

For this reason even the Roman Catholic Church appeals to a dogmatic utterance according to which the bishops of Rome are the sole successors of Peter.[50] We do not need to return again to the question how far this utterance lacks basis either in Scripture or in the most ancient tradition. We should, however, ask this question: Is it not another and final begging of the question, *a petitio principii*, when this very assertion, which is so notably basic for the Roman claim, is founded only upon later dogmas? For the exclusive claim to *proclaim dogmas through the possession of sole apostolic authority* is nevertheless dependent on this very dogma of the legal succession to Peter. What is involved here is not just another dogma; it is that dogma that is meant to justify completely the exclusive right of the Roman Catholic Church to promulgate dogmas. In such a situation,

---

[50] See the sentence from the *Vaticanum* cited above in note 39. The most thorough presentation of the Roman Catholic doctrine seems to me to be offered by the already mentioned work of Ch. Journet, *L'Eglise du verbe incarné*, 1941. See, especially, pp. 522 ff. See also his book, *Primauté de Pierre dans la perspective protestante et dans la perspective catholique*, 1953; it appeared in reply to the first edition of my book on Peter, and I plan to discuss it in my reply to Catholic critics which will appear later under the title *Peter and the Pope*.

Q

can every other basis be lacking, above all the witness of Scripture, which does not mention Rome at all in connection with Peter? Can *ancient* tradition also be lacking? It knows nothing of a government of the Church at large from Rome by Peter, and also knows nothing of a transfer of his succession to the Roman bishops.

We reach the following conclusion of these doctrinal and theological discussions:

In so far as Peter is the Rock, he is such in the temporal sense of laying the foundation as an apostle. In every generation Christ intends to build his Church on the foundation of the apostles, and among them Peter is the most important.

In so far as he is the leader of the Primitive Church in Jerusalem, this also has chiefly temporal significance, and in this respect his bearing for the redemptive history of all later time consists in the fact that in the beginning he held the leadership of the original Church.

If we wish to derive further from the saying that after Peter also there must be in the Church a universal leadership that administers the keys, the binding and loosing, this cannot take place in the sense of a limitation to the future occupants of one episcopal see. This principle of succession cannot be justified either from Scripture or from the history of the ancient Church. In reality the leadership of the Church at large is not to be determined by succession in the sense of a link with one episcopal see. The significance of individual churches for the Church at large comes a goes. But the Rock, the foundation for all churches of all times, rema the historical Peter. At that time he was especially chosen by Jesus fr among the Twelve; he was given special distinction as a witness of Jesu life and death and as the first witness of his resurrection. On him Christ, who is himself the cornerstone, will keep building his Church as long as there is such a Church on earth.

INDEXES

# INDEX OF AUTHORS CITED

# INDEX OF BIBLICAL PASSAGES